The Possibility of Practical Reason

The Possibility
of Practical Reason

J. DAVID VELLEMAN

CLARENDON PRESS · OXFORD

OXFORD

UNIVERSITY PRESS

Great Clarendon Street, Oxford OX2 6DP

Oxford University Press is a department of the University of Oxford.
It furthers the University's objective of excellence in research, scholarship,
and education by publishing worldwide in

Oxford New York

Athens Auckland Bangkok Bogotá Buenos Aires Calcutta
Cape Town Chennai Dar es Salaam Delhi Florence Hong Kong Istanbul
Karachi Kuala Lumpur Madrid Melbourne Mexico City Mumbai
Nairobi Paris São Paulo Singapore Taipei Tokyo Toronto Warsaw

and associated companies in Berlin Ibadan

Oxford is a registered trade mark of Oxford University Press
in the UK and certain other countries

Published in the United States
by Oxford University Press Inc., New York

British Library Cataloguing in Publication Data

Data available

Library of Congress Cataloging-in-Publication Data

Velleman, James David.
The possibility of practical reason /J. David Velleman.
p. cm.
Includes bibliographical references and index.
1. Act (Philosophy) 2. Agent (Philosophy) 3. Reason. I. Title.
B105.A35 V435 2000   128'.4–dc21   00-25246

ISBN 0-19-823825-8
ISBN 0-19-823826-6 (Pbk.)

Typeset by Best-set Typesetter Ltd., Hong Kong
Printed in Great Britain
on acid-free paper by
T.J. International Ltd
Padstow, Cornwall

For my parents

PREFACE

This volume contains the work that I have done in the philosophy of action since completing the book *Practical Reflection*. One of the papers, 'Epistemic Freedom,' is an expanded version of a chapter in the book; it was written after the book went to press, though it was published first. I have included it here because I think that it significantly improves on the corresponding portions of the book. One or two of the other papers are attempts to build upon or renovate the theory set down in the book, but most of them are attempts to dig beneath it. Without even referring to that theory, I have tried to unearth more fundamental reasons for wanting a theory of its general form—reasons for thinking that there ought to be a theory of its kind.

In most cases, I have done my digging in areas familiar to philosophers of action: problems about agent causation, internal and external reasons, direction of fit, the normative force of formal decision theory, and the rationality of resolute choice. The papers therefore do more to situate my view on the philosophical map than I previously could, though they do less by way of filling in the details.

The Introduction is an attempt to fashion a single narrative out of the main themes that appear in the rest of the collection. In concentrating on the flow of this narrative, I have tended to gloss over argumentative details, relying on the other papers to provide them. I have tried to indicate in the footnotes where detailed versions of the arguments can be found in the other chapters. The Introduction also records recent changes of mind about various issues.

I have not revised or updated the previously published material in substantive respects. (I have made some minor adjustments in Chapters 9 and 10.) I have also retained the acknowledgements that originally appeared with the papers, thus ensuring that each paper contains at least one true statement—namely, that of my indebtedness to friends and colleagues. I have several debts, however, that are not adequately represented in those acknowledgements, and I would like to mention them here.

Although each paper thanks many of my colleagues individually, none records my debt to the collective that they make up: the Department of Philosophy at the University of Michigan, Ann Arbor. Whatever virtues my work displays are largely a reflection of the intellectual community in which it was carried out. I also want to thank those colleagues who have chaired the Department during my tenure here—Jaegwon Kim, Allan Gibbard, Stephen Darwall, and Louis Loeb—each of whom has provided significant support to my research.

Michael Bratman is the person who first suggested that I publish this collection. Michael's contributions to the philosophy of action include not only many important publications but also many years of good-natured advice and encouragement to others working in the field. I am fortunate to have been a beneficiary of his intellectual generosity since the very beginning of my career.

Finally, I want to thank Ted Hinchman for help with the Bibliography and Index; James Bell for help with proofreading; Nancy Higginbotham for copyediting; and, at Oxford University Press, Peter Momtchiloff, Enid Barker, and Charlotte Jenkins.

Ann Arbor
October 1999

CONTENTS

I

Introduction

Behavior, Activity, Action

Philosophers of action have traditionally defined their topic by quoting a bit of Wittgensteinian arithmetic: "What is left over if I subtract the fact that my arm goes up from the fact that I raise my arm?"[1] The difference between my arm's rising and my raising it is supposed to illustrate the difference between a mere occurrence involving my body and an action of mine. And the difference between mere occurrences and actions is what the philosophy of action seeks to explain.

Yet there is reason to doubt whether Wittgenstein's computation has a unique result. As Harry Frankfurt has pointed out, my raising an arm may be something less than an action:[2]

> Actions are instances of activity, though not the only ones even in human life. To drum one's fingers on the table, altogether idly and inattentively, is surely not a case of passivity: the movements in question do not occur without one's making them. Neither is it an instance of action, however, but only of being active. . . . One result of overlooking events of this kind is an exaggeration of the peculiarity of what humans do. Another result, related to the first, is the mistaken belief that a twofold division of human events into action and mere happenings provides a classification that suits the interests of the theory of action.

Frankfurt's distinction between action and mere activity reveals a potential ambiguity in the above quotation from Wittgenstein. "The fact that I raise my arm" can denote an instance of action, such as my signaling a request to be recognized by the chair of a meeting; but the same phrase can also denote an instance of mere activity, such as my idly and inattentively—perhaps even

For comments on earlier drafts of this Introduction, I am grateful to Joel Anderson, Pamela Hieronymi, Sigurdur Kristinsson, R. Jay Wallace; and to Philip Clark and other members of the Philosophy Department at Kansas State University.

[1] *Philosophical Investigations*, trans. G. E. M. Anscombe (Oxford: Blackwell, 1972), §621.

[2] 'Identification and Externality,' in *The Importance of What We Care About* (Cambridge: Cambridge University Press, 1988), 58–68, at 58. The second half of this quotation appears in the original as a footnote to the first.

unwittingly—scratching my head while engrossed in a book. When the fact that my arm goes up is subtracted from something called "the fact that I raise my arm," what is left will depend on whether the minuend is a case of action or mere activity.

Unfortunately, most philosophy of action is premised on the mistaken belief pointed out by Frankfurt, that human events can be divided without remainder into actions and mere happenings. The result is that the prevailing theory of action neglects the difference between action and activity.[3]

This difference is also illustrated by behaviors that call for psychoanalytic explanation.[4] Consider an example from Freud's *Psychopathology of Everyday Life*:[5]

> My inkstand is made out of a flat piece of Untersberg marble which is hollowed out to receive the glass inkpot; and the inkpot has a cover with a knob made of the same stone. Behind this inkstand there is a ring of bronze statuettes and terra cotta figures. I sat down at the desk to write, and then moved the hand that was holding the pen-holder forward in a remarkably clumsy way, sweeping on to the floor the inkpot cover which was lying on the desk at the time.
>
> The explanation was not hard to find. Some hours before, my sister had been in the room to inspect some new acquisitions. She admired them very much, and then remarked: 'Your writing table looks really attractive now; only the inkstand doesn't match. You must get a nicer one.' I went out with my sister and did not return for some hours. But when I did I carried out, so it seems, the execution of the condemned inkstand. Did I perhaps conclude from my sister's remark that she intended to make me a present of a nicer inkstand on the next festive occasion, and did I smash the unlovely old one so as to force her to carry out the intention she had hinted at? If that is so, my sweeping movement was only apparently clumsy; in reality it was exceedingly adroit and well-directed, and understood how to avoid damaging any of the more precious objects that stood around.

This explanation is simpler than many of Freud's, in that it portrays his action as a realistically chosen means to a desired end, rather than a symbolic wish-

---

[3] In 'What Happens When Someone Acts?' (Chap. 6, below), I tried to distinguish between action that is full-blooded, or fully human, and action that is something less. I now regard the terms "action" and "activity" as preferable for drawing the distinction that I had in mind.

[4] See Richard Wollheim, *The Thread of Life* (Cambridge, Mass.: Harvard University Press, 1984), 59–61; and Sebastian Gardner, *Irrationality and the Philosophy of Psychoanalysis* (Cambridge: Cambridge University Press, 1993), 188–9. As Gardner notes, this distinction is probably co-extensive with the distinction drawn by Brian O'Shaughnessy between sub-intentional and intentional action (*The Will*, vol. ii (Cambridge: Cambridge University Press, 1980), ch. 10). The distinction is also discussed by Jonathan Lear in his critical notice of Gardner, 'The Heterogeneity of the Mental,' *Mind* 104 (1995) 863–79. Note, however, that Wollheim and Gardner do not draw the distinction between action and activity as I shall draw it. They accept the desire-belief model as adequate to characterize action, whereas I shall argue that it at most characterizes a kind of activity.

[5] *The Standard Edition of the Complete Psychological Works of Sigmund Freud*, trans. James Strachey et al. (London: Hogarth Press, 1960), VI: 167–8.

fulfillment or the enactment of a phantasy. The agent wanted to destroy the inkstand so as to make way for his sister to give him a new one; and his desire to destroy the inkstand moved him to brush its cover onto the floor, thereby destroying it.

Freud's point about bungled actions is that they are no accidents: they serve an intention or purpose. Because there was a purpose for which the agent brushed the inkstand's cover onto the floor, his doing so cannot be classified as something that merely happened to him. He didn't just suffer or undergo this movement of his hand; he actively performed it.

Nevertheless, Freud acknowledges that a bungled action somehow differs from a normal attempt to accomplish the same purpose with the same bodily movement. This admission is clearest in Freud's explanation for a famous slip of the tongue:[6]

> You probably still recall [writes Freud's source] the way in which the President of the Lower House of the Austrian Parliament *opened* the sitting a short while ago: "Gentlemen: I take notice that a full quorum of members is present and herewith declare the sitting *closed!*" His attention was only drawn by the general merriment and he corrected his mistake.

In commenting on this case (which he does several times during his career), Freud sometimes emphasizes the similarity between the President's initial slip and his subsequent correction.[7]

> The sense and intention of his slip was that he wanted to close the sitting. 'Er sagt es ja selbst' we are tempted to quote: we need only take him at his word. . . . It is clear that he wanted to open the sitting, but it is equally clear that he also wanted to close it. That is so obvious that it leaves us nothing to interpret.

Here Freud implies that the President's utterance of the word "closed" was motivated by a desire to close the sitting, just as his subsequent utterance of the word "open" was motivated by a desire to open it. In other passages, however, Freud draws a contrast between the two utterances. In the first case, he points out, the President "said the contrary of what he intended," whereas "[a]fter his slip of the tongue he at once produces the wording which he originally intended"—and which he now presumably intends again.[8] The correction is therefore intentional in a sense that the slip was not. Indeed, Freud ultimately implies that the slip was committed not only unintentionally but

---

[6] *Ibid.*, 59. Freud is quoting R. Meringer, 'Wie man sich versprechen kann,' *Neue Freie Presse*, 23 Aug. 1900.

[7] *Introductory Lectures on Psychoanalysis*, SE XV: 40, 47.

[8] *Introductory Lectures*, 47; see also 'Some Elementary Lessons in Psycho-Analysis,' SE XXIII: 284.

unwillingly, since he says that the desire to close the session "succeeded in making itself effective, against the speaker's will."[9]

Thus, Freud's explanation of the slip as purposeful leaves unchallenged the speaker's own sense that his power of speech ran away with him, or that his words "slipped out." The explanation would contradict the speaker only if he went to the extent of denying that it was indeed his power of speech and his words that were involved. The Freudian explanation would then force the speaker to admit that "I declare the sitting closed" was something that he said—not, for example, a noise forced from his throat by a spasm. But the Freudian explanation still allows him to claim that he said it despite himself, and that it was therefore a slip, however motivated.

Such cases require us to define a category of ungoverned activities, distinct from mere happenings, on the one hand, and from autonomous actions, on the other. This category contains the things that one does rather than merely undergoes, but that one somehow fails to regulate in the manner that separates autonomous human action from merely motivated activity. The philosophy of action must therefore account for three categories of phenomena: mere happenings, mere activities, and actions.

Making Things Happen

The boundaries separating these categories mark increments in the subject's involvement as the cause of his own behavior. A slip of the tongue differs from a spasm of the larynx, we observed, in that it doesn't just issue from the subject: he produces it. But then, of course, there is also a sense in which his utterance is produced despite him, by a desire that he didn't intend to express. Similarly, a person can knock something off a desk in a manner that is adroitly clumsy— perfectly aimed, on the one hand, and yet also out of his conscious control, on the other.

Mere activity is therefore a partial and imperfect exercise of the subject's capacity to make things happen: in one sense, the subject makes the activity happen; in another, it is made to happen despite him, or at least without his concurrence. Full-blooded human action occurs only when the subject's capacity to make things happen is exercised to its fullest extent. To study the nature of activity and action is thus to study two degrees in the exercise of a single capacity.

This capacity merits philosophical study because it seems incompatible with our conception of how the world works more generally. We tend to think that

---

[9] 'Some Elementary Lessons,' *loc. cit.*

whatever happens either is caused to happen by other happenings or *just* happens, by chance: events owe their occurrence to other events or to nothing at all. But if we make things happen, those events owe their occurrence to us, to persons. How can people give rise to events?

On the answer to this question hangs the viability of innumerable concepts indispensable for everyday life—concepts of human agency, creativity, and responsibility. Nothing that happens can genuinely be our idea, our doing, or our fault unless we somehow make it happen. Without a capacity to make things happen, we would never be in a position to choose or reject anything, to owe or earn anything, to succeed or fail at anything. We would simply be caught up in the flow of events, and our lives would be just so much water under the bridge.

We don't seem to be adrift in the flow events: we seem to intervene in it, by producing some events and preventing others. Yet our intervention invariably consists in thoughts and bodily movements, which either happen by chance or are caused to happen by other thoughts and movements, which are themselves events taking place in our minds and bodies. Our intervening in the flow of events is just another part of that flow. So how can it count, after all, as an intervention—or, for that matter, as ours?

The Standard Model

The standard answer to this question goes like this. We want something to happen, and we believe that some behavior of ours would constitute or produce or at least promote its happening. These two attitudes jointly cause the relevant behavior, and in doing so they manifest the causal powers that are partly constitutive of their being, respectively, a desire and a belief. Because these attitudes also justify the behavior that they cause, that behavior eventuates not only *from causes* but *for reasons*. And whatever we do for reasons is consequently of our making.

Thus, for example: I want to know the time; I believe that looking at my watch will result in my knowing the time; and these two attitudes cause a glance at my watch, thus manifesting their characteristic causal powers as a desire and a belief. The desire and belief that cause my glance at the watch are my reasons for glancing at it; and because I engage in this behavior for reasons, I make it happen.[10]

---

[10] The example is borrowed from Donald Davidson, 'How is Weakness of the Will Possible,' in *Essays on Actions and Events* (Oxford: Clarendon Press, 1980), 21–42, at 31. Davidson is, of course, the foremost exponent of the standard model.

This model seems right in several respects. To begin with, it treats my making something happen as a complex process composed of simpler processes in which events are caused by other events. I can make something happen even though it is caused by other events, according to this model, because their role in its production can add up or amount to mine. If the model identifies events whose causal role really does amount to mine, then it will have succeeded in reconciling my capacity to make things happen with the causal structure of the world.

The model is at least partly successful on this score. The events that it picks out in the causal history of my behavior are closely associated with my identity, and the causal operations of these events consequently implicate me, at least to some extent. What I want and what I believe are central features of my psychology, which is central to my nature as a person. My wantings and believings are therefore central features of me, and whatever they cause can be regarded as caused by me, in some sense.

The question remains, however, whether the causal role of my desires and beliefs adds up to the role that I play in producing an action or whether alternatively, it amounts to the role that I play in producing a mere activity. The claim made for the standard model is that it is a model of action, in which my capacity to make things happen is exercised to its fullest extent. Is this claim correct?

The standard model is at least correct, I think, about what this claim will require for its vindication. The model assumes that the processes constituting a person's role in producing an action must be the ones that connect his behavior to reasons in such a way that it is based on, or performed for, those reasons. If a person's constitution includes a causal mechanism that has the function of basing his behavior on reasons, then that mechanism is, functionally speaking, the locus of his agency, and its control over his behavior amounts to his self-control, or autonomy.[11]

Why would behavior produced by such a mechanism be any more attributable to the person than that produced by other causes? The answer is that a person is somehow identified with his own rationality. As Aristotle put it, "Each person seems to be his understanding."[12] Hence causation via a person's rational faculties qualifies as causation by the person himself. Of course, this statement raises more questions than it answers; but I hope to answer those questions, too, by the end of this Introduction. For now,

---

[11] The terms 'autonomy' and 'autonomous' are ambiguous. On the one hand, they express a property that distinguishes action from mere behavior and (I claim) from mere activity as well. On the other hand, they express a property that differentiates among actions, or styles of action. To be subservient or conformist is to lack autonomy in the latter sense. But subservience and conformism can be displayed in actions that are still autonomous in the sense that distinguishes them from mere behavior or activity.   [12] *Nicomachean Ethics* 1178a.

I simply want to endorse this inchoate intuition underlying the standard model of agency.

One might object, at this point, that responding to reasons is the function of an entire person, not of a causal mechanism within him. The phrase "responding to reasons," one might insist, already describes something done by the agent and hence cannot describe a mere chain of events.

To be sure, the concept of basing behavior on reasons belongs to the same conceptual vocabulary as that of performing an action or making things happen, and so it cannot provide the desired reduction of those concepts into the vocabulary of event-causation. But it isn't meant to provide that reduction. "Basing behavior on reasons" is not proposed as an event-causal replacement for agential concepts; rather, it is proposed as that agential concept whose reduction will be the key to reducing the others. In order for a chain of events to constitute a person's making things happen, in the fullest sense of the phrase, it will have to constitute, more specifically, his doing something for a reason.

So says the standard model of action—rightly, in my view. But my agreement with the standard model ends here. The model goes on to say that the chain of events constituting a person's doing something for a reason is that in which his behavior is caused by a desire and belief in the manner that's characteristic of those attitudes. I think that this aspect of the model runs afoul of obvious counterexamples.

Failings of the Standard Model

The standard model already contains a clause designed to rule out some counterexamples, in which behavior is caused by a desire and belief but fails to constitute an action performed for reasons. This clause appears in my formulation as the requirement that the desire and belief causing behavior must exercise the causal powers that are characteristic of those attitudes.

Here is an example in which desire and belief operate uncharacteristically. A speaker's desire to win the sympathy of his audience, and his belief that nothing short of tears would suffice, might frustrate him to the point of tears. In causing behavior through the medium of frustration, his desire and belief would not manifest their characteristic causal powers. Characteristically, these attitudes cause whatever behavior is specified in the content of the belief as conducive to the outcome desired.[13] But the speaker in this case could have

---

[13] We can imagine a version of this case in which the speaker, upon sensing the purely involuntary flow of tears, is moved to exploit it by actively crying, thus transforming a mere bodily event into an activity. The point is that the difference between the initial event and the

been frustrated to the point of tears by many different beliefs about the difficulty of attaining his goal. It's just an accident that the belief frustrating his desire, and thereby producing tears, is a belief about the necessity of tears. The mechanism thus actuated—that is, the mechanism of frustration—would not in general conform the subject's behavior to the instrumental content of his belief. Hence his motives do not exercise their characteristic powers in causing his behavior.

Adherents of the standard model believe that by ruling out such cases, in which behavior is caused but not motivationally guided by a desire and belief, they have succeeded in narrowing their analysis to behavior that is caused in the right way to qualify as an action performed for reasons. I think that they have made considerable progress in narrowing their analysis to behavior that qualifies as motivated activity. But I do not think that motivated activity necessarily constitutes an action performed for a reason.

Recall the first Freudian slip examined above.[14] The agent wants to destroy his inkstand and he is thereby moved to do what he knows will destroy it. His behavior thus satisfies the standard model, but it doesn't qualify as an action: it's a defective instance of the agent's making something happen.

Note that this example is not ruled out by the requirement that desire and belief exert their characteristic powers in causing behavior. In Freud's explanation of his mishap these characteristic powers are indeed at work. It's no accident that the agent is caused to do what's specified in the content of his belief as conducive to the desired outcome of obtaining a new inkstand: the instrumental content of his belief is what's governing his behavior. So the agent really does brush the inkstand's cover off the desk for the purpose of

---

subsequent activity would be—not *that* the latter was caused by the speaker's desire and belief—but rather *how* it was caused by them.

[14] Note, by the way, that the second slip does not fit the standard model, because the President knows that he cannot close the session simply by uttering the words "I declare the session closed." Hence his utterance is not motivated by the belief that it will accomplish the desired result.

Other slips of the tongue do fit the standard model, however. Consider, for example, a case reported to Freud by Viktor Tausk. Tausk committed his slip of the tongue when the hostess entertaining him and his young sons began to rail against the Jews, unaware that Tausk himself was Jewish. On the one hand, Tausk wanted to set his sons an example of moral courage in the face of anti-Semitism; on the other hand, he wanted to avoid a scene, which could potentially have ruined the family's vacation. Deciding to hold his tongue, he tried to dismiss the boys from the room, lest they precipitate the confrontation that he had reluctantly decided to avoid: 'I said: "Go into the garden *Juden* [Jews]", quickly correcting it to '*Jungen* [youngsters]''. The others did not in fact draw any conclusions from my slip of the tongue, since they attached no significance to it; but I was obliged to learn the lesson that the "faith of our fathers" cannot be disavowed with impunity if one is a son and has sons of one's own' (*Psychopathology of Everyday Life*, 92–3). Tausk wanted to show his sons how they should declare their Jewish ancestry when under social pressure to conceal it; and he was moved to say something that amounted to just such a declaration.

destroying it, unlike the frustrated speaker imagined above, whose tears are shed out of frustration and hence not for any purpose.

In sum, the agent's movement is caused in the way that's designated as right by the standard model; and yet it is only an activity. The standard model thus appears to specify the wrong "right way" for behavior to be caused. It specifies the way in which behavior must be caused in order to qualify as a purposeful activity, but not the way it must be caused in order to qualify as an autonomous action.

If we want to know why the standard model has failed to specify the right way for autonomous action to be caused, we need look no farther than the requirements that the model set for itself. The idea behind the model, remember, is that the causal processes constitutive of action will be the ones in virtue of which behavior is based on or performed for reasons. Those processes are the ones that the model aspires to specify as the right way for action to be caused. But the model has not lived up to its own aspirations: it hasn't specified the processes in virtue of which behavior is based on reasons.

A reason for acting is something that warrants or justifies behavior. In order to serve as the basis for the subject's behavior, it must justify that behavior to the subject—that is, in his eyes—and it must thereby engage some rational disposition of his to do what's justified, to behave in accordance with justifications. When someone just knocks over something that he unconsciously wants to destroy, or blurts out something that he unconsciously wants to say, he has not necessarily seen any justification for his behavior, nor has his rationality been engaged, although he has indeed been motivated by a desire.So although his behavior has been caused by something that may in fact be a reason, it has not been caused in the right way to have been done for that reason.

This flaw in the standard model is papered over, in some versions, by a characterization of desire itself as entailing the grasp of a justification for acting. Engagement of the agent's rationality is thus claimed to be inherent in the very nature of desire.

Desiring something entails regarding it as *to be brought about*, just as believing something entails regarding it as *having come about*, or *true*. And regarding something as to be brought about sounds as if it entails seeing a justification for acting. Proponents of the standard model therefore claim that if a subject desires something, and believes some behavior conducive to it, then he already sees a justification for that behavior, and his responsiveness to reasons is thereby engaged.

Unfortunately, this argument trades on confusions in the language of "seeing" and "regarding as." To say that desiring something entails regarding it as to be brought about is simply to describe the so-called direction of fit that's characteristic of desire. Desire has what is called a mind-to-world direction of fit, in that its propositional object functions as a model for what it represents rather than as modeled after it. When the President wants the session of the Senate to be closed, for example, he has a mental representation of the session's being closed, and that representation serves as an archtype for the state of affairs that it represents rather than as an ectype of it. But to regard the session's closure as to be brought about in this sense is not to think of it as appropriate or fitting or correct to bring about: it is not to judge that the session's closure is desirable or good. It's simply to hold the thought "session closed" in a conative rather than cognitive mode. Thus, wanting the session to be closed does not entail seeing any justification or warrant for behavior conducive to closing it.

The objection therefore stands that the standard model fails to specify the way in which action involves causation by reasons, although it succeeds in specifying the way in which purposeful activity involves causation by desires and beliefs. The standard model is a model of activity but not of action.[15]

Let me pause for a brief summary. I began by drawing a distinction between mere activity and action, which differ with respect to the degree of the subject's agency—the degree to which he makes things happen. I then posed the question how a person can make things happen, in a world where events are caused by other events. An answer to this question, I suggested, would have to show how causation by events could add up to or amount to causation by a person.

I next examined a standard model of agency, which rests on the premise that a person causes his behavior when it is caused by reasons in such a way that it is based on or performed for those reasons. The model claims that behavior is performed for reasons whenever it is caused by desire and belief in the characteristic way. But some instances of characteristic desire-belief causation yield no more than mere activity, because the resulting behavior is not based on the desire and belief as reasons. Hence the standard model is sufficient for motivated activity but not for autonomous action.

I shall now consider a proposal for improving the standard model by adding to it. This proposal will bring us closer to an account of agency, but still not close enough. My critique of this proposal will suggest a third—and, in my view, correct—account of agency.

Adding to the Standard Model

I have argued that when desire and belief cause behavior in such a way as to operate as its motives, they do not necessarily operate as its reasons—that is,

---

[15] The argument of this section is developed more fully in 'The Guise of the Good,' (Chap. 5, below).

as reasons for which the behavior is performed. But I do not claim that their being motives for acting somehow excludes their also being reasons; nor do I claim that their operating as motives somehow excludes their also operating as reasons. All I claim is that their operating in the one capacity doesn't amount to their operating in the other. Autonomous action requires something more than motivation by desire and belief, as is demonstrated by motivated slips that are not autonomous; but the "something more" that's required can be provided by the same motivating desire and belief, operating in an additional capacity.

Consider an alternative version of Freud's story, in which the agent not only is motivated by his desire to destroy the inkpot but also acts on the grounds of that desire, in its capacity as a reason. In acting on that desire as a reason, let us suppose, he is aware of the desire and regards it as justifying a movement of his hand; and he makes the movement partly because of seeing it as justified. His desire thus causes his behavior via his disposition to behave in accordance with perceived justifications—a mechanism that wasn't operative in the original story, where the agent was unaware of the justifying desire.

Yet even in the alternative version of the story, where the desire influences the agent via his perception of it as justifying action, it can continue to operate as a motive, as it did when it was hidden from view. The new influence that it now exerts in its capacity as a reason can be to enlist some reinforcement for, or remove some inhibition of, its own motivational force. Even when the subject is persuaded by rational reflection on his desire—a process different from simply being moved by its inherent force—his response to being persuaded can be to acquiesce in being so moved. On the grounds of his desire conceived as warrant, he may accede to its impetus as a motive.

The interaction of these causal mechanisms is not as mysterious as it may sound. Suppose that you were charged with the task of designing an autonomous agent, given the design for a mere subject of motivation.[16] If you like, you can imaginatively assign yourself to divine middle-management as project leader for the sixth afternoon of creation; or you may prefer to take the role of natural selection over the corresponding millennia. In either case, you face a world already populated with lower animals, which are capable of motivated activity, and your task is to introduce autonomous agents.

In neither case would you start from scratch. Rather, you would add practical reason to the existing design for motivated creatures, and you would add

---

[16] Michael Bratman has pointed out to me that the methodology of "creature design" was first proposed by Paul Grice, in his Presidential Address to the APA, 'Method in Philosophical Psychology (From the Banal to the Bizarre),' *Proceedings and Addresses of the APA* 48 (1975) 23–53. Bratman uses the same methodology, to reach different conclusions, in a paper entitled 'Valuing and the Will,' (MS).

it in the form of a mechanism modifying the motivational forces already at work. You would design practical reason to survey a creature's motives, to block or inhibit some of them, and to reinforce others.

A creature endowed with such a mechanism would reflect on forces within him that were already capable of producing behavior by themselves, as they do in nonautonomous creatures or in his own nonautonomous behavior. His practical reasoning would be a process of assessing these springs of action and intervening in their operations—which intervention would require an additional, rational spring of action capable of modifying or redirecting the force exerted by the other springs.

The Hierarchical Model

Actually, you would already have come close to equipping motivated creatures with such a mechanism as soon as you had endowed them with self-awareness. For if creatures already have the capacity to desire—that is, to represent things as *to be brought about*—and if they subsequently gain the capacity to represent their own desires, then they will be able to desire states of affairs involving their own desires. They will be capable of wanting to have some desires but not others, and to be actuated by some desires but not by others. And then the latter, lower-order desires, upon coming to their notice, will be either reinforced or opposed by the force of the higher-order desires directed at them.

The result would be the hierarchical model of agency, as it is often called.[17] In the hierarchical model, the behaviors that a person makes happen, in the fullest sense, are the ones that are caused by his first-order motives as reinforced by higher-order motives. Autonomous action, according to this model, is behavior motivated by the desires and beliefs by which the subjects wants, or is at least content, to be motivated.

I regard the hierarchical model of agency as an improvement on the standard model, because it requires the subject to be reflectively aware of his motives in order to act autonomously. A Freudian slip takes its agent by surprise, thereby casting him in the passive role of observer. This behavior takes its agent by surprise because its motive is unconscious: he is not aware of wanting to do what he does. Such a lack of self-awareness would not have disqualified the resulting behavior from being an autonomous action according to the standard model, but it is indeed disqualifying according to the hierarchical model. For an agent cannot want or be content to be motivated by a desire that he is unaware of having.

---

[17] The originator of this model is Harry Frankfurt, in *The Importance of What We Care About*. See also Frankfurt's *Volition, Necessity, and Love* (Cambridge: Cambridge Univ. Press, 1999), especially 'The Faintest Passion.'

Even so, the hierarchical model of autonomous action still seems inadequate. In this model, the subject's awareness of his first-order desires arouses second-order desires as to whether they should motivate him, but the latter desires are not necessarily a response to the rational force of the former: they aren't a response to first-order desires in their capacity as reasons for acting. Hence the subject's higher-order desires play a causal role from which he can once again be dissociated.

Suppose that the President, in Freud's second example, had been aware of his desire to close the session rather than open it; and that he had even liked the idea of being motivated by that desire as he spoke. His desires might have been due to an overwhelming sense of depression or *ennui* at the prospect of the new session.[18] Also out of boredom or depression, the President might have taken perverse satisfaction in being moved to speak inappropriately; he might even have taken a further, perverse satisfaction in the perversity of his own satisfaction; and so on. According to the hierarchical model, his indifferent mood would have enhanced his autonomy, by forestalling any higher orders of dissatisfaction with his first-order motives. He would have been motivated by a first-order desire with which he was satisfied, and satisfied to be satisfied, and so on. The hierarchical model would therefore have classified his behavior as autonomous.

As this example suggests, however, higher-order satisfaction with one's motives doesn't necessarily make for autonomy. Insofar as the President's satisfaction with his own motivational state was attributable to depression or *ennui*, it would not have been an expression of his own will. If anything, it would have expressed a lack of will on his part, under the weight of a psychic force that is usually regarded as pathological or alien.

The reason why the hierarchical model would classify this behavior as autonomous is that the model doesn't distinguish sufficiently among the subject's responses to his own motivation. A favorable disposition toward his first-order motives automatically implicates the subject in causing their behavioral results, according to this model, irrespective of why or how he is favorably disposed toward those motives. It doesn't matter, in the hierarchical model, whether the subject is satisfied with his first-order motives because of depression or boredom or laziness—or, alternatively, because he is responding to their force as reasons.

But this distinction ought to matter in the constitution of autonomous action. A motive cannot be taken up into the subject's will by just any favorable response to it. It can be taken up into the subject's will only by a

---

[18] This counterexample to the hierarchical model is adapted from one introduced by Michael Bratman in 'Identification, Decision, and Treating as a Reason,' *Faces of Intention; Selected Essays on Intention and Agency* (Cambridge: Cambridge Univ. Press, 1999), 185–206.

favorable response to it as a reason for acting—a response mounted by the subject's rationality. What autonomy seems to require, then, is not just the capacity for higher-order motives in general but particular higher-order motives, which would reinforce the agent's first-order motives insofar as the latter were perceived as reasons.

We thus arrive at a third model of action, avoiding the faults of the other two.[19] Unlike the standard model, this third model would exclude from the category of actions those unforeseen movements to which a person is impelled by motives of which he is unaware. Unlike the hierarchical model, it would also exclude movements produced by those motives which the agent endorses without regarding them as reasons. This model would define action as behavior whose first-order motives are perceived as reasons and are consequently reinforced by higher-order motives of rationality.

Higher-Order Motives of Rationality

What sort of higher-order motives can we imagine for this role? One possibility would be to posit a higher-order desire, on the part of every agent, to be actuated by those of his lower-order motives which constitute the best reasons for him to act. This desire would move a person to survey and evaluate his motives as reasons for acting, and it would then add its motivational force to whichever combination of motives impressed him as rationally superior.

I am going to argue in favor of positing something like a desire to be actuated by the best reasons—something that might imprecisely be described as such. But first I am going to argue against positing the desire that would fit the description precisely.[20]

In order to fit this description precisely, a desire would need to have a *de dicto* content that included the concept of motives that constitute reasons for acting.

---

[19] A model of this kind is also favored by Bratman in 'Identification, Decision, and Treating as a Reason.'

[20] Unfortunately, this point is somewhat obscured by the division of topics among the papers in this volume. In 'What Happens When Someone Acts?' I speak of a desire to act in accordance with reasons, remarking in a footnote that, in my view, the desire in question is not the one to which this description would apply *de dicto*. My argument for this remark appears in 'The Possibility of Practical Reason' (Chap. 8, below) and is summarized in the following section of this Introduction.

An additional argument, which I do not give, is that a *de dicto* interpretation of the "the desire to act in accordance with reasons" would yield a view that ruled out weakness of will. For if autonomous action were behavior guided in part by the desire to act in accordance with reasons so described, then an agent could never autonomously do something other than what he believed he had most reason for doing. My conception of the relevant desire allows for this possibility. (See n. 34, below.)

It would have to be a desire to be actuated by reason-constituting motives so described—described, that is, as constituting reasons. And there are serious problems with the notion that such a desire mediates an agent's response to reasons.

One problem with this notion is that it would require a person to have the concept of a reason for acting in order to have the desire whose reinforcement of his other motives would turn their behavioral output into full-blooded actions. The notion would thus require a person to have the concept of a reason in order to be capable of acting at all. Indeed, it would require him to have, not only the generic concept of a reason, but a specific conception of what counts as a reason, and what makes some reasons better than others. Without such a conception, a person would never draw any conclusions about which motives were rationally superior, and his desire to be actuated by rationally superior motives would never be engaged. Agency itself would therefore require a fairly advanced level of intellectual sophistication.

A further problem emerges from consideration of how a person might form his conception of what counts as a reason for acting. What *does* count as a reason for acting, and how can a person tell that it does? In order to answer this question, we shall have to suspend our inquiry into the causal structure of practical reason, so that we can consider its logic.

I should pause, at this point, to beg for patience with the arguments that follow. When the dust settles, these arguments will have yielded a new account of agency. But the dust won't settle for several pages, during which the outlines of the final product will remain obscure.

The Logic of Reasons

A reason is a consideration that justifies, and to justify something is to show that it is just, in the old-fashioned sense meaning "correct." Something is subject to justification only if it is subject to a *jus*, or norm of correctness; and it is then subject to reasons in the form of considerations showing it to satisfy the norm.

Thus, a belief can be justified only because it can be correct or incorrect by virtue of being true or false. Reasons for a belief are considerations that show the belief to be correct by this standard, insofar as they show it to be true. The question, then, is what serves as the standard of correctness for action, in the same way as truth serves as the standard of correctness for belief.

There is a temptation to think that the norm of correctness for actions is that they should be supported by the strongest reasons. But this thought leads in a vicious circle. What counts as a reason for acting depends on what justifies action; which depends on what counts as correctness for action; which cannot depend, in turn, on what counts as a reason. Action must have an independent norm of correctness—a standard not dependent on the concept of reasons—before it can provide the sort of normative context in which reasons exist.[21]

Ideally, the norm of correctness for action should be exempt from deliberative criticism. That is, the norm should not leave open any question about whether to act in accordance with it. If such a question could be raised, it would have to be answered by appeal to reasons for acting in accordance with the norm; whereas the norm is supposed to determine what counts as a reason for acting, in the first place. If there had to be reasons for acting in accordance with the norm that determines what counts as a reason for acting, then practical reasoning would again be circular.[22]

Here the analogy with theoretical reasoning suggests a solution. The norm of correctness for belief is not open to question because it is internal to the nature of belief itself. The concept of belief just is the concept of an attitude for which there is such a thing as correctness or incorrectness, consisting in truth or falsity. For a propositional attitude to be a belief just is, in part, for it to be capable of going right or wrong by being true or false. Philosophers have traditionally accounted for this feature of belief by saying that belief constitutively aims at the truth.[23]

If there were something at which action constitutively aimed, then there would be a norm of correctness internal to the nature of action. There would be something about behavior that constituted its correctness *as* an action, in the same way as the truth of a propositional attitude constitutes its correctness as a belief. This standard would not be open to question: actions meeting the standard would be correct on their own terms, so to speak, by virtue of their nature as actions, just as true beliefs are correct by virtue of their nature as beliefs. And this norm of correctness for action would in turn determine what counts as a reason for acting.[24]

Let me be clearer about the relation between the constitutive aim of belief and the norm that applies to belief in light of that aim.[25] To say that belief aims at

---

[21] The argument of this paragraph is developed more fully in 'The Possibility of Practical Reason'.

[22] On the topic of practical reasons for obeying norms of practical reason, see 'Deciding How to Decide' (Chap. 10, below).

[23] See Bernard Williams, 'Deciding to Believe' in *Problems of the Self* (Cambridge: Cambridge University Press, 1973), 136–51.

[24] My reasons for thinking that action must have a constitutive aim are developed more fully in 'The Possibility of Practical Reason'.

[25] My views on the truth-directedness of belief are developed more fully in 'On the Aim of Belief' (Chap. 11, below).

the truth is not simply to re-express the norm stipulating that a belief must be true in order to be correct; rather, it is to point out a fact about belief that generates this norm for its correctness.

Belief aims at the truth in the normative sense only because it aims at the truth descriptively, in the sense that it is constitutively regulated by mechanisms designed to ensure that it is true. Belief also bears a more fundamental relation to the truth, in that it is an attitude of regarding a proposition as true; but in this respect it is no different from other cognitive states, such as assuming or imagining, which share the same direction of fit, in that they take their objects as true. What distinguishes a belief from other states that take their propositional objects as true is that, unlike assumption or fantasy, belief tends to track what *is* true, when its regulatory mechanisms are functioning as designed. If a cognitive state isn't regulated by mechanisms designed to track the truth, then it isn't a belief: it's some other kind of cognition. That's why aiming at the truth is constitutive of belief.

Belief thus aims at the truth in the same sense that the circulation aims to supply body tissues with nutrients and oxygen. Not just any movement of fluids within the body counts as the circulation, but only those movements which are under the control of mechanisms designed to direct them at supplying the tissues. Hence the aim of supplying the tissues is constitutive of the circulation, just as the aim of being true is constitutive of belief.

If action were to have a constitutive aim in the same sense, that aim would have to be a function of mechanisms that produce and control action, and constitutively so. What could those mechanisms be?

Well, we have already envisioned such mechanisms, in our third model of action, outlined above. That model characterizes action as behavior that is motivated by lower-order desires and beliefs as regulated by a particular higher-order motive. The model thus implies that it is constitutive of action to be regulated by a particular motive. The object of that motive, whatever it is, should qualify as action's constitutive aim.

Our inquiry into the logic of practical reason has thus led us back to the causal mechanisms involved. Action would be logically subject to justification, we find, if it had a constitutive aim, in relation to which it could be correct or incorrect merely by virtue of its nature as action. But the constitutive aim of action would have to be something at which it was in fact *aimed*; and its being aimed, in some direction or other, would be a fact about the mechanisms causing and controlling it—in particular, the mechanisms whose causing and controlling it were constitutive of its being action. And we previously posited such a mechanism, in the form of a higher-order, rational motive.[26]

---

[26] This section supplies the connection between two of my papers, 'What Happens When Someone Acts?' and 'The Possibility of Practical Reason'. The former argues that action must have a constitutive motive; the latter argues that action must have a constitutive aim. The

We were wondering whether this higher-order, rational motive could consist in a desire to be actuated by whichever motives provide the best reasons for acting. That question prompted our digression into the logic of reasons; and the digression has now put the answer within reach.

What's in question is the content of that higher-order motive which turns mere behavior into autonomous action by regulating how it is motivated. We have now seen that this higher-order motive, in constitutively regulating action, would lend it a constitutive aim in relation to which it would be subject to justification and reasons. But if this motive consisted in a desire to be actuated by reasons, then being actuated by reasons would be the constitutive aim of action—which is impossible, as we have also seen. For if the constitutive aim of action were that it be actuated by reasons, then the aim of action and the nature of reasons for acting would be caught in a vicious circle. What counted as a reason for acting would depend on what counted as correctness for actions as such; but what counted as correctness for actions would depend on what counted as a reason for acting.

We are hoping to find that action is constituted by a substantive aim, just as belief is constituted by the substantive aim of being true. The aim of belief is substantive in the sense that it is conceptually independent of reasons for believing; our hope for action must be, similarly, that it turn out to be constituted by an aim conceptually independent of reasons for acting. What turns out to lend action its constitutive aim, we must hope, is a higher-order motive whose content does not include the concept of a reason.

Yet we have also said that the higher-order motive constitutively regulating action must be a rational motive, embodying the subject's responsiveness to reasons, so that its role in producing behavior will be inescapably his. The question therefore arises how a motive can be rational, and embody the subject's responsiveness to reasons, if its content doesn't include the concept of a reason. The answer is that the motive constitutively regulating action will constitute the subject's responsiveness to reasons simply because the considerations to which it responds will *ipso facto* count as reasons for acting.

Let me resort again to the analogy with belief. Indicators of truth count as reasons for belief because truth is the aim of belief; but truth's being the aim of belief just consists in the way that the mechanisms of belief are designed to regulate it—which they do by responding to indicators of truth. Ultimately, then, indicators of truth count as reasons for belief because they are the considerations in response to which belief is designed to be regulated. The aim of belief and reasons for belief are fixed simultaneously, the one being determined by the way in which belief is constitutively regulated in response to the other.

connection is that if action has a constitutive motive, then the object of that motive is something at which it will be constitutively aimed.

So, too, we are hoping that considerations of a particular kind will count as reasons for acting because of action's constitutive aim; but action's having that aim must consist in the way that its mechanisms are designed to regulate it—which they must do in response to considerations of that kind. Thus, we must hope for considerations of a kind that count as reasons for acting because they are the kind in response to which action is designed to be regulated. The aim of action and reasons for action must be fixed simultaneously, the one being determined by the way in which action is regulated in response to the other.

Again, the considerations in response to which action is constitutively regulated will need to have something in common other than being reasons for acting, since their being reasons for acting will just consist in action's being constitutively regulated in response to them. Whatever regulates action in response to these considerations may turn out to be describable, imprecisely, as a desire to be actuated by reasons. But there will have to be something else about them to which this regulatory mechanism responds, since its responsiveness to them will be what constitutes them as reasons, and hence cannot depend on their already being reasons.

Indeed, the analogy between action and belief suggests that this mechanism need not literally be a desire.[27] We conceived of it as a desire because we appended it to the hierarchical model of agency, which characterizes action as regulated by higher-order motives. The problem with the hierarchical model, we found, is that it can be satisfied by any higher-order motive at all, whereas the mechanism that constitutively regulates action must somehow connect it to reasons for acting. That's why we posited a higher-order motive of rationality.

Yet consider the case of belief. Here the analogous role may be played by the subject's desire to arrive at the truth; but it may also be played by sub-personal cognitive systems that are designed to track the truth, independently of the subject's desires. Truth must be the aim of belief, but it need not be an aim on the part of the believer; it may instead be an aim implicit in some parts of his cognitive architecture. When his beliefs change in the face of evidence or argument, he might be described as trying to arrive at the truth, as if he were motivated by a desire. But this description might be a personification of aims that are in fact sub-personal.

Similarly, an agent's responsiveness to reasons for acting may only sometimes be due to a desire for the relevant aim while, at other times, being due

---

[27] The ideas in this section are not contained in any of the following papers, all of which assume that the constitutive aim of action is provided by a higher-order, rational motive. Objections pressed by Philip Clark have recently led me to see that this assumption is mistaken, for reasons that I had myself applied to the analogous case in 'On the Aim of Belief'.

to psychological mechanisms in which that aim is implicit. Whenever someone acts, he might then be described as trying to arrive at that aim, as if motivated by a desire for it. As in the case of belief, however, this description might sometimes be a personification of aims that are in fact sub-personal. I shall therefore stop speaking of a higher-order, rational motive and speak instead of a higher-order, rational aim, which may or may not be imparted to action by a motive on the part of the agent.

The Constitutive Aim of Action

I have now arrived at a highly abstract schema for a theory of agency—so abstract, I fear, as to lack any intuitive appeal. So let me return to a more concrete level of thought. Let me return, in particular, to the examples with which I initially illustrated the difference between action and mere activity. I want to see whether a theory of agency can be developed directly from reflection on those examples. (The dust should finally begin to settle.)

Consider the slip of the tongue committed by the President in Freud's anecdote: "I herewith declare the sitting closed!" This behavior was less than an autonomous action precisely because it was a slip. But what do we mean in calling the President's utterance a slip, or in saying that it slipped out? What we mean, I think, is that it slipped *past* something—that it *gave the slip* to something that should have held it back. To what restraint did this utterance give the slip?

The relevant restraint is indirectly revealed, I believe, in the next sentence of the story: "His attention was only drawn by the general merriment and he corrected his mistake." What this sentence tells us is that the speaker didn't know what he had said until the laughter of his audience brought it to his attention. He came to know what he had said only by having his attention drawn to what he had heard himself say. And the reason why he came to know it in this manner is that *as he said it, he didn't know what he was saying.*

The same is true of any slip of the tongue, including one that immediately draws the speaker's attention without any help from the audience. Even when a speaker immediately catches his own mistake, the fact remains that he catches it: he receives it passively, in the manner of a surprised audience. And he is obliged to catch his faulty remark precisely because he let it fly without knowing what it was.

Unwitting speech of this sort is often inhibited. We often proceed under an inhibition with a content something like this: "Keep your mouth shut unless you know what you're going to say." This inhibition, I suggest, is what our words slip past on those occasions when they slip out: they slip past our inhibition against saying what we don't yet know that we're going to say.

Not saying what we don't know we're going to say is clearly a means of ensuring that when we open our mouths to say something, we already know what it is. Our inhibition against saying we-know-not-what is thus the negative manifestation of a positive aim: the aim of knowing what we're (already) saying. The words that slip out are the ones that escape regulation by this aim—which explains why we learn of them only by hearing ourselves say them.

Knowing what we're saying is rarely our end-in-view, of course, but I'm not suggesting that it is; I'm claiming only that it is an aim regulating our verbal behavior. It is what might be called a *sub-agential* aim,[28] which is not represented in our practical reasoning. Our behavior is regulated by many sub-agential aims. For example, our movements through the world are generally regulated by the aim of avoiding pain, even though pain-avoidance becomes our end-in-view only on rare occasions, when we are deliberately being careful. We are usually inhibited from bumping into furniture or stepping on sharp objects, without thinking about the pain to be avoided. Our behavior is thus regulated by an aim that isn't our end. I am suggesting that our behavior is similarly regulated by the sub-agential aim of knowing what we're saying, which inhibits us from speaking until we know what we're going to say.

In many cases, of course, we speak without already knowing the precise words that we're going to use, or even the precise meaning that we're going to express. All that we already know, in these cases, is the gist of what we're about to say, or perhaps some mental images associated with the thought to be articulated. Our precise wording is then something that we learn only by listening to ourselves.

But the reason why we have to listen for our words on such occasions, I suggest, is merely that the cognitive aim regulating our speech has been scaled back, not that it has disappeared. The aim that's operative on these occasions is merely to know what thought we're expressing, rather than the words in which we're expressing it; and so we are inhibited from speaking only until we know which thought we're going to express. At that point, we simply let the words come out, without knowing which words they'll be. But our verbal behavior has already been regulated by the cognitive aim of knowing our own drift, which is still, in modest form, the aim of knowing what we're saying.

A natural thing to observe about these occasions is that we speak without choosing our words: to produce words without knowing what they'll be is, in effect,

---

[28] An aim's being *sub-agential* is different from its being *sub-personal*, in the sense used on 19, above. If the aim consists in a desire on the part of the subject, then it is an attitude of the person; but it still may fail to operate as a reason for the agent. In that case, it may be personal but sub-agential. In my view, the aim currently under discussion is sometimes personal and sometimes sub-personal, but it is only rarely agential.

not to choose them. The times when we choose our words are times when we don't utter them until we have them properly in mind—which, I have suggested, are times when they are regulated by the aim of knowing what we're saying.

This observation suggests that there may be a connection between choosing our words and uttering them under the regulation of this sub-agential aim. In fact, it suggests that there may be a connection between choosing our behavior in general and producing it under the regulation of the corresponding, general aim. The general aim corresponding to that of knowing what we're saying would be this: the aim of knowing what we're doing.

I suggest that you go back to the drawing-board and add this aim to your design for autonomous creatures. To their existing capacities for motivation and self-awareness, add the sub-agential aim of knowing what they're doing. Now what sort of creatures have you designed?

Of course, your creatures still have first-order motives for doing various things on particular occasions. But because their behavior is now regulated by the aim of knowing what they're doing, they will be inhibited from doing anything until they have an idea of what they're going to do. And once they have an idea of what they're going to do, they will gain an additional inclination to do it, rather than anything else, since doing something else would result, at least momentarily, in their not knowing what they were doing. Their antecedent motives for doing various things will thus be restrained, until there's something that they expect themselves to do; whereupon the balance of forces will be decisively tilted in favor of doing the expected thing. Your creatures are therefore in a position to expect themselves to do any one of the things toward which they are antecedently motivated, in the confidence that they'll do whatever they expect.[29]

Your creatures now seem to share our capacity for choice or decision-making. When we choose or decide what we are going to do, we settle that question in our minds and we thereby settle the same question in fact. We make up our minds that we are going to do something, and we thereby make it the case that we're going to do it. Similarly for your redesigned creatures: settling in their minds what they are going to do is a way of settling that question in fact. For they will be inhibited from doing anything until they think they are going to do it, and then they will be prompted to do what they think.

---

[29] The mechanism described in this paragraph is similar to various mechanisms of self-prediction examined by empirical psychologists. Research on these mechanisms is surveyed in Mark Snyder, 'When Belief Creates Reality,' *Advances in Experimental Social Psychology* 18 (1984) 247–305, esp. p. 283. See also Eric R. Spangenberg and Anthony G. Greenwald, 'Social Influence by Requesting Self-Prophecy,' *Journal of Consumer Psychology* 8 (1999) 61–89. For another example, see S. J. Sherman, 'On the Self-erasing Nature of Errors of Prediction,' *Journal of Personality and Social Psychology* 39 (1980) 211–21.

Your creatures should also share our sense of having an open future or a meta-physically free will.[30] I don't say that they have a metaphysically free will or open futures—only that they should share our sense of having them. I assume that your creatures will be governed by deterministic laws of nature, under which their futures are fixed by facts about the past. I therefore assume that their futures are not in fact open, and their wills are not in fact free in the meta-physical sense.

But when these creatures contemplate what they are going to do next, there is nothing that they must think they'll do, in order to think correctly. There are many different things that they would be correct in expecting themselves to do, because they would do whichever one they expected. There is of course only one of these things that they are actually going to do; but they are going to do it only because they are going to expect so. They would do otherwise if they expected otherwise, and so they aren't epistemically barred from those alternative expectations.

There is consequently an epistemic sense in which the future is open, from these creatures' perspective. When they imagine various alternative futures for themselves, they would be correct to believe in any one of them, since the future that they end up believing in will be the future that they end up having. And being in a position to believe correctly in any one of several different imaginable futures feels like being in a position to *have* any one of several different imaginable futures. Thus, an epistemically open future is easily misperceived as metaphysically open. In reality, your creatures aren't in a position to have any one of several different futures, only to believe in them correctly. But the confusion is understandable.

The fact that your creatures would now perceive themselves as free, or their futures as open, is indirect evidence for the hypothesis that they have in fact been endowed with a capacity for choice or decision-making. What makes us feel free, after all, is our own capacity to make choices. If you have given your creatures the same feeling by endowing them with a particular higher-order aim—which, as it happens, also enables them to settle what they are going to do—then you must have endowed them with something very like our own capacity for choice.

My examination of a Freudian slip has now led me to an hypothesis about the nature of choices or decisions. I first identified the inhibition that fails when we commit a slip: it's the inhibition against doing things without knowing what they are. I then imagined this inhibition as being exerted by a second-order aim of knowing what we're doing, which would regulate what we do, by guiding

---

[30] The claims made in this section are developed further in 'Epistemic Freedom' (Chap. 2, below).

us toward things that we already know about. In the mechanism thus envisioned, we would have a kind of expectation that functioned in a peculiar way: it would settle in our minds the question what we were going to do, and it would thereby settle the same question in fact. Because this is exactly the function of a choice, I have arrived at the hypothesis that a choice consists in just such a self-fulfilling expectation.

One might wonder how we can come to expect behavior that isn't going to occur unless we already expect it. There would seem to be, antecedently, nothing to expect.

But that's the beauty of it: there *isn't* antecedently anything to expect, if "something to expect" means some future event waiting for us to expect it. Our expectation of doing something embodies an invention rather than a discovery. For we can simply adopt the expectation that we're going to do any one of the things for which we have some antecedent motives, and this expectation will modify the balance of forces so as to make itself true. We are thus in a position to *make up* our forthcoming behavior. Making up what we will do is, in fact, our way of making up our minds to do it.

Choice and Belief

I may at this point seem to have misappropriated terms like 'expectation' and 'knowledge'. An expectation, after all, is a belief; and knowledge is true and reliably justified belief. How can we simply make up true and reliably justified beliefs? In order to answer this question, I shall need to examine the similarities and differences between the mental states of belief and choice.[31]

The relevant similarities and differences between these attitudes occur on three related dimensions, two of which I have already mentioned—namely, the attitudes' directions of fit and their constitutive aims. I'll begin with the first of these dimensions.

An attitude's direction of fit, remember, consists in whether the attitude treats its propositional object as true or to be made true. The desire to act, on the one hand, and the belief that one will act, on the other, are attitudes toward the same proposition—i.e., that one will act—but the belief accepts the proposition as a representation of how things *are* arranged, whereas the desire projects it as a representation of how things are *to be* arranged. Their different directions of fit are what distinguish belief as cognitive from desire as conative.

---

[31] This section summarizes material contained in 'The Guise of the Good,' 'The Possibility of Practical Reason,' and 'On the Aim of Belief'.

Because choosing entails settling a question in one's mind, it requires more than representing an answer as *to be* arranged. If it were still to be arranged that I was going to act, then it would not yet be settled that I was going to act; and insofar as I regarded it as to be arranged, I would not yet regard it as settled. Settling on a future action thus requires representing the action as arranged: my choice makes it true that I'm going to act, by representing it as true that I'm going to act. It therefore has the same direction of fit as a belief.

Where choice differs from ordinary beliefs is in a feature that might be called its direction of guidance. An attitude's direction of guidance consists in whether the attitude causes or is caused by what it represents.

Now, there is a temptation to assume that if a mental state is cognitive, representing how things are, then it must be caused by how they are; whereas if it causes what it represents, then the state must be conative, representing how things are to be. This assumption implies that a cognitive direction of fit entails a passive direction of guidance; and, conversely, that only states with a conative direction of fit can be active or practical.

But when I make a choice, a question is resolved in the world by being resolved in my mind. That I am going to do something is made true by my representing it as true. So choice has the same direction of fit as belief but the same direction of guidance as desire: it is a case of practical cognition.

Choice has a third essential feature, which it shares with belief. Like belief, choice aims at the truth.

Note that accepting a proposition as true and aiming at the truth are two distinct features of belief. Mental states such as imagining and assuming also regard their propositional objects as true—that is, as representing how things *are* arranged rather than how they are *to be* arranged. But belief is regulated by the aim of regarding something *as* true only if it really *is* true; whereas imagining and assuming entail accepting a proposition fancifully or hypothetically, with some aim other than getting at the truth. The latter states thus share belief's direction of fit but not its constitutive aim.

When I form a choice or decision, however, I aim to settle a question in my mind only insofar as I can thereby settle it in fact; I aim, that is, to avoid representing an arrangement that I am not thereby managing to make. In the face of compelling evidence that I'm not going to do something, my mind cannot remain made up that I'm going to do it: the decision to do something, like the belief that I'm going to, cannot withstand evidence to the contrary. It thus represents things as having been arranged in some way, with the aim of representing how they really have been arranged, albeit by this very representation. It has the cognitive direction of fit and the associated aim of being true, despite having a practical direction of guidance.

A state that represents something *as* true, with the aim of so representing what *is* true, ought to count as knowledge if it attains its aim in the right way. And it ought to count as belief whether or not it attains its aim.

I do not want to quibble over the terms 'knowledge' and 'belief', however, if anyone insists on withholding them from states with a practical direction of guidance. By the same token, I can expect to be allowed the provisional use of these terms, given that I have explained how they can be replaced by descriptions of the mental state in question. The full description of this state is that it represents as true that we are going to do something; that it aims therein to represent something that really is true; and that it causes the truth of what it represents.

Reasons for Acting

I have suggested that what you should add to subjects of motivation, in order to create agents, is the higher-order aim of knowing what they're doing. Just design your creatures to gravitate toward knowing what they're doing, and they will do only those things which they have made up their minds that they're going to do; and so they will act by choice.

This design specification implies that self-knowledge is the constitutive aim of action. And in my schema for a theory of agency, the constitutive aim of action determines an internal criterion of success for action, in relation to which considerations qualify as reasons for acting. The question therefore arises what sort of reasons apply to action as constituted by this aim.

The answer is this: the considerations that qualify as reasons for doing something are considerations in light of which, in doing it, the subject would know what he was doing. They are, more colloquially, considerations in light of which the action would make sense to the agent.

Now, there is a definition of 'making sense' under which it is a term of practical rationality. What makes sense for someone to do, by this definition, is whatever he has reason for doing. The statement that reasons for an action are the considerations in light of which the action would make sense can therefore sound like a tautology. But I do not mean to speak tautologically.

When I speak of "making sense," I am borrowing the phrase from the domain of theoretical reason, where it is used to characterize phenomena as susceptible to explanation and understanding. What makes sense to someone, theoretically speaking, is what he can explain. This is what I mean when I say that reasons for doing something are considerations in light of which it would make sense. I mean that they are considerations that would provide the subject with an explanatory grasp of the behavior for which they are reasons.

Here I may seem to have changed my mind about the cognitive aim under dis-cussion. I initially said that the aim constitutive of action is to know what we are doing; I have now suggested that considerations qualify as reasons insofar as they provide an explanatory grasp of what we are doing. And knowing what we're doing may seem slightly different from being able to explain it.

But the difference is more apparent than real. The ostensibly descriptive terms in which we aim to know what we're doing are in fact descriptions of activities—that is, of behavior as actuated by particular motives under particu-lar circumstances—and so they are in fact explanatory as well. The sort of self-knowledge at which we aim is embodied in descriptions such as "declaring the session closed" or "getting rid of an old inkstand," and these descriptions carry implications as to the causes and conditions of the bodily movements to which they apply.[32] To know what we are doing is thus to grasp our bodily move-ments under concepts that set them in an explanatory context of motives and circumstances.

Considerations of these motives and circumstances are what qualify, in my view, as reasons for acting. They are the considerations out of which we can fashion a description that would embody a knowledge of what we were doing, if we applied that description to ourselves in the way that would prompt us to behave accordingly. Reasons provide us with an account of what we could be doing and, indeed, *would* be doing if we adopted an expectation to that effect.[33]

[32] A number of research programs in social psychology are based on the postulation of such an aim. This postulate is stated by the psychologists Shawn McNulty and William Swann as follows: "[O]ut of a desire to make their worlds predictable and controllable, people strive to verify and sustain their self-views" ('Psychotherapy, Self-Concept Change, and Self-Verification,' in *The Relational Self; Theoretical Convergences in Psychoanalysis and Social Psychology*, ed. Rebecca C. Curtis (New York: Guildford Press, 1991), 213–37, at 213). Perhaps the first version of this postulate was stated by Prescott Lecky (*Self-Consistency: A Theory of Personality* (The Shoe String Press, 1961), 152): "We propose to apprehend all psychological phenomena as illus-trations of the single principle of unity or self-consistency. We conceive of the personality as an organization of values which are felt to be consistent with one another. Behavior expresses the effort to maintain the integrity and unity of the organization." See also Arthur W. Combs and Donald Snygg, *Individual Behavior: A Perceptual Approach to Behavior* (New York: Harper & Brothers, 1959); Seymour Epstein, 'The Self-Concept Revisited; Or a Theory of a Theory,' *American Psychologist* 28 (1973) 404–416; Ruth Thibodeau and Elliot Aronson, 'Taking a Closer Look: Reasserting the Role of the Self-Concept in Dissonance Theory,' *Personality and Social Psychology Bulletin* 18 (1992) 591–602; Abraham K. Korman, 'Toward an Hypothesis of Work Behavior,' *Journal of Applied Psychology* 54 (1970) 31–41. I regard this empirical work as sup-portive of my view. Achieving consistency, or avoiding dissonance, between one's behavior and one's self-concept is a way of making sense to oneself. I discuss this research in 'From Self-Psychology to Moral Philosophy,' forthcoming.

[33] Relevant here is psychological research on "Action Identification" by Daniel M. Wegner and Robin R. Vallacher (*Handbook of Motivation and Cognition*, ed. Richard M. Sorrentino and E. Tory Higgins (New York: Guilford Press, 1986), 550–82). These authors propose three princi-ples: first, "that people do what they think they are doing," by framing a "prepotent act iden-tity" and then instantiating it in action (552); second, that "[p]eople search for meaning in action, and they find it by identifying the action at higher and higher levels" (555–6); and third, that the

In this sense, reasons provide us with a *rationale* under which we can choose to act.[34]

Another way of putting the point is this: reasons for acting are the elements of a possible storyline along which to make up what we are going to do.[35] The story might be this: "My sister has just pointed out that my inkstand seems out of place beside my new antiquities, and I want to make way for a new one, which I suspect that she plans to buy for my birthday; so I'll knock the old inkstand off my desk."

Of course, this particular story is borrowed from an historical incident in which it notably failed to the play the role of rationale. In this incident, recounted by Freud, the agent was indeed moved by the attitudes and cir-

---

difficulty of performing an act under higher-level descriptions may force descent to a lower, less meaningful level of description. The first two of these principles are a close approximation to my view. When people "search for meaning" by framing a "prepotent identity" for their forthcoming action at a "higher level," they are framing the sort of explanatory description that I would call a rationale; and when they subsequently "do what they think" by instantiating that prepotent identity, they are being guided by the rationale that they have framed. See also Vallacher and Wegner, "What Do People Think They're Doing? Action Identification and Human Behavior," *Psychological Review* 94 (1987) 3–15.

[34] I can now complete the discussion of *akrasia* begun in n. 20, above. The motive whose guidance renders behavior autonomous, in my view, is the agent's desire to know what he is doing. What engages this desire is the agent's sense of grasping an action—of knowing what he would be doing if he did it—and he gets this sense from having a rationale. But this sense can diverge from the agent's *de dicto* beliefs about what he has reason for doing, or even his beliefs about what he has a rationale for doing.

First, the agent may have a misguided view about what constitutes a reason for acting. If so, he may respond to the force of reasons that he doesn't explicitly believe to be reasons, with the result that he autonomously contravenes his (mistaken) belief as to what reasons he has. Alternatively, the agent's beliefs about the relative strengths of competing reasons, so described, may fail to reflect their actual impact on his perception of what would make sense to do, and hence on his desire to know what he's doing. He may then autonomously act on reasons that he (mistakenly) judges to be overridden or outweighed. Finally, an agent may have the elements of a rationale for acting, and he may know that he has them, and yet he may still lack a sense of knowing what he would be doing if he performed the corresponding action; for he may not have assimilated the rationale to the point where it renders the action intelligible to him, just as he may still fail to understand a natural event that he has the materials to explain. In this case, he may autonomously refrain from doing something for which he (correctly) believes himself to have sufficient reason. He *has* the reason in the sense that he knows its content, but he doesn't appreciate the force of the reason, because his knowledge of it hasn't coalesced into a felt grasp of the relevant action. All of these cases would result in genuinely akratic action.

[35] See Jerzy Trzebinski, 'Narrative Self, Understanding, and Action,' in *The Self in European and North American Culture: Development and Processes*, ed. A. Oosterwegel and R. A. Wicklund (Dordrecht: Kluwer, 1995), 73–88: "Constructing self-narratives is the mode of searching for a meaning . . . . To find meaning, and more often just to maintain meaning and avoid disruption of the ordered world, an individual has to move in a specified way within the narrated events. In this way the active schema . . . not only directs the individual's interpretations of on-going and foreseen events, but also pushes him toward specific aspirations, decisions, and actions. By particular moves within the events an individual elaborates, fulfils, and closes important episodes in the developing self-narrative. Personal decisions and actions are inspired by, and take strength from self-narratives—devices for meaning searching."

cumstances mentioned in the story, but he was thereby moved to act without knowing what he was doing. The story itself occurred to him only after the fact. That's why the activity motivated by his desire and belief did not amount to an autonomous action. He didn't make up this particular piece of his personal history; he was obliged to discover it.

In order to have acted autonomously, the agent would need to have been actuated not only by the desire and belief mentioned in the story but also by the story itself, serving as his grasp of what he was doing—or, in other words, as his rationale. He would need, first, to have been inhibited from acting on his desire and belief until he knew what he was up to; and then guided to act on them once he had adopted this story. He would then have acted autonomously because he would have acted for a reason, having been actuated in part by a rationale.

This conception of reasons as rationale requires considerable elaboration. What makes one reason better or stronger than another? How do we deliberate with the reasons so characterized?

Answers to these questions will have to come from the philosophy of action, if my schema for a theory of agency is correct. Reasons will have to qualify as better or stronger in relation to the constitutive aim of action, which lends reasons their normative force. Roughly speaking, the better reason will be the one that provides the better rationale—the better potential grasp of what we are doing.

If the agent in Freud's anecdote had become aware of a desire to destroy his inkstand, he would immediately have realized that such an activity was contrary to various other motives of his, as well as to some of his customs, emotions, and traits of character. So even though he would subsequently have known that he was destroying the inkstand, in moving his arm, he might still have wondered, "What am I doing?" That is, he might still have been puzzled as to how a person like him, with a makeup like his, would come to act on such motives; and so he wouldn't really or fully have known what he was up to.

This lack of self-knowledge would have indicated to the agent that he would have had a better idea of what he was doing if he had chosen to do something else instead. That is, he could have adopted, and consequently enacted, a more intelligible story. And insofar as there was a more intelligible story for him to enact, by choosing to do something else, there was a better rationale for doing that thing instead.

Conclusion

I have now brought my discussion back to its point of departure: the difference between autonomous action and mere purposeful activity. Purposeful activity is motivated by desire and belief, but it may or may not be regulated by the subject's grasp of what he is doing. Autonomous action is activity regulated by that reflective understanding, which constitutes the agent's rationale, or reason—the reason for which the action is performed, and whose role as its basis is what makes it an action rather than a mere activity.

The arguments by which I have reached this conclusion are developed further in the essays reprinted here. They expand on ideas originally contained in my book *Practical Reflection*.[36]

One of the following papers departs from the present line of argument in an important respect. In the title essay, "The Possibility of Practical Reason," I identified the constitutive aim of action as autonomy itself, partly because I liked the Kantian ring of that claim and partly because I had hopes of forestalling criticism of my view as oddly intellectualist, or as portraying an autonomous agent to be unduly self-absorbed. Unfortunately, I think that the resulting version of my view is unworkable, as becomes evident, I think, in the final, tortured sections of that paper.[37]

Perhaps this result is not so unfortunate, after all. The intuition with which I began, in writing about the philosophy of action, is that autonomy is an expression of the drive to wrap your mind around things—an expression, in particular, of that drive as directed at yourself. You govern yourself, it seems to me, when you seek to grasp yourself as part of an intelligible world and consequently gravitate toward being intelligible.

The appeal of this view, for me, is that it locates autonomy in a part of the personality from which you truly cannot dissociate yourself. This part of your personality constitutes your essential self, in the sense that it invariably presents a reflexive aspect to your thinking: it invariably appears to you as "me" from any perspective, however self-critical or detached.[38]

That's what Aristotle means, I think, when he says that each person seems to be his understanding.[39] You can dissociate yourself from other springs of action within you, by reflecting on them from a critical or contemplative distance. But you cannot attain a similar distance from your understanding, because it is something that you must take along, so to speak, no matter how

[36] (Princeton: Princeton Univ. Press, 1989). Because this book has recently gone out of print, I am making it available on the World Wide Web. It is linked to my personal home page at http://www-personal.umich.edu/~velleman.

[37] The drawbacks of this version didn't become clear to me until I read a paper by Philip Clark, arguing that if autonomy were the constitutive of aim of action, then every instance of action (as opposed to what I here call activity) would turn out to be a success. Another issue on which I have recently revised my view is the use of the first-person plural in the expression of shared intentions. (See Chap. 9) My revised view is explained in a review of Michael Bratman's *Faces of Intention*, to appear in *The Philosophical Quarterly*.

[38] I discuss this conception of the self in 'Identification and Identity,' forthcoming.

[39] Quoted at n. 12, above.

far you retreat in seeking a perspective on yourself. You must take your understanding along because you must continue to exercise it in adopting a perspective, where it remains identified with you as the subject of that perspective, no matter how far off it appears to you as an object. Your understanding is therefore like that point between your eyes which constitutes the visual standpoint from which you see whatever you see, even when you view that point itself in the mirror, at a distance. Just as that point is always "here," at the origin of your visual images, even when it's also "over there," in the mirror; so your understanding is always "me" in your reflective thinking, even when you regard it externally, as "it." It's your inescapable self, and so its contribution to producing your behavior is, inescapably, your contribution.

It's an intellectualist view, all right. But we are intellectual creatures, and our autonomy may well be a function of our intellect.

2

Epistemic Freedom[1]

Epistemic freedom is the freedom to affirm any one of several incompatible propositions without risk of being wrong.[2] We sometimes have this freedom, strange as it seems, and our having it sheds some light on the topic of free will and determinism.

I think that there are two equally important reasons why we seek an alternative to determinism as an account of how our actions come about. One reason is phenomenological: we just feel free. Determinism seems incompatible, in the first instance, with what it's like to be an agent. Our other reason for seeking an alternative to determinism is conceptual. We fear that if determinism is true, then we shall have no grounds for applying concepts such as responsibility and desert to ourselves and our fellows.

The conceptual reason for worrying about determinism has tended to take precedence in the writings of philosophers, but I think that the phenomenological reason deserves equal attention. My own view is that explaining what it's like to be an agent is just as interesting, philosophically, as finding room in the world for punishment and blame. And even those who disagree with me on this score should consider that the experience of freedom serves, in some philosophical theories, as a datum from which conceptual consequences are derived.[3] The conceptual problem of freedom thus becomes intertwined with the phenomenological problem.

[1] This chapter originally appeared in *Pacific Philosophical Quarterly* 70 (1989) 73–97 and is reprinted by permission of the University of Southern California. For comments on the material contained in this chapter, I am indebted to Paul Boghossian, Jaegwon Kim, Louis Loeb, Larry Powers, Dan Velleman, and Nicholas White. I also wish to thank various audiences to whom I have presented versions of the chapter, including the philosophy departments of Wayne State University, Indiana University, and The Ohio State University, as well as participants in a seminar on the philosophy of action that I conducted at the University of Michigan. Portions of this chapter appear in my *Practical Reflection* (Princeton: Princeton University Press, 1989), ch. 5.
[2] I use the vague word 'affirm' in this definition in order to encompass both assertions and beliefs. In this paper I shall confine my attention to epistemically free assertions, since epistemically free beliefs pose additional problems that I do not have the space to discuss. I allude to some of these problems in n. 17, below.
[3] See, e.g., C. A. Campbell, *On Selfhood and Goodhood* (London: Allen & Unwin, 1957), 158–79; Richard Taylor, *Metaphysics* (Englewood Cliffs, N.J.: Prentice-Hall, 1983), 23–50; and Roderick M. Chisholm, 'Human Freedom and the Self' in *Free Will*, ed. Gary Watson (Oxford: Oxford Univ. Press, 1982), 24–35.

This paper sketches a potential explanation for our feeling of freedom. It identifies a kind of freedom that we might have and that might cause us to feel free. The paper is therefore addressed primarily to the phenomenological problem of freedom, but it also has an indirect bearing on the conceptual problem. The freedom that I postulate is not causal but epistemic (in a sense that I shall define), and the result is that it is quite compatible with determinism. I therefore claim that insofar as we feel metaphysically free—free in a sense that would be incompatible with determinism—we are mistaking the epistemic freedom that we have for a kind of freedom that we may lack. This claim will lead me, at the end of the paper, to a projectivist account of moral responsibility. Ascriptions of moral responsibility, I shall suggest, should be treated in the same way as ascriptions of color or other secondary qualities.

The idea that our experience of freedom is occasioned by epistemic rather than causal freedom first appeared, I believe, in Hume's account of what he called "the *false sensation* . . . of the liberty of indifference."[4] According to Hume, we feel that our past doesn't determine our forthcoming behavior because of "a certain looseness which we feel in passing or not passing from the idea of one to that of the other." Here Hume seems to suggest that what makes us feel free is not a freedom to *do* any one of various things but rather a license to *think* any one of various things about what we are going to do. Hume contends that when we interpret this experience as a perception of gaps in causality, we're simply making a mistake.

Like Hume, I shall argue that our feeling of freedom is erroneous; and my diagnosis of the error, like Hume's, is that we mistake the license to affirm any one of various things about what we'll do for the possibility that we might do any one of those things. At the end of the paper, I shall discuss an occurrence of this confusion in the philosophical literature. First, however, I must establish that it is indeed a confusion; and my arguments to this end are somewhat different from Hume's.

The Openness of the Future

The experience that I shall explain is often described, in particular, as the experience of openness in our future. Whenever we face a decision, we feel that our future is partly undetermined and thus leaves something for us to decide. This feeling seems to be a perception of real indeterminacy in the course of future events; how much indeterminacy is a difficult question. One might think

---

[4] David Hume, *A Treatise of Human Nature*, L. A. Selby-Bigge and P. H. Nidditch (eds.) (Oxford: Oxford Univ. Press, 1978), 408.

that our sense of deciding an aspect of the future intimates that there is no antecedent fact of the matter as to how that aspect will turn out. Alternatively, one might think that our sense of deciding an aspect of the future doesn't intimate that there is no fact about it but only that any such fact isn't causally determined by the present state of the world. Under either interpretation, the experience is taken to contain a denial of determinism, the first denial being considerably stronger than the second.

My thesis is that under either interpretation, the experience is an understandable illusion. Our sense of an open future is occasioned by a genuine indeterminacy, I believe, but the indeterminacy that occasions it is not the metaphysical indeterminacy that the experience represents to us. Our future is undetermined, I shall argue, in a way that explains our feeling of freedom without conflicting with determinism.

Of course, to say that indeterminacy doesn't conflict with determinism sounds like a stark contradiction. The reason why it isn't a contradiction is that talk of indeterminacy is ambiguous. There is a sense in which the indeterminacy of the future would falsify determinism, and then there is a sense in which it doesn't. These senses seem inseparable, but they can in fact come apart.

Here are the two different senses in which our future might be undetermined. On the one hand, there may be no particular way that the future is going to turn out—or at least, no way that's necessitated, under the laws of nature, by the present state of the world. In that case, the future would be metaphysically or causally open. On the other hand, there may be no particular way that we must describe the future as turning out, in order to describe it correctly—or at least, no way that's necessitated, under the laws of nature, by a correct description of the present state of the world. In that case, the future would be, as I put it, epistemically open. So formulated, these two kinds of indeterminacy seem inextricably linked. We naturally assume that if there is a way that the future will turn out, then that's the way we must describe it as turning out, in order to give a true description of it; and we assume that if the present will determine the future, under the laws of nature, then a true description of the present will determine, under the same laws, how we must describe the future in order to describe it correctly.

I shall argue that these assumptions, however plausible, are false. For in some cases, even if the future is going to turn out in a particular way, we don't have to describe it as turning out that way in order to describe it correctly, since there are several other, incompatible ways in which we would be equally correct to describe it as turning out. Similarly, even if the present determines how the future will be, a correct description of the present needn't dictate how we must describe the future as being in order to describe it correctly.

Here I have purposely made my claim sound implausible, to say the least. My reason for doing so is not that I wish to be credited with proving a startling claim. My reason is rather that I want to familiarize the reader with the strength of his own resistance to the idea of a divergence between the two indeterminacies that I have defined. My ultimate thesis, after all, is that we continually mistake epistemic indeterminacy, as I have defined it above, for causal indeterminacy; and this thesis gains support from any evidence that the two are generally perceived as inseparable. The reader's resistance to the thought of epistemic indeterminacy without causal indeterminacy is, if you will, a piece of psychological evidence for my claim that an experience of the one might be mistaken for an experience of the other.

In reality, the cases in which these indeterminacies diverge are not particularly startling, once they have been pointed out. Like most exceptions to specious generalizations, they hide in plain sight. Nevertheless, I shall continue to describe these cases in deliberately paradoxical-sounding ways, in order to heighten the reader's appreciation of their potential for causing confusion. I want the reader to realize that the confusion between causal and epistemic freedom, like the paradoxical sound of the cases in which they diverge, never entirely goes away, no matter how well it is understood.

Self-fulfilling Predictions

Why would we sometimes be correct in describing the future in any one of several incompatible ways? The reason is that our descriptions would sometimes amount to self-fulfilling predictions.

Self-fulfilling predictions are more common than most people think. A famous example is a case discussed by G. E. M. Anscombe in the first pages of her book *Intention*. Anscombe imagines a doctor saying to a patient, in the presence of a nurse, "Nurse will now take you to the operating theater." The patient interprets this utterance as a straight-forward assertion of fact; the nurse interprets it as an implicit command and complies, thereby making the assertion true.[5]

---

[5] *Intention* (Ithaca: Cornell Univ. Press, 1963), 3. I shall follow Anscombe in saying that the doctor's utterance serves two functions, as both an assertion to the patient and a command to the nurse. However, nothing of significance hangs on characterizing this utterance as a command. Anscombe's story can be retold in such a way that the doctor's utterance is self-fulfilling even though its only illocutionary force is that of an assertion. For even if the doctor's utterance isn't intended or interpreted as a command, the nurse might still have motives for fulfilling it. The nurse might be afraid of undermining the patient's faith in the doctor, or of incurring the doctor's wrath by making him look like a fool. If the doctor is aware of these motives, he can count on his utterance to elicit the corresponding behavior whether or not it is an implicit command.

The point of the story, for my purposes, is that although the doctor is correct in asserting that the nurse will take the patient to the operating theater, he would have been equally correct in asserting that the nurse would take the patient to the lab, or to any other destination, within reason.[6] Insofar as the nurse stands ready to do whatever the doctor says, the doctor can truly assert any one of several incompatible things; and to that extent, he is epistemically free.

Of course, the epistemic freedom involved in this case is freedom enjoyed by the doctor in relation to the actions of the nurse. Because the subject of freedom here is not the agent, his freedom would seem to have little bearing on the question of free will. Yet the doctor in this case does, in a sense, decide what the nurse is to do; and his epistemic freedom attaches to the very utterance in which he formulates his decision. Perhaps, then, the present case is not as irrelevant to the question of free will as it seems.

I therefore plan to proceed as follows. First, I shall examine the epistemic freedom of the doctor in Anscombe's story, bringing to bear upon it various philosophical tools that have been developed for the analysis of predictability and determinism. I shall then suggest how the lessons learned in this case might be transferred to cases in which agents experience the distinctive feeling of freedom.

Epistemic Freedom and Determinism

The doctor's epistemic freedom entails that the nurse's future is open from his perspective, in the sense that there is no one future that he has to predict in order to predict correctly. What's odd is that the nurse's future is open from the doctor's perspective even if it is predetermined. For if the nurse is predetermined to take the patient to the operating theater, in the case that I have described, then the reason must be that the doctor is predetermined to say so—which cannot change the fact that the nurse would take the patient elsewhere if the doctor said otherwise.

The doctor's epistemic freedom therefore amounts to the fact that he would be correct in predicting events that aren't actually going to occur. These events

[6] Within reason, I say. This qualification imposes a limit on the doctor's epistemic freedom—the limit of what the nurse would do if he predicted it. The nurse would probably take the patient to the lab, the lobby, the x-ray room, and several other places simply at the doctor's say-so. But if the doctor said "Nurse will now wheel you into the broom closet," he would be wrong. His prediction is therefore constrained by prior evidence about what a nurse, or this nurse, is likely to do on implicit instructions. I won't repeat this qualification, but it applies throughout the following discussion.

aren't going to occur only because he isn't going to predict them; and so if he did predict them, they would occur, and his predictions would be true.

Note, however, that although the doctor would be correct in predicting events that won't in fact occur, he doesn't directly confront the future nonoccurrence of the events in question. All that the doctor confronts is the present state of the world, which provides evidence about the events in question—potentially conclusive evidence, if determinism is true. What occasions the doctor's experience of freedom, then, is not that the future cannot determine how he should describe it but rather that the present cannot determine how he should describe the future. What makes him feel free, in short, is his freedom from the evidence.

The idea that an agent's descriptions of his own future actions are not constrained by evidence is hardly original with me. It has arisen periodically in the philosophy of action, especially since Anscombe's *Intention* and Stuart Hampshire's *Thought and Action*. Unfortunately, however, the philosophers who have discussed an agent's freedom from the evidence have usually linked it to epistemological or metaphysical views that are hard for the rest of us to accept. Some have contended, for example, that an agent's projections of his actions aren't constrained by evidence because they constitute a unique species of knowledge, "a kind . . . of knowledge to which the notion of evidence is irrelevant."[7] Others have contended that freedom from the evidence entails contracausal freedom of the will.[8] The idea of freedom from the evidence has therefore become associated, in the minds of most philosophers, with unacceptable conceptions of knowledge or causality. My hope is to make the idea respectable, by dissociating it from any suspect epistemology or metaphysics.

Freedom from the Evidence

Anscombe says that the statement of the doctor in her story isn't "founded on evidence," even in its capacity as information to the patient. I believe that this characterization of the statement is mistaken. I say that the doctor's assertion to the patient is indeed based on evidence—namely, the evidence that the nurse is herewith getting implicit instructions to take the patient to the operating theater, that nurses usually understand and obey such instructions, and that this nurse has no inhibition against obeying this particular instruction. What

[7] Stuart Hampshire and H. L. A. Hart, 'Decision, Intention, and Certainty,' *Mind* 67 (1958) 1.

[8] Carl Ginet, 'Can the Will be Caused?', *Philosophical Review* 61 (1962) 49–55, and Richard Taylor, 'Deliberation and Foreknowledge,' *American Philosophical Quarterly* 1 (1964) 73–80.

Anscombe should have said, I claim, is that the evidence on which the doctor bases his assertion didn't and couldn't have dictated that assertion, since it wasn't at hand until the assertion was made. Until the doctor said that the nurse would take the patient to the operating theater, he had no particular evidence that the nurse would do so. All he had was evidence that the nurse would take the patient to the operating theater if he said so; and he had similar evidence about many alternative actions, each of which the nurse would have performed if he predicted it. Hence the doctor's evidence couldn't have dictated to him what to predict.

So stated, my argument sounds as if it relies on the doctor's ignorance, since his lack of compelling evidence sounds like something that would easily be remedied by more information. If determinism is true (as I shall henceforth assume for the sake of argument), then there is some action that the nurse is predetermined to perform; and which action the nurse will perform can in principle be extrapolated from the present state of the world. The nurse's future behavior is already in the cards, so to speak, and we assume that to anyone who is in a position to read those cards, they will dictate a determinate prediction. We are therefore inclined to think that if the doctor's prediction is underdetermined by his evidence, the reason must be that he can't see all of the cards—that his evidence is incomplete.

So we are inclined to think, but we're wrong. Let the nurse's behavior be causally predetermined; let the doctor know and fully appreciate all of the relevant laws and facts; let those laws and facts entail that the nurse will inevitably take the patient to the operating theater. Even so, the doctor is equally licensed to say "Nurse will take you to the lab" instead. Indeed, the evidence proving that the patient will be taken to the operating theater includes the very information that licenses the doctor to predict that the patient will be taken to the lab, since the way it proves that the patient will be taken to the operating theater is precisely by invoking the nurse's disposition to do what the doctor says—a disposition that would lead the nurse to take the patient to the lab if the doctor so predicted.

In the case of other observers, of course, the complete body of evidence indicates that they would be wrong to make an alternative prediction. It indicates that if they want to speak the truth, they must predict that the nurse will take the patient to the operating theater. The evidence thereby dictates a prediction to them, by showing that they mustn't diverge from it, on pain of error. But the evidence dictates this prediction to others by demonstrating that the nurse will fulfill it because of the doctor's making it. And to the doctor this evidence shows, not that he must make the prediction, on pain of error, but precisely the reverse—that no matter what he predicts, within reason, he can't go wrong. The evidence therefore contains one component that licenses the doctor to contradict what all of the evidence, taken together, conclusively proves. This component of evidence shows that the doctor would be correct in predicting whatever he likes, within reason, irrespective of what the totality of evidence demonstrates is bound to occur.

The crucial component of the evidence is the part that supports various counterfactuals specifying the various places to which the nurse would take the patient if the doctor said so. This evidence includes facts about the nurse's dispositions to understand and obey implicit instructions, as well as facts about the absence of conditions inhibiting the nurse from taking the patient to the destinations in question. If the doctor is aware of this central component of the evidence, then he knows that although the complete body of evidence may indicate what the nurse will actually do, it cannot indicate that he must predict accordingly in order to predict correctly. The central evidence shows the doctor that even if the totality of evidence guarantees one outcome, he would still be correct in predicting others. It shows, in short, that he is epistemically free.

Causal Versus Epistemic Freedom

Let me forestall a possible misunderstanding about what kind of freedom I am claiming for the doctor. I am claiming that one component of the evidence licenses the doctor to assert propositions even in the face of more extensive evidence guaranteeing their falsity; I am not claiming that the doctor's asserting one of those propositions is a physical or psychological possibility. The doctor has a license to say "Nurse will take you to the lab," but his saying it isn't causally possible given the antecedent facts.

After all, the doctor is in a particular conjunction of psychological states, which include his knowing that the nurse will do as he says, within reason, and his wanting the nurse to take the patient to the operating theater. Given the conjunction of these mental states, and the absence of any opposing forces, the doctor is predetermined to say "Nurse will take you to the operating theater." His license to say "Nurse will take you to the lab" is thus a license that he is predetermined not to invoke.

One might wonder about the point of having such a license. Indeed, one might wonder whether this license is anything more than a sham, issued only because the licensee is guaranteed never to invoke it. But the license involved here is not a sham. It is of course moot, in the sense that it isn't going to be invoked. But moot or not, it is still well worth having; it's worth having because it excuses the doctor from consulting evidence that would otherwise be pertinent to his prediction.

The evidence that the doctor is excused from consulting is the evidence that would indicate which destination, among the ones to which the patient might reasonably be taken, is the one to which he will be taken in fact. For the purpose of making a true prediction, the doctor needn't investigate whether the nurse will take the patient to the lab rather than the operating theater, or to the x-ray room rather than the lab, so long as he is in possession of the central evidence indicating that the nurse will take the patient to whichever one of these destinations he names. To be sure, the doctor is predetermined to name the operating theater, and so his license to predict a trip to the lab is already moot. Yet to say that such a license is moot is not to say that it's a fake—that if the doctor attempted to invoke it, it would be revealed as invalid. No, the doctor's license to name the lab in his prediction is just as valid as his license to name the operating theater, since it indicates that naming the lab would result in an equally true prediction. The doctor is therefore entitled to name either destination without the support of evidence favoring it over the other.

One might think, alternatively, that the only reason the doctor needn't consult such evidence is that the prediction it would dictate is the one he's predetermined to make in any case. He can let his preferences determine his prediction, one might think, only because he knows that his preferences are guaranteed to yield that prediction which the evidence already supports.

One would be right that the doctor's preferences are guaranteed to yield such a prediction, but one would be wrong in thinking that this guarantee is of any significance. The fact is that the doctor needn't make a prediction that's congruent with the prior evidence about where the patient will be taken; for if he made a prediction contrary to that evidence, he would thereby have refuted it. The crucial evidence for saying that the patient will be taken to the operating theater is evidence that the doctor will say so. If he said otherwise, he would have proved this evidence false, thereby vindicating himself in contravening it.

As I have said, the doctor will not and cannot contravene this evidence. But to portray him as relying on the fact that he cannot contravene it is to imply that conformity to such evidence is a desideratum for him—which it isn't. Contravening the evidence about where the patient will be taken is impossible for him, but it's epistemically permissible; and precisely because it's permissible, he needn't rely on its impossibility.

Complete versus Incomplete Evidence

Of course, the doctor's license to make alternative predictions consists in what I have called the central component of evidence, the component showing that various predictions on the doctor's part would prompt various actions on the nurse's. If the doctor lacks this component of the evidence, then other evidence may well dictate a determinate prediction to him.

In order to illustrate this possibility, let me introduce a familiar prop of philosophical fiction. I shall ask you to imagine that there is a chronicle of the nurse's activities from birth to death, compiled and recorded in advance by a superhuman author. Imagine, further, that the doctor has obtained this book and has fully tested its reliability. For months, he has been surreptitiously trailing the nurse around the hospital in order to test the book's predictions, and he has found them to be exhaustive and unerring. Gradually, the doctor realizes that he is in possession of the genuine article, a book of life.[9]

One day the doctor enters a patient's room for a routine examination and finds himself face to face with the nurse whom he has been studying from a distance for all these months. During a lull in the subsequent conversation, the doctor extracts the nurse's book of life from his pocket in order to see what happens next. Leafing to the entry for the present date and time, he reads this: "Takes patient to operating theater." The doctor hasn't bothered to consider for himself what the nurse might do next; all he knows is that the book is always right. He thinks, "The operating theater, is it? Well, then, I'd better tell the patient"—whereupon he reports his discovery by saying, "Nurse will take you to the operating theater." The nurse, who knows nothing about books of life, interprets the doctor's utterance as a command and immediately complies.

In this version of the story, the doctor's prediction is dictated by the evidence available to him. In the absence of any other information, the book's proven reliability forbids him to gainsay the next entry. His information indicates that if he wants to speak the truth about the nurse's actions, he had better go by the book.

Yet the doctor's prediction is dictated by his evidence in this case only because that evidence is incomplete. In particular, the evidence dictating the doctor's prediction doesn't include information about his own role in causing the events predicted. The doctor therefore becomes the unwitting collaborator of the nurse's anonymous biographer, in somewhat the same way that Jocasta and Laius, the parents of Oedipus, became unwitting collaborators of Fate when they reacted to the prophecy about their infant son. The difference, of course, is that Oedipus' fate would have been fulfilled no matter what—or

---

[9] The classic discussion of books of life is in chapter 6 of Alvin I. Goldman's *A Theory of Human Action* (Princeton: Princeton Univ. Press, 1970). Goldman is primarily interested in the question whether the predictions in a book of life defeat themselves, if the subject reads them, by making him decide to prove them false. The same question is discussed in D. M. MacKay, 'On the Logical Indeterminacy of a Free Choice,' *Mind* 69 (1960) 31–40; David P. Gauthier, 'How Decisions are Caused,' *Journal of Philosophy* 64 (1967) 147–51; David P. Gauthier, 'How Decisions are Caused (But Not Predicted),' *Journal of Philosophy* 65 (1968) 170–1; and John O'Connor, 'How Decisions Are Predicted,' *Journal of Philosophy* 64 (1967) 429–30. I am interested in a different question, involving self-fulfilling rather than self-defeating predictions.

so the myth asks us to believe[10]—whereas, the biographer's prediction about the nurse would not have been fulfilled without the doctor's collaboration. And the doctor feels compelled by the biographer's prediction only because he doesn't realize that without his collaboration it won't be fulfilled.[11]

For consider another version of the story, in which the nurse's biographer has recorded, not just the nurse's future actions, but also the chains of causes leading up to them—the chains down which the author himself must have peered in order to foresee the actions, in the first place. In this version, the doctor finds a more informative entry for the present date and time. He reads, "Hears the doctor say, 'Nurse will take you to the operating theater,' and is prompted to comply." Reading this entry, the doctor realizes that the nurse will take the patient to the operating theater only because he's going to say so. Does he now say to himself "I'd better tell the patient"? Does he feel that in order to warn the patient of impending events, he must echo the prediction written in the book? Surely not. He realizes that unless and until he repeats the book's prediction, it won't be fulfilled—and so he doesn't have to repeat it in order to warn the patient. He also realizes that he can utter an alternative prediction without fear of a mistake.

Of course, even in this version of the story, the doctor says "Nurse will take you to the operating theater." If he didn't, the book of life would contain an error, whereas the story presupposes that the book is infallible. But when the doctor says "Nurse will take you to the operating theater" in this version of the story, he says it because he wants the nurse to take the patient to the operating theater, or for some such reason, and not because he thinks that he had better repeat what's in the book in order to warn the patient of coming events.

Indeed, the nurse's superhuman biographer must have realized that if he was going to reveal the causal inferences behind his entries in the book, then he couldn't write an entry whose truth depended on the doctor's thinking that he had better repeat it to the patient. The reason is that the doctor would never think this about an entry if it was explicitly based on the premise that he was going to think so. After all, the doctor wouldn't think that such an entry was worth repeating for the patient's information if he didn't think that its stated premise was true; but its stated premise, in this case, would be that he'd think the entry was worth repeating for the patient's information. Hence the doctor

---

[10] Consider how the myth would change if it were merely deterministic instead of fatalistic. In that case, the seer Tiresias would be the villain of the story, causing Oedipus' downfall by uttering a self-fulfilling prophecy of it.

[11] Note that in this version of the story, the biographer's prediction must have been based on his knowledge that the doctor would find the prediction compelling and consequently report it to the others, thereby unwittingly securing its truth. Evidently, then, the biographer could have written many other entries for the relevant date and time, in the knowledge that the doctor would feel compelled to report whatever was written, and that the nurse would be prompted to comply. Hence the biographer himself wasn't compelled by prior evidence. But that's another story.

wouldn't think that the entry was worth repeating unless he thought it was worth repeating; and so he wouldn't have to think so, if he didn't want to. If the nurse's book of life said to him, in effect, "The following prediction is true because you are going to find it worth repeating for the patient's information," he would read the prediction and rightly think, "Why should I repeat that? If I thought that the author had some *other* grounds for his prediction, I might think that it was true, and hence worth repeating to the patient. But if his only grounds for the prediction was that I would find it worth repeating to patient, then I don't."[12] The author must therefore have realized that in order to make a true prediction for which he could record his causal inferences, he would have to make a prediction that did not rely on the doctor's feeling compelled to repeat it.

What the author could rely on, and must have known he could rely on, was that if he alerted the doctor to his potential influence over the nurse, then the doctor would feel free, even in the face of a reliable prediction, to say what he wanted about the nurse's next action. Hence the author must have realized that so long as he made sure to write his entry in such a way as to reveal the doctor's potential influence, he could figure out what else to write simply by figuring out which action the doctor would want to prompt the nurse to perform.[13] In recording his causal inferences, the author must therefore have written, "Doctor wants nurse to take patient to the operating theater, and therefore says, 'Nurse will take you to the operating theater' . . ." and so on. Reading this, the

---

[12] Once again, the doctor might feel that the prediction was worth repeating if the evidence offered for it was incomplete. Suppose the doctor began to suspect that the nurse's biographer must have possessed, not only infallible foresight about his subject, but also hypnotic power over his readers. If the doctor then read "You are going to repeat, 'Nurse will take you to the operating theater'," he might regard it as conveying a threat that the author was capable of carrying out. The doctor might then say to himself, "He's going to compel me to say that the nurse will take the patient to the operating theater. But if I say that, the nurse will do it. I'd better warn the patient." The doctor would thereupon blurt out, "Nurse will take you to the operating theater"—realizing too late that he had just been tricked into fulfilling the author's threat. Of course, if the author had recorded the psychological processes by which he expected to trick the doctor, the doctor would never have fallen for the trick.

[13] More precisely, the author would have needed to figure out, not just an action that the doctor would want to prompt, but an action that the doctor would want to prompt even after reading a prediction that he would do so. If the doctor is overwhelmingly averse to being anticipated, of course, there may be nothing that he would still want to do after reading a prediction of his doing it. If so, there may have been no prediction about the doctor that the author would have been correct to record, given that the doctor was going to read it.

My argument does not rely on the assumption that the author could always circumvent such perversity on the part of his subject. All I am claiming is that the author's recorded prediction, if explicitly based on the premise that the doctor would repeat it, could not put the doctor in the position of being epistemically compelled to repeat it—that is, of having to repeat it on pain of failing to make a correct prediction. In order to illustrate this claim, I have assumed that the author could have found some prediction that the doctor would want to repeat for reasons other than correctness, even if he had read a prediction of his making it. But this assumption is not crucial to my argument.

doctor thinks—not "I'd better tell the patient"—but rather "That *is* what I want to say. How clever of him!" And then he proceeds to say what he wants, and to say it only because he wants to.

Thus, the addition of further information to the first book of life undermines the book's authority to dictate a prediction to the doctor, without undermining the book's claim to be true. Once the book contains the central component of evidence, it shows that the doctor needn't predict what it predicts in order to predict correctly, even though its prediction is, in fact, correct.

Questions and Answers

But suppose that the doctor reads the relevant entry in the more complete book of life on the previous evening. He is then compelled to conclude that when the time comes, he is going to say, "Nurse will take you to the operating theater," and that the nurse is going to comply. The doctor therefore knows that the nurse is going to take the patient to the operating theater; and he can retain that knowledge until the moment of his utterance arrives. Surely, if he already knows that the nurse will take the patient to the operating theater, he isn't entitled to say "Nurse will take you to the lab."

Surely he is. "Nurse will take you to the lab," in his mouth, would still be just as true as "Nurse will take you to the operating theater," and for precisely the same reasons. He is therefore fully entitled to say it.

You mean that he's entitled to say what he already knows to be false?

Yes. The doctor is entitled to say what he knows to be false—not in the sense that he's entitled to say something while knowing it to be false even as he speaks, but rather in the sense that something he now knows to be false is something that he's nevertheless entitled to say, because it wouldn't be false if he said it.

But if it wouldn't be false, then how could he have known it to be false?

The answer is that if it wasn't false, then he would not have known it to be false, after all. He does, in actuality, know it to be false, since he believes it to be false, with reliable justification, and it is false. But it's false only because he isn't going to say it. If he did say it, then it would be true, and his belief that it was false would not have constituted knowledge. In saying it, then, he would be saying something that he does (in actuality) know to be false but that he wouldn't (in the circumstances) have known to be false. His utterance would be incompatible with what he actually knows but not with what he would know in that counterfactual case. Hence the doctor can know something to be false and still be entitled to say it simply because *if* he said it, he would not have known it to be false, after all.

There are two potential sources of confusion here. One is my claim that the doctor's asserting what he knows to be false would result in his not having known it to be false—a claim that seems to credit the doctor with the magical power of altering the past. All the claim actually attributes to the doctor, however, is the power of altering the epistemic status of past beliefs about events that still lie in the future; and this power requires no magic. If the doctor believes that the nurse won't take the patient to the lab, he will always have believed that proposition, even if he subsequently contradicts it. His having believed the proposition will henceforth be a fact about the past, which cannot be changed. But the doctor's having *known* the proposition will not yet be a fact about the past, since it involves a relation between the doctor's belief and the nurse's action, which is still to come. If the doctor were now to contradict his belief, his utterance would affect the nurse's behavior, thus affecting whether his earlier belief was true and hence whether it constituted knowledge. Thus, even though the doctor knows that the nurse won't take the patient to the lab, it can still be the case that if he contradicted that proposition, he wouldn't have known it, after all.[14]

Another potential source of confusion is that I seem to be saying that the evidence contained in the book supports mutually contradictory propositions—namely, the proposition that the doctor learns from the book and the alternative proposition that it licenses him to assert. But I am not saying that the book supports both propositions in the sense of showing both propositions to be true. Rather, I am saying that the book gives the doctor knowledge of one proposition by showing it to be true and licenses an assertion of the other proposition by showing that it would be true if asserted. Ordinarily, there is no difference between what evidence shows to be true and what it shows would be true if someone asserted it. Consequently, there is ordinarily no contradiction between the knowledge that evidence provides and the assertions that it licenses. In the case of self-fulfilling predictions, however, there can be a contradiction between what's actually true and what would be true if someone said it, since there are things that aren't true because the person isn't going to say them but that would be true if he did. And where there's a contradiction between what is true and what would be true if asserted, a person can know something on the basis of evidence that simultaneously licenses him to contradict it.

Here again, my point may seem academic, in the derogatory sense of the word, since it's about the potential truth of an assertion that the speaker is

---

[14] A more concise way of expressing the point of this paragraph is this. The claim that if the doctor contradicted what he knows, then he wouldn't have known it, sounds like an illicitly backtracking counterfactual. But it isn't one, because the antecedent, though phrased in the past tense, doesn't express a fact that's strictly about the past. (See David K. Lewis, 'Counterfactual Dependence and Time's Arrow,' *Noûs* 13 (1979) 455–76.)

predetermined not to make. But as I have argued, the potential truth of this utterance has implications for the speaker's actual position. Because the central evidence shows that he *would* be correct in making an alternative assertion, it shows that he *is*—in reality–entitled to make it. And if he is thus entitled to make any one of several different assertions, he may make one without consulting the evidence that would discriminate between them.

You have conceded that even if the doctor told the patient "Nurse will take you to the lab," he would still have believed that the nurse would take the patient to the operating theater. You are therefore claiming that the doctor has a license to say something that he not only does believe to be false but also would have believed false even if he said it. Aren't you thereby claiming that he has a license to lie?

The answer to this question has two parts. On the one hand, I haven't said that the doctor's asserting "Nurse will take you to the lab" wouldn't alter his belief: all I've said is that it couldn't alter the facts about what he antecedently believed. If the doctor said "Nurse will take you to the lab," and if he knew what he was saying, then he'd come to believe what he was saying, on the grounds that he was saying it. He would thus change his mind about what the nurse was going to do. Saying what he antecedently believed false would therefore entail changing his belief; and so it wouldn't entail saying something while still believing it to be false.

On the other hand, I recognize the possibility of the doctor's saying "Nurse will take you to the lab" without realizing that he was saying it, and hence without altering his antecedent belief. (The doctor might suffer a slip of the tongue and think that he was saying "operating theater" when he was actually saying "lab.") In that case, the doctor would indeed be saying something even as he believed that it was false. Yet even if we call the resulting assertion a lie, we must admit that it would be an inadvertent one. More importantly, we have to question whether the usual strictures against lying would still apply. Surely, the strictures against lying are based on the principle that a person ought to speak the truth, to the best of his ability. And in order to yield an injunction against saying something while believing it false, the principle that one should do one's best to speak the truth must be combined with the assumption that the best one can do, by way of speaking the truth, is to say what one justifiedly believes. In the case of self-fulfilling predictions, however, saying what one justifiedly believes is no more reliable a means of speaking the truth than saying what one justifiedly disbelieves. One can speak the truth by contradicting one's well-founded beliefs as well as by affirming them. Hence the principle that one ought to speak the truth, to the best of one's ability, doesn't yield an injunction against contradicting one's own beliefs.

You have assumed that the causal inferences recorded in the nurse's book of life refer to psychological states and events. But if anyone actually wrote a book of life, he would probably base his predictions on physics, which yields better predictions than psychology. And if the book cited the motions of particles and fields as causes of the nurse's actions, then the doctor might not realize that the causes cited were actually his own attitudes and utterances. Hence he wouldn't recognize his own role in causing the events predicted; and so he would once again be compelled to echo the book's prediction.

I concede this point. But it's just another instance in which evidence would be compelling because it lacked the central component. In order to derive predictions about the nurse from premises about particles and fields, the author would have needed to know which microevents constituted which actions on the nurse's part. And if only he had cited similar correspondences for the doctor's actions, the doctor wouldn't have been in the dark about his causal role. The doctor's evidence would dictate his prediction, then, only because it failed to include the psychophysical relations necessary to complete the central component.

Further Debate

Whenever I present the thesis of epistemic freedom, I encounter opponents of two kinds. One opponent says that the thesis of epistemic freedom is obviously false; the other says that it is true, but trivially so. My first inclination is to answer either opponent by introducing him to the other. For how can the truth of a thesis be trivial, I wonder, if the thesis strikes some people as obviously false? And how can its falsity be obvious if it strikes others as trivially true? Of course, this reply never satisfies either party, and so the debate continues, along the following lines.

The opponent who calls the thesis of epistemic freedom trivial tends to compare my examples to cases of assertions that are more immediately and obviously self-fulfilling. In the eyes of this opponent, my claim that the doctor would be correct in saying "Nurse will take you to the lab," even though the nurse will actually take the patient to the operating theater, seems no more remarkable than the claim that even when the doctor isn't actually talking he would be correct in saying "I am talking." The opponent asks how such a trivial case can have interesting implications.

My initial response to this question is to admit, with pleasure, that the logic of "I am talking" is similar to that of "Nurse will take you to the operating theater" as it appears in Anscombe's story. The only significant difference between these assertions is that there is no obvious alternative to "I am talking" that the doctor would be equally correct in asserting, whereas there are clear alternatives to "Nurse will take you to the operating theater" that would be equally correct in the doctor's mouth.

Having admitted the similarity, however, I argue that the apparent triviality of the assertion "I am talking" does not prevent the case from having significant implications. The case demonstrates that a person can sometimes be licensed to make an assertion despite having conclusive evidence that it is false. For even if a person is not about to talk, and even if he has conclusive evidence to this effect, what deters him from saying "I am talking" cannot be this knowledge of the statement's falsity, since that knowledge doesn't imply that he would be wrong to make the statement. He may have evidence of conditions that will prevent him from saying "I am talking"—or from saying anything else—but that evidence cannot forbid him to say "I am talking." A person can therefore feel entitled to say "I am talking" at any time without having consulted evidence about whether he is about to talk.

(At this point in the debate, I turn to my other opponent, who said that epistemic freedom was impossible, and I ask whether he can still think so, in light of this obvious case. Often he grants the existence of epistemic freedom and immediately joins forces with the opponent who calls it trivial.)

My first opponent now says that the implications I draw from the case of "I am talking" are well-known: epistemic freedom is therefore nothing new. Here I can only say that if it is nothing new, it is at least unfamiliar to some; and in any case, its relevance to the problem of free will has not been generally recognized. Its relevance to the problem of free will, I claim, is that when we have the distinctive experience of free will, we may be experiencing nothing more than epistemic freedom. Hence our feeling of freedom may be perfectly compatible with determinism.

The relevance of epistemic freedom to the problem of free will has not yet been demonstrated, however. I therefore turn to that task.

Freedom in the First-Person

From the perspective of the doctor in Anscombe's story, the nurse's forthcoming action is undetermined. I don't mean that the doctor can truly say, "The nurse's forthcoming action is undetermined." If determinism is true, as I am assuming, then the nurse's action is determined, and the doctor cannot truly say otherwise. What's undetermined, for the doctor, is which action to say that the nurse will perform: it's undetermined in the sense that there is no one action that the doctor must predict in order to predict correctly. Insofar as the action to be predicted by the doctor is undetermined, there is a recognizable sense in which the action itself is undetermined from his perspective. In the doctor's eyes, the nurse's immediate future is open, simply because he is entitled to predict that it will turn out however he likes.

I believe that the openness the doctor sees in the nurse's future is a perfect analog for the openness that he sees in his own. For I think that the openness that a person sees in his future is just the openness of epistemic freedom. Of course, the openness that the doctor sees in his own immediate future would ordinarily be thought of as reflecting his freedom to decide his next action rather than his freedom to predict it. But I believe that the traditional distinction between predicting and deciding breaks down in the case of self-fulfilling predictions.

Let me illustrate this phenomenon with a modest story of my own. My story is this. You go to a restaurant for lunch. The waiter gives you time to peruse the menu and then asks, "What will you have?" You reply, "I'll have a club sandwich." The end.

I take it to be uncontroversial that your utterance in this case expresses your decision about what to have for lunch. I propose, somewhat more controversially, that your utterance is also a self-fulfilling assertion. Just as the doctor asserted "Nurse will take you to the operating theater" in such a way as to bring about the patient's being taken there, so you assert "I'll have a club sandwich" in such a way as to bring about your having a club sandwich. You say that you'll have a club sandwich on the assumption that if you say so, then a club sandwich is what you'll get, and consequently what you'll have.

Some may object that your utterance in my story is a request or a command rather than an assertion; but this interpretation strikes me as inaccurate. If you said "I'll have a club sandwich" and the waiter replied "We're all out of turkey," then a natural thing for you to say would be "Then I guess I won't have a club sandwich"—which goes to show that you would regard your utterance as having misfired because of being false. (If you had started off with "Please bring me a club sandwich," the waiter's reply would not similarly lead you to say, "Then please don't bring me one.") I therefore feel safe in saying that your utterance purports to be true and, to that extent at least, qualifies as an assertion.

Now suppose that you were carrying a copy of your book of life, which you had tested and authenticated in the usual way. When the waiter asked "What will you have for lunch?" would you feel the need to consult the book before giving an answer that purported to be true? If you had already read that you were going to have a club sandwich, would you feel required to say so, on pain of speaking falsely? Would you be afraid to say "I'll have a chef's salad," lest your answer misfire? Certainly not. The reason, as I hope is now clear, is that you are epistemically free in relation to your reply, and you know it. When the question is "What will you have for lunch?" you are entitled to say whatever you like (within reason), because you'll have whatever you say.

The Feeling of Freedom

Now, my claim is that confronting the waiter's question "What will you have for lunch?" makes you feel that your future is open. You feel your future to be open, in respect to what you'll have for lunch, because you know that there isn't one, predetermined thing that you must say you are going to have, in order to speak the truth. You feel free to decide what you'll have for lunch because you know that there is, in your mouth, no unique true answer to the question "What will you have?" Yet as I have shown, the fact that there isn't one, pre-determined thing that you must say you'll have, in order to speak the truth, is perfectly compatible with the fact that there is something that you're prede-termined to have. There isn't a unique true answer for you to give, but there may still be a unique truth of the matter.

I do not claim, of course, that you are aware of the compatibility between your epistemic freedom and determinism; quite the reverse. The evident lack of a unique true answer for you to give in response to the waiter's question makes you feel that what you are going to have for lunch is metaphysically undetermined—that your luncheon selection is still open. But in feeling that your luncheon selection is open, you are mistaking epistemic for causal freedom. *All that's open is, not what you are going to have for lunch, but rather what you would be correct in saying you are going to have.* You mistake your license to say any one of various things about what you'll have for the possi-bility that you'll have any one of various things.

Here I am not making the familiar but, to my mind, less convincing claim that you feel free because of mere ignorance. According to that claim, the reason why you think that you might do any one of various things is simply that you don't know which of them you'll do. But the difference between not being sure what will happen and there being nothing that's sure to happen is perfectly clear in most cases. Why, then, should it elude you in this instance? My view is that if the experience of freedom is mistaken, it ought to rest on a more likely mistake. And although the difference between ignorance and meta-physical freedom is hard to miss, the difference between epistemic and meta-physical freedom is not. There being no unique answer to the question "What will I do?"—unlike your mere ignorance of the answer—is easy to mistake for there being no unique thing that you'll do.

Can't the Will be Caused?

This mistake is so easy to make, in fact, that it appears in the work of some philosophers, who have argued that a person's decisions require an openness that's incompatible with their being caused. One such argument is given by

Carl Ginet, as follows. A person cannot predict an action and then decide whether to perform it, according to Ginet, because his prediction would imply that the question to be decided was closed, and would thus preempt his decision. If a person's decisions were caused, however, there would be grounds on which he could predict them; and if he could predict the decisions, then he could also predict the resulting actions. But as Ginet has just claimed, a person cannot predict actions that he is to decide; and so Ginet concludes that a person's decisions must not be caused.[15]

As some critics have pointed out, the most that this argument can show is that in order for a set of conditions to be sufficient to cause a decision, they must be sufficient to prevent the decider from actually predicting it.[16] My criticism of the argument is different, however. I say that the argument fails to recognize the possibility of epistemic freedom.

Ginet's argument relies on the assumption that the agent's predicting an aspect of the future would preempt any decision about it, by closing the question how it would turn out. But I have argued that a person's prior knowledge does not close that question if he enjoys epistemic freedom. Even if you knew that you were going to say "I'll have a club sandwich" —and hence that you were going to have a club sandwich—you would still be in a position to say otherwise without risk of being wrong. And even if you then said "I'll have a club sandwich," as you knew you would, the reason would not be that your knowledge left you no permissible alternative. The evidence that you were going to have a club sandwich would have shown that you were going to have one because you were going to say so, and hence that you would have been equally correct in saying something else.

Ginet's argument would seem to imply, to the contrary, that if you knew that you were going to have a club sandwich, then you would be restricted to a single permissible answer when asked what you'd have. What I have shown is that even if you knew what you were going to have, you would be entitled to say that you'd have something else. From your perspective, then, the question "What will you have?" would remain open.

Naturally, this account of your feeling of freedom would be uninteresting— and, indeed, highly implausible—if it applied only to the small subset of

---

[15] Carl Ginet, 'Can the Will be Caused?'. Related arguments appear in Richard Taylor, 'Deliberation and Foreknowledge,' *American Philosophical Quarterly* 1 (1964) 73–80. See also John Canfield, 'Knowing About Future Decisions,' *Analysis* 22 (1962) 127–9, J. W. Roxbee Cox, 'Can I Know Beforehand What I am Going to Decide?', *Philosophical Review* 72 (1963) 88–92, Andrew Oldenquist, 'Causes, Predictions and Decisions,' *Analysis* 24 (1964) 55–8, David Pears, 'Predicting and Deciding,' *Proceedings of the British Academy* 50 (1964) 193–227, David L. Perry, 'Prediction, Explanation and Freedom,' *Monist* 49 (1965) 234–47, Roy A. Sorensen, 'Uncaused Decisions and Pre-Decisional Blindspots,' *Philosophical Studies* 45 (1984) 51–6, and the works cited in n. 9, above.

[16] Roy A. Sorensen, 'Uncaused Decisions and Predecisional Blindspots.'

decisions that are formulated aloud as self-fulfilling assertions. But I believe that all decisions are self-fulfilling predictions of one sort or another, spoken or unspoken;[17] and so I believe that all decisions enjoy epistemic freedom. My purpose here is not to defend the proposition that decisions are self-fulfilling predictions, however.[18] My purpose has rather been to show that there is a kind of freedom that might explain the felt openness of your future without contradicting determinism. If your decisions were such as to enjoy this brand of freedom, then your experience of free will could be explained without resort to any metaphysical premises. Whether they actually do enjoy it is a question for another occasion.

Freedom as a Secondary Property

Before concluding, however, I want to outline how my solution to the phenomenological problem of freedom may bear upon the conceptual problem. I

[17] In particular, I believe that most decisions consist in self-fulfilling beliefs. However, the epistemic freedom of beliefs is inextricably tangled up with issues that I wanted to avoid for the purposes of this paper. Let me say briefly what those issues are.

One important difference between utterances and beliefs is that our ability to say what we like is relatively uncontroversial, whereas our ability to believe what we like is not. (See Bernard Williams 'Deciding to Believe' in *Problems of the Self* (Cambridge: Cambridge Univ. Press, 1973); Stuart Hampshire, *Freedom of the Individual* (Princeton: Princeton Univ. Press, 1970); Brian O'Shaughnessy, *The Will: A Dual Aspect Theory* (Cambridge: Cambridge Univ. Press, 1980) vol. 1, 21 ff.) If we cannot believe what we like, then we have no use for a license to believe what we like about our future, which is what epistemic freedom would amount to in application to beliefs. I think, however, that the arguments against our ability to believe what we like are undermined in the case of potentially self-fulfilling beliefs. Most of those arguments involve the claim that a "belief" formed at will would not present itself to the subject as being reliably connected to the truth, and for that very reason would not qualify as a full-blooded belief. But a self-fulfilling belief can present itself simultaneously as having been formed at will and yet as reliably connected to the truth. Hence the main reason that has been adduced for denying that beliefs can be formed at will doesn't apply to those beliefs which would be epistemically free. This exception to arguments about believing at will is noted briefly by Jon Elster in *Ulysses and the Sirens; Studies in Rationality and Irrationality* (Cambridge: Cambridge Univ. Press, 1979), 48.

Another issue raised by the notion of epistemically free beliefs has to do with the ethics of belief. For as William James argues in 'The Will to Believe,' *Essays on Faith and Morals* (New York: New American Library, 1974), the possibility of self-fulfilling beliefs requires us to reconsider the commonsense notion that "It is wrong always, everywhere, and for every one, to believe anything upon insufficient evidence" [p. 39, quoting Clifford]. What needs reconsideration here, in my view, is the preposition 'upon', which turns out to be ambiguous. Talk about believing something *upon* evidence can refer either to believing the thing in response to evidence or to believing it with evidentiary support. Self-fulfilling beliefs, though subject to the requirement that they have evidentiary support, may well be exempted from the usual requirement of being prompted by evidence.

[18] I assert this proposition in 'Practical Reflection,' *Philosophical Review* 94 (1985) 33–61. I offer some defense in 'The Doxastic Theory of Intention,' in *Reasoning About Actions and Plans*, ed. Michael P. Georgeff and Amy L. Lansky (Los Altos, Cal.: Morgan Kaufmann, 1987). I defend the proposition at greater length in Velleman, *Practical Reflection*, ch. 4.

believe that my explanation of the phenomena yields a means of improving on the traditional compatibilist account of moral responsibility.

Traditional compatibilism about moral responsibility is unsatisfying, I think, because it insists on misconstruing what we mean when we say that a person has acted freely. Traditional compatibilists claim that moral responsibility can be said to require freedom, but only because 'freedom', in this context, means nothing metaphysical. When an ascription of responsibility is at stake, according to these compatibilists, the claim that a person has acted freely means, not that his action resolved some metaphysical indeterminacy, but only that it satisfied various conditions that are necessary for there being something to gain from subjecting the agent to praise or blame, reward or punishment. The problem with this theory is that it gets the meaning of the relevant discourse so obviously wrong. When we say that a person has acted freely, we mean that his action was metaphysically free, and no philosophical theory is going to convince us otherwise.

In my opinion, however, compatibilism can afford to leave the meaning of our discourse as it is. For if my explanation for the phenomena of freedom is correct, then metaphysical freedom is like a secondary quality, such as color. And in that case, compatibilism can take its cue from a projectivist account of secondary qualities, an account that interprets ascriptions of those qualities as systematically false and yet instrumentally justifiable.

The version of projectivism that I have in mind here is the one that says, not only that the color qualities that objects appear to have are merely projected onto them by our visual experience, but also that these qualities are the ones that are expressed by color predicates in ordinary discourse, and hence that our ascriptions of colors to objects are false.[19] According to this view, no external object has the quality that it is seen as having when it looks red or that it is said to have when it is called red.

Now, I believe that metaphysical freedom is a secondary property in the same sense. It's a property that we experience as being in the world, but only because we project it onto the world, by projecting a property of our predictions onto the actions predicted, thereby mistaking epistemic for metaphysical freedom. The metaphysical freedom that we consequently experience our actions as having, I want to say, is the property that we ascribe to those actions when we call them free. Hence our ascriptions of freedom, like our ascriptions of color, are systematically false: no action has the property that it is felt to have when it feels free or that it is said to have when it is called free.

I thus part company with the traditional compatibilists, who wish to interpret ascriptions of freedom in such a way as to make them come out true. I

---

[19] Paul Boghossian and I defend this version of projectivism in 'Color as a Secondary Quality,' in *Mind* 98 (1989) 81–103.

ally myself with the compatibilists, however, for the purpose of justifying—in my case, salvaging—the ascriptions of freedom that I have just condemned as false.

Here again, my view is modeled on the projectivist theory of color. The projectivism that I have in mind says that although color is an illusion, it is a sufficiently reliable and intersubjective illusion to be highly useful for everyday purposes. This illusion enables us to recognize objects, and to describe them in ways that make them recognizable to others, by adverting to the colors that the objects falsely appear to have. What's more, these purposes can be served equally well—indeed, better—if we ignore the distinction between an object's merely appearing to have a color (under standard conditions)[20] and its actually having one. We cannot go wrong, for the purpose of identifying objects, by believing the false testimony of our eyes or by reporting that testimony to others as if it were true, so long as everyone goes by the testimony of his eyes; for everyone's eyes conspire in precisely the same system of falsehoods.[21] Hence the falsity of color ascriptions is no reason for abandoning them or for assigning them a reformed meaning that would render them true.

I wish to vindicate ascriptions of freedom along parallel lines. I say that the feeling of metaphysical freedom, though illusory, does tend to track a real class of actions—namely, the actions in respect to which the agent is epistemically free. And I say that we have a legitimate interest in identifying actions belonging to that class, because they are the actions for which there will be something to gain from subjecting the agent to praise or blame, reward or punishment. The reason—which I cannot expound here—is that epistemically free actions are the ones that get performed only because the agent thinks he'll perform them, and wouldn't be performed if the agent thought otherwise; and such actions are precisely the ones whose performance could be influenced by the agent's application of the moral principles expressed in the practices of blame and punishment.

As I have said, I cannot defend this claim here. I state it only for the sake of showing where I think the compatibilist doctrine of responsibility can properly be applied. Its proper application is in explaining why we have a legitimate interest in the class of actions that falsely appear, from the agent's perspective, to be metaphysically free. Yet since everyone recognizes the actions in that class by their illusory metaphysical freedom—just as everyone recognizes objects by their illusory colors—there is no harm in treating the illusion as the truth for everyday purposes. Hence our ascriptions of freedom,

---

[20] Henceforth I omit this qualification.

[21] Here I am ignoring the possibility of spectrum inversion, of course. My reason for ignoring it is that it doesn't alter the value of describing objects by the colors that they appear to have. Indeed, the fact that it doesn't alter the value of such descriptions is precisely what makes spectrum inversion a problem, in the first place.

like our ascriptions of color, needn't be abandoned or reinterpreted. All that they require is an instrumentalist justification, along the lines suggested by compatibilism.

Of course, there are out-of-the-ordinary purposes for which these ascriptions, either of color or of freedom, can be disastrous. For example, if we attempt a scientific explanation of how our eyes detect the colors of objects, on the assumption that those colors are the properties that they appear to be, then we are bound to meet with failure.[22] If colors were as they appear, then our eyes would have to function as mere windows, transmitting those colors to some inner observer. This explanation is the one that informs our ordinary awareness of colors, I think, but it doesn't comport with the facts of physics or physiology.

Similarly, if we attempt a philosophical explanation of why blame and punishment are properly applied to free actions, on the assumption that the freedom of such actions is what it is felt to be, we are bound to meet with a corresponding failure. Again, we do have a commonsense notion of the connection between metaphysical freedom and desert—just as we have a commonsense notion of our eyes as windows on the colors of the world—but that notion won't stand up to philosophical scrutiny.

---

[22] Here I am accepting the projectivist account of visual experience. Other accounts attempt to argue that colors appear to be properties of a sort that external objects could have and that our eyes could detect. Arguments against such accounts appear in Boghossian and Velleman 'Color as a Secondary Quality' and 'Physicalist Theories of Color,' *Philosophical Review* 100 (1991) 67–106.

3

Well-Being and Time[1]

A person can fare well either over an extended period or at a particular moment. We evaluate how well a person fares over an extended period when we speak of him as having a good day, a good year, or a good life, or when we speak of such a period as going well for him. We evaluate how a person fares at a particular moment when we say that he is doing well just then. We favor different idioms in these two kinds of evaluation: we are more inclined to speak of a person as having a good life than as having a good moment; and, conversely, we are more inclined to use the terms 'welfare' or 'well-being' to express how well things are going for him at a particular moment than to evaluate how well his life goes as a whole. Nevertheless, evaluations of both kinds are judgments of relational value—of what's good for the person or good in relation to his interests—and so they are both judgments of the person's welfare.[2]

What is the relation between the welfare value[3] of a temporal period in someone's life and his welfare at individual moments during that period? And what is the relation between the value of a period and that of the shorter periods it comprises? Is a good day just a day during which one is frequently

[1] This chapter originally appeared in *Pacific Philosophical Quarterly* 72 (1991) 48–77 and is reprinted by permission of the University of Southern California. For comments on earlier drafts of this chapter, I am indebted to Elizabeth Anderson, Fred Feldman, Jonathan Lear, Brian Leiter, Peter Railton, Connie Rosati, Michael Slote, and Nicholas White.
    [2] In this chapter I assume that a person's welfare is defined by his interests, or what's good for him. According to some theories of the good, however, a person can have interests that do not bear on his well-being, since his interests are not all self-regarding, and his well-being depends only on the fulfillment of self-regarding interests. These theories imply that what has value for a person and what improves that person's welfare are not necessarily coextensive.

In my view, proponents of such theories should recognize two distinct ways of measuring the relational value attaching to a person's life: first, the extent to which the life fulfills the person's interests, broadly construed; and second, the extent to which the life fulfills the person's self-interest, or welfare interests. Although I ignore this distinction, I believe that it could be introduced into my arguments with only a loss of simplicity. (Thanks to Peter Railton for bringing this point to my attention.)

   [3] Henceforth I shall frequently drop the modifier and speak simply about the value of someone's life. In all cases, however, I shall be referring to the welfare value of the life—that is, how well it goes for the person living it—rather than to its being morally praiseworthy, aesthetically pleasing, or endowed with significance. (See also ns. 8 and 18 below.) I shall also refer to the welfare value of someone's life as his "lifetime well-being."

well off?[4] Is a good week just a week in which the good days outweigh the bad? Is a good life just a string of good years?

The answer to these questions would be yes if well-being were additive. If the welfare value of a time-period in one's life were equivalent to the sum of momentary well-being that one enjoyed during that period, then a good period would indeed be a period during which one was, on balance, well off, and a good life would be a life composed, on balance, of good periods. But I doubt whether well-being is additive in this way.

Of course, I do not mean to rule out the possibility that the amount of momentary welfare accruing to someone during his life and the welfare value of that life might turn out to be the same. I am simply saying that their being the same would ordinarily be an accident, because the welfare value of a life is not in general determined by, and cannot be inferred from, the amount of momentary well-being that the life contains.[5]

Here I am not merely denying that the value of a life can be computed by the addition of values antecedently assigned to its constituent moments. Computing the value of the whole in this manner, by composition, might be impossible only because the values of the parts had to be computed, inversely, by decomposition. If the only way to assess someone's well-being at a particular moment was to compute the fraction of his life's value that was being realized at the time, then the value of the whole would have to be computed first, and couldn't be derived from the values of the parts.[6] In that case, however, well-being might still be additive in the sense that interests me, since the values of the parts and the value of the whole might still be such that the latter had to

---

[4] Amartya Sen interprets the phrase 'being well off' as referring to something other than well-being. "The former," he says, "is really a concept of opulence" ('Well-Being and Freedom,' the second lecture in 'Well-Being, Agency and Freedom: The Dewey Lectures 1984,' *Journal of Philosophy* 82 (1985) 195 ff.). Without necessarily rejecting Sen's intuitions about the meanings of these terms in ordinary parlance, I shall stipulate, for the purposes of the present paper, that 'being well off' refers to the state of having well-being.

[5] This statement requires one minor qualification. I can imagine a kind of life whose welfare value would be determined by the amount of momentary welfare accruing to its subject. This would be a life with virtually no narrative structure at all—say, the life of someone who is maintained, from birth to death, in a state of semiconsciousness and inactivity. That this particular life would be only as good as the sum of its good and bad moments is perfectly compatible with my claim that a life's value is not *in general* a function of momentary well-being.

[6] I believe that James Griffin denies additivity in this sense. He initially says, "We can never reach final assessment of ways of life by totting up lots of small, short-term utilities. . . . It has to take a global form: this way of living, all in all, is better than that" (*Well-Being: Its Meaning, Measurement and Moral Importance* (Oxford: Clarendon Press, 1986), 34–5). But Griffin then goes on to say that the values of a life's components should be assessed in terms of the components' contributions to the value of the whole, in such a way that "aggregation" is preserved (see esp. 36). Thus, Griffin's objection to the "totting-up model," as he calls it, is an objection to computing values by composition rather than decomposition. (See also 88, 104–5, 144–6.).

equal the sum of the former. What I wish to deny is that well-being is additive in even this sense.

My claim thus militates equally against evaluating a whole life by composition and evaluating its parts by decomposition. In my view, just as assigning values to someone's moments of existence and adding them will not necessarily yield the value of his life; so assigning a value to his life and dividing it among his moments of existence will not necessarily yield their values, either.

My strategy will be to criticize these alternative computations in turn. First I shall presuppose a rough understanding of momentary well-being, and I shall argue, on rather intuitive grounds, that the value of a life need not be the sum of the momentary well-being enjoyed within it. Then I shall argue, on more theoretical grounds, against regarding a person's well-being at a particular moment as a currently realized fraction of his life's value. In neither phase of the argument will I presuppose any particular theory of individual well-being; rather, I'll apply what I take to be commonsense notions of faring well, either over one's entire life or within the confines of a particular moment.

Intuitively speaking, the reason why well-being isn't additive is that how a person is faring at a particular moment is a temporally local matter, whereas the welfare value of a period in his life depends on the global features of that period. More specifically, the value of an extended period depends on the overall order or structure of events—on what might be called their narrative or dramatic relations.[7]

Consider two different lives that you might live. One life begins in the depths but takes an upward trend: a childhood of deprivation, a troubled youth, struggles and setbacks in early adulthood, followed finally by success and satisfaction in middle age and a peaceful retirement. Another life begins at the heights but slides downhill: a blissful childhood and youth, precocious triumphs and rewards in early adulthood, followed by a midlife strewn with disasters that lead to misery in old age. Surely, we can imagine two such lives as containing equal sums of momentary well-being. Your retirement is as blessed in one life as your childhood is in the other; your nonage is as blighted in one life as your dotage is in the other.

Yet even if we were to map each moment in one life onto a moment of equal well-being in the other, we would not have shown these lives to be equally good. For after the tally of good times and bad times had been rung up, the fact would remain that one life gets progressively better while the other gets pro-

---

[7] The notion that the value of a life depends on its narrative structure appears in many works, including Alasdair MacIntyre's *After Virtue* (Notre Dame: University of Notre Dame Press, 1984), ch. 15; and Charles Taylor's *Sources of the Self: The Making of the Modern Identity* (Cambridge: Harvard Univ. Press, 1989), 47 ff.

gressively worse; one is a story of improvement while the other is a story of deterioration. To most people, I think, the former story would seem like a better life story—not, of course, in the sense that it makes for a better story in the telling or the hearing, but rather in the sense that it is the story of a better life.[8]

Note that I am not committed to the truth of this value judgment, in particular. I offer it merely as an intuitively plausible illustration of the possibility that periods containing equal sums of momentary welfare can have different overall welfare values. (The same goes for most of the value judgments offered below.) Even those who don't agree with the present value judgment, or can imagine disagreeing with it, will at least acknowledge that it is a reasonable judgment to entertain; whereas it would be ruled out *a priori* if well-being were additive.

One who thinks that a life's value is the sum of the momentary well-being enjoyed therein may seek to explain the outcome of this thought experiment as due to subconscious assumptions that violate the experiment's terms. That is, one may claim that a preference between lives stipulated to contain equal amounts of momentary well-being must arise from a silent refusal to grant the stipulation. Those who prefer the uphill climb to the downhill slide, one may say, are simply assuming that the highs and lows encountered in maturity are more extreme than those encountered in childhood, and that the intensifying effects of age, or mitigating effects of youth, make the goods of one life better and the evils of the other life worse.

But I doubt whether our preference between these lives can be traced to a denial of their supposed symmetry. We don't necessarily assume that the best retirement is better than the best childhood, or that the miseries of age are worse, at their worst, than the miseries of youth. If asked why we prefer the life of improvement, we would be unlikely to express such views; we would be more likely to say, "A life that gets better is, other things being equal, better than a life that gets worse."[9] We would then be expressing a preference between

---

[8] Michael Slote has pointed out to me that my view is at risk of being confused with a view sometimes attributed to Nietzsche, to the effect that literary or aesthetic considerations determine the value of a life. (See Alexander Nehamas, *Nietzsche: Life as Literature* (Cambridge: Harvard Univ. Press, 1985).) I am grateful to Brian Leiter for guidance on this subject.

[9] Our preferences among trends in well-being are not confined to that for improvement over deterioration. I think that one may have reason to prefer variety and intensity to consistency and moderation—that is, a life of great joys and sorrows to one of uninterrupted contentment—even if the sum of momentary well-being were the same in both lives; or there may be reasons supporting the opposite preference. (Amartya Sen favors equality of well-being among the different moments in one's life. See 'Utilitarianism and Welfarism,' *Journal of Philosophy* 76 (1970) 407 f.). As I have said, my argument doesn't depend on showing one such preference to be more rational than another. I am arguing against a view that would deny the possibility of reasons supporting either preference, given the equal amounts of momentary well-being accumulated in the two lives.

trends, as opposed to sums, of momentary well-being, a preference that is entirely natural and yet at odds with the view that a life's value is the sum of the values of its constituent moments.

This preference can be further sustained by reflection on the counter-intuitive consequences of the opposing view.[10] If the value of a life were additive, then a life could be forever spoiled or saved by its initial segment. Every year of well-being would raise the minimum value to which one's life could possibly fall; every year of suffering would lower the maximum value to which one's life could possibly rise. An unfortunate childhood would therefore make for a bad start in life, not only by leaving one emotionally or physically ill-equipped for future challenges, but also by permanently lowering the level of lifetime well-being to which one could reasonably aspire. Conversely, a fortunate childhood would provide not only the personal resources with which to succeed in the future but also so much lifetime well-being in the bank, so to speak, insuring the value of one's life against subsequent reverses. But surely, we do not think, after reading the first few chapters of a biography, that they have placed limits on how well or how badly the subject's life might possibly turn out. We don't think, "He's already fifteen years to the good," or ". . . fifteen years in the hole," as if registering credits or debits that will necessarily be reflected in the subject's final accounts. Yet we do think that we know how well the person fared during the first fifteen years of his life.

My remarks thus far may differ only slightly from, and add only slightly to, what Michael Slote has said in his essay "Goods and Lives."[11]

---

[10] The point made in this paragraph is borrowed from Connie Rosati, who makes it in a somewhat different context. See her 'Mortality, Agency, and Regret' (MS).

Rosati has pointed out to me that people sometimes regret having started too late on a particular career or relationship, as if the value of their lives has been permanently reduced by this delay in their success or happiness. But I am not committed to denying that there can ever be a bad start that permanently depresses the value of one's life. I am committed only to denying that early misfortunes necessarily depress the value of one's life, as they necessarily would if well-being were additive.

What's more, I suspect that the view of well-being as additive cannot properly account for the cases that Rosati has in mind. What these people regret is not the level of well-being that they enjoyed in youth but rather their delay in embarking on a particular project that (as they now realize) will provide an important theme or plot for their life's story. Hence their regret can be understood only as an attitude toward the narrative structure of their lives.

[11] In *Goods and Virtues* (Oxford: Clarendon Press, 1983), originally published in *Pacific Philosophical Quarterly* 63 (1982) 311–26. Recently the additivity of well-being has also been challenged by John Bigelow, John Campbell, and Robert Pargetter, in 'Death and Well-Being, *Pacific Philosophical Quarterly* 71 (1990) 119.

Nick White has pointed out to me that an early argument against the additivity of well-being appears in C. I. Lewis's *An Analysis of Knowledge and Valuation* (La Salle, IL: Open Court Publishing Co., 1946), ch. XVI. In reading Lewis, I have difficulty separating (1) the claim that the juxtaposition of events in a life affects the value of the whole; (2) the claim that it affects the intrinsic character of the events themselves, which are colored by the recollection

There Slote offers an example closely resembling the cases I have discussed:[12]

> A given man may achieve political power and, once in power, do things of great value, after having been in the political wilderness throughout his earlier career. He may later die while still "in harness" and fully possessed of his powers, at a decent old age. By contrast, another man may have a meteoric success in youth, attaining the same office as the first man and also achieving much good; but then lose power, while still young, never to regain it. Without hearing anything more, I think our natural, immediate reaction to these examples would be that the first man was the more fortunate. . . .

Slote goes on to say that our natural reaction to such a case "seems to suggest a time preference for goods that come late in life."

Whether Slote is describing the phenomenon that I have in mind depends on how this last remark is to be interpreted. On the one hand, a preference for goods that come late in life may reflect the view that one and the same commodity, as measured in purely descriptive terms, often adds more to one's well-being if it is received later. In that case, however, the preference in question is perfectly compatible with the view that a life's value is the sum of the momentary well-being enjoyed therein. For even if a particular quantity of pleasure or money or fame gives a greater boost to one's momentary welfare if it is received later in life, what the commodity adds to one's total momentary welfare, whenever it is received, may still exhaust its contribution to the value of one's life overall. On the other hand, the goods among which Slote's temporal preference discriminates might be equilibrated as goods rather than as commodities—that is, in terms of their impact on one's welfare at the time of their receipt. In that case, the preference reflects the view I am defending, that one and the same increment in one's momentary well-being may have greater or lesser effect on the value of one's life, depending on when and how it occurs. Although Slote sometimes appears to favor the former view,[13] only the latter would place him in disagreement with Sidgwick's principle that "a smaller present good is not to be preferred to a greater future good"[14]—a principle with which Slote claims to disagree. I shall therefore interpret Slote's "pure time preference" as implying that a life's value is not equivalent to a sum of momentary well-being.

and anticipation of other events; and (3) the claim that the value of a life depends on its character as a diachronic *experience* that is not reducible to a succession of momentary experiences. My defense of (1) does not depend on claims like (2) or (3). My argument can thus be viewed as a generalization of Lewis's, in which I abstract from Lewis's experiential conception of value. [12] In *Goods and Virtues*, 23–4.

[13] e.g., when saying that "a good may itself be greater for coming late rather than early in life" (*ibid.*, 25).

[14] *The Methods of Ethics* (Indianapolis: Hackett Publishing Co., 1981), 381.

I hope to build on Slote's observations in two ways. First, I would like to suggest a deeper explanation than Slote's for the preferences cited in his article. While I agree with Slote that two benefits of equal momentary value may contribute differently to the welfare value of one's life, I doubt whether they can do so merely because of their timing. They can do so, I think, because they can belong to different life stories, which coincidentally place them at different times.

Second, I hope to draw out the consequences of this phenomenon for various issues in moral psychology and moral philosophy. Among the issues I shall discuss are the evil of death, the nature of prudence, and the value of desire-satisfaction.

Consider the theoretical conclusion that Slote hopes to illustrate with the case cited above:[15]

> When a personal benefit or good occurs, may make a difference to how fortunate someone is (has been), quite independently of the effects of such timing in producing other good things and of the greater importance we attach to the distinctive goals and interests of certain life periods. And I believe, in particular, that what happens late in life is naturally and automatically invested with greater significance and weight in determining the goodness of lives.

While I agree with Slote's evaluative intuitions about the case, I do not agree with this explanation of them. The reason why later benefits are thought to have a greater impact on the value of one's life is not that greater weight is attached to what comes later. Rather, it is that later events are thought to alter the meaning of earlier events, thereby altering their contribution to the value of one's life.

Suppose that we drew one of Slote's politicians behind a veil of ignorance about his life and put to him the following proposition. He is to have ten years of political success, but he can choose whether his fortunate decade is to occur in his fifties or his thirties. How strong a preference would he have between the alternatives thus described? I suspect that he would be indifferent.[16] If he had any preference at all, it would be neither as strong nor as stable as the preference he would have if we described the alternative careers more fully,

---

[15] Michael Slote, *Goods and Virtues*, 23.

[16] Here I am assuming that the veil of ignorance deprives the subject of information about his current age. For if he knew that he was currently in his forties, then he may have a preference arising out of what Parfit calls the bias toward the future (*Reasons and Persons* (Oxford: Clarendon Press, 1984), 165 ff.). Note, then, that the time preferences considered by Slote are different in structure from those considered by Parfit. Parfit is concerned with a preference between past and future, whereas Slote is concerned with a preference between early and late. As the subject's temporal relation to an event changes, the former preference yields a different attitude toward the event, but the latter does not.

Connie Rosati has suggested to me that a person might prefer earlier success because it would be a sign of genius. But this suggestion strikes me as only proving my point. The person so described would not prefer earlier success merely by virtue of its timing; he would prefer it only because he values the meaning of some story that its early occurrence would subserve.

as they are described in Slote's example. Merely postponing a fixed amount of well-being until later in life wouldn't strike him as an obvious means of making it more valuable; indeed, he might reasonably regard well-being as more valuable if enjoyed in youth. Surely, then, the preference elicited by Slote's example must depend on something other than the effects of mere timing.[17]

In order to reproduce the preference elicited by Slote's example, we would have to tell the aspiring politician that the later successes being offered to him would be the culmination of a slow ascent, whereas the earlier successes would be the prelude to a sudden decline. That is, we would have to tell him, not only about the timing of the rewards in question, but also about their place in a larger trend. He wouldn't care whether a particular bundle of goods was to be encountered early or late in the game; what he would care about is whether they were to be encountered at the top of a chute or the top of a ladder.

Why would a person care about the placement of momentary goods on the curve that maps his changing welfare? The answer, I believe, is that an event's place in the story of one's life lends it a meaning that isn't entirely determined by its impact on one's well-being at the time. A particular electoral victory, providing a particular boost to one's current welfare, can mean either that one's early frustrations were finally over or that one's subsequent failures were not yet foreshadowed, that one enjoyed either fleeting good luck or lasting success—all depending on its placement in the trend of one's well-being. And the event's meaning is what determines its contribution to the value of one's life.[18]

The meaning attached to a quantity of momentary well-being is determined only in part by its place in the overall trend.[19] The meaning of a benefit depends not only on whether it follows or precedes hardships but also on the specific narrative relation between the goods and evils involved. Slote's politician would

---

[17] Bigelow, Campbell, and Pargetter also express doubts about Slote's treatment of this case. See 'Death and Well-Being,' 122–3.

[18] To say that the meaning of an event determines its contribution to the value of one's life is not to equate a valuable life with a meaningful one. To be sure, meaningfulness is a valuable characteristic in a life, and it, too, is probably a function of the life's narrative structure. But we can conceive of meaningful lives that aren't particularly good ones for the people who live them; and we may be able to conceive of good lives that aren't particularly meaningful. What's more, the meaning, or narrative role, that determines an event's contribution to a life's value, in my view, must not be confused with the event's meaningfulness, in the evaluative sense. To say that a particular increment in momentary well-being adds more to the value of a particular life if it has the meaning of a well-earned reward than that of a windfall is not to say that rewards are necessarily more meaningful events; it's simply to say that their contribution to the life's value depends on their being rewards.

[19] Here I disagree with Bigelow, Campbell, and Pargetter, who believe that the value of someone's life, though not reducible to the sum of the momentary well-being enjoyed throughout that life, nevertheless supervenes on the pattern of the person's momentary well-being through time. (See 'Death and Well-Being,' 127–8, 136–7.) Indeed, these authors believe that momentary well-being just *is* that property—whatever it may be—whose profile through time determines the value of a person's life (*ibid.*, 128). My reasons for rejecting this view are expounded in greater detail below.

have experienced an improvement in his well-being whether his years of toil were capped by electoral victory or merely cut short by his winning the lottery and retiring young. But the contribution of these alternative benefits to the overall value of his life wouldn't be determined entirely by how well-off each would make him from one moment to the next. Their contribution to his life's value would also be determined by the fact that the former would be a well-earned reward, and would prove his struggles to have been a good investment, whereas the latter would be a windfall in relation to which his struggles were superfluous. Thus benefits that would effect equal improvements in his momentary well-being might contribute differently to the value of his life, by virtue of lending and borrowing different meanings in exchange with preceding events.

The most familiar illustration of this principle is the commonly held belief in the importance of drawing lessons from one's misfortunes. If a life's value were a sum of momentary well-being, learning from a misfortune would be no more important than learning from other sources, since every lesson learned would add so much value and no more to the sum of one's well-being. On being invited to learn from a personal tragedy, one would therefore be entitled to reply, "No, I think I'll read a book instead." Edification would offset the losses incurred in the tragedy, but its having been derived from the tragedy wouldn't render edification more valuable, either intrinsically or extrinsically. Any lesson of equal value would offset one's losses equally.[20]

The point of learning from a misfortune, surely, is to prevent the misfortune

---

[20] In some cases, of course, what we hope to learn from a misfortune is how to avoid repeating some mistake that occasioned it. But why do we think it more important to learn how to avoid repeating a past mistake than to learn a different lesson, about how to avoid committing a novel mistake? The reason isn't that we regard the consequences of a repeated mistake as necessarily worse than those of a mistake committed for the first time. We might prefer committing a novel mistake to repeating a past mistake even if their consequences would be equally bad. Surely, the reason is that we regard the story of committing the same mistake repeatedly as worse than that of committing different mistakes—a value judgment that depends on more than the momentary costs of the mistakes themselves.

One might think that our interest in learning from misfortunes, and the mistakes that occasion them, is based on the assumption that the mistakes a person has already committed are the ones that he's most likely to commit in future, and hence that lessons learned from them are the ones that are most likely to be useful. I disagree. We value learning from mistakes even if we know that the opportunity to repeat them will never arise. And we value learning from misfortunes, such as grave illnesses or freak accidents, that are not in any way attributable to mistakes.

Finally, one might think that learning from a misfortune is valuable only because it is a means to a more pleasant consciousness of the misfortune—a means of "coming to terms" or "making peace" with it. But why not simply forget about the misfortune entirely, or turn one's thoughts to something else? If making peace with a misfortune were valuable only as a means to pleasurable consciousness, then any alternative pleasure would serve just as well. Making peace with a misfortune is valuable not just because it entails acquiring so much peace of mind but because it entails acquiring peace of mind in a way that draws a fitting conclusion to one's past. (All of the objections considered in this note were suggested to me by Connie Rosati.).

from being a total loss. Learning from the misfortune confers some value on it, by making it the means to one's edification. But how could this be the point? The instrumental value of a means is not to be counted as additional to the intrinsic value of the end. (Otherwise, we would be obliged to pursue our ends as circuitously as possible, so as to accumulate the most instrumental value along the way.) Since the value of a means is not additional to that of the end, turning a misfortune into a means of learning a lesson doesn't produce any more value than that inherent in the lesson itself, a value not necessarily greater than that of any alternative lesson one might have learned. So how can the point of learning from a misfortune, in particular, be to confer instrumental value on it?

The answer, I believe, is that conferring instrumental value on a misfortune alters its meaning, its significance in the story of one's life. The misfortune still detracted from one's well-being at the time, but it no longer mars one's life story as it formerly did. A life in which one suffers a misfortune and then learns from it may find one equally well-off, at each moment, as a life in which one suffers a misfortune and then reads the encyclopedia. But the costs of the misfortune are merely offset when the value of the latter life is computed; whereas they are somehow cancelled entirely from the accounts of the former. Or rather, neither misfortune affects the value of one's life just by adding costs and benefits to a cumulative account. The effect of either misfortune on one's life is proportionate, not to its impact on one's continuing welfare, but to its import for the story. An edifying misfortune is not just offset but redeemed, by being given a meaningful place in one's progress through life.[21]

The same point can be illustrated with other examples. In one life your first ten years of marriage are troubled and end in divorce, but you immediately remarry happily; in another life the troubled years of your first marriage lead to eventual happiness as the relationship matures. Both lives contain ten years of marital strife followed by contentment; but let us suppose that in the former, you regard your first ten years of marriage as a dead loss, whereas in the latter you regard them as the foundation of your happiness.[22] The bad times are just

---

[21] Charles Taylor remarks on our concern for whether the past "is just 'temps perdu' in the double sense intended in the title of Proust's celebrated work, that is, time which is both wasted and irretrievably lost, beyond recall, in which we pass as if we had never been" (*Sources of the Self*, 43). Taylor goes on to say that our desire to prevent the present from becoming lost in this sense is a desire for "the future to 'redeem' the past, to make it part of a life story which has sense or purpose." Taylor continues: "A famous, perhaps for us moderns a paradigm, example of what this can mean is recounted by Proust in his *A la recherche du temps perdu*. In the scene in the Guermantes's library, the narrator recovers the full meaning of his past and thus restores the time which was 'lost' in the two senses I mentioned above. The formerly irretrievable past is recovered in its unity with the life yet to live, and all the 'wasted' time now has a meaning, as the time of preparation for the work of the writer who will give shape to this unity" (50–51).

[22] Of course, we can also imagine a life in which an unsuccessful first marriage teaches you lessons instrumental to the success of your second. But in that case, I would claim, your life would be better than it would have been if the first marriage had been a dead loss.

as bad in both lives, but in one they are cast off and in the other they are redeemed. Surely, these two decades can affect the value of your life differently, even if you are equally well off at each moment of their duration. From the perspective of your second marriage, you may reasonably think that your life would have gone better if you could have made your first marriage work out; and you may reasonably think so without thinking that the first marriage, if successful, would have been better from day to day than the second. You can simply think that a dead-end relationship blots the story of one's life in a way that marital problems don't if they lead to eventual happiness.

Of course, your desire for a successful first marriage is fulfilled in the latter life, whereas in the former it is given up and replaced by the desire for a successful second marriage. In a sense, then, the former life differs from the latter by virtue of containing more unfulfilled desires. Doesn't this difference in desire fulfillment explain the difference in perceived value between these lives?

I doubt whether a difference in desire fulfillment can do this explanatory job. Suppose, for example, that in both versions of the story your early desire to achieve happiness with your first mate was accompanied by an equally strong, competing desire to start afresh with someone else. The only difference between these desires, let us say, was that during your ten years of trying to fulfill the former, the latter remained an idle yearning on which you never acted. Now the two endings of your story no longer differ in respect to the fulfillment of your youthful desires: each ending fulfills one and frustrates one of the desires that you harbored throughout your first marriage. Do they consequently result in equally valuable lives? I am inclined to say not. For I am still inclined to prefer the ending in which your initial efforts are redeemed over the ending in which they are abandoned. Fulfilling a desire on behalf of which you have struggled may be more important than fulfilling a desire in which you have made no investment. Hence desire fulfillment *per se* is not what's valuable; what's valuable is living out a story of efforts rewarded rather than efforts wasted.[23]

Insofar as the fulfillment of one's past desires is valuable, I am inclined to say, its value depends on that of life stories in which desires are eventually fulfilled. For I cannot see how a difference in the fulfillment of past desires can yield any difference in momentary well-being. Let us cancel the assumption that you always wanted to change mates, and return to the assumption that the beginning of your story, in either version, includes only a desire to make a go of your first marriage—a desire that's fulfilled in one version but abandoned

---

[23] Peter Railton has pointed out to me that I seem to be appealing to a desire that was omitted from my calculation of desire-fulfillment—namely, your desire for a life in which your efforts are rewarded. But I do not think that your desire for a life in which your efforts are rewarded is contingent on the assumption of your having that desire in the life under consideration.

in the other. The question remains when you are rendered worse off, in the version that involves a second marriage, by the abandonment of your hopes for the first. Once you abandon those hopes, you acquire new ones—for success in the second marriage—and these are richly fulfilled. You are therefore just as well off in your second marriage, from day to day, as you would have been in your first, had it flourished. To be sure, you are no longer achieving what your former self wanted you to achieve—namely, success in the first marriage—but this failure can hardly make your former self worse off retroactively. The daily well-being of your former self is a feature of the past, beyond alteration. Failure to fulfill your previous desires thus impinges on your interests without affecting your welfare at any particular moment.

Oddly enough, several philosophers have affirmed the possibility of retroactive effects on well-being—often in order to explain when a person suffers the evil of death.[24] According to these philosophers, a person's death can make him worse off during the immediately preceding portion of his life, by preventing the fulfillment of the desires he has during that period.

These philosophers argue that our resistance to the idea of being currently harmed by future events is based on the false assumption that one cannot be harmed by things that don't affect one's conscious experiences. But acknowledging the possibility of unexperienced harms should not necessarily lead us to acknowledge the possibility of present harms due to future events. For even if a person's current welfare is not determined entirely by facts within his experience, it may still be determined entirely by facts within the present.

This restriction on the determinants of momentary well-being cannot be inferred directly from the impossibility of backward causation. Future events could affect one's present well-being if present well-being were a relation between one's present desires and the states of affairs that fulfilled or failed to fulfill them. In that case, retroactively harming someone would no more require retrograde causation than retroactively "making a liar" of him. But momentary well-being is ordinarily conceived as a temporally local matter, determined by a person's current circumstances, whether experienced or unexperienced. We think of a person's current well-being as a fact intrinsic to the present, not as a relation that he currently bears to his future. We don't say, of a person who dies in harness, that he fared progressively worse toward the end, simply because he was acquiring more and more ambitions that would go unfulfilled.

---

[24] These philosophers include Joel Feinberg (*Harm to Others* (New York: Oxford University Press, 1984), 79 ff.); and Bigelow, Campbell, and Pargetter ('Death and Well-Being,' 134–5, 138). Note that in rejecting the notion of retroactive effects on a person's momentary well-being, I do not necessarily reject the notion that the value of a person's life can be influenced by events after his death. The reason is that I regard the value of a person's life as a feature of his life story, and a person's life story may not end at his death.

Nor do we say, of a person raised in adversity, that his youth wasn't so bad, after all, simply because his youthful hopes were eventually fulfilled later in life.[25] We might say that such a person's adulthood compensated for an unfortunate youth; but we wouldn't say that it made his youth any better. Because the belief in retroactive welfare effects would entail such judgments, it strikes me as highly counterintuitive.

Thus, the reason why it is generally in your interests to promote the fulfillment of your current desires for the future cannot be that their future fulfillment will make you better off now. Nor can it be that their future fulfillment will make you better off then—that is, better off than you would be if you replaced them with different desires that got fulfilled.[26] The reason why it is in your interests to promote the fulfillment of your current desires for the future is rather that a life story of ambitions conceived, pursued, and fulfilled may be a better life story than one of ambitions conceived, discarded, and replaced. And the one life is better than the other even though they may include equal amounts of momentary well-being.[27]

My view of lifetime well-being provides a different explanation from Slote's for the discrepancy in our attitudes toward early and late stages in life. My explanation begins with the observation that events in a person's life can borrow significance from both preceding and succeeding events. A particular success can be either a windfall or a well-earned reward, depending on the amount of effort that preceded it; the expenditure of a particular effort can be either a good investment or a waste, depending on the degree of success that ensues. Retrospective significance—that which is gained from subsequent events—is often responsible for the discrepancy between total momentary well-being and lifetime value. For when subsequent developments alter the meaning of an event, they can alter its contribution to the value of one's life, but they cannot retroactively change the impact that it had on one's well-being at the time.

From the perspective of practical reasoning, in which the past is fixed but the future remains open, earlier events seem more susceptible to retroactive

---

[25] Indeed, I don't see how Feinberg or Bigelow *et al.* can say that such a person's life gets better at all if, in adulthood, he desires that his youth had gone differently.

[26] Many philosophers have noted the absence of any rational requirement to satisfy desires that one had in the past (Derek Parfit, *Reasons and Persons*, ch. 8; Richard Brandt, 'Two Concepts of Utility,' in *The Limits of Utilitarianism*, ed. Harlan B. Miller and William H. Williams (Minneapolis: Univ. of Minnesota Press, 1982), 180). To my knowledge, these philosophers do not raise the further question of why one has any present reason to promote the fulfillment of one's desires for the future, given that one may have no reason to promote their fulfillment at the time. See also Amartya Sen, 'Plural Utility,' *Proceedings of the Aristotelian Society* 81 (1981) 202–4.

[27] C. I. Lewis offers many suggestive remarks to the effect that striving and achieving have value only as related to each other in a diachronic whole (*Analysis of Knowledge and Valuation*, 498 ff.). As I have noted, however, Lewis's remarks often rely on the notion that the *experiences* of striving and achieving suffuse one another or add up to an irreducible diachronic experience.

changes of significance. Even after the events of one's youth have occurred, their import for one's life story remains undetermined, since the events from which they will gain significance or to which they will lend significance lie primarily in the future. By contrast, the events of one's old age occur in the determinate context of one's past, with which they exchange fixed implications that are unlikely to be significantly modified in what remains of one's life. Thus, one looks forward to a lifetime in which to redeem one's youth, but confronts events of middle age as having a single, determinate significance once and for all.

The result is, not that later events are more important, but that one sees less latitude for arranging them within the requirement of a good life. By middle age, one finds oneself composing the climax to a particular story—a story that is now determinate enough to be spoiled. Virtually any beginning might have been the beginning of a good life; but given one's actual beginnings, there may now be only a few good ways of going on.[28]

Because one will confront one's prime with relatively narrow criteria of success, one is required to devote more care to planning it and to ensuring that it turns out as planned. The extraordinary attention paid to this stage in life may be misinterpreted as indicating that it is more important—that the events of middle age contribute more to a life's value than events at other stages. The reason for paying more attention to one's prime, however, is not that the possibilities at middle age are worth more than at other stages but rather that in relation to a fixed youth, fewer of the possibilities will result in a life that's any good at all.

My account of the value judgments canvassed above amounts to the claim that the value of one's life is what might be called a strongly irreducible second-order good.[29] A second-order good is a valuable state of affairs consisting in some fact about other goods. Of course, corresponding to every good that someone might attain is the potential fact of his having thereby attained something good; and his having attained something good would undeniably be a good state of affairs consisting in a fact about other goods. There is therefore a second-order good corresponding to every attainable good of the first order. But such a second-order good is reducible to the first-order good implicated in it, in the sense that it has no value over and above that of the implicated first-order good. That is, when someone attains a good, he is not enriched by its value plus some additional value attaching to the fact of his having thereby

---

[28] Subsequently, such constraints may relax to some extent, since the events of one's retirement may be less intimately related to the other events in one's life than those occurring at the culmination of one's active career. A life story that has only one fitting climax may have more than one fitting denouement.

[29] As Michael Stocker points out, the value of a life is what Moore would have called an "organic whole," *Plural and Conflicting Values* (Oxford: Clarendon Press, 1990), 300–2, 323.

attained something good. (If he were, then he would be infinitely enriched, since the second-order good would generate a good of the third order, and so on *ad infinitum*.)

In order for a second-order good to be irreducible, it must at least possess value over and above that of its component first-order goods. A possible example of such a good in the realm of social value is that of a just distribution of benefits. Some people think that there can be value in redistributing benefits among the members of a society even if the redistribution doesn't increase the total amount of good accruing to individuals. This thought implies that the resulting distribution has a value over and above that of the goods being distributed, and hence that the new distribution is an irreducible second-order good.

There is yet a stronger form of irreducibility that may or may not attach to a second-order good whose value is additional to that of its components. Consider two possible views about the second-order value of a just distribution. On the one hand, we might judge that a distribution of individual benefits has a second-order value that depends entirely on the proportions among the shares of benefits distributed; on the other hand, we might judge that the justice of a distribution, and hence its value, depends on whether individuals deserve their shares by dint of their actions or characters. The first view implies that the value of a just distribution, though additional to that of the benefits distributed, can still be computed from the amounts in which those benefits are distributed. The view thus implies that facts about second-order value are still, in a sense, reducible to facts about mere quantities of first-order goods. By contrast, the second view implies that no facts about quantities of first-order goods can fully determine the facts about second-order value, since the latter also depend on facts about the conduct and characters of individuals. The second view thus implies that the second-order value of a just distribution is irreducible in a stronger sense.

The existence of second-order goods that are irreducible in either sense entails the existence of more than one dimension of value. If social justice is an irreducible second-order good, for example, then there must be a dimension of value other than total individual welfare—a dimension of social value, as it might be called—along which value can be produced even while total individual welfare remains constant.

In the case of distributing benefits among the periods in someone's life, however, the corresponding implication may initially seem odd. If we regard a particular temporal distribution of well-being as having irreducible second-order value for a person, we would seem committed to claiming that its value lies along a dimension distinct from that of total individual well-being, since we shall have said that value can be produced by a redistribution that leaves total well-being constant. Yet the distribution in question is supposed to be good specifically for the person, and so its value would seem to lie along the dimension of individual well-being rather than along any alternative dimension. We are therefore confronted with a puzzle. If a temporal redistribution of benefits produces no additional benefits for the person, how can it be beneficial to him? How can a person be better off under an arrangement that affords him no additional benefits?

The answer to this question is that the value of a temporal distribution of benefits needn't lie along a dimension of value distinct from that of individual well-being; its dimension of value must be distinct only from that of *momentary* individual well-being, since momentary benefits are the benefits whose total remains constant under the envisioned redistribution. Thus, regarding a temporal distribution of benefits as an irreducible second-order good requires the assumption that a person's well-being has both a synchronic and a diachronic dimension. The value of someone's life lies along the dimension of diachronic welfare, which is distinct from, and irreducible to, how well off he is at each moment therein.

Here we find, in a new guise, the value judgment with which I began— namely, that two lives containing equal sums of momentary well-being need not be equally good lives if their momentary benefits stand in different temporal or, more generally, different narrative relations. We can now see what this intuitive judgment implies: it implies that self-interest is not a unitary dimension of value. Rather, a person has two distinct sets of interests, lying along two distinct dimensions—his synchronic interests, in being well off at particular moments, and his diachronic interests, in having good periods of time and, in particular, a good life.

Although Slote regards a life's value as weakly irreducible, he doesn't regard it as irreducible in the stronger sense.[30] Slote analyzes the values of lives in terms of weights assigned to momentary goods in accordance with the time of their occurrence. He says that some periods of life are more important than others, and hence that the goods and evils occurring in those periods are accorded greater weight when the value of a life is computed. His view therefore amounts to the claim that facts about the value of a life can be reduced to facts about the amounts and temporal order of the momentary benefits enjoyed therein—in short, to facts about temporal patterns of momentary benefits.

---

[30] The same goes for Bigelow, Campbell, and Pargetter, who argue that the value of someone's life supervenes on the pattern of his momentary well-being through time. They say, "Surely if two people have had the same temporal well-being at all times of their life-spans of equal length, they are to be seen to have had equal global well-being" ('Death and Well-Being,' 137). I say, Surely not. For if one person's later good fortune redeemed his earlier sufferings and the other's did not, the value of their lives might well differ.

In my view, however, the facts about a life's value are not even reducible to this extent. Some of the value judgments considered above are incompatible with any reduction of diachronic well-being to synchronic well-being, no matter how sophisticated an algorithm of discounting and weighting is applied. Because an event's contribution to the value of one's life depends on its narrative relation to other events, a life's value can never be computed by an algorithm applied to bare amounts of momentary well-being, or even to ordered sequences of such amounts, in abstraction from the narrative significance of the events with which they are associated. How the value of one's life is affected by a period of failure combined with a period of success, for example, cannot be computed merely from the timing of these periods and the amounts of well-being they contain. Their impact on the value of one's life depends as well on the narrative relations among the successes and failures involved. Were one's travails in the political wilderness ended by ascent to high office? or were they ended by a lucky ticket in the lottery and a round-the-world cruise? Was one's perseverance through rocky times vindicated or discredited by the particular way in which one eventually attained domestic happiness? Our evaluative intuitions about the importance of learning from misfortunes, or of salvaging one's projects, thus imply that the value of a life is more strongly irreducible than Slote suggests.

The degree of irreducibility between second- and first-order goods determines the degree of independence between the corresponding dimensions of value. If we analyze the second-order value attaching to different patterns of benefits in terms of weights attached to those benefits, we shall continue to regard diachronic well-being as reducible to synchronic well-being, albeit by means of a time-weighted algorithm. The implication will therefore remain that the greater weight attached to some goods and evils, because of their occurring at important times, can be offset by a greater amount of goods and evils occurring at times of less importance. The second-order value of a benefit's timing will thus be conceived as exchangeable for a greater amount of that or any other first-order benefit.

Thus, if the problem with a downward trend in well-being were that more importance attached to what happens in one's prime, then there would have to be some amount of childhood happiness that was sufficient to compensate for midlife misfortunes even after the appropriate weights had been applied. Childhood well-being would still amount to so much credit earned toward a good life, even if that credit was computed at a discounted rate. Hence a life that took a slide would still be a good one if it started from a sufficient height.

If we suppose, however, that the second-order value of a life is simply not computable from the amounts and temporal order of the momentary benefits that it contains, then we must conclude that some second-order goods may not be exchangeable for goods of the first order (and vice versa). That is, there may be some undesirable turns of plot whose disvalue simply cannot be offset by greater amounts of momentary well-being in the associated prelude or denouement. I find this implication more consonant with our evaluative intuitions than the implications of Slote's view. It explains why we think that the value of someone's life remains almost entirely undetermined even after he has passed an especially happy or unhappy childhood; and why we are inclined to perceive some wisdom in Solon's refusal to declare Croesus happy without knowing how his life would ultimately turn out.[31]

I therefore favor the principle that a person's self-interest is radically divided, in the sense that he has an interest in features of his life that aren't at all reducible to, and hence cannot be exchanged with, patterns of momentary well-being. Let me briefly suggest two possible applications for this principle.

First, I think that this principle, if correct, justifies a revision in the philosophical conception of prudence and imprudence.[32] Imprudence has traditionally been conceived as an irrational preference for momentary goods that are closer in time, and prudence as a rational indifference toward the timing of such goods. Prudence and imprudence have thus been conceived as dispositions to value momentary goods differently. In my view, however, we should consider the hypothesis that imprudence is rather an undue concern for momentary goods altogether; and prudence, a rational appreciation for the second-order value of a good life—a disposition that cannot be constituted out of any appreciation for patterns of momentary goods. According to this hypothesis, a person can be imprudent no matter how carefully he balances momentary goods of the present against those of the future, if he does so without regard to the value of the resulting life, a value not reducible to temporal distributions of momentary goods; and a person can be prudent even if he pursues present benefits at the expense of future benefits, so long as the value of his life is thereby enhanced. Preferring the lesser but nearer good to that which is greater but more remote may sometimes be the prudent thing to do, if done in the service of one's irreducible second-order interest in a good life.

A second application for the principle of divided self-interest has to do with the evil of death. A prevalent view about death is that it is bad for a person if,

---

[31] Herodotus, I. 30–3. This story is cited by Aristotle (*Nicomachean Ethics* I.x. 1–2), whose final definition of happiness (at I.x. 15) also betrays an inclination to agree with Solon to some extent.

[32] Some philosophers seem to regard 'prudence' as synonymous with "self-interested rationality" or "practical wisdom." In this paragraph I am discussing prudence in a narrower sense, in which it denotes a specific aspect of practical wisdom—namely, a rational attitude toward the future.

but only if, his continued survival would add to his accumulation of momentary well-being. The choice between heroic medical treatment and passive euthanasia is therefore frequently said to require so-called quality-of-life considerations. Whether days should be added to or subtracted from a patient's life is to be judged, according to the prevalent view, by whether the days in question would be spent in a state of well-being or hardship.[33]

In my view, however, deciding when to die is not (despite the familiar saying) like deciding when to cash in one's chips—not, that is, a decision to be based on the incremental gains and losses that one stands to accumulate by staying in the game. It is rather like deciding when and how to end a story, a decision that cannot be dictated by considerations of momentary well-being. Hence a person may rationally be willing to die even though he can look forward to a few more good weeks or months;[34] and a person may rationally be unwilling to die even though he can look forward only to continued adversity. The rationality of the patient's attitude depends on whether an earlier or later death would make a better ending to his life story.

Thus far I have presupposed a prior understanding of what it is to be well off at a particular moment, and I have argued that the value of a person's life is not reducible to his momentary well-being, so understood. The reader might be moved to object, however, that I am not entitled to my initial presupposition. One might think that the only legitimate conception of a person's well-being is that of his life's value; and that any conception of his well-being at a particular moment must therefore be illegitimate insofar as it fails to capture the portion of his life's value being realized at that moment.

I shall argue against this suggestion on grounds more theoretical than those of my previous arguments. First I shall offer a more theoretical explanation of why a person's momentary well-being might fail to be additive. The reason, I shall claim, is that a person's well-being at each moment is defined from the perspective of that moment, and values defined from different perspectives cannot necessarily be added together. This explanation will prompt the suggestion that the successive perspectives defining momentary well-being simply

---

[33] For a clear presentation of this view, see Fred Feldman, 'Some Puzzles About the Evil of Death,' *Philosophical Review* 100 (1991) 225–7. Feldman's own view on the matter may not correspond to the view that he presents in this paper, since the paper adopts a simplistically additive hedonism merely for the sake of arguing with Epicureans. What Feldman does believe is that the evil of a particular death must be computed as the difference between the value of the actual life in which it occurs and that of the same life in the nearest possible world in which the death doesn't occur. I do not in general accept this method of computing the value of events in someone's life, since I believe that events have a momentary value that's distinct from their contribution to the value of the subject's life as a whole. Since death has no momentary disvalue, however, my view about it coincides with Feldman's. I discuss this subject further below.

[34] Griffin expresses doubts about this view in n. 33, p. 355, of *Well-Being*.

distort the true values of things, which are properly defined from the comprehensive perspective of an entire life. I shall then argue against this suggestion, by defending the independent validity of momentary perspectives. Finally, I shall explore some further implications of these theoretical results.

That momentary well-being might not add up should come as no surprise: values are rarely additive. Notoriously, the value of two things together need not be the sum of their individual values.[35] The value of having two egg rolls on one's plate is less than the sum of the values of having one or the other of them; and the value of having one egg roll and a dollop of plum sauce is more than the sum of the values of having either an egg roll or plum sauce alone. To be sure, the value of having two egg rolls is indeed the sum of their marginal values: marginal values are additive. But marginal values are additive only because they are defined by decomposition of total value, to begin with. That is, the marginal value of one's second egg roll is defined as the amount by which its acquisition increases one's total well-being; and this definition guarantees that the acquisition of a second egg roll increases one's well-being by the addition of its marginal value. The point previously made by saying that the values of egg rolls aren't additive can then be made by saying that the marginal values of two successive egg rolls aren't the same.

Of course, what's currently at issue is not additivity in the value of some commodity such as food but additivity in well-being itself. The question is not whether two egg rolls are twice as good as one but whether being well off at two different times is twice as good as being well off at one time. And we might have thought that although successive helpings of food can vary in their impact on one's well-being, and hence in their marginal value, successive helpings of well-being cannot.

This thought might have been correct if the helpings in question were defined in relation to the same context of evaluation. But since helpings of momentary well-being are defined in relation to different contexts, they aren't additive at all. Let me explain.

The reason why the marginal value of successive egg rolls varies is that the value of acquiring an egg roll depends on the context in which the acquisition occurs. One's second egg roll is worth less than the first because it is acquired in the context of one's already having the first. Of course, once the second egg roll is assigned a marginal value, that value needn't be further adjusted because of its being acquired in the context of the well-being that's already, so to speak, on one's plate; the egg roll's marginal value already reflects the only adjustment necessitated by the context.

---

[35] See Griffin, *Well-Being*, 36, 144–6.

Nevertheless, we often restrict the context in which judgments of value are made. For example, we make distinct assessments of how well off someone is in different respects—assessments of his financial well-being, say, or his emotional well-being, and so on. And such evaluations are made within restricted contexts. An assessment of someone's financial well-being may take account of the diminishing marginal value of dollars:[36] his second million needn't be thought to make him twice as well off, financially speaking, as the first. But our assessment of someone's financial well-being does not take account of interactions between his finances and other goods. The impact of a million dollars on someone's overall well-being may depend not only on how much wealth he already has but also on his emotional state or his health. But the potential interactions between wealth and these other goods are screened off from assessments of specifically financial well-being. Two people with equal assets and liabilities (and, perhaps, similar attitudes towards money) are judged to be equally well off, financially speaking, even if those assets and liabilities affect their overall welfare differently, by virtue of their differing emotional or physical circumstances.[37]

Consequently, we cannot compute a person's overall well-being at a particular moment by adding up his concurrent financial well-being, emotional well-being, physical well-being, and so on. The problem is not simply that we don't know how to commensurate among wealth, health, and sanity—that is, how to bring these commodities under a common unit of value for the purposes of addition and subtraction. The problem is that such restricted assessments of well-being are made in isolation from potential interactions among the goods involved. Our assessment of the person's financial well-being doesn't reflect how his emotional and physical circumstances affect the marginal value of his wealth; our assessment of his emotional well-being doesn't reflect how his physical and financial circumstances affect the marginal value of his sanity; and so forth. Thus, even if we could establish an equivalence of value between a helping of financial well-being and a helping of physical well-being, we wouldn't have established that the combination of the two was worth twice as much as either one alone, since our measures of financial and physical well-being would not reflect potential interactions between the values of the underlying commodities.

---

[36] In speaking of financial well-being, of course, I am assuming that wealth has intrinsic value for a person. Nothing in my argument depends on this assumption. Emotional, social, or physical well-being can be substituted in my arguments, *mutatis mutandis*, for financial well-being.

[37] Assessments of emotional, physical, and professional well-being thus involve what Sen would call "informational constraints"—that is, constraints on which sorts of information are relevant. In Sen's terms, the reason why people with equivalent financial holdings have the same level of financial well-being is that they belong to the same "isoinformation set" as defined by the applicable informational constraint. See 'Moral Information,' the first lecture in 'Well-Being, Agency and Freedom,' 169–84.

We can easily forget this limitation on evaluative calculations if we imagine value itself to be a commodity. If we picture financial well-being as an elixir distilled from piles of money, we shall think of it as having an independent existence; and we shall then be inclined to think that when financial well-being is added to the values distilled from physical health or emotional stability, the resulting brew must simply be the sum of its ingredients. But an amount of financial well-being is not a quantity of stuff; it is rather a property of one's financial state. Indeed, it's a property that one's financial state possesses only in relation to other possible financial states, just as one's overall well-being at a particular moment is a relation of one's overall state to the other states that one might be in. And there is no reason to assume that the relation of one's overall state to its possible alternatives can be computed from the relations of its parts or aspects to theirs.

The problem of compounding values is analogous, in many respects, to problems in the compounding of chances. Notoriously, the probability of a person's having the trait *p or q* is not necessarily equal to the probability of having *p* plus that of having *q*, since the latter probabilities may not be independent; and for the same reason, the probability of having the trait *p and q* is not necessarily equal to the product of the probabilities of having the component traits. Consequently, we cannot estimate how unusual a person is by compounding the degrees to which he is physically unusual, psychologically unusual, socially unusual, and so on. The product of these probabilities may not reflect the extent to which the person possesses physical and psychological traits that are individually rare but often combined, or vice versa. This computation would therefore count someone with red hair and a hot temper as doubly unusual,[38] even if these two unusual traits tend to go hand in hand; and it would correspondingly underestimate the rarity of someone who is both beautiful and modest. In estimating how physically unusual a person is, we do take account of interactions among the probabilities of physical traits (red hair and freckles); in estimating how psychologically unusual he is, we take account of interactions among the probabilities of psychological traits (hot temper and romantic passion); but in neither case do we consider interactions between physical and psychological probabilities. Because these estimates of probability are thus confined to different contexts, they cannot be added or multiplied together.

In short, calculating someone's overall well-being by adding up his physical and emotional welfare is no more appropriate than calculating how unusual he is by compounding his physical and emotional quirkiness. My view is that momentary well-being lacks additivity for the same reasons. Estimates of momentary well-being are made within a restricted context—namely, the

---

[38] For ease of expression, I have chosen to compare probabilities on a logarithmic scale. That is, I call *p* doubly unlikely in relation to *q* if the probability of *p* is equal to the probability of *q* squared.

context of the events and circumstances of the moment. How well off someone is judged to be at one moment doesn't reflect potential interactions between the value of what obtains and happens then and the value of earlier or later events. Hence evaluations made in the context of one moment cannot be added to evaluations made in the context of another. Being well off on two occasions doesn't necessarily make a person doubly well off, any more than being both physically and psychologically unusual makes him doubly unusual.[39]

Again, we shall tend to forget this limitation on evaluative calculations if we imagine an amount of momentary well-being as a quantity of stuff, derived from the facts of the moment but then having an independent existence of its own. In reality, one's well-being at each moment is a relation between the facts of the moment and alternative possibilities; and there is no reason to assume that the relations of successive facts to their alternatives determine the relation of the entire succession to its alternatives.

My claim that momentary well-being is assessed from a restricted perspective might seem to undermine my earlier claim that a person's self-interest is divided. Doesn't my latest argument show that a person's synchronic interests are divided from his diachronic interests only in the sense that his financial interests, say, are divided from his interests as a whole? Either division, one might think, is merely an artifact of the restrictions placed on the context in which synchronic or financial interests are assessed: a person's interests, comprehensively considered, are still unified.

Although I agree that the division between synchronic and diachronic interests results from the difference between the perspectives from which they are assessed, I hesitate to assume that the more comprehensive of these perspectives has exclusive authority. In the case of a person's financial interests, of course, I am inclined to say that insofar as they diverge from his interests overall, they should be regarded as a figment of a restricted perspective and should be ignored. Although a person can limit his attention and concern to financial matters from time to time, the resulting value judgments, even if correct, have no independent authority on which to stand in competition with more comprehensive judgments of his interests.

A person's synchronic interests, however, strike me as having an independent claim that is not necessarily overridden by that of his diachronic interests. The reason, I think, is that a person himself has both a synchronic and a diachronic identity. The perspectives from which synchronic interests are assessed, unlike the financial perspective, are not optional points of view that a person may or may not adopt from time to time. They are perspectives that a person necessarily inhabits as he proceeds through life, perspectives that are

---

[39] See the preceding note.

partly definitive of who he is. An essential and significant feature of persons is that they are creatures who naturally live their lives from the successive viewpoints of individual moments, as well as from a comprehensive, diachronic point of view.

To think that the more comprehensive of these perspectives must have greater authority is, I believe, to mistake how perspectives bear on questions of relational value. When we choose between competing theories about one and the same phenomenon, the more comprehensive theory may be preferable, other things being equal. But the different perspectives currently in play aren't competing theories about the same phenomenon: they're partly constitutive of different phenomena—that is, different modes of relational value. Because well-being is a relational value, it is constituted, in part, by a point of view—namely, the point of view inhabited by the creature whose well-being is in question. What's good for that creature, in particular, depends on what point of view it inhabits by virtue of being the particular creature it is.

Thus, although the perspective of a particular creature is less comprehensive than that of the entire universe, evaluations relative to the creature's perspective aren't any less authoritative than those relative to the universe's point of view. Evaluations relative to a particular creature's perspective are authoritative about what's good for that creature; and what's good for a particular creature is really and truly good for that creature, even if it isn't good for the universe. These two perspectives aren't two competing theories about one and the same mode of value; they're constitutive of two different modes of value.

Similarly, evaluations from the perspective of a single moment in someone's life needn't be less authoritative than those which are relative to the perspective of his life as a whole. Both are judgments of relational value, which is constituted in either case by a particular point of view; and evaluations relative to either point of view are authoritative about what's good from that point of view.

The question, then, is not whether what's good from the perspective of a moment in someone's life is really good, since it really *is* good from that perspective. The question is rather whether the perspective in question has a subject—whether there really is a creature whose perspective it is and who therefore is the subject of the values it constitutes. To this latter question, I think, the answer is yes. By virtue of being who you are, you unavoidably occupy successive momentary viewpoints as well as a diachronic one; and just as what's good from the latter viewpoint is good for you as protagonist of an ongoing life, so what's good from the former viewpoints is good for you as subject of successive moments within that life.[40]

---

[40] This argument is in the same spirit as the following remarks of Thomas Nagel's: "Human beings are subject to . . . motivational claims of very different kinds. This is because they are

Note that in arguing for the validity of synchronic perspectives, I am not defending or attacking any thesis about time preferences.[41] I am not trying to show that one is entitled to take a greater interest in the present moment than in other moments in one's life. In my view, no one momentary perspective takes precedence over any other. My brief is on behalf of all momentary perspectives equally, against the assumption that their deliverances are to be overridden by those of the diachronic perspective that subsumes them. I am trying to show that the value something has for someone in the restricted context of a single moment in his life is a value that genuinely accrues to him as the subject of that moment, even if interactions with events at other times result in its delivering a different value to him in his capacity as the protagonist of an entire life. The good that something does you now is not just the phantom of a restricted method of accounting; it's an autonomous mode of value.

If I am right about the autonomy of synchronic interests, then a person's well-being at a particular moment cannot be computed from the fraction of his life's value being realized at the time, any more than the value of the whole can be computed from the values of its parts. To assess the benefits that someone is currently receiving in terms of their share in the value of his life would be to evaluate everything in the more comprehensive context. Such a method of evaluation might be appropriate for Tralfamadorians, who don't live one moment at a time,[42] but it isn't appropriate for human beings. Just as evaluating a life by adding up the values of its component moments entails neglecting the perspective that encompasses the unity of those moments, so evaluating moments in a life by dividing up the value of the whole entails neglecting the perspectives that preserve their individuality. Each moment in a life is, momentarily, the present. And for a human being, the present is not just an excerpt

complex creatures who can view the world from many perspectives . . . and each perspective presents a different set of claims. Conflict can exist within one of these sets, and it may be hard to resolve. But when conflict occurs between them, the problem is still more difficult. . . . [Such conflicts] cannot, in my view, be resolved by subsuming either of the points of view under the other, or both under a third. Nor can we simply abandon any of them. There is no reason why we should. The capacity to view the world simultaneously from [different points of view] is one of the marks of humanity" ('The Fragmentation of Value,' in *Mortal Questions* (Cambridge: Cambridge Univ. Press, 1979), 134). (Here I have made strategic deletions from Nagel's remarks in a way that may exaggerate their similarity to my view.)

[41] I am therefore making a somewhat different point from one made by Bernard Williams. When Williams says, "The correct perspective on one's life is *from now*," he is criticizing the principle that one should "distribute consideration equally over [one's] whole life" ('Persons, Character and Morality,' in *The Identities of Persons*, ed. Amélie Oksenberg Rorty (Berkeley: Univ. of California Press, 1976), 206, 209).

[42] Kurt Vonnegut, *Slaughterhouse Five* (New York: Dell Publishing, 1969), 23: "The Tralfamadorians can look at all the different moments just the way we can look at a stretch of the Rocky Mountains. . . . They can see how permanent all the moments are, and they can look at any moment that interests them. It is just an illusion we have here on Earth that one moment follows another one. . . ."

from a continuing story, any more than the story is just a concatenation of moments.[43]

What if a creature cannot adopt a perspective that encompasses a particular combination of goods? How then do we assess what value the combination has for him or how the values of its components interact?

Consider a nonhuman animal, such as a cow or a pig. I assume that a cow cannot conceive of itself as a persisting individual and consequently cannot conceive of itself as enjoying different benefits at different moments during its life. What the cow cannot conceive, it cannot care about; and so a cow cannot care about which sequences of momentary goods it enjoys. The cow cannot care twice as much about faring well at two distinct times than it cares about faring well right now—not because it can care only less than twice as much, but rather because it cannot care at all, being unable to conceive of itself as persisting through a sequence of benefits.

The upshot is that any judgment we make about the value that a particular sequence of benefits has for a cow will bear no relation to how the cow would or should or even could feel about that sequence of benefits. And this result seems incompatible with even a weak form of internalism about value, which would at least rule out the possibility that something can be intrinsically good for a subject if he is constitutionally incapable of caring about it. I am not sympathetic to stronger versions of internalism, which make a thing's intrinsic value for someone contingent on his being disposed to care about it under specified or specifiable conditions; but I am inclined to think that unless a subject has the bare capacity, the equipment, to care about something under some conditions or other, it cannot be intrinsically good for him.[44]

Of course, we can adopt yet a weaker form of internalism, which allows for intrinsic goods that the subject cannot care about, so long as they are compounded out of goods that he can. But this version of internalism will be unstable, for two reasons.

One reason is that this version will commit us to constrain some of our judgments about intrinsic relational value within the bounds of internalism and yet to make other, similar judgments that exceed the same bounds. If we assume that what cannot be of concern to a creature can nevertheless have intrinsic value for that creature, provided that it is divisible into components that can be of concern, then we shall need to adopt some method for combining the

---

[43] C. I. Lewis also defends the autonomy of momentary value (*Analysis of Knowledge and Valuation*, 503 ff.). Again, Lewis's argument is based on an experiential conception of value.

[44] I defend this view in Chap. 4, below. Note that internalism applies only to matters of intrinsic value. Obviously, something that's beyond a person's powers of comprehension can still be good for him extrinsically, since it can be conducive to things that are good for him intrinsically.

values of the components. In order to add up the momentary goods enjoyed by a cow, for example, we shall have to make some assumption about how the values of those goods interact, so that we can compute their combined value. And this assumption will constitute another judgment of intrinsic relational value. To suppose that a cow's momentary well-being consists in this or that feature of its current circumstances is one value judgment; but to suppose that the values of the cow's good moments can be combined in this or that way is a further value judgment, a judgment to the effect that two moments containing the relevant feature are this much or that much better for the cow than one.

Whether we say that one moment of such-and-such a kind is good for a cow, or that two such moments are thus-and-so much better for the cow, we are making a judgment of intrinsic relational value. Yet the proposed version of internalism will say that the validity of the former judgment depends on the cow's ability to care about the object of evaluation, whereas the validity of the latter does not. On what grounds can this distinction be drawn? Surely, whatever intuitive reasons we have for applying the internalist constraint to the first value judgment are likely to be reasons for applying it to the second.

Another, related instability in the resulting view is that it is at odds with a fundamental intuition about relational value—namely, that the value something has for a particular creature is somehow grounded in or determined by that creature's point of view.[45] Insofar as we commit ourselves to combining the values accruing to a subject from goods whose combinations exceed his comprehension, we shall find ourselves making relational value judgments that are not appropriately related to the subject's perspective. There is nothing about the perspective of a cow that supports one assumption rather than another about how the value of two momentary benefits stands to the value of either benefit alone, given that sequences of such benefits are beyond the cow's ken and thus, as it were, nothing to the cow. The combined value would therefore have no claim to represent what's good for the cow, or what's good from the cow's perspective.[46]

---

[45] Of course, the intuition expressed here may not be independent of that expressed in internalism. Indeed, there are some interpretations of internalism according to which the two intuitions are one and the same. I separate them here because I regard internalism as resting on a rather different intuition. See Chap. 4, below.

[46] This point follows most clearly from desire-based conceptions of well-being, which will define how valuable different sequences of harms and benefits are for a cow in terms of how much the cow wants those sequences, or would want them under some ideal conditions. Since a cow cannot care about sequences of harms and benefits, and wouldn't be able to care about them except under conditions that transformed it into something other than a cow, these definitions imply that temporal sequences cannot be assigned a value specifically for a cow.

Although my point thus follows from desire-based conceptions of relational value, it does not presuppose that relational value is desire-based. Judgments of relational value must somehow be relativized to the subject's perspective—if not by being made to depend on the subject's actual

Note that this problem is equally acute for all possible assumptions about how the cow's momentary benefits should be combined. Even the assumption that two equally good moments in the cow's life are twice as valuable as one presupposes a flat curve of marginal value;[47] and this presupposition has no basis in the cow's point of view. Such a straightforward method of adding benefits may have the advantages of simplicity and salience in comparison with other methods, but these advantages shouldn't be mistaken for truth. In respect to truth, any method of combining the values of a cow's good and bad moments will be purely arbitrary and consequently defective, insofar as it fails to represent what values things have specifically for the cow rather than from some other perspective.

I therefore think that we should refuse to combine the momentary benefits and harms accruing to a cow; we should conclude, instead, that a cow can fare well or ill only at particular moments. Good and bad things can befall a cow, but they are good or bad for it only at particular times and thus bear only a time-indexed sort of value. There is no timeless dimension of value along which the cow progresses by undergoing successive benefits and harms. Hence the various benefits accruing to a cow at different moments must not add up to anything at all, not even to zero: they must simply be unavailable for addition.

As before, if we imagine the cow's momentary well-being as a commodity, then we shall be puzzled by the claim that amounts of this commodity cannot be added together. But once we realize that the cow's momentary well-being is a relation that the cow's current state bears to other possible states, the air of mystery is dispelled. For there is nothing odd about the suggestion that a relation obtaining between momentary states of a cow cannot obtain between sequences of those states. One moment can be better or worse for a cow than

or counterfactual desires, then by some other means. And any strategy for relativizing evaluations of temporal sequences to the perspective of a cow will run into the same obstacle—namely, that the perspective of a cow doesn't encompass temporal sequences at all.

(One might think that Peter Railton's version of the desire-based conception would have the resources to circumvent this problem, since it would define what's good for the cow in terms of what an idealized cow would want its actual self to desire ('Moral Realism,' *The Philosophical Review* 95 (1986) 163). The idealized cow, one might think, could acquire the ability to conceive of, and form preferences among, temporal sequences of harms and benefits while still doing so on behalf of its cognitively limited and hence fully bovine self. This suggestion strikes me as out of keeping with Railton's theory, for various reasons, of which one will suffice for now. The cognitively enhanced cow, once fully informed, would realize that its actual self was unable to want temporal sequences of harms and benefits, and would therefore not bother wanting its actual self to have any such desires.)

[47] See Griffin, *Well-Being*, 145: "Even when one does tot up, say, many small-scale pleasures to get an overall aggregate value, the value of the life containing these many local pleasures is fixed in comparison with competing forms of life, and so the finally effective magnitudes are fixed by global desires." My point is that a cow is incapable of having the requisite global desires.

another moment, but one sequence of moments cannot be better for a cow than another sequence, because a cow cannot care about extended periods in its life. This conclusion seems mysterious only if we imagine one moment as better for the cow than another by virtue of containing more of a special stuff that cannot help but accumulate.

For a lower animal, then, momentary well-being fails not only of additivity but of cumulability by any algorithm at all. Consequently, the totality of this subject's life simply has no value for him, because he cannot care about it as such, and because its constituent moments, which he can care about, have values that don't accumulate.

This conception of a lower animal's interests is supported, I think, by its fruitfulness in accounting for our intuitions about the moral difference between killing animals and killing people. For in relation to an animal's interests, as I have now described them, the traditional Epicurean arguments about death are correct. That is, there is no moment at which a cow can be badly off because of death, since (as Lucretius would put it) where death is, the cow isn't;[48] and if there is no moment at which a cow is harmed by death, then it cannot be harmed by death at all. A premature death doesn't rob the cow of the chance to accumulate more momentary well-being, since momentary well-being isn't cumulable for a cow; nor can a premature death detract from the value of the cow's life as a whole, since a cow has no interest in its life as a whole, being unable to care about what sort of life it lives.

Of course, a person can care about what his life story is like, and a premature death can spoil the story of his life. Hence death can harm a person but it cannot harm a cow.[49]

---

[48] *De Rerum Natura*, III, 870 f., 898 f., cited by Bernard Williams in 'The Makropulos Case,' *Problems of the Self* (Cambridge: Cambridge Univ. Press, 1973), 83, n. 2.

[49] Here I am not saying that a premature death is bad for a person because he wants or would want his life to be longer. Rather, I am saying that because a person *can* want his life to be longer, the judgment that a premature death is bad for him satisfies the requirements of internalism. To cite a person's actual or potential desires as evidence that a value judgment is compatible with internalism is one thing; to cite those desires as the value judgment's truth-makers is quite another.

These brief remarks on the evil of death were inspired by Thomas Nagel's essay 'Death,' in *Mortal Questions*, 1–10. Nagel points out that the Epicurean argument assumes that if death harms its victim, it must harm him at a particular time. Nagel argues that this assumption is false. (So does Fred Feldman, in 'Some Puzzles About the Evil of Death.') My claim is that although the assumption is indeed false in application to persons (which is the application that Nagel has in mind), it is true in application to lower animals.

4

Is Motivation Internal to Value?

Introduction

Various philosophers have thought that the truth-conditions of some normative statements—the statement that something is good for a person, or that an
action is morally required of him, or that there is some reason for him to act—
include or entail that the person would be moved to act accordingly under some
conditions.[1] I want to argue that there are good reasons for accepting one
version of internalism, as this thesis is usually called; but that if these reasons
are all that can be said for internalism, as I suspect, then its scope and implications are more limited than they are often conceived to be.

The version of internalism that I'll try to vindicate is restricted to statements about what's intrinsically good for a person. One reason for focusing on
intrinsic value for a person is that it is, of all the normative properties, the one
of which internalism seems most likely to be true. The norms of morality and
rationality aren't tailored to suit individual tempers; and so we can imagine an
agent expressing indifference to morality, and perhaps even to rationality, by
saying that they aren't for him. But a person's own good is indeed tailored to
him, and we cannot imagine him saying that his good is not for him, since its
being for him seems essential to its being specifically his good.[2] As Peter Railton
has said, "it would be an intolerably alienated conception of someone's good
to imagine that it might fail in any [. . .] way to engage him."[3] My strategy,

This chapter originally appeared in *Preferences*, ed. Christoph Fehige, Georg Meggle, and Ulla
Wessels (Berlin: de Gruyter, 1998). For comments and discussion, I am grateful to the participants in the *Preferences* conference, and especially to my commentator, Georg Meggle.

[1] For general discussions of this view, see W. D. Falk, *Ought, Reasons, and Morality* (Ithaca:
Cornell Univ. Press, 1986); William K. Frankena, 'Obligation and Motivation in Recent Moral
Philosophy,' in A. I. Melden (ed.), *Essays in Moral Philosophy* (Seattle, Wash.: Univ. of Washington Press, 1958); Stephen L. Darwall, *Impartial Reason* (Ithaca: Cornell Univ. Press, 1983),
51–61 et passim.

[2] For the idea that a person's good is tailored to him, see Connie Rosati, 'Naturalism, Normativity and the Open-Question Argument,' *Noûs* 29 (1995) 46–70.

[3] Peter Railton, 'Facts and Values,' *Philosophical Topics* 14 (1986) 5–31, p. 9. Note, however,
that my ellipsis materially affects Railton's meaning. What Railton says is that it would be an
alienated conception of someone's good "to think that it might fail in any *such* way to engage

then, will be to examine what truth there is in internalism about a person's good, on the assumption that there will be some truth in that version of internalism if there is any truth in the doctrine at all.

The Intuitive Basis of Internalism

I think that Railton puts his finger on the intuitive basis of internalism about the good in the following passage:[4]

> [N]otions like good and bad have a place in the scheme of things only in virtue of facts about what matters, or could matter, to beings for whom it is possible that something matter. Good and bad would have no place within a universe consisting only of stones, for nothing matters to stones. Introduce some people, and you will have introduced the possibility of value as well. It *will* matter to people how things go in their rock-strewn world.

These reflections imply that the existence of value entails the existence of beings to whom things can matter. And this conclusion sounds like a version of internalism about the good.

Railton's intuition is similar to one that other philosophers have adduced in support of very different conclusions. Sidgwick, for one, claimed that things "are not ultimately and intrinsically desirable [. . .] when considered apart from any relation to conscious existence"—a claim that sounds very much like Railton's.[5] "For example," Sidgwick said, "we commonly judge some inanimate objects [. . .] to be good as possessing beauty, and others bad from ugliness: still no one would consider it rational to aim at the production of beauty in external nature, apart from any possible contemplation of it by human beings."[6] One can almost hear Sidgwick adding that aesthetic value would have no place in a universe consisting merely of stones.

Unlike Railton, however, Sidgwick employed this intuition in the service of hedonism. From the premise that things have intrinsic value only "in relation to conscious existence" he concluded that the requisite relation is that of identity, in the sense that states of consciousness are the only things capable of having value. And this conclusion seems more than the intuition by itself (or perhaps any reasonable intuition) can support.

---

him," the way in question being "if he were rational and aware" (my emphasis). I think that a person's good might still fail to engage him under these particular conditions—for example, if he were himself suffering alienation, which is perfectly compatible with rationality and awareness. I discuss these issues at greater length below.   [4] *Ibid.*

[5] Henry Sidgwick, *The Methods of Ethics*, seventh ed. (Indianapolis: Hackett Publishing, 1981), 401.   [6] *Ibid.*, 114.

In light of the uses to which the intuition expressed by Railton has been put, then, we would be wise to consider carefully what exactly it implies. If Railton has accurately identified the intuitive basis of internalism, the question remains what exactly that basis will support. What are we entitled to conclude from the intuition that a world of stones would be devoid of value?

What the Intuitive Basis Will Support

One might claim that we're entitled to draw no more than the weakest conclusion, to the effect that nothing can be good or bad unless there is someone to whom something can matter. This conclusion would not require that the power of mattering to a creature be vested in the object that has value; nor would it stipulate that an object can have value only for those creatures to whom it can matter. So long as something can matter to someone, according to this conclusion, anything can be good or bad for anyone, or valuable absolutely.

Yet this conclusion is surely less than Railton's intuition calls for. Railton's story of the unpopulated world suggests, to begin with, that introducing potential subjects of concern into a world lays a basis for value only in the potential objects of their concern, since objects that can't arouse their concern remain, as before, in an affective vacuum. Things that cannot matter to the only creatures to whom anything can matter might as well be back among the stones.

The story also suggests that introducing potential subjects of concern into a world lays a basis for value only by introducing potential subjects of value— that is, creatures for whom things can be good or bad. The arrival of sentient beings in a world of stones wouldn't render anything potentially good or bad *for* the stones, since the stones would remain as impassive as before. And if things could have value absolutely—a value that didn't consist in being good or bad for someone—then why would that value depend on their chances of mattering to sentient beings? Absolute value is precisely the sort of value that something ought to possess even if it were the only thing in the world. If having value requires bearing a relation to the potential concerns of sentient beings, then value would appear to be essentially relational.

Thus, Railton's story suggests the stronger conclusion that nothing is good or bad unless it can matter to someone, and that it is then good or bad specifically for him. The story suggests, in other words, that a valuable object must itself be a potential object of concern and has value only for the potential subjects of that concern.

Now, I am not currently interested in whether value can be absolute or must instead be relative to a subject. The question that interests me is whether value entails a relation to anyone's potential concerns. And if any kind of value is likely to entail such a relation, as I've already suggested, it's the kind that's relative to the subject in question. That is, the kind of goodness that's most likely to depend on whether the object possessing it can matter to a creature is the quality of being good for that creature.

The Concept of What Can Matter to Someone

The conclusion that nothing can be good for someone unless it can matter to him is still relatively weak, in various respects. For instance, it does not say that in order for something to be good for someone, he must be disposed to care about it under particular conditions that are specifiable without reference to the good. All it says is that his caring about it must be a possibility.

Furthermore, Railton's story suggests that the requisite possibility may be relatively remote. What distinguishes stones from people is that stones are necessarily devoid of concern: nothing capable of caring about anything would qualify as a stone. All that Railton's story implies, then, may be that something can't be good for someone if he's constitutionally incapable of caring about it—if caring about it is beyond the affective capacities of a creature like him. And this conclusion allows that the thing can be good for him so long as the possibility of his caring about it isn't ruled out by his very nature.

The resulting conclusion doesn't entirely lack significant consequences. Some sentient creatures are constitutionally incapable of caring about some things, because those things are necessarily beyond their grasp. For example, a cat cannot care about being famous; nothing capable of caring about fame would qualify as a cat (rather than as a person in feline form). The present conclusion therefore implies that fame is not intrinsically good for a cat—a consequence that might bear significantly, say, on the humane treatment of show animals.[7]

Unfortunately, we cannot similarly specify the analogous consequences that this conclusion might yield for people. If some things lack human value because they lie beyond human grasp, we humans are in no position to say what they are. There might of course be things that lie within our comprehension but beyond the possible scope of our concern; and the present conclusion would be a premise from which to prove that such things cannot be good or bad for us. But one is hard pressed to think of interesting examples.

---

[7] For an argument of this form, see Chap. 3, above.

Mattering vs. Motivating

The present conclusion is also weak in that it speaks of what matters to a creature rather than what the creature wants or is moved to pursue. Hence the version of internalism suggested by Railton's story doesn't posit a connection between having value and motivating; it posits a connection between having value and mattering.[8]

The difference is that what matters to a creature includes things that have already come about, whereas desire and motivation are ordinarily restricted to things that haven't. You cannot want something to be the case, or be moved to make it the case, if you know that it already is the case. But you can still be glad that it is the case; and if you're glad about it, then it matters to you, even if you cannot retrospectively desire it and couldn't have desired it in advance.

Suppose there were a kind of experience that you would have to imagine in order to want, and that you would have to undergo at least once in order to imagine. You might then be constitutionally incapable of desiring your very first experience of this kind. For until you'd had the first such experience, you'd be unable to want it yet, because you couldn't imagine it; and once you'd had the first one, you'd be unable to want that one any more, since you would unmistakably have had it.[9] Would we say that your first experience of this kind couldn't be good for you, because you were incapable of wanting it? Surely, your capacity to care about the experience retrospectively, by being glad to have had it, should satisfy any reasonable constraint on what can have value for you.

I am therefore tempted to reject the formulation of internalism as a thesis about the relation between value and motivation. I am inclined to formulate it instead as a thesis about the relation between value and affect, which encompasses motivation and more.

Why We Need Two Concepts of a Person's Good

The distinction between interpreting internalism as a thesis about motivation and interpreting it as a thesis about affect corresponds, I think, to a distinction between senses of the phrase 'a person's good'. In one sense, this phrase refers

[8] On the difference between mattering and motivating, see Elizabeth Anderson, *Value in Ethics and Economics* (Cambridge, Mass.: Harvard Univ. Press, 1993), ch. 2.

[9] See James Griffin, *Well-Being* (Oxford: Oxford Univ. Press, 1986), 11: "I might get something I find that I like but did not want before because I did not know about it, nor in a sense want now simply because I already have it." See also Richard M. Hare, 'Brandt on Fairness to Happiness,' *Social Theory and Practice* 15 (1989) 59–65.

to whatever constitutes a person's welfare or well-being. But philosophers sometimes use the phrase in a different sense, with very different implications.

Consider, for example, Sidgwick's claim that "a man's future good on the whole is what he would now desire and seek on the whole if all the consequences of all the different lines of conduct open to him were accurately foreseen and adequately realised in imagination at the present point of time."[10] Some qualifications must be read into this passage, since Sidgwick has previously limited his discussion to "what a man desires for itself—not as a means to an ulterior result—and for himself—not benevolently for others."[11] Yet even so qualified, Sidgwick's account cannot mean that whether a particular future outcome will be good for a person depends on whether he would want and work toward that outcome at present. For in that case, the account would attach different and incompatible values to future outcomes as changes occurred in a person's present dispositions to desire and pursue them. You can be alternately attracted and repelled by the prospect of some future event; but that event cannot be both your future good and your future ill, in a sense that would entail its being both good and bad for you at the time of its future occurrence.

Of course, Sidgwick's account would identify your future good with what you would desire only after being informed about the motivational changes that you were due to undergo (among other matters); but it would still make your future good depend on how that information would impress you as you are now. Suppose that you were once disposed to desire and pursue some future state of affairs even in light of the knowledge that you were destined to lose that disposition, and even though you did in fact lose it. In that case, the state in question was your future good at one time, according to Sidgwick's account, but then ceased to be your future good. Yet if that state of affairs comes about, it will then either be or not be a state of well-being for you, in what was at both times your future. Hence what would constitute someone's welfare in the future cannot be what Sidgwick means by the phrase "a man's future good."[12]

---

[10] Sidgwick, *The Methods of Ethics*, 111 f.

[11] *Ibid.*, 109. Here Sidgwick implies that the structure of desires is more complex than is sometimes acknowledged. All philosophers recognize the possibility of wanting one thing for the sake of something else that one wants. In this case, the former object is desired extrinsically, as a means, and one's desire for it is psychologically dependent on one's desire for the end. What Sidgwick suggests, however, is the possibility of wanting something intrinsically but for the sake of a person. In this case, the phrase "for the sake of" does not introduce a relation of dependence between two desires whose objects are regarded as end and means. Rather, it introduces, so to speak, an indirect object of the desire, in the form of a person for whom something is wanted.

[12] The problem I have raised is cited by Brandt as a reason for rejecting desire-based conceptions of utility or well-being ('Two Concepts of Utility,' in Harlan B. Miller and William H. Williams (eds.), *The Limits of Utilitarianism* (Minneapolis, Minn: Univ. of Minnesota Press,

What's more, the things that a person is currently disposed to desire and seek may not exhaust the constituents of his welfare, because his welfare may include things whose value depends on their having been unanticipated and unsought.[13] If there are windfalls that would be good for a person precisely in virtue of being windfalls—things such as unsolicited affection or spontaneous merriment—then no amount of reflection on the consequences of potential actions would lead the person to desire or seek them, since the constituents of these goods would lose their attraction when considered as consequences of his own efforts.[14]

The latter problem disappears, however, if Sidgwick's phrase "a man's good" is interpreted to mean "the proper object of self-interest"—that is, the goal that would be rational for a person to aim at for his own sake, insofar as he aims at anything for himself.[15] What a person would pursue in a spirit of self-interest under conditions of full information may well be all that he rationally ought to pursue in that spirit, even if other things might make for his well-being when acquired without effort.

The proposed interpretation may also remove the former problem, since it

1982), 169–85). I prefer to regard the problem as an indication that there is more than one sense of the phrase 'a person's good'. In 'Fairness to Happiness,' *Social Theory and Practice* 33 (1989) 40, he suggests that conceptions of utility based on fully informed desires may elude this problem, because the fully informed desires that a person is disposed to have at different times would in fact tend to converge. But this empirical claim is inadequate to solve the problem. For we do not conceive of well-being as something whose determinateness depends on some contingent fact about a convergence among one's past dispositions to desire.

[13] See Griffin, *Well-Being*, 22: "Good things can just happen; manna from heaven counts too." I am making the somewhat stronger suggestion that the value of things may sometimes depend on the very fact that they "just happen"—on their being not only manna but manna *from heaven*. See Elster *Sour Grapes; Studies in the Subversion of Rationality* (Cambridge: Cambridge Univ. Press, 1983), 44–52. The phenomenon at issue here is related to what Derek Parfit calls 'self-effacingness' in *Reasons and Persons* (Oxford: Oxford Univ. Press, 1984).

[14] Immediately before the passage that I first quoted, Sidgwick considers a slightly different objection: "[A] prudent man is accustomed to suppress, with more or less success, desires for what he regards as out of his power to attain by voluntary action—as fine weather, perfect health, great wealth or fame, etc.; but any success he may have in diminishing the actual intensity of such desire has no effect in leading him to judge the objects desired less 'good'" (*The Methods of Ethics*, 110). Sidgwick therefore modifies his initial account by identifying a person's good with what he would want "if it were judged attainable by voluntary action" (p 111). But for reasons that I don't fully understand, this seemingly essential qualification drops out in Sidgwick's final formulation of the account, which specifies only that the agent is to consider the possible consequences of actions that are actually open to him. In any case, the qualification in question wouldn't solve the problem that I have raised in the text.

[15] Here I am assuming, with Sidgwick, that we can speak of desiring and pursuing something "for oneself," and I am referring to such attitudes as constituting one's self-interest. See n. 11, above.

Note also that the terms 'ought' and 'rational' are here being used in their prudential senses. Hence when I speak of what a person ought to pursue self-interestedly, or what would be rational for him to pursue self-interestedly, I mean what the norms of rational self-interest would recommend that he self-interestedly pursue.

renders "a person's future good" as "the proper future object of a person's self-interest"—meaning, that future goal which would be rational for him to pursue for himself. Although one and the same future state cannot both be and not be a state of well-being for a person at the time of its occurrence, it can still be rational for him to pursue at one time and not at another. For there can be (prudential) reasons for pursuing something self-interestedly other than the fact that one would benefit from the thing's attainment. The self-interested pursuit of something may be intrinsically valuable for a person, since the pursuit itself may be one component of a good life; or it may have the extrinsic value of providing incidental satisfactions and opportunities for growth.

Consequently, a person sometimes regards the attainment of his former goals as not truly in his interest without regretting that he pursued them, and without wishing that he had always preferred the goals that he now prefers. Indeed, a person may even be glad that he didn't make a youthful beeline for what he has now resolved to pursue self-interestedly; and he may be quite confident that his pursuing it now is rational, even though he's uncertain whether its future attainment will serve his interests later on.

Thus, for example, I came to my career in philosophy circuitously, via several years of preparation for a career in a different field. I now believe that being a classicist in my thirties—which is what I originally aimed at—would not have been at all good for me. Yet I'm glad that I aimed at it and that I didn't initially set out to be a philosopher instead. For I think that my actual life, in which I set out to become a classicist and then became a philosopher, has turned out to be better than either sticking with the Classics or starting out in Philosophy would have been. And I think so largely because I think that seeking to be a classicist was the better way for me to spend my twenties—and that the person who wanted to be a classicist was the better person for me to be in my twenties—even though being a classicist wouldn't have been a good way to spend my thirties. I therefore think that being a classicist now, though not in my interest now, was the proper future object of my self-interest fifteen years ago and was therefore, in a sense, my future good at the time. In this sense, my future good can change from one time to another, even though I can have only one future and only one future set of interests.

Two Concepts of the Good, Two Versions of Internalism

Reflection on Sidgwick's account of a person's future good thus reveals that we speak of a person's good in two subtly different senses, corresponding to two different perspectives in which personal evaluations take place. On the one hand, a person deliberates about what to aim at for his own sake, and we consider how to advise him in such deliberations or how to judge his success in them. From this perspective, the person's good is whatever he ought to seek for himself—what I have called the proper object of his self-interest—including things whose pursuit is valuable independently of their attainment, but not things whose value depends on their not being pursued.

On the other hand, we sometimes evaluate how well someone is doing, or how a particular action on our part would impinge on his welfare. From that perspective, our concern is not to guide the person's own self-interested motives to their proper object; it is simply to evaluate how the person is faring or would fare under various possible outcomes. Things that the person rationally ought to seek for his own sake might not benefit him by their occurrence; whereas he might benefit from the occurrence of things that he has no reason to seek. Hence the person's good appears slightly differently from this latter perspective.

These two senses of "a person's good" might be labeled the agent's and patient's senses, since one is grounded in the perspective of practical reasoning, and the other, in the perspective of the person as he is affected by events. But since a person's good in the patient's sense is also what we ordinarily call his well-being, I shall mark the distinction by referring to a person's practical good, on the one hand, and his well-being, on the other.

Now, if we plan to apply internalism to a person's practical good, we may want to formulate it as a thesis about the relation of value to motivation rather than affect in general. A person's practical good, after all, is the proper object of his self-interested motives, and we might therefore expect that it can exist only in relation to such motives, whatever the relevant relation may be. Since a person's well-being is not necessarily the proper object of any motives, it should require no relation to motives.

Yet a person's well-being is the proper object of his self-regarding affect in some sense, since it is intrinsically valuable for him and hence something he ought to value for himself—something about which he ought to be at least retrospectively glad, for his own sake, though not necessarily prospectively desirous. Perhaps, then, a person's well-being depends, not on a relation to his self-interested motives, but rather on a relation to his self-interested affect in general.

Internalism as an Instance of 'Ought' Implying 'Can'

This thought can be formulated more clearly as follows. Say that a person's practical good is that which ought to be the object of his self-interested motives—what he ought to desire and be inclined to pursue for his own sake; whereas his well-being is that which ought to be the object, more generally, of his self-regarding affect, or self-concern—what he ought to cherish or treasure or be glad about, in the same, self-regarding spirit. Naturally, what *ought* to be the object of an attitude must be something that *can* be the object of that attitude: it cannot be the case that a person ought to have some attitude toward an object if he's constitutionally incapable of having it. Hence a person's practical good must be something that he's capable of being moved to pursue for his own sake; and his well-being must consist in things that he's capable of caring about at all for his own sake. The version of internalism that's suggested by Railton's story thus emerges as an instance of the principle that 'ought' implies 'can'.

I'll admit that deriving internalism from the principle that 'ought' implies 'can' may seem like damning it with a faint premise. The rule of inferring from 'ought' to 'can' is highly controversial, and the grounds on which this rule was accepted by moralists of an earlier generation have been widely criticized.[16] But the case for internalism does not require the principle that 'ought' implies 'can' always and without exception. All it requires is a weaker principle, which I would formulate by saying that 'ought' can imply 'can'.

This weaker principle reflects the fact that inability sometimes is the reason why a person isn't obligated to do something. Arguments over whether inability always entails a lack of obligation have not undermined the intuition that it sometimes does. No one has yet denied, for example, that the reason why a person is never obligated to perform acts of telepathy or telekinesis or levitation is precisely that he can't.[17]

I am not going to present a detailed account of how and when inability entails a lack of obligation. Any such account would require fine discriminations among kinds of obligation, on the one hand, and kinds of ability, on the other, followed by an assessment of the connections obtaining among their various permutations.[18] What can be said in advance, I think, is that obligatoriness must attach to things that are options, in some sense of the word, and that something's being impossible threatens its status as an option. The property of being obligatory is that of bearing a particular status in the context of practical

---

[16] See, e.g., Michael Stocker, ' "Ought and Can",' *Australasian Journal of Philosophy* 49 (1971) 308–10; Walter Sinnott-Armstrong, ' "Ought" Conversationally Implies "Can",' *Philosophical Review* 93 (1984) 249–62. For an excellent critical survey of the views of Sidgwick, Ross, Prichard, and others, see William K. Frankena, 'Obligation and Ability,' in Max Black (ed.), *Philosophical Analysis* (Ithaca: Cornell Univ. Press, 1950), 157–75.

[17] But suppose that I promised you that I would read someone's mind. Am I not then obligated to do so? I think not, although I am of course guilty of having made a lying promise.

[18] Again, I recommend Frankena's 'Obligation and Ability' (n. 16 above) as a prolegomenon to such a project.

reasoning; and if something isn't an option, it may be excluded from that context and hence ineligible to have any status within it.

'Prima Facie Ought' and 'Prima Facie Can'

These general (and admittedly vague) remarks imply nothing about the substantive issues that philosophers have sought to resolve with the principle that 'ought' implies 'can'—issues such as whether a person's obligations can ultimately conflict, or whether ignorance can exempt a person from duty. Yet they do enable us to make some headway on the question at hand, which is whether internalism about a person's good may ultimately rest on some version of the principle that 'ought' implies 'can'.

We can note, to begin with, that insofar as 'good' means "such as one ought to want" or ". . . pursue" or ". . . care about," the occurrence of 'ought' in the *definiens* expresses a prima facie obligation. Some things that are good for a person may not, in the final analysis, be such as he ought to pursue or even care about for his own sake, since the final analysis may encompass competing and more pressing claimants for his attention. That something is good for a person entails only that he ought to pursue or care about it in the first instance, other things being equal.

Some philosophers have argued that prima facie obligations fall outside the intended range of the principle that 'ought' implies 'can'.[19] But William Frankena suggests that prima facie obligations do require latent ability, if nothing more.[20] I think that a case can be made for a version of Frankena's position.

That case begins with the observation that the concept of prima facie status can be applied to options as well as to obligations. Some things that are impossible in the final analysis are nevertheless prima facie options, in the sense that their impossibility isn't settled in advance of practical reasoning about whether and how to undertake them. Impossibility will eventually exclude these things from practical evaluation, but their exclusion will consist in their being thrown out of court, so to speak, rather than in their never being admitted in the first place. Hence their impossibility isn't such as to exclude them from consideration in some initial phase of deliberation, or from having some status within that context. Being prima facie options, then, they are eligible to be prima facie obligatory. Other things, however, are impossible in ways that exclude them from even the most preliminary consideration, and these things are not even prima facie options. They include actions of which

---

[19] See Stocker, ' "Ought and Can".'   [20] Frankena, 'Obligation and Ability,' 175.

the agent is constitutionally incapable, things that are not within the behavioral repertoire of his species or kind. Such things cannot be obligatory even prima facie.

I am thus prepared to hypothesize that whatever isn't at least a prima facie option cannot be even prima facie obligatory.[21] And this hypothesis entails that something cannot be good, in either sense, for a creature who is constitutionally incapable of caring about it self-interestedly, in the corresponding way.[22] For if a creature is incapable of caring about something, then caring about it is not a prima facie option for him, and so he cannot be under even a prima facie obligation to care about it. And unless the creature ought prima facie to care about the thing self-interestedly, it isn't intrinsically good for him. Thus can a plausible version of internalism about the good be derived from a plausible version of the principle that 'ought' implies 'can'.

What This Derivation Implies

This derivation of internalism about the good reorients the doctrine on the metaethical map. It suggests, for one thing, that the plausibility of internalism about the good isn't due to any general connection between normativity and motivation or affect. Rather, the plausibility of internalism about the good is now traced to a peculiarity in the normativity of value—namely, that value is normative specifically for motivation and affect.[23] Being good is being valuable, and being valuable is being such as one ought prima facie to value or care about. That goodness is normative fundamentally for affect, in this sense, may be the only reason why it is contingent on a creature's affective capabilities.

Thus, the plausibility of internalism about the good may provide no support to internalism about the right, since the two doctrines may not be relevantly analogous. Rightness is not normative for affect in the first instance: there is no term of affective obligation that's synonymous with 'right', as 'valuable' is synonymous with 'good'. There is consequently no reason to expect the normativity of rightness to bear any connection to affect—not, at least, if the connection in the case of goodness is mediated by the principle that 'ought' can imply 'can'.

---

[21] Note, once again, that this assertion has no bearing on the question whether obligations can ultimately conflict, since it is about prima facie rather than ultimate obligations.

[22] Similarly, Frankena concludes that 'ought' implies "is latently able" in the case of our obligations to have particular feelings (Frankena, 'Obligation and Ability,' 161). Note that I shall henceforth dispense with the distinction between a person's practical good and his welfare.

[23] The idea that value is normative for affect in the first instance, and for action only secondarily, is central to the work of Elizabeth Anderson. See her *Value in Ethics and Economics*.

Another implication of deriving internalism from this principle is that our current, weak version of internalism about the good may be the strongest version that's true. In particular, we should not expect to find any truth in those versions which say that something's being good for a person depends on his having a positive disposition to care about it under conditions specifiable without reference to the good, such as his being rational and fully informed about nonevaluative matters.[24] What's prerequisite to a thing's being good for a person is simply that which is prerequisite to its being such as he prima facie ought to care about for his own sake; what's prerequisite to its being such as he prima facie ought to care about is that his caring about it be a prima facie option; and his caring about it is a prima facie option so long as caring about it is possible for a creature like him—meaning, I take it, so long as there are some conditions or other under which a creature like him would care about it. Even if he wouldn't care about the thing under one set of conditions, such as his being fully informed and rational, there may yet be other conditions under which he would, and so the thing may satisfy the only prerequisite to possessing value.

This implication accords with arguments that have recently been raised against the conventional wisdom about the relation between value and affect. Michael Slote has pointed out that a person is rationally permitted, and may even be rationally obligated, not to desire some things that are intrinsically good for him and that he even recognizes as such.[25] The reason, Slote argues, is that moderation in desires—wanting to have enough of what's good rather than wanting to have it all—is rightly considered to be a virtue and must therefore be compatible with, or indeed a component of, rationality in desire. Thus, what a person would desire if he were fully informed and rational may not include everything that's intrinsically good for him.

Conclusion

Of course, I have not proved that the plausibility of internalism about the good is in fact due the connection between 'ought' and 'can'. I've only offered this derivation as an hypothesis, which proves nothing; but it does shift various burdens of proof. Those who wish to reject internalism altogether should now be prepared to explain why the connection between 'ought' and 'can' shouldn't lead us to believe that in order for something to be good for a person, it must be something that he's constitutionally capable of caring about

---

[24] Railton favors this version of internalism about the good. See n. 3, above.
[25] Michael Slote, *Beyond Optimizing* (Cambridge, Mass.: Harvard Univ. Press, 1989).

self-interestedly—either by desiring it, in the case of his practical good, or at least by being glad about it, in the case of his well-being. And those who wish to adopt a broader or stronger version of internalism should not appeal to the intuitive plausibility of internalism, unless they are prepared to explain why that plausibility should not be attributed to the connection between 'ought' and 'can', which doesn't support internalism about the right or strong internalism about the good.

5

The Guise of the Good[1]

The agent portrayed in much philosophy of action is, let's face it, a square. He does nothing intentionally unless he regards it or its consequences as desirable. The reason is that he acts intentionally only when he acts out of a desire for some anticipated outcome; and in desiring that outcome, he must regard it as having some value.[2] All of his intentional actions are therefore directed at outcomes regarded *sub specie boni*: under the guise of the good.[3]

This agent is conceived as being capable of intentional action—and hence as being an agent—only by virtue of being a pursuer of value. I want to question whether this conception of agency can be correct. Surely, so general a capacity as agency cannot entail so narrow a cast of mind. Our moral psychology has characterized, not the generic agent, but a particular species of agent, and a particularly bland species of agent, at that. It has characterized the earnest agent while ignoring those agents who are disaffected, refractory, silly, satanic, or punk. I hope for a moral psychology that has room for the whole motley crew.

I shall begin by examining why some philosophers have thought that the attitudes motivating intentional actions involve judgments of value. I shall then argue that their conception of these attitudes is incorrect. Finally, I shall argue that practical reason should not be conceived as a faculty for pursuing value.

[1] This chapter originally appeared in *Noûs* 26 (1992) 3–26, and is reprinted by permission of Blackwell Publishers. The material in this chapter was presented, in various forms, at the University of Michigan, Yale University, and the University of Dayton. I am grateful to these audiences for their comments. I am also indebted to Rüdiger Bittner, Paul Boghossian, Jennifer Church, Carl Ginet, Jonathan Lear, Richard Miller, Donald Regan, Connie Rosati, Geoffrey Sayre-McCord, Sydney Shoemaker, Michael Slote, Michael Smith, and Dennis Stampe for comments on earlier drafts or discussion of related issues. Thanks are also due to Lloyd Humberstone for allowing me to read the manuscript of a paper entitled 'Direction of Fit,' which was subsequently published in *Mind* 101 (1992) 59–83.
[2] G. E. M. Anscombe, *Intention* (Ithaca: Cornell Univ. Press, 1963), 70 ff.; Donald Davidson 'Intending,' reprinted in *Essays on Actions and Events* (Oxford: Clarendon Press, 1980), 97, n. 7; Dennis Stampe, 'The Authority of Desire,' *The Philosophical Review* 96 (1987), 355; Alvin I. Goldman, *A Theory of Human Action* (Princeton: Princeton Univ. Press, 1970), 94.
[3] See Ronald B. De Sousa, 'The Good and the True,' *Mind* 83 (1974) 534–51; see also Donald Davidson, 'How is Weakness of the Will Possible?', reprinted in *Essays on Actions and Events*, 22; David Pears, *Motivated Irrationality* (Oxford: Clarendon Press, 1984), 198.

One source of the view that intentional actions are aimed at the good has been a desire, on the part of moral psychologists, to reconcile two seemingly incompatible stories about how human action originates. These might be called the story of motivation and the story of rational guidance.[4]

The story of motivation says that an action is caused by a desire for some outcome and a belief that the action will promote it. The agent wants to know the time, for example, and believes that looking at his watch will result in his knowing the time; and he consequently looks at his watch.[5] The desire and belief cited in this story are conceived as propositional attitudes. That is, each is thought to consist in the agent's grasping and being somehow disposed toward a proposition. He is, so to speak, desirous toward the proposition "I know the time" and credent toward the proposition "Looking at my watch will result in my knowing the time." These attitudes combine to cause a new attitude—a desire toward the proposition "I look at my watch." And since looking at his watch is something that the agent can just do if he wants, this desire causes him to act.

The story of rational guidance tells how an agent acts for a reason. According to this story, a reason for acting is a proposition whose truth would reflect well on, count in favor of, recommend, or in some other sense justify an action.[6] A reason for performing an action exists so long as a proposition justifying the action is true.[7] But an agent cannot act for this reason unless he has mental access to it—unless he believes the proposition or at least grasps it in some related fashion. And even if he has appropriately grasped the reason, and is therefore in a position to act for it, he doesn't ultimately act for the reason unless his grasp of it results in his being influenced or guided by its justifying force. An agent acts for a reason, then, when the action-justifying character of a proposition prompts his action via his grasp of that proposition.[8]

---

[4] Michael Smith refers to these two stories as the "intentional perspective" and the "deliberative perspective" ('Valuing: Desiring or Believing?', in David Charles and Kathleen Lennon (eds.), *Reduction, Explanation and Realism* (Oxford: Oxford Univ. Press, 1992), 323–60). I understand that Rüdiger Bittner is also working independently on the relation between these stories.

[5] I have borrowed this example from Davidson, 'How is Weakness of the Will Possible?', 31 ff. I shall presently discuss Davidson's own analysis of the case.

[6] I realize, of course, that some philosophers would deny that genuine propositions justify action, independently of their actually or potentially exerting some motivational influence on the agent. I discuss this view briefly below, under the name of noncognitivism.

[7] I shall avoid giving an example of an action-justifying proposition, so as to remain neutral on the precise nature of practical reason.

[8] To say that acting for a reason entails being influenced by the intrinsic action-justifying character of a belief is not to say that it requires the operative belief to have intrinsic motivational force that's independent of any desires. One may have a desire to perform actions that are justified, or to perform actions that are related to one's circumstances in particular ways, which are in fact justifying. Any belief that gains motivational force from such a desire will also owe that motivational force, in part, to its own action-justifying character, and will therefore fulfill the story of rational guidance. I thus assume that beliefs can be intrinsically justifying even

The apparent discrepancy between these stories lies in the relation posited between the agent's action and the propositional objects of his attitudes. In the story of motivation, the objects of the agent's attitudes are propositions that do not in themselves justify his action. They do, of course, help to determine which action he is moved to perform. The agent would not be moved to look at his watch if he didn't want, in particular, to know the time and if he didn't believe, in particular, that looking at his watch would result in his knowing the time. Yet the content of these attitudes doesn't in any way reflect well on, count in favor of, or otherwise justify looking at his watch. Indeed, the propositions "I know the time" and "Looking at my watch will result in my knowing the time" do not reflect more favorably on watch-consulting behavior than on watch-ignoring behavior. When the agent's attitudes toward these propositions move him to consult his watch, he is not responding to any action-justifying property of the propositions themselves; he is simply manifesting the valence of his attitude toward the former proposition. Because the agent has a desire toward "I know the time," he is moved to look at his watch; whereas if he had an aversion toward the same proposition, he would be moved to ignore his watch instead. The content of his attitudes is in itself neutral between these alternatives.

The action performed in the story of rational guidance is also determined in part by the nature of the agent's attitudes and not merely by their content. When the protagonist of this story acts for a reason, he acts partly because of grasping the reason in an attitude something like belief. But more than the nature of the agent's attitude toward his reason must work in favor of his action. When an agent acts for a reason, he acts not only because his attitude toward the reason is more like belief than disbelief but also because the proposition involved militates in favor of his action rather than against it. The agent's attitudes are thus conceived as having propositional objects that intrinsically favor a particular action, and their favoring the action is conceived as crucial to their behavioral influence.

This aspect of rational guidance is what makes rationally guided behavior, as we conceive it, comparable to the conclusion of an inference. The premises of an inference are propositions whose truth guarantees or makes probable the truth of the conclusion; and in this sense they favor believing the conclusion solely by virtue of their content, antecedently to any attitude in which one might fix them. In order for a particular set of premises to become one's reasons for drawing a conclusion, one must somehow be influenced, in grasping them, by their antecedently favorable relation to the conclusion. Similarly, in order

---

if they cannot be intrinsically motivating. Here I differ with, e.g., Thomas Nagel, *The Possibility of Altruism* (Princeton: Princeton Univ. Press, 1970), and John McDowell, 'Are Moral Requirements Hypothetical Imperatives?', *Proceedings of the Aristotelian Society* (1978, supp. Vol.) 13–29.

for a particular reason to become one's reason for performing an action, one must be influenced by its bearing favorably on that action. To be motivated by a desire, by contrast, is to be guided by attitudes toward propositions that do not in themselves favor anything.

This fundamental difference between motivation and rational guidance wouldn't necessarily render the two stories incompatible if neither purported to be the complete explanation of an action. One and the same action could be due to a confluence of motivation and rational guidance. Yet philosophers have tended to interpret each story as purporting to be the whole story; and they have therefore assumed that the apparent discrepancy between these stories has to be removed. They have sought to remove the discrepancy by slightly retelling one story or the other.

Noncognitivists, for example, retell the story of rational guidance in such a way that it collapses into the story of motivation. According to their version of the story, the agent's reason for acting is the proposition "Looking at my watch will result in my knowing the time," a proposition that recommends looking at his watch, not by virtue of its content, but rather because his belief in it inclines him to look at his watch, given his desire to know the time. Noncognitivists thus deny that the propositions constituting an agent's reasons for acting are intrinsically favorable to his action. Propositions recommend acting, they think, only in relation to desires that lend motivational force to the agent's belief in those propositions.[9]

Some noncognitivists may resent the suggestion that they are hereby retelling or revising anything—that there ever was any other story of rational guidance than theirs. But the noncognitivist story diverges from the common-sense story of rational guidance in one important respect: it reverses the order of explanation between justificatory and motivational force. In the common-sense story, the agent is moved toward an action because his reasons justify it; whereas in the noncognitivist story, his reasons justify the action in virtue of moving him toward it. The noncognitivist thus treats motivation as a constituent rather than an effect of justification.[10]

I shall not consider here whether this departure from the commonsense story of rational guidance is defensible. What suffices for my purposes is that

---

[9] This approach can be traced back at least as far as Hobbes's definition of deliberation, at *Leviathan*, Part I, chapter vi.

[10] The noncognitivist cannot remove the discrepancy by pointing out that he conceives of justificatory force as a disposition to motivate, which can indeed explain particular instances of motivation. In the commonsense story, the justificatory force of a reason explains (rather than consists in) the reason's disposition to motivate as well as its motivating on particular occasions.

My remarks on the noncognitivist view echo much that is said in W. D. Falk 'Action-Guiding Reasons,' (1963), reprinted in *Ought, Reasons, and Morality* (Ithaca: Cornell Univ. Press, 1986), 82–98. Yet Falk does not ultimately reject noncognitivism, since he, too, believes that reasons "are . . . choice-supporting in proportion to their choice-influencing potential" (p. 92).

some philosophers have preferred to avoid it, by adopting a different strategy for reconciling the two stories of human action. Rather than characterize rational guidance noncognitively, so that it collapses into motivation, they characterize motivation cognitively, so that it amounts to something like rational guidance; and they thereby introduce the evaluative conception of agency that interests me.

Proponents of this alternative strategy portray motivation itself as an inference, governed in part by action-justifying content to be found in the motivating attitudes. To this end, they incorporate the valence of desire into its content, by describing desire, not as a favorable attitude toward the representation of some outcome, but rather as an attitude toward a favorable representation of the outcome. The agent who wants to know the time is said, not to be favorably disposed toward "I know the time," but rather to accept a proposition such as "My knowing the time would be good." The content of this attitude and the content of the agent's belief, "Consulting my watch would result in my knowing the time," are sufficient to justify the conclusion "Consulting my watch would be good." And the agent's accepting this favorable representation of consulting his watch is now conceived as constituting a desire to consult his watch. Hence his transition from a desire to know the time to a desire to consult his watch appears to be dictated, in the fashion of an inference, by a privileged logical relation between the contents of the attitudes involved.

The leading contemporary proponent of this latter strategy is Donald Davidson. Consider the following passage, in which Davidson is discussing an agent who is moved to add sage to his stew by a desire to improve the taste:[11]

> [L]et us suppose [the agent] wants to improve the taste of the stew. But what is the corresponding premise? If we were to look for the proposition toward which his desire is directed, the proposition he wants true, it would be something like: He does something that improves the taste of the stew (more briefly: He improves the taste of the stew). This cannot be his premise, however, for nothing interesting follows from the two premises: Adding sage to the stew will improve its taste, and the agent improves the taste of the stew. The trouble is that the attitude of *approval* which the agent has toward the second proposition has been left out. It cannot be put back in by making the premise 'The agent wants to improve the taste of the stew': we do not want a *description* of his desire, but an *expression* of it in a form in which he might use it to arrive at an action. The natural expression of his desire is, it seems to me, evaluative in form; for example, 'It is desirable to improve the taste of the stew,' or, 'I ought to improve the taste of the stew'. We may suppose different pro attitudes are expressed with other evaluative words in place of 'desirable'.

In this passage Davidson subjects the story of motivation to the retelling that I have just described. He demands that the outcome of motivation—the act of

adding sage—be justified by some propositional content of the agent's attitudes, as if it were a conclusion following from premises. And he obtains the
required content by incorporating the valence of the agent's attitude toward
"I improve the taste" into a new proposition: "Improving the taste is desirable." The story of motivation is thus transformed into the story of an inference, in which the agent is under genuinely rational guidance.

Here, then, is one way in which rational agency comes to be conceived as a
capacity for pursuing value. Desires are conceived as value judgments, with
intrinsic justificatory force, so that the desire motivating an agent can be identified with the reason guiding him. The result is that all actions performed for
reasons are conceived as arising from favorable value judgments, and hence as
being aimed at the good.

This reconciliation of motivation and rational guidance comes under pressure from two different directions. If the cognitivist seriously means to characterize desire as an attitude toward an evaluative proposition, then he implies
that the capacity to desire requires the possession of evaluative concepts. Yet
a young child can want things long before it has acquired the concept of their
being worth wanting, or desirable. Surely, the concept of desirability—of
something's being a correct or fitting object of desire—is a concept that children need to be taught. And how would one teach this concept to a child if
not by disciplining its antecedently existing desires?[12]

This problem may explain Davidson's apparent efforts to avoid saying that
evaluations serve as the contents or propositional objects of desire. Davidson
often favors alternative formulations, as in the passage quoted above, where
he says that the relevant evaluation is "the natural expression of [the agent's]
desire" rather than its propositional object.

But this qualification leaves the cognitivist open to a different objection,
since it seems to undermine his attempt to reconcile the stories of motivation
and rational guidance. According to the latter story, acting for a reason entails
being influenced by the force of a mentally grasped justification of one's action.
According to Davidson's qualified formulation, however, a proposition that's
essential to the justification of the action—namely, the proposition that the
action's expected consequences are desirable—is merely a proposition that
would naturally be used to express the agent's desire. And the agent can be

---

[12] Of course, the young child may not be susceptible to rational guidance, either; but this point
hardly counts in Davidson's favor. When Davidson characterizes belief-desire motivation as
equivalent to rational guidance, he leaves no room for agents who are moved by desires without
being guided by reasons. The fact that children, who pursue desired ends, can nevertheless be
too young for rational guidance is therefore a point against Davidson, on a par with my point that
they can be too young for the concept of the desirable. (For an alternative argument against identifying desires with evaluative judgments, see David Lewis, 'Desire as Belief,' *Mind* 97 (1988)
323–42.)

moved by his desire without either being able to express it or grasping the proposition with which it would naturally be expressed. He can therefore satisfy Davidson's story of motivation without having mentally accessed anything that justifies his action. Hence the resulting story of motivation no longer corresponds to the story of rational guidance.[13]

These two objections seem to leave no room for the cognitivist strategy. But they do not rule out a sophisticated version of cognitivism—a version that is suggested, in any case, by an important feature of propositional attitudes in general. The feature in question is the so-called direction of fit that distinguishes conative attitudes such as desire from cognitive attitudes such as belief.[14] As we shall see, reflection on this feature naturally leads to a version of cognitivism that escapes the foregoing objections.

The term "direction of fit" refers to the two different ways in which attitudes can relate propositions to the world. In cognitive attitudes, a proposition is grasped as patterned after the world; whereas in conative attitudes, a proposition is grasped as a pattern for the world to follow. The propositional object of desire is regarded not as fact—not, that is, as *factum*, having been brought about—but rather as *faciendum*, to be brought about; it's regarded not as true but as to be made true.

There is a temptation to think that regarding something as to be brought about or made true is tantamount to holding a value judgment about it. Perhaps, then, when philosophers say that to want something is to regard it as good or desirable, they are thinking of the attitude's direction of fit—of the distinctive way in which a proposition is regarded when it's the object of desire rather than belief.[15]

---

[13] I think that Davidson sometimes betrays an uncomfortable awareness of this difficulty. He wants to avoid the implausibly strong claim that desires consist in value judgments. (See, e.g., the discussion of wanting to drink a can of paint in 'Actions, Reasons, and Causes,' reprinted in *Essays on Actions and Events*, 4.) And yet he senses that he is committed to that claim by his strategy of equating motivation with rational guidance. See, e.g., 'Intending,' 102; (desires "constitute" value judgments); 'How is Weakness of the Will Possible?', 31 (desiring something is "setting a positive value" on it); 'Intending,' 97, n. 7 (desiring something entails "holding" it to have "some positive characteristic").

[14] The reader will find that I use the term "direction of fit" in a somewhat different sense from others who have used the term—including, for example, John Searle, *Intentionality: An Essay in the Philosophy of Mind* (Cambridge: Cambridge Univ. Press, 1983), 7 ff.; and Mark Platts, *Ways of Meaning* (London: Routledge and Kegan Paul, 1979), 257. See also G. E. M. Anscombe, *Intention* (Ithaca: Cornell Univ. Press, 1963), 56. The definition offered by these authors will be explained and criticized in the text below.

[15] Direction of fit is clearly what Dennis Stampe has in mind in his version of this claim: "[W]hile the belief and the desire that *p* have the same propositional content and represent the same state of affairs, there is a difference in the *way* it is represented in the two states of mind. In belief it is represented *as obtaining*, whereas in desire, it is represented as a state of affairs *the obtaining of which would be good*," 'The Authority of Desire,' *The Philosophical Review* 96 (1987) 355.

I shall argue presently that the use of an evaluative term like "good" to express desire's direction of fit is a potential source of confusion. For the moment, however, I shall adopt that usage, in order to examine precisely what it might mean and where it might lead.

As for the meaning of this usage, note that even if desiring something entails making a value judgment about it, by regarding it as good, this attitude qualifies as a value judgment in only a rather unusual sense of the phrase, a sense corresponding to that in which a belief might be called a "truth judgment." The desire that p is here conceived as a value judgment in the sense that it involves regarding p as to be brought about and hence, supposedly, as good, just as the belief that p involves regarding p as true. But to say that belief in p involves regarding p as true is not to say that it consists in a judgment whose object is the proposition "p is true." That way lies a vicious regress of propositional attitudes. Similarly, to say that the desire involves regarding p as good is not to say that it consists in a judgment with an evaluative proposition as its object.

Expressions like "regarding . . . as true" and "regarding . . . as good" are intended to describe belief and desire in a way that elucidates the difference in their directions of fit. Because we conceive of belief and desire as alike in being attitudes toward propositions, and as differing in their treatment of the fit between propositions and the world, we unavoidably describe them with a common attitudinal verb ("regarding") and different predicate adjectives ("as true," "as good"). But this construction—attitudinal verb plus differentiating predicate—must not be interpreted as invoking a further attitude directed toward a proposition containing that predicate. The desire that p is not to be analyzed as an attitude toward the proposition that p is good; it must be analyzed as an attitude toward p as good.[16]

Even so, the resulting conception of desire does seem to allow for a reconciliation between the stories of motivation and rational guidance. For although

---

[16] What psychological realization, if any, attends the predicates used to characterize propositional attitudes? A behaviorist might insist that regarding a proposition as true is nothing more than being disposed to behave as would be appropriate if the proposition were true. Alternatively, one might imagine that regarding a proposition as true entails having a representation of it in a particular mental compartment, which might be called the "true" box, because of its role in the mental architecture. Another alternative would be to give a phenomenological rather than functional account of the relevant mental posture toward a proposition—whatever such an account might be. The most attractive alternative, for present purposes, is a stance of neutrality among these and other models of propositional attitudes. One needn't adopt any particular model of propositional attitudes in order to adopt the descriptions whose realization is the point of contention among such models. One can thus insist that whatever believing that p consists in, it must be something that would appropriately be called regarding p as true; and whatever desiring that p consists in, it must be something that would appropriately be called regarding p as to be made true. For further discussion of this issue, see Chap. 11.

the desire that *p* doesn't entail grasping a proposition that justifies action conducive to *p*, the desire itself may appear to constitute an attitude that justifies such action, if it consists in regarding *p* as good.

Once we recognize that a propositional attitude must be characterized, not only by the proposition that embodies its content, but also by a predicate expressing how that proposition is regarded—that is, whether it's regarded as *factum* or *faciendum*, as true or to be made true—we are less inclined to insist that the justificatory force influencing reason-guided behavior be lodged in the propositional objects of the agent's attitudes. When the valence of a desire that *p* is represented by the expression "regarding *p* as good," valence takes on the form of a content-like phenomenon and begins to seem like a potential bearer of justificatory force. For even if no action is justified by the fact that *p*, some action might well be justified by the *faciendum* that *p*—by *p*'s being something to be brought about.

Thus, if an attitude combines the propositional object *p* with a direction of fit expressible by the predicate "good," then it would seem to harbor justificatory force—not in its propositional object alone but rather in the combination of its propositional object and its direction of fit. And the agent can be imagined as having mental access, not only to the propositions that he grasps in various attitudes, but also to the attitudes' direction of fit, as expressed by their constitutive predicates.

We may therefore be inclined to revise the story of rational guidance, by replacing its references to the agent's grasp of action-justifying propositions with references to his action-justifying attitudes. We might say, for example, that an agent is mentally in touch with a justification for looking at his watch not only if he believes that knowing the time would be good but also if he regards it as good that he know the time—an attitude that supposedly constitutes a desire. We might also say that being guided by a desire's direction of fit entails being guided by its evaluative aspect, which lends the desire its mentally accessible justificatory force. We might then conclude that being motivated by a desire can amount to acting for a reason.[17]

This version of cognitivism, like the previous version, implies that every action that's motivated by a desire—or, equivalently, performed for a reason—is guided by some favorable value judgment, and hence that intentional action is always aimed at the good. The judgment involved is no longer conceived as an attitude toward an evaluative proposition; but it is still conceived as having the

---

[17] This version of cognitivism is articulated by Dennis Stampe: "Desires constitute reasons for us to act because their contents are represented as states of affairs the realization of which would be good" (*ibid.*). I do not know whether Davidson accepts or would accept this formulation. His accepting it would explain why he says both that desires are and that they are expressed by value judgments.

recommending force of an evaluation, so that it can serve as the agent's reason for acting.

I believe that this version of cognitivism is an improvement on its predecessor, but that it is not ultimately more successful. For even if desiring something entails regarding it as good in some sense, regarding something as good in that sense does not in fact amount to making a value judgment about it. An agent's motivating desire consequently lacks the justificatory force that the cognitivist attributes to it for the sake of identifying it with the agent's reason for acting. The cognitivist strategy for reconciling motivation and rational guidance, and the resulting conception of intentional action as aimed at the good, thus turn out to rest on a mistake.

Before I attempt to demonstrate this mistake, however, I had better define more clearly what sort of mistake it is. When I deny that desire has the justificatory force with which it is credited by the cognitivist, I am not necessarily denying that having a desire provides one with reason for acting. It often does. Yet the cognitivist doesn't merely claim that desire provides reason for acting; he claims that being moved by a desire amounts to acting for a reason. And this claim implies, as we have seen, that to fall under a desire's motivational influence is to fall under the rational influence of a mentally grasped justification.

Yet one can agree that having a desire—and *a fortiori* being moved by a desire—sometimes entail the existence of a reason for acting, while denying that they entail being in the appropriate mental rapport with that reason. Suppose, for example, that the reason generated by a desire is the fact that one has the desire, a fact to which one can be utterly oblivious even as the desire moves one to act. In that case, one can have a desire and be moved by that desire without having grasped the reason that it generates; and so one can have and be moved by a desire without being in a position to be guided by the associated reason for acting.[18]

How the fact that one has a desire might justify action, and how an agent might be influenced by this justification, are questions that lie beyond the scope of this paper.[19] I mention this view of the matter only for the sake of distinguishing the sense in which I concede that a motivating desire justifies action from the sense in which I deny it. I concede that desire can justify action objectively, by making true a proposition that could guide one's actions if one gained

---

[18] Davidson seems to entertain a view like this when he says, "[I]f someone acts with an intention, he must have attitudes and beliefs from which, *had he been aware of them* and had the time, he *could* have reasoned that his action was desirable" ('Intending,' 85, emphasis added). Here Davidson seems to suggest that the agent needs to become aware of his attitudes in order to be in a position to draw a conclusion about the desirability of his action. I do not understand, however, how this suggestion squares with Davidson's claim that an intentional action constitutes the agent's conclusion that the action is desirable ('Intending,' 99). For how can his action constitute a conclusion that he might not have been in a position to draw?

[19] But see the discussion of the issue in my *Practical Reflection* (Princeton: Princeton Univ. Press, 1989).

appropriate access to it; but I deny that desire justifies action subjectively, by constituting an evaluative attitude whose justificatory force is already available to guide one's actions. I thus deny that desire amounts to an evaluation, and that motivation consequently amounts to rational guidance, in the sense proposed by the cognitivist.[20]

The cognitivist thinks that desire provides a mentally accessible justification for acting because it harbors justificatory force in its direction of fit, as expressed by its constitutive predicate, which he takes to be a term of evaluation. But why would one think that the constitutive predicate of desire was "good" or "desirable" or some other evaluative term?

One reason, I suspect, is a tendency to psychologize various extrinsic descriptions of mental states. For example, to desire something is to be disposed toward it in a way that would be appropriate if the thing were good; and a person who desires something can therefore be said to regard or treat it *as if* it were good or, more concisely, *as* good. But this description of the person's attitude, which cites a purely extrinsic fact about it, should not be mistaken as expressing a psychological aspect of the attitude itself. That someone's attitude would be appropriate if its object were good is not something to which he has mental access simply by virtue of having the attitude; and so it's not something whose justificatory force is necessarily available to guide him. Treating something as good in this sense is no more a value judgment than treating someone like dirt is a soil-judgment.

Similarly, a person who desires something can be said to find it attractive, but this description does not necessarily mean that he makes an attractiveness-judgment about it. It may mean simply that he is attracted to the thing and thereby has an experience that's indicative of, or evidence for, its attractiveness. Although the combination of "to find" with a predicate adjective has the superficial grammar of an attitudinal verb, it doesn't necessarily express the content or valence of an attitude. Someone can find his dinner indigestible, for instance, without having any attitude toward it whatever: he may simply have a cramp. To say that he finds his dinner indigestible in this case is not to describe his cramp as an attitude; it's to describe the cramp in terms of what it indicates. Of course, the phrase "find attractive" does describe an attitude when it's applied to desire; but it may still describe the attitude in extrinsic terms, as evidence of its object's attractiveness, rather than in terms of the attitude's content or direction of fit. Hence the subject's finding something attractive may not entail that he has mental access either to a proposition about attractiveness or to an attitude that takes "attractive" as its constitutive predicate.

---

[20] That Davidson regards desire as justifying action subjectively is confirmed by passages such as this: "Thus there is a certain irreducible—though somewhat anaemic—sense in which every rationalization justifies: *from the agent's point of view* there was, when he acted, something to be said for the action" ('Actions, Reasons, and Causes,' 9, italics mine.)

These subtleties in our descriptions of propositional attitudes are compounded by the fact that predicates like "attractive" and "desirable" can have both normative and nonnormative senses. Calling something desirable can have the normative meaning that the thing is correct or fitting to desire; but it can also have the purely psychological meaning that the thing tends to be desired, that it's easy or natural to desire. We must therefore be doubly careful with the observation that someone who desires something can be said to find it desirable. Desiring something may sometimes entail having an experience indicative of the thing's being easily or naturally desired; and in such a case, it entails finding the thing desirable, in some sense. But to have an experience that's evidence of something's tendency to be desired is not necessarily to think of the thing as readily desired, much less to think of it as correct to desire or worth desiring. Hence we mustn't assume that someone who finds something desirable thereby makes a desirability-judgment that would subjectively justify action.

Although I think that some such confusion is responsible for the use of "good" or "desirable" as the constitutive predicate of desire, I also think that this usage can be harmless, if properly understood. I am not opposed to describing desire as the attitude of regarding something as good, so long as this description is taken merely to express the attitude's direction of fit. Unfortunately, the description is also taken to imply that desire has the justificatory force of a value judgment; and in this respect, the description is misleading.

The resulting confusion can best be explained by analogy to a related misunderstanding about the justificatory force of belief. We are inclined to think that belief qualifies as a judgment of a proposition's truth, and carries the justificatory force of a truth judgment, simply because it entails regarding the proposition as true. Yet to say that belief entails regarding a proposition as true doesn't exhaust the relation between belief and the truth. There are many cognitive attitudes other than belief, attitudes that have the same direction of fit and consequently take the same constitutive predicate. Hypothesizing that p, assuming that p, fantasizing that p, and the like are all attitudes in which p is regarded, not as a representation of what is to be brought about, but rather as a representation of what is. The propositional object of these attitudes is thus regarded as true. Yet fantasizing that p doesn't amount to a judgment on the truth of p, and it lacks the justificatory force that would attach to such a judgment. Hence the reason why belief qualifies as a truth judgment cannot be simply that its constitutive predicate is "true."

One might be inclined to say that fantasizing and hypothesizing don't involve regarding anything as *really* true. But to say this is simply to acknowledge that there is more than one way of regarding a proposition as true. The sense in which hypotheses aren't regarded as really true is, not that they aren't regarded as true at all, but rather that they are only hypothetically so regarded. Fantasies aren't regarded as really true because it is only imaginatively, or in imagination, that they are regarded as true—not because they aren't so regarded at all. To regard something as "really" true must therefore be a particular way of regarding it as true—and, in particular, some way other than imaginatively or hypothetically.

My point here is not the purely grammatical point that imagining or assuming something entails imagining or assuming it to be true; after all, wanting something entails wanting it to be true, as well. In this construction, "true" attaches, trivially, to all propositional attitudes, simply by virtue of their being attitudes toward the bearers of truth values. My point is rather that what distinguishes belief from desire distinguishes assumption, hypothesis, and imagination from desire, too—namely, that they treat their propositional objects as reflecting antecedently fixed conditions rather than as dictating conditions to be achieved, as *facta* rather than *facienda*. To be sure, these attitudes don't treat their propositional objects as reflecting *the actual* facts. But they still treat those propositions as factual reports rather than practical dictates—as being already true of some completed, though unreal, states of affairs rather than as to be made true by the completion of such states. These attitudes therefore share the distinctively cognitive direction of fit.

The definition that philosophers have traditionally offered for direction of fit has somewhat obscured the difference between cognitive and conative attitudes, as well as the differences among the attitudes within either category.[21] Direction of fit has traditionally been defined in terms of the locus of responsibility for correspondence between an attitude and the world. Whether an attitude has one direction of fit or the other is said to depend on whether the attitude is responsible for conforming itself to the world or makes the world responsible for conforming itself to the attitude. The difference in direction of fit between an expectation and an intention is thus supposed to entail that when an expectation isn't fulfilled, the fault lies with the expectation, whereas when an intention isn't fulfilled, the fault lies with the world.[22]

This definition doesn't accurately characterize the difference between cognition and conation. A lack of correspondence between the world and an assumption, for example, doesn't constitute a failure for which one party or the other must be to blame. If the assumption is made solely for the sake of argument, then it neither takes responsibility for fitting the world nor makes the world responsible for fitting it. Fit between such an assumption and the world is of no importance and is therefore neither party's responsibility. Yet

---

[21] In this paragraph and the next I have benefitted from Lloyd Humberstone's manuscript 'Direction of Fit.'   [22] See the references to Searle, Platts, and Anscombe in n. 14, above.

an assumption is still like an expectation, and unlike an intention, in that what's assumed is regarded as true rather than as to be made true, as modelled after its intentional object rather than a model for it. Thus, an assumption still possesses the cognitive direction of fit, even though neither it nor the world is responsible for conforming itself to the other.

Where the traditional definition goes wrong, then, is in presupposing that whenever a proposition is regarded as true or to be made true, its truth thereby comes to constitute a success—and its falsity, a failure—for which either the attitude or the world must bear responsibility. Not every attitude of regarding something as true, or to be made true, has the thing's being or coming true as a criterion of success. I shall now argue that different criteria of success—or, as I shall now put it, different constitutive aims—help to account for the differences among attitudes with the same direction of fit.

Let us say that to regard a proposition as true, in the sense that applies to all cognitive attitudes, is to accept the proposition. We can then distinguish believing that p from assuming or fantasizing that p, for example, as follows. Assuming or fantasizing that p consists in accepting it irrespective of whether it is really true; whereas believing that p requires accepting it as if in response to its being true. Thus, belief bears a double relation to the truth. Believing a proposition entails not only regarding the proposition as true but, in addition, so regarding it in a manner designed to reflect whether it really is true.[23] The latter relation to the truth is part of what distinguishes believing from the other cognitive attitudes, in which a proposition is regarded as true without concern for whether it really is.

The clearest way to analyze such differences between belief and the other cognitive attitudes is in terms of the subject's dispositions to regulate his acceptance of a proposition. When someone assumes a proposition, he or his cognitive faculties are disposed to regulate his acceptance of it in ways designed to promote the ends of argument or inquiry: he comes to accept the proposition when doing so seems conducive to scoring a point or making a discovery, and he is disposed to continue accepting it only insofar as doing so seems to serve such polemical or heuristic purposes. When someone fantasizes, his acceptance of propositions is regulated in ways designed to whet his appetites, stimulate his mind, or provide a substitute for the fulfillment of his wishes: he accepts whatever propositions promise to provide the appropriate excitement or vicarious satisfaction.

---

[23] For an explication of this expression, see the following note. The expression gives, at most, a necessary condition of belief, not a sufficient condition. Indeed, even to call it a necessary condition may still be too strong. My suspicion is that attitudes qualify as beliefs or desires or intentions, etc., by virtue of approximating to a paradigm or ideal specimen. What are usually called the necessary conditions for belief or desire are in fact a definition of the paradigm case; and instances that fail to meet one condition may still qualify as beliefs or desires if they sufficiently resemble the relevant paradigm in other respects. (See my *Practical Reflection*, 136.)

When someone believes a proposition, however, his acceptance of it is regulated in ways designed to promote acceptance of the truth: he comes to accept the proposition, for example, when evidence indicates it to be true, and he's disposed to continue accepting it until evidence indicates otherwise. Part of what makes someone's attitude toward a proposition an instance of belief rather than assumption or fantasy, then, is that it is regulated in accordance with epistemic principles rather than polemics, heuristics, or hedonics. An attitude's identity as a belief depends on its being regulated in a way designed to make it track the truth.[24]

Although the dispositional explication of this difference between belief and the other cognitive attitudes is perhaps the clearest, its import can be expressed, as I expressed it above, in attitudinal terms. That is, regulating one's acceptance of the proposition by the exigencies of argument can be described as accepting the proposition without regard to its truth but rather with polemical or heuristic intent. And regulating one's acceptance of a proposition by evidence of its truth can be described as accepting the proposition with an eye to its truth, or with truth as one's aim. Belief and assumption are then described as two-tier attitudes, combining the first-order attitude of acceptance with different second-order attitudes—namely, the different aims or intentions with which a proposition can be accepted.[25]

We thus arrive at the familiar dictum that belief aims at the truth.[26] Properly understood, this dictum means that belief combines the attitude of regarding something as true with the aim of regarding *as* true what really *is* true—of getting the truth right. Hence belief not only has truth as its constitutive

[24] What do I mean when I describe a cognitive mechanism as "designed to track the truth"? I don't mean that it's designed in such a way that it succeeds in tracking the truth, since beliefs can be false. Rather, I mean that its design is governed by the goal of tracking the truth, although it may not attain that goal invariably or completely. And I am of course assuming that the concept of design encompasses the work of the pseudo-designer known as evolution.

In the text I have assumed that a mechanism designed to track the truth would operate in response to evidence, as it probably would if designed by evolution. But other mechanisms might also qualify as being designed to track the truth—particularly if they were designed by the subject himself, in accordance with an alternative epistemology. For example, someone who believes that the truth about something is to be found by consulting scripture or seeking revelation may regulate his acceptance of the relevant propositions by those means. The resulting attitudes will qualify as beliefs, however, since the method of their regulation will be designed to track the truth, in the requisite sense. (I am indebted to Michael Slote for pointing out this possibility.)

[25] Note that the aim or intention with which a proposition is accepted may belong to the subject's cognitive faculties rather than to the subject himself, depending on who or what is regulating the subject's acceptance of propositions. I shall henceforth ignore this distinction. In 'Direction of Fit,' Lloyd Humberstone cites J. O. Urmson, 'Memory and Imagination,' *Mind* 76 (1967) 83–91, as offering a similar account of the difference between imagining and remembering.

[26] The notion that belief aims at the truth figures prominently in the literature on believing at will. See, e.g., Bernard Williams, 'Deciding to Believe,' reprinted in *Problems of the Self* (Cambridge: Cambridge Univ. Press, 1970).

predicate but also has correctness in matters of truth—or, as one might put it, the "real" truth—as its constitutive aim.[27]

The difference between the constitutive aim of belief and those of other cognitive attitudes can also be expressed, even less clearly, by being incorporated into the constitutive predicates of these attitudes. Once we conceive of belief as a two-tier attitude, we tend to think of the second tier as having a constitutive predicate of its own, or as modifying the constitutive predicate of the entire attitude. Accepting a proposition is the attitude of regarding it as true; but accepting a proposition with the aim of accepting what's really true must entail regarding the proposition's acceptance as a means to that end. If one is aiming to get the truth right when one comes to regard p as true, then one must in effect regard p not only as true but also as something to be regarded as true for the sake of getting the truth right. The double relation between belief and truth can thus be expressed, somewhat obscurely, in the thought that believing a proposition entails regarding it as something that one is right to regard as true. Surely, that's what we mean when we say that believing p entails regarding p as "really" true; we mean that it entails regarding p not only as true but also as correct to regard in this way. Belief can thus be conceived as having a constitutive predicate that expresses its own correctness.[28]

The constitutive aim of belief is necessary to belief's being a judgment on the truth of a proposition, since nothing would count as a judgment on p's truth if it didn't aim at getting right whether p is true. The constitutive aim of belief is also essential to the attitude's justificatory force as a premise of inferences.

Consider, for example, why my believing that p and that $p \rightarrow q$ gives me subjective justification for believing that q. The answer cannot be simply that believing these propositions entails regarding them as true, and that the truth of the premises guarantees that of the conclusion. After all, fantasizing that p

---

[27] This aspect of belief is, I suspect, what leads Davidson to say, "Someone cannot have a belief unless he understands the possibility of being mistaken" ('Thought and Talk,' reprinted in *Essays on Actions and Events*, 168). Because believing entails aiming to get the truth right, it would seem to entail understanding the possibility of a mistake. But the soundness of this argument depends on the assumption that the constitutive aim of belief must be an attitude of the believer rather than a purpose inherent in the design of his cognitive faculties. I have suggested that a person's acceptance of a proposition can be aimed at getting the truth right—and hence qualify as a belief—so long as it is regulated by a mechanism designed to track the truth. (See n. 24, above.) In that case, the believer himself might lack the conceptual resources for framing the requisite aim in an attitudinal sense.

[28] Or, more precisely, the correctness of the acceptance involved in the belief. The view that belief involves an intimation of its own correctness is similar to the view of judgment that Hannah Ginsborg attributes to Kant. Ginsborg argues that reflective judgment, for Kant, is "the capacity for taking one's states of mind in the perception of given objects to be universally valid" ('Kant on Judgment,' (MS)). See also Ginsborg's 'Reflective Judgment and Taste,' *Noûs* 24 (1990) 63–78.

also entails regarding p as true, but fantasies justify nothing whatever, not even other fantasies.

The reason why one belief has subjective justificatory force for other beliefs is that the attitude of belief involves not only regarding a proposition as true but also doing so with the aim of getting the truth right. Because my belief that p is an attempt at tracking the truth, it makes a *prima facie* claim to be on the right track; and with this claim, the belief offers itself as a guide for other attitudes, provided that they, too, aim to track the truth. One belief guides the others because the latter aim at getting the truth right and the former represents my best efforts thus far toward the same end.

Those who have noted that belief aims at the truth are often inclined to think (mistakenly, I shall argue) that desire correspondingly aims at the good.[29] What are the consequences of the assumption that desire and belief are analogous in this respect?

Well, desire is like belief in being only one of many attitudes with its characteristic direction of fit. Wishing, hoping, and the like are also attitudes in which a proposition is regarded as a pattern for the world to follow, as something to be brought about or made true. Let us say that these attitudes are different ways of approving a proposition, just as the cognitive attitudes are different ways of accepting one. Suppose, then, that the difference between desire and other modes of approval was analogous to that between belief and other modes of acceptance.[30] In that case, wishing that p, for example, might entail regarding p as to be brought about, but so regarding it irrespective of whether it really was to be brought about; whereas desiring that p would entail regarding p as to be brought about, and doing so with an eye to whether it really was.[31] The analogy between desire and belief would thus lead to the conclusion that, just as belief aims at tracking the actual facts, so desire aims at tracking the actual *facienda*.

Such an attitude would indeed have the justificatory potential claimed for it

---

[29] See Anscombe, *Intention*, 76: "Truth is the object of judgment and good the object of wanting. . . ." See also DeSousa, 'The Good and the True,' *Mind* 83 (1974) 538: "[T]ruth and good are the *targets* of belief and want."

[30] Note that the distinction developed here is different from Pears's distinction between "weak" and "strong" value judgments, even though Pears regards his distinction as defining the line between those value judgments which are and those which are not necessarily implicated in preference and noncompulsive intentional action (*Motivated Irrationality*, 196 ff.). "Weak" value judgments, in Pears's terminology, are still *judgments*; what distinguishes them from their "strong" counterparts is the set of interests on which they are based. My distinction, by contrast, divides value judgments from valuings or preferrings that aren't judgments at all.

[31] What would it mean to say that something really was to be brought about? I'm not sure. This phrase is generated when the formula describing the constitutive aim of belief is adapted for the purpose of attributing an analogous aim to desire. Since I reject the analogy, I needn't take responsibility for the language it generates.

in Davidson's theory of rational guidance. As an attempt to track the actual *facienda*, it would present itself as a guide for one's actions, representing one's best efforts to identify what really was to be brought about. What's more, the feature lending justificatory force to this attitude would also give the attitude a constitutive predicate expressing its correctness. For if desiring something entailed regarding it as to be brought about, with the aim of so regarding what really was to be brought about, then it would entail regarding the thing as correct to regard in that way—as correct to approve.

We would thus arrive in the vicinity of Davidson's claim that to desire something is to regard it as desirable.[32] This claim seems to say that to desire something is to have an attitude toward it as worthy of that very attitude. We can now see that such a claim would make sense if it rested on the assumption that desire, like belief, had correctness as its constitutive aim.

Yet when the use of an evaluative term as the constitutive predicate of desire was first introduced, it was understood merely as a way of expressing the attitude's direction of fit—as a colorful alternative to the predicates "to be brought about" or "to be made true." Now a different interpretation has emerged. The claim that to desire something is to regard it as desirable is now being interpreted to imply, not just that the propositional object of desire is regarded as something to be made true or brought about, but also that it is so regarded with the aim of getting things right.

This implication can easily infiltrate our understanding of every evaluative term used to express a desire. Whereas the word "good" in "regarding *p* as good" was initially taken as a synonym for "to be brought about," a phrase that merely expressed the attitude's direction of fit, it can easily be understood as meaning "*really* to be brought about" or "correct to approve"—phrases expressing the aim of tracking the actual *facienda*. Regarding *p* as good can thus be thought to entail a potentially action-guiding judgment as to what is worth bringing about or making true.

In order to assess the validity of this new interpretation, we must ask whether desire really has a constitutive aim analogous to that of belief. The answer, I'm afraid, is no. When we consider how desire differs in aim from other modes of conation, we find that the difference is not analogous to that between belief and other modes of cognition. The difference in aim between desire and other conative attitudes appears to be that desire aims, not at the good, but rather at the attainable.[33]

One cannot desire something if it seems impossible or if it seems already to have come about; one can desire that *p* only if *p* seems attainable, in the sense

---

[32] I say "in the vicinity" because to regard something as worthy of approval is not quite to regard it as worth desiring—approval and desire being slightly different attitudes.

[33] For this point I am indebted to Geoffrey Sayre-McCord.

of being a possible future outcome. Yet the obstacle to desiring what seems unattainable, or already attained, is not that such things cannot be objects of approval. One can wish that *p* even if the truth of *p* seems quite impossible, and one can hope that *p* when *p* already seems to be true. Thus, one can approve the unattainable or the attained, and what prevents one from desiring them must be something else.

The obstacle, I would suggest, is that desire has the attainable as its constitutive aim. That is, unless approval is regulated in a way designed to track what's attainable, it doesn't qualify as desire; and approval isn't being regulated in a way designed to track the attainable if it's directed at what already seems actual or impossible.[34]

Although this explanation for the limits on desire is only an hypothesis, I think that it is clearly more plausible than the alternative hypothesis about desire's constitutive aim. The grounds that I have just outlined for thinking that desire aims at the attainable are not matched by any comparable grounds for thinking that it aims, more narrowly, at what really is to be brought about. Nothing other than allegiance to the cognitivist program would tempt us to think that desire must be regulated in a way designed to track the *facienda*.

The upshot is that nothing about desire entitles us to credit it with the justificatory force of a value judgment. A judgment on something's value would be an attempt to get things right, and it would consequently have the standing to guide one's actions. But even if desiring something consists in regarding the thing as good, in a sense synonymous with "to be brought about," it isn't an attempt at getting right whether the thing really is to be brought about, and so it doesn't amount to a judgment on the thing's goodness. Desiring something consists in regarding it as to be made true only in the sense that imagining something consists in regarding it as true. Hence desire has the same subjective justificatory force as fantasy—that is, none at all.

That desire doesn't aim at correctness explains why desire can be perverse.[35] As Michael Stocker has pointed out, one can often desire things conceived as worthless, or even bad, and desire them precisely under those descriptions.[36]

---

[34] Note, as before, that an attitude's constitutive aim should be treated as a necessary but not a sufficient condition. An instance of approval must have other features—including, perhaps, actual or counterfactual behavioral manifestations—in order to qualify as a desire. Compare n. 23, above, for further qualifications.

[35] Although I believe that we can indeed have perverse desires (and shall assume so in the text), I am not strictly committed to this empirical claim. I am committed only to the claim that desires can *in principle* be perverse, in the sense that there is nothing about the concept of desire that would prevent a perverse attitude from satisfying it. That is, an attitude can qualify as a desire even if it is perverse. This conceptual claim would be compatible with there being some contingent feature of human psychology that prevented us from having perverse desires.

[36] 'Desiring the Bad: An Essay in Moral Psychology,' *Journal of Philosophy* 76 (1979) 738–53.

A tendency to desire things under negative descriptions is an essential element of various emotions and moods such as silliness, self-destructiveness, or despair. A mood of playfulness is, in part, a disposition to form desires for things conceived as having no particular value; a self-destructive mood is, in part, a disposition to form desires for things conceived as harms; and so on. None of these desires could retain its characteristic idleness or perversity if it involved an attempt at getting things right.

After all, what makes a desire perverse is that its propositional object implies that it is inappropriate. That is, the perverse subject desires that something undesirable occur, and its being undesirable is part of the description under which he desires it. He thus holds the attitude of desire toward something under the description that it is unworthy of that attitude. This discrepancy between his attitude toward an object and his conception of the object's deserts would be impossible in an attitude whose nature was to aim at getting things right and whose constitutive predicate consequently implied the attitude's correctness. Correctness in approval simply cannot be one's aim when one approves of something under the description that it is unworthy of approval.

Consider, by way of analogy, the prospects for perversity in belief. Because belief entails not only regarding a proposition as true but, in addition, doing so with the aim of getting the truth right, belief cannot be transparently perverse. That is, one cannot believe a proposition that presents itself as false— say, the proposition "I am five inches taller than I really am."[37] The reason why one cannot believe such a proposition is not that one is incapable of accepting it. The reason is rather that the only way of accepting such a self-evident falsehood would be to accept it irrespective of its truth; and accepting a proposition irrespective of its truth wouldn't amount to believing it. If one accepts this proposition irrespective of its truth, one will then be assuming it, as one might do for the sake of reasoning counterfactually ("Let's assume that I'm five inches taller than I really am . . .").

In short, a proposition that presents itself as false cannot be the object of an attitude that aims at getting the truth right. Similarly, a prospect that presented itself as bad could not be the object of an attitude that aimed at correctness in regarding things as to be brought about. Thus, if aiming at correctness were constitutive of desire, as it is of belief, perverse desire would be inconceivable.

The assumption that desire aims at the good forces the cognitivist to misdescribe examples of perverse desire. Consider, for a particularly vivid example, the figure of Satan in *Paradise Lost*, who responds to his defeat with the cry, "Evil be thou my Good."[38] Satan is here resolving to desire and pursue evil,

---

[37] The word 'really' in this proposition rigidly designates our world, so that the proposition is evidently false in this world but true in some other possible world.

[38] Book IV, line 110.

and hence—as he himself puts it—to regard evil as good. But he cannot reasonably be interpreted as adopting new estimates of what's valuable—that is, as resolving to cease judging evil to *be* evil and to start judging it to be good. If Satan ever loses sight of the evil in what he now desires, if he ever comes to think of what he desires as really good, he will no longer be at all satanic; he'll be just another well-intentioned fool. The ruler of Hell doesn't desire what he wrongly thinks is worthy of approval; he desires what he rightly thinks isn't. He thereby illustrates my point that regarding something as good, in the sense requisite to desiring it, does not amount to making a favorable judgment on its value.

See how Satan's horns are blunted when his desires are misinterpreted as full-blooded value judgments, in this passage from Elizabeth Anscombe's *Intention*:[39]

> 'Evil be thou my good' is often thought to be senseless in some way. Now all that concerns us here is that 'What's the good of it?' is something that can be asked until a desirability characterisation has been reached and made intelligible. If then the answer to this question at some stage is 'The good of it is that it's bad', this need not be unintelligible; one can go on to say 'And what's the good of its being bad?' to which the answer might be condemnation of good as impotent, slavish, and inglorious. Then the good of making evil my good is my intact liberty in the unsubmissiveness of my will.

What sort of Satan is this? He is trying to get things right, and so he rejects the good only because he has found respects in which it is unworthy of approval. He rejects the good, that is, only because it is slavish and inglorious, and hence only because shunning the good is a means to liberty and glory. But then he isn't really shunning the good, after all, since the goods of liberty and glory remain his ultimate goals. Anscombe's Satan can desire evil only by judging it to *be* good, and so he remains, at heart, a lover of the good and the desirable—a rather sappy Satan.

Let me summarize my argument thus far by updating one of Anscombe's own devices for analyzing the difference between cognition and conation. Anscombe suggests that the difference between cognition and conation is analogous to that between an inventory and a shopping list.[40] An inventory is modelled after one's existing stock: it represents things as being on the shelves, having already been obtained. A shopping list is a model for one's stock to follow: it represents things as not yet on the shelves but to be obtained.

What I have argued, in effect, is that Anscombe's analogy neglects differences within the categories of possible inventories and possible shopping lists. When a list of items falls into our hands, we must of course ascertain whether

---

[39] *Intention*, 75.   [40] *Ibid.*, 56 ff.

it represents those items as having been obtained or as to be obtained. But we must also ascertain the aims with which the contents of the list have been regulated. A list of things on the shelves may have been compiled in a way designed to represent what's actually on the shelves, but it may also have been compiled in a way designed to include whatever *might* be on the shelves, as a checklist against which the actual contents of the shelves can then be compared. A checklist is also an inventory; it's just a hypothetical inventory. Similarly, a list of things to be obtained may have been compiled in a way designed to track what's actually needed, but it may also have been compiled in way designed to lend excitement to one's bet on the lottery. A wish-list is also a shopping list; it's just a fantasy shopping list.

Thus, to find a list headed "Things in stock" is not yet to have grounds for any conclusions about what's available for dinner; and to find a list headed "Things to buy" is not yet to have grounds for making purchases. If the inventory is hypothetical—merely a checklist—then it doesn't embody a judgment of what's in stock and doesn't justify any conclusions about what's available; and if the shopping list is fantastical—merely a wish-list—then it doesn't embody a judgment of what to buy and doesn't justify any purchases. Judgmental and justificatory force attaches only to those lists whose entries have been compiled and regulated with the aim of getting things right.

The cognitivist conception of desire as an action-justifying value judgment thus depends on a misinterpretation of the sense in which desiring something entails regarding it as good. Properly understood, the use of "good" as desire's constitutive predicate doesn't support the cognitivist conception of desire as a value judgment of the sort that would subjectively justify action; and it therefore doesn't support identifying an agent's motivating desire with his guiding reason.

Of course, to show that desire lacks the subjective justificatory force of a value judgment is not to show that such force may be lacking from whatever else might constitute an agent's reason for acting. Indeed, one might think that my arguments thus far prove only that desire cannot be what constitutes an agent's reason for acting, precisely because his reason, whatever it may be, must somehow present his action as a good thing to do.[41] One might

---

[41] For the view that evaluation is embedded in the very concept of a reason, see, e.g., Kurt Baier, 'Rationality, Reason, and the Good,' in *Morality, Reason and Truth*, ed. D. Copp and D. Zimmerman (Totowa, N.J.: Rowman & Littlefield, 1984), 202. "What I call 'cognitive' reasons are employed in the activity of examining what to believe, and 'practical' ones are employed in the activity of examining what to do. The specific aim of the first is beliefs that are true; the second is intentions or acts that are good. We could say that the aim in the case of the first is the true and in the case of the second the good." See also E. J. Bond, *Reason and Value* (Cambridge: Cambridge Univ. Press, 1983), 2–3. For a persuasive attack on this view, see Anderson, 'Pluralism, Deliberation, and Rational Choice.'

then continue to claim that an action performed for a reason must be aimed at the good, without assuming that the guiding evaluation is embodied in a desire.

Yet I think that one of my arguments against identifying reasons with desires suggests an argument against identifying reasons with value judgments in any form. In that argument, I explained the capacity of desires to be perverse in terms of their not being aimed at the good; here I shall contend that reasons for acting can be perverse as well. That is, an agent's reason for doing something can be that it's a bad thing to do; and so its justificatory force cannot depend on that of a favorable evaluation.

Suppose that I have suffered a profound disappointment that has cast me into a mood of bitterness and despair. In this mood, the very thought of ameliorating my condition, or the condition of the world, strikes me as a sick delusion. All attempts at constructive action seem absurd. No more earnest efforts for me, I say to myself, no more worthy endeavors: to hell with it all.[42]

Being in despair doesn't prevent me from being moved to act, however. I am moved to stay at home, refuse all invitations, keep the shades drawn, and privately curse the day I was born. I may even be moved to smash some crockery—though not in order to feel better, mind you, since trying to feel better seems just as ludicrous a project as any other. (Someone who smashes crockery in order to feel better didn't feel all that bad to begin with.) What's more, I engage in these actions not only *out of* despair but also *in light of* and *on the grounds of* despair. That is, despair is part of my reason as well as part of my motive for acting.

But do I regard my actions, in light of my despair, as good or desirable or positive things to do? Far from it. I am determined never to do a good or desirable or positive thing again. If smashing things seemed like a good thing to do, I would pointedly avoid it; even if it seemed good only for someone in despair, I would still avoid it; indeed, it's seeming good for someone in despair would count most strongly against it, since doing things that are good for someone in my condition is exactly what, in light of that condition, makes sense for me to avoid.[43] I'm smashing things because this seems like an utterly worthless act, worthless from every perspective but especially from mine. My reason for acting thus includes not only my mood but also an unconditionally negative evaluation of the action.

To be sure, there is a kind of perversity that would preclude my acting for reasons; but the perversity that would preclude acting for reasons is not a counter-evaluative state of mind but rather a counter-rational one. That is, I cannot act for reasons if I don't care about doing what's justified or (as I would prefer to put it) what makes sense. But I can still care about doing what makes

---

[42] Again, see Stocker, 'Desiring the Bad,' 745.   [43] *Ibid.*, 748.

sense even if I don't care about the good. This possibility is demonstrated by my capacity to be guided by what makes sense in light of a counter-evaluative mood such as despair, since what makes sense in light of such a mood just is to do what's bad rather than what's good.

Yet pursuing the bad on the grounds of despair would be impossible if every reason for an action had to present that action as a good thing to do. The problem is not that the badness of an action could never make the action seem good. The problem is that if the badness of an action weighed with me by making the action seem good, then I would be once again engaged in pursuing the good—a pursuit incompatible with the very mood that helps to constitute my reason for acting. Just as Satan would have to shed his satanism in order to value evil *sub specie boni*, so I would have to shed my despair in order to pursue a self-destructive course under that positive guise. If I were swayed toward an action because its badness made it seem like a good thing to do, then I'd be in the business of finding silver linings, a business that's closed to me so long as I am truly acting out of despair.

If my arguments are correct, then practical reasoning is nothing like what it has traditionally been conceived to be. Desires lack the evaluative force that is thought to make them reasons for acting; and the justificatory force of reasons is not evaluative, in any case. Since reasons do not recommend an action by presenting it as a good thing to do, actions performed for reasons need not be performed under the guise of the good.

6

What Happens When Someone Acts?[1]

What happens when someone acts?

A familiar answer goes like this. There is something that the agent wants, and there is an action that he believes conducive to its attainment. His desire for the end, and his belief in the action as a means, justify taking the action, and they jointly cause an intention to take it, which in turn causes the corresponding movements of the agent's body. Provided that these causal processes take their normal course, the agent's movements consummate an action, and his motivating desire and belief constitute his reasons for acting.

This story is widely accepted as a satisfactory account of human action—or at least, as an account that will be satisfactory once it is completed by a definition of what's normal in the relevant causal processes. The story is widely credited to Donald Davidson's *Essays on Actions and Events* (1980), but I do not wish to become embroiled in questions of exegesis.[2] I shall therefore refer to it simply as the standard story of human action.

I think that the standard story is flawed in several respects. The flaw that will concern me in this paper is that the story fails to include an agent—or, more precisely, fails to cast the agent in his proper role.[3] In this story, reasons cause an intention, and an intention causes bodily movements, but nobody— that is, no person—*does* anything. Psychological and physiological events take place inside a person, but the person serves merely as the arena for these events: he takes no active part.[4]

[1] This chapter originally appeared in *Mind* 101 (1992) 461–81 and is reprinted by permission of Oxford University Press. The material in this chapter was originally presented to a seminar in the philosophy of action at the University of Michigan. I am grateful to the participants in that seminar for their comments and questions. A very different paper was presented under a similar title to the philosophy departments of Yale University and the University of Dayton; this chapter shows the benefit of comments from those audiences as well. For comments on earlier drafts, I am grateful to Paul Boghossian, Sarah Buss, Daniel Cohen, John Martin Fischer, Harry Frankfurt, Carl Ginet, Brian Leiter, Connie Rosati, and several anonymous reviewers for *Mind*.

[2] The story can be traced back at least as far as Hobbes, *Leviathan*, Part I, chapter vi.

[3] I discuss another problem with the standard story in my 'The Guise of the Good' (Chap. 5, above).

[4] A critique along these lines, with special reference to Hobbes, appears in N. J. H. Dent, *The Moral Psychology of the Virtues* (Cambridge: Cambridge Univ. Press, 1984), ch. 4. See, e.g., p. 99: "a weighty reason does not, like a weighty brick, fall upon one and impart a certain push to one's body".

To be sure, a person often performs an action, in some sense, without taking an active part in it; examples of such actions will be discussed below.[5] But these examples lack that which distinguishes human action from other animal behavior, in our conception of it if not in reality. I shall argue that the standard story describes an action from which the distinctively human feature is missing, and that it therefore tells us, not what happens when someone acts, but what happens when someone acts halfheartedly, or unwittingly, or in some equally defective way. What it describes is not a human action *par excellence*.

Those who believe the story will of course contend that the events recounted in it add up to the agent's participating in his action, as components add up to a composite. The story doesn't mention his participation, they will explain, simply because his participation isn't a component of itself. Complaining that the agent's participation in his action isn't mentioned in the story is, in their view, like complaining that a cake isn't listed in its own recipe.

But this response strikes me as inadequate, because I don't accept the claim that the events recounted in the story add up to a person's activity. Various roles that are actually played by the agent himself in the history of a full-blooded action are not played by anything in the story, or are played by psychological elements whose participation is not equivalent to his. In a full-blooded action, an intention is formed by the agent himself, not by his reasons for acting. Reasons affect his intention by influencing him to form it, but they thus affect his intention by affecting him first. And the agent then moves his limbs in execution of his intention; his intention doesn't move his limbs by itself. The agent thus has at least two roles to play: he forms an intention under the influence of reasons for acting, and he produces behavior pursuant to that intention.

Of course, the agent's performance of these roles probably consists in the occurrence of psychological states and events within him. To insist that the story mention only the agent himself as the object of rational influence, or as the author and executor of intentions, would be to assume a priori that there is no psychological reduction of what happens in rational action. One is surely entitled to hypothesize, on the contrary, that there are mental states and events within an agent whose causal interactions constitute his being influenced by a reason, or his forming and conforming to an intention.

---

[5] Here I part company with some philosophers of action, who believe that nothing counts as an action unless the agent participates in it. (See, e.g., J. Bishop, *Natural Agency: An Essay on the Causal Theory of Action* (Cambridge: Cambridge Univ. Press, 1989), 41.) Of course, every action must be someone's doing and must therefore be such that an agent participates in it, in the sense that he does it. But this conception of agential participation doesn't require anything that is obviously missing from the standard story. What's missing from that story is agential participation of a more specific kind, which may indeed be missing from doings that count as cases—albeit defective or borderline cases—of action.

True enough. But the states and events described in a psychological reduction of a fully human action must be such that their interactions amount to the participation of the agent. My objection to the standard story is not that it mentions mental occurrences in the agent instead of the agent himself; my objection is that the occurrences it mentions in the agent are no more than occurrences in him, because their involvement in an action does not add up to the agent's being involved.

How can I tell that the involvement of these mental states and events is not equivalent to the agent's? I can tell because, as I have already suggested, the agent's involvement is defined in terms of his interactions with these very states and events, and the agent's interactions with them are such as they couldn't have with themselves. His role is to intervene between reasons and intention, and between intention and bodily movements, in each case guided by the one to produce the other. And intervening between these items is not something that the items themselves can do. When reasons are described as directly causing an intention, and the intention as directly causing movements, not only has the agent been cut out of the story but so has any psychological item that might play his role.[6]

At this point, defenders of the standard story might wish to respond that it includes the agent implicitly, as the subject of the mental and physiological occurrences that it explicitly describes.[7] The reasons, intention, and movements mentioned in the story are modifications of the agent, and so their causal relations necessarily pass through him. Complaining that the agent takes no part in causal relations posited between reasons and intention, they might claim, is like complaining that the ocean takes no part in causal relations posited between adjacent waves.

But reflection on the phenomena of action reveals that being the subject of causally related attitudes and movements does not amount to participation of the sort appropriate to an agent.[8] As Harry Frankfurt has pointed out,[9] an agent's desires and beliefs can cause a corresponding intention despite him, and hence without his participation. When an addict's desire for a drug causes his decision to take it, Frankfurt reminds us, "he may meaningfully make the analytically puzzling [statement] that the force moving him to take the drug is a force other than his own," (p. 18) and so he may be "a helpless bystander to the forces that move him" (p. 21). Similarly, an agent can fail to participate when his intention causes bodily movements. A frequently cited example is the

---

[6] *Ibid.*, 72: "Intuitively, we think of agents as carrying out their intentions or acting in accordance with their practical reasons, and this seems different from (simply) being caused to behave by those intentions or reasons."

[7] See A. I. Goldman, *A Theory of Human Action* (Princeton: Princeton Univ. Press, 1970), 80 ff.

[8] See C. Ginet, *On Action* (Cambridge: Cambridge Univ. Press, 1990), 6–7. "For a person S to cause E, it is not enough for S to be the subject of just any sort of event that causes E."

[9] *The Importance of What We Care About* (Cambridge: Cambridge Univ. Press, 1988).

assassin whose decision to fire on his target so unnerves him as to make his trigger-finger twitch, causing the gun to fire.[10] In such a case, the agent's intention has caused corresponding movements of his body, but it has done so without the agent's participation.

Proponents of the standard story believe that the agent's participation is lacking from these cases only because the train of causes leading from his motives to his intention, or from his intention to his behavior, is somehow abnormal.[11] They therefore deny that these cases demonstrate the inadequacy of the standard story. The story is committed only to the claim that the causal sequence from motives to behavior will involve the agent himself when it proceeds in the normal way.

In my view, however, the discussion of "deviant" causal chains has diverted attention from simpler counterexamples, which omit the agent without lapsing into causal deviance; and it has thereby engendered a false sense of confidence in the requirement of causal normality, as sufficient to protect the standard story from counterexamples. In reality, an agent can fail to participate in his behavior even when it results from his motives in the normal way. Consequently, no definition of causal normality will fix what ails the standard story.

Suppose that I have a long-anticipated meeting with an old friend for the purpose of resolving some minor difference; but that as we talk, his offhand comments provoke me to raise my voice in progressively sharper replies, until we part in anger. Later reflection leads me to realize that accumulated grievances had crystallized in my mind, during the weeks before our meeting, into a resolution to sever our friendship over the matter at hand, and that this resolution is what gave the hurtful edge to my remarks.[12] In short, I may conclude that desires of mine caused a decision, which in turn caused the corresponding behavior; and I may acknowledge that these mental states were thereby exerting their normal motivational force, unabetted by any strange perturba-

---

[10] The most recent discussion of such "deviant causal chains" appears in Bishop, *Natural Agency*, chs. 4 and 5. See also G. Harman, 'Practical Reasoning,' *Review of Metaphysics* 29 (1976) 445; C. Peacocke, 'Deviant Causal Chains,' *Midwest Studies in Philosophy* 4 (1979) 124; R. Taylor, *Action and Purpose* (Englewood Cliffs, N.J.: Prentice-Hall, 1966), 248; Goldman, *A Theory of Human Action* 54; and Donald Davidson, *Essays on Actions and Events* (Oxford: Clarendon Press, 1980), 79.

[11] See e.g., Davidson, *ibid.*, pp. xiii, 79, 87.

[12] We can assume that this causal relation was mediated by any number of subconscious intentions—intentions to sever the friendship by alienating my friend, to alienate my friend by raising my voice, to raise my voice now . . . etc. So long as we assume that these intentions subconsciously crystallized as the conversation progressed (which is not hard to assume) we preserve the intuition that I'm currently trying to evoke—namely, that I did not participate in the resulting action. And surely, this intuition doesn't depend on the assumption that the causal links between these intentions and my behavior weren't "sensitive" to counterfactual differences in them (in the sense defined by Bishop, *Natural Agency*, ch. 5). Thus, we can conceive of cases in which reasons cause intentions, intentions cause behavior in all the "right ways," and yet the agent doesn't participate.

tion or compulsion. But do I necessarily think that I made the decision or that I executed it? Surely, I can believe that the decision, though genuinely motivated by my desires, was thereby induced in me but not formed by me; and I can believe that it was genuinely executed in my behavior but executed, again, without my help. Indeed, viewing the decision as directly motivated by my desires, and my behavior as directly governed by the decision, is precisely what leads to the thought that as my words became more shrill, it was my resentment speaking, not I.[13]

Of course, to say that I was not involved in the formation and execution of my intention is to concede that these processes were abnormal in some sense. My point, however, is that they were not abnormal in respect to the causal operation of the motives and intention involved. When my desires and beliefs engendered an intention to sever the friendship, and when that intention triggered my nasty tone, they were exercising the same causal powers that they exercise in ordinary cases, and yet they were doing so without any contribution from me. Hence what constitutes my contribution, in other cases, cannot be that these attitudes are manifesting their ordinary causal powers. When I participate in an action, I must be adding something to the normal motivational influence of my desires, beliefs, and intentions; and so a definition of when their influence is normal still won't enable the standard story to account for my participation.

In omitting the agent's participation from the history of his action, the standard story falls victim to a fundamental problem in the philosophy of action—namely, that of finding a place for agents in the explanatory order of the world.[14] Our concept of full-blooded human action requires some event or state of affairs that owes its occurrence to an agent and hence has an explanation that traces back to him. As I have already noted, not all actions are full-blooded—witness the aforementioned raising of my voice, which owed its occurrence to my attitudes but not to me. Such an occurrence may still count

---

[13] I don't mean to suggest that these reflections absolve me of responsibility for my action. I have an obligation to be vigilant against unconsidered intentions and to keep my voice down, no matter what may be causing it to rise. The fact remains, however, that my responsibility for the action in question arises from my having failed to prevent or control it rather than from my having truly initiated it. And I am responsible for having failed to prevent or control the action because it would have yielded to various measures of self-scrutiny and self-restraint that I could have initiated. Thus, my responsibility depends on my capacity to intervene among events in a way in which I failed to intervene among my desires, intentions, and movements in this instance. If my behavior could come about only in the manner described here—that is, springing directly from intentions that have simply come over me—nothing would owe its occurrence to either my participating or failing to participate in events, and I might bear no responsibility for anything.

[14] I believe that this problem is distinct from the problem of free will, although the two are often treated together. For my views on the latter problem, see Chap. 2, above.

as the behavioral component of an action, as something that I did; but it lacks those features which seem to set human action apart from the rest of animal behavior, and which thus provide the philosophy of action with its distinctive subject matter. What makes us agents rather than mere subjects of behavior—in our conception of ourselves, at least, if not in reality—is our perceived capacity to interpose ourselves into the course of events in such a way that the behavioral outcome is traceable directly to us.

The question whether our practical nature is as we conceive it in this respect—or in any other, for that matter—should be clearly distinguished from the question what we conceive our practical nature to be. Carl Ginet has recently argued[15] that what happens when someone acts is that his behavior is caused by a mental event whose intrinsic qualities include feeling as if it issues directly from him; but that this feeling corresponds to no actual feature of the event's causal history or structure. Even if Ginet's account correctly describes what actually happens in all or most of the episodes that we describe as actions, the question remains whether it correctly expresses what we mean to say about those episodes in so describing them.

Indeed, Ginet's account strongly suggests that what we mean to say about an event, in calling it an action, is unlikely to be what the account itself says, since it says that an action begins with a mental event that feels as if it were something that, according to this account, it is not—namely, a direct production of the agent. If our actions always begin with mental events that feel as if they are of agential origin, then one might expect the notion of agential origin to crop up in our commonsense concept of action; whereas one wouldn't expect a commonsense concept to include the philosophical critique of this notion, as having no realization in the history or structure of events. Ginet's account therefore suggests that we are likely to conceive actions as traceable to the agent in a sense in which, according to Ginet, they actually are not.

Of course, if actions can fail to be as we conceive them, then the philosopher of action must specify whether his object of study is the concept or the reality. Does the philosopher seek to explain what we ordinarily mean when we call something an action, or does he seek to explain what something ordinar-

---

[15] *On Action*, 11–15. Ginet thinks that actions other than simple mental actions do issue from the agent in the sense that they involve the agent's causing something. But he thinks that something can be caused by an agent only insofar as it is caused by one of the agent's actions. And he thinks that the resulting regress, of actions in which things are caused by other actions, must terminate in a simple mental action—usually, the act of willing—which qualifies as an action only because it feels as if it was caused by the agent himself, although it hasn't in fact been caused by him in any sense. Thus, Ginet thinks that complex actions issue from the agent only in the sense that their component behavior is ultimately caused by a mental event that misleadingly feels as if it issued from the agent. Since the agential ancestry of complex action is thus inherited from a simple mental act whose agential ancestry is itself illusory, the ancestry of all actions would seem to be tainted by illusion.

ily is when so called?[16] My aim is to explain the former, at least in the first instance. For I suspect that our practices of deliberation, rationalizing explanation, and moral assessment are designed for action as we conceive it to be, and that any account of a reality substantially different from this conception will not help us to understand the logic of these practices.

In saying that my aim is to explicate our concept of action, as opposed to the reality, I do not mean to imply that I have given up hope of finding that the two are in accord. All I mean is that the concept has an antecedently fixed content that doesn't depend on what actually goes on in all or most or even a privileged few of the cases to which it's applied, and hence that correspondence between concept and reality will count as a cognitive achievement on our part. As for this cognitive achievement, however, I do hope to show that we need not despair of having attained it. For I hope to show that our concept of full-blooded action, as involving behavior that's ultimately traceable to an agent, can be understood in a way that may well be realized in the world, as we otherwise understand it.[17]

The obstacle to reconciling our conception of agency with the possible realities is that our scientific view of the world regards all events and states of affairs as caused, and hence explained, by other events and states, or by nothing at all. And this view would seem to leave no room for agents in the explanatory order.

---

[16] Here, of course, I assume that the term 'action' does not function like the Kripkean name of a natural kind, referring to whatever shares the essential nature of all or most or a privileged few of the episodes to which it is applied. I assume that 'action' has a *de dicto* meaning in virtue of which it may in fact fail to be a correct description of anything to which it is applied.

[17] I therefore think that Ginet dismisses the causal conception of action too quickly. I do agree with Ginet that an agent, as a persisting entity, is the wrong sort of thing to cause particular events. (Ginet cites C. D. Broad, *Ethics and the History of Philosophy*, (London: Routledge & Kegan Paul, 1952), 215, as the source of this objection.) But this objection militates only against a non-reductive theory of agent-causation. It leaves open the possibility that the causation of events by the right sort of things—that is, by other events—may in some cases amount to, or deserve to be described as, their being caused by the agent himself. It therefore leaves open the possibility of agent-causation that's reducible to, or supervenient on, causation by events. (I discuss this possibility, and its implications, in the next section of the text.) Ginet argues against a conception that characterizes action in terms of event causation (pp. 11–13). But Ginet's argument suffers from two flaws. Ginet's argument is that we can conceive of a simple mental act, such as mentally saying a word, without conceiving of it as comprising a structure of distinct, causally related events. ("I mean that it is not *conceptually required* to have such a structure, under our concept of it as that kind of mental act" (p. 12).) Yet this point doesn't speak to the hypothesis that we conceive of the act in question as comprising behavior caused by the agent, and that the behavior's being caused by the agent supervenes on its causal relation to other events. Our concept of action may include agent-causation without including the supervenience base thereof. What's more, the illustrations that Ginet provides for his argument—pairs of mental causes and effects whose structure is clearly different from that of the mental act in question—are all cases in which the imagined cause is itself a mental act. But someone who thinks that a mental act consists in mental behavior caused by the agent, in a sense that supervenes on it's being caused by another event, is not likely to think that the causing event is yet another act.

As Thomas Nagel puts it, "Everything I do or that anyone else does is part of a larger course of events that no one 'does', but that happens, with or without explanation. Everything I do is part of something I don't do, because I am a part of the world."[18]

I implicitly endorsed this naturalistic conception of explanation when I conceded, earlier, that the standard story of action cannot be faulted merely for alluding to states and events occurring in the agent's mind. Any explanation of human action will speak in terms of some such occurrences, because occurrences are the basic elements of explanation in general.

Some philosophers have not been willing to concede this point. According to Roderick Chisholm,[19] for example, the explanatory order must include not only occurrences but also agents, conceived as additional primitive elements. The causation of occurrences by agents, rather than by other occurrences, is what Chisholm calls "agent-causation."

If the phrase "agent-causation" is understood in Chisholm's sense, then the naturalistic conception of explanation implies that agent-causation doesn't exist. Yet those who endorse the naturalistic conception of explanation, as I do, may still want to reconcile it with our commonsense conception of full-blooded action, in which behavior is traced to the agent himself rather than to occurrences within him. Such a reconciliation will have to show how the causal role assigned to the agent by common sense reduces to, or supervenes on, causal relations among events and states of affairs. And the agent's being a supervenient cause of this sort might also be called agent-causation, in a more relaxed sense of the phrase. If "agent-causation" is understood to encompass this possibility as well as the one envisioned by Chisholm, then naturalists may want a theory of agent-causation, too.

This broader understanding of the phrase "agent-causation" is in fact endorsed by Chisholm himself, in a passage whose obscure provenance justifies extended quotation. Chisholm says:

> [T]he issues about "agent-causation" . . . have been misplaced. The philosophical question is not—or at least it shouldn't be—the question whether or not there is "agent-causation". The philosophical question should be, rather, the question whether "agent-causation" is reducible to "event causation". Thus, for example, if we have good reason for believing that Jones . . . kill[ed] his uncle, then the philosophical question about Jones as cause would be: Can we express the statement "Jones killed his uncle" without loss of meaning into a set of statements in which only events are said to be causes and in which Jones himself is not said to be the source of any activity? And can we do this without being left with any residue of agent-causation—that is, without being left with some such statement

---

[18] T. Nagel, *The View from Nowhere* (Oxford: Oxford Univ. Press, 1986), 114; cf. Bishop, *Natural Agency*, 39 ff.

[19] R. Chisholm, *Person and Object: a Metaphysical Study* (London: Allen & Unwin, 1976).

as "Jones raised his arm" wherein Jones once again plays the role of cause or partial cause of a certain event?[20]

As the failings of the standard story reveal, we may have difficulty in meeting this challenge even if we help ourselves to a rich inventory of mental events and states. We could of course make the problem even harder, by asking how statements about Jones's action can be reexpressed, not just in terms of occurrences, but in terms of physical occurrences taking place among particles and fields. In that case, we would be worrying, in part, about the mind-body problem. But the problem of agent-causation lingers even if the mind-body problem can be made to disappear. For let there be mental states and events in abundance—motives, reasons, intentions, plans—and let them be connected, both to one another and to external behavior, by robust causal relations; still, the question will remain how the existence and relations of these items can amount to a person's causing something rather than merely to something's happening in him, albeit something mental.[21] The problem of agency is thus independent of, though indeed parallel to, the mind-body problem. Just as the mind-body problem is that of finding a mind at work amid the workings of the body, so the problem of agency is that of finding an agent at work amid the workings of the mind.[22]

Now, Chisholm's non-reductionist solution to the problem of agency hasn't been taken seriously by many philosophers, nor do I intend to accord it serious attention here. However, I do sympathize with Chisholm's complaint that those who smirk at his solution do so unjustly, since they haven't taken seriously the problem that it is intended to solve. Chisholm says:

> Now if you can analyze such statements as "Jones killed his uncle" into event-causation statements, then you may have earned the right to make jokes about the agent as [a primitive] cause. But if you haven't done this, and if all the same you do believe such things as that I raised my arm and that Jones killed his uncle, and if moreover you still think it's a joke to talk about the agent as cause, then, I'm afraid, the joke is entirely on you. You are claiming the benefits of honest philosophical toil without even *having* a theory of human action.[23]

[20] R. Chisholm, 'Comments and Replies,' *Philosophia* 7 (1978) 622–3.

[21] Cf. Bishop, *Natural Agency*, 43.

[22] The standard story of rational action has also illustrated that the problem is more than that of casting the agent in the role of cause. In explaining an action, we trace its history back to the agent who brought the action about; but then we trace back further, to the reasons that persuaded him to do so. And as Donald Davidson has argued ('Actions, Reason, and Causes,' in *Essays on Actions and Events*), the reasons cited in the explanation of an action must be, not just reasons that were available to the agent, but reasons for which he acted, the difference being precisely that the latter are the reasons that induced him to act. The reasons that explain an action are thus distinguished by their having exerted an influence upon the agent. In the explanation of an action, then, the agent must serve not only as an origin of activity, or cause, but also as an object of rational influence—and hence, in a sense, as an effect.

[23] *Ibid.* Note the need to insert the word "primitive" in Chisholm's phrase "the agent as cause,"

Here I think that Chisholm has come as close as anyone ever has to speaking frankly about a philosophical disagreement. And I hope that he would recognize it as a token of my respect for this accomplishment if I adopt his locution and declare that the proper goal for the philosophy of action is to earn the right to make jokes about primitive agent-causation, by explaining how an agent's causal role supervenes on the causal network of events and states.[24]

The best sustained attempt at such an explanation, I think, is contained in a series of articles by Harry Frankfurt.[25] These articles begin with the question of what constitutes a person, but the focus quickly narrows to the person as an element in the causal order.[26] What primarily interests Frankfurt, as I have mentioned, is the difference between cases in which a person "participates" in the operation of his will and cases in which he becomes "a helpless bystander to the forces that move him."[27] And this distinction just is that between cases in which the person does and does not contribute to the production of his behavior.

In attempting to draw this distinction, Frankfurt is working on the same problem as Chisholm, although he is seeking a reductive solution rather than a solution of the non-reductive sort that Chisholm favors. What's odd is that Frankfurt conceives of the problem in a way that initially appears destined to frustrate any reductive solution. In the following sections, I shall first explain why Frankfurt's project can thus appear hopeless; and I shall then suggest a conception of agency that might offer Frankfurt some hope.

Frankfurt's strategy for identifying the elements of agent-causation is to identify what's missing from cases in which human behavior proceeds without the agent as its cause. Frankfurt figures that if he can find what's missing from instances of less-than-full-blooded action, then he'll know what makes it the case, in other instances, that the agent gets into the act.

---

which illustrates that Chisholm has reverted to understanding agent-causation in a narrower sense.

[24] See Bishop, *Natural Agency*, 69: "Of course action differs from other behavior in that the agent brings it about, but the problem is how to accommodate such bringing about within a naturalist ontology."

[25] 'Freedom of the Will and the Concept of a Person,' 'Three Concepts of Free Action,' 'Identification and Externality,' 'The Problem of Action,' 'Identification and Wholeheartedness,' all in Frankfurt, *The Importance of What We Care About* (Cambridge: Cambridge Univ. Press, 1988). Frankfurt has recently returned to the topic, in his 1991 Presidential Address to the Eastern Division of the APA, entitled 'The Faintest Passion.' I shall not be discussing the new suggestions contained in this address.

[26] Frankfurt says that the "essential difference between persons and other creatures" that he wishes to discuss "is to be found in the structure of a person's will" (*ibid.*, 12). And he later suggests that if someone becomes unable to exercise his will in the relevant way, this inability "destroys him as a person" (p. 21).

[27] *Ibid.*, 21–2. In another essay Frankfurt formulates the distinction in terms of a person's "activity or passivity with respect to . . . states of affairs" (p. 54).

The cases of defective action that occupy Frankfurt's attention are cases in which the agent fails to participate because he is "alienated" from the motives that actuate him and which therefore constitute his will, or (as Frankfurt calls it) his "volition." And what's missing when an agent is alienated from his volition, according to Frankfurt, is his "identifying" or "being identified" with it.

Although Frankfurt draws this observation from cases in which the agent consciously dissociates himself from the motives actuating him—cases involving addiction or compulsion—it can equally be drawn from cases of the more familiar sort that I illustrated above. When my latent resentments against a friend yield an intention that causes my voice to rise, for example, I am not consciously alienated from that intention, perhaps, but I do not identify with it, either, since I am simply unaware of it. Hence Frankfurt might say that I do not participate in raising my voice because, being unaware of my intention, I cannot identify with it.

From this analysis of defective actions, Frankfurt draws the conclusion that what makes the difference between defective and full-blooded actions must be that, in the case of the latter, the agent identifies with the motives that actuate him.[28] Here Frankfurt casts the agent in a role of the general sort that I envisioned in my critique of the standard story. That is, he doesn't think of the agent as entering the causal history of his action by displacing the motivational force of his desires or intentions; rather, he thinks of the agent as adding to the force of these attitudes, by intermediating among them. Specifically, the agent interacts with his motives, in Frankfurt's conception, by throwing his weight behind some of them rather than others, thereby determining which ones govern his behavior.

Frankfurt thus arrives at the conclusion that if a causal account of action is to include the agent's contribution to his behavior, it must include the agent's identifying himself with his operative motives. He therefore looks for mental events or states that might constitute the agent's self-identification.

Frankfurt's first candidate for the role is a second-order motive. The agent's identifying with the motive that actuates him, Frankfurt suggests, consists in his having a second-order desire to be actuated by that motive, whereas his being alienated from the motive consists in his having a desire not to be so actuated. These higher-order desires either reinforce or resist the influence of the agent's operative motive, and they thereby "*constitute* his activity"—that is, his throwing his weight behind, or withholding his weight from, the motive that actuates him, and thereby making or withholding a contribution to the resulting behavior (p. 54).

As Gary Watson has pointed out[29] and Frankfurt has conceded,[30] however,

[28] *Ibid.*, pp. 18 ff., 54.
[29] G. Watson, 'Free Agency,' in his *Free Will* (Oxford: Oxford Univ. Press, 1982), 205–20.
[30] *The Importance of What We Care About*, 65–6.

the same considerations that show the standard story to be incomplete can be applied to this enhanced version of it. For just as an agent can be alienated from his first-order motives, so he can be alienated from his second-order desires about them; and if his alienation from the former entails that they operate without his participation, then his alienation from the latter must entail similar consequences. Yet if the agent doesn't participate when a second-order desire reinforces his operative motive, then how can its doing so constitute his identifying with that motive and contributing to the resulting behavior? The occurrence that supposedly constitutes the agent's contributing to his behavior seems itself to stand in need of some further contribution from him. Hence Frankfurt has failed to identify a mental item that necessarily implicates the agent in producing his behavior.

Watson and Frankfurt have subsequently sought alternative candidates for the role. Watson argues that Frankfurt's references to second-order desires should be replaced with references to the agent's values. What is distinctive about behavior in which the agent isn't fully involved, according to Watson, "is that the desires and emotions in question are more or less radically independent of [his] evaluational systems."[31] Watson therefore suggests that the agent's contribution to an action is the contribution made by his system of values.

But this suggestion solves nothing. A person can be alienated from his values, too; and he can be alienated from them even as they continue to grip him and to influence his behavior—as, for instance, when someone recoils from his own materialism or his own sense of sin.[32] Hence the contribution of values to the production of someone's behavior cannot by itself be sufficient to constitute his contribution, for the same reason that the contribution of his second-order desires proved insufficient.[33]

Frankfurt has made an attempt of his own to solve the problem, in subsequent papers, but with no more success.[34] Frankfurt now suggests that the agent's involvement in his behavior can be provided by "decisions" or "decisive commitments" to his operative motives, since these mental items are indi-

---

[31] Watson, 'Free Agency,' 110. For a recent discussion of Watson's view, see S. Wolf, *Freedom Within Reason* (Oxford: Oxford Univ. Press, 1990), ch. 2.

[32] I owe the latter example to Elizabeth Anderson, 'The Source of Norms,' (MS).

[33] Of course, Watson refers not just to values lodged in the agent but to the agent's evaluational system; and he might argue that values are no longer integrated into that system once the agent becomes alienated from them. But in that case, Watson would simply be smuggling the concept of identification or association into his distinction between the agent's evaluational system and his other, unsystematized values. And just as Frankfurt faced the question how a volition becomes truly the agent's, Watson would face the question how a value becomes integrated into the agent's evaluational system.

[34] Again, the discussion that follows deals only with Frankfurt's published work on the subject, not his 1991 Presidential Address to the Eastern Division of the American Philosophical Association, in which he outlines a somewhat different solution.

visible from the agent himself. Frankfurt writes, "Decisions, unlike desires or attitudes, do not seem to be susceptible both to internality and to externality"—that is, to identification and alienation—and so "[i]nvoking them . . . would appear to avoid . . . the difficulty" (p. 68, n. 3). Yet the example of my unwitting decision to break off a friendship shows that even decisions and commitments can be foreign to the person in whom they arise.[35] How, then, can a decision's contribution to behavior guarantee that the agent is involved?

One might wonder, of course, why Frankfurt and Watson assume that the agent's identifying with his operative motives must consist in a mental state or event specifiable in other terms, as a particular kind of desire, value, or decision. Perhaps identifying with one's motives is a mental state or event *sui generis* rather than a species of some other genus.

Tempting though this suggestion may be, it is really just an invitation to beg the question of agent-causation. The question, after all, is how an agent causally contributes to the production of his behavior; and to observe that he sometimes identifies with the motives producing that behavior is to answer this question only if identifying with motives entails somehow making a causal contribution to their operation—throwing one's weight behind them, as I put it before. Other kinds of identification may not at all guarantee that the agent gets into the act.

Frankfurt seems to think that an agent cannot fail to get into the act when he identifies with a motive. "It makes no sense," he says, "to ask whether someone identifies himself with his identification of himself, unless this is intended simply as asking whether his identification is wholehearted or complete" (p. 54). What this remark shows, however, is that Frankfurt is using the term "identification" in a specialized sense, since ordinary talk of identifying with something often denotes a mental event or state from which the subject can indeed be alienated. For example, you may find yourself identifying with some character in a trashy novel, even as you recoil from this identification. Identifying with the character may then seem like something that happens to you, or comes over you, without your participation.

One might think that such a case is what Frankfurt has in mind when he says that an agent's identification of himself may not be "wholehearted" or "complete," but I think not. For if it were, then Frankfurt would in effect be conceding that self-identification can sometimes occur without the agent's

---

[35] I can of course imagine defining a phrase "decisive commitments" denoting only those commitments which an agent actively makes. In that case, decisive commitments will indeed be such as cannot fail to have the agent's participation; but in what that participation consists will remain a mystery, and the claim that the agent participates in his actions by way of decisive commitments will be uninformative. A related criticism of Frankfurt's solution appears in J. Christman, 'Autonomy and Personal History,' *Canadian Journal of Philosophy* 21 (1991) 8–9.

participation; and in that case, he could no longer claim that self-identification alone is what distinguishes the actions in which the agent participates from those in which he doesn't. An agent who identifies with a motive needn't be implicated in the behavior that it produces if he can somehow dissociate himself from the identification.

I think that what Frankfurt means, when he refuses to ask whether someone identifies with his self-identification, is that identifying oneself with a motive is unlike identifying with a character in a novel precisely in that it cannot happen at all without one's participation. Identifying with another person is, at most, a matter of imagining oneself in his skin, whereas identifying with a motive entails taking possession of it in fact, not just in imagination. Frankfurt therefore assumes, I think, that identifying with a motive is a mental phenomenon that simply doesn't occur unless one participates, although one may participate halfheartedly or incompletely.

Having put our finger on this assumption, however, we can see that for Frankfurt to posit self-identification as a primitive mental phenomenon would be to beg the question of agent-causation. For if self-identification is something that cannot occur without the agent's contributing to it, then it cannot occur without agent-causation, and we cannot assume that it occurs without assuming that agent-causation occurs—which is what we set out to show, in the first place. The question is whether there is such a thing as a person's participating in the causal order of events and states, and we can't settle this question simply by positing a primitive state or event that requires the person's participation.

Lest the question be begged, then, "self-identification" must not be understood as naming the primitive event or state that provides the needed reduction of agent-causation; it must be understood, instead, as redescribing agent-causation itself, the phenomenon to be reduced. When Frankfurt says that an agent participates in an action by identifying with its motives, he doesn't mean that self-identification is, among mere states and events, the one in virtue of which the agent gets into the act; rather, he is saying that if we want to know which are the mere states and events that constitute the agent's getting into the act, we should look for the ones that constitute his identifying with his motives. Frankfurt and Watson are therefore correct in trying to reduce self-identification to desires, values, or decisions—that is, to mental phenomena whose existence we can assume without presupposing that agent-causation occurs.

But how can such a reduction ever succeed? If we pick out mental states and events in terms that do not presuppose any causal contribution from the agent, then we shall have picked out states and events from which the agent can in principle dissociate himself. Since the occurrence of these items will be conceptually possible without any participation from the agent, we shall have no grounds for saying that their occurrence guarantees the agent's participation in the causal order.

The only way to guarantee that a mental state or event will bring the agent into the act is to define it in terms that mandate the agent's being in the act; but then we can't assume the occurrence of that state or event without already assuming the occurrence of agent-causation. Hence we seem to be confronted with a choice between begging the question and not answering it at all.

We may be tempted to slip between the horns of this dilemma, by characterizing some mental items in terms that are sufficiently vague to carry an assumption of agent-causation while keeping that assumption concealed. I suspect that Watson's appeals to "the agent's system of values" and Frankfurt's appeals to "decisive commitments" seem to succeed only insofar as they smuggle such an assumption into the story.[36] But a genuine resolution of the dilemma will require a more radical change of approach.

The main flaw in Frankfurt's approach, I think, is that substituting one instance of agent-causation for another, as the target of reduction, does not advance the reductionist project. Since self-identification won't serve our purpose unless it's conceived as something to which the agent contributes, rather than something that happens to him, reducing self-identification to mere events and states is unlikely to be any easier than reducing action itself.

The way to advance the reductionist project is not to substitute one agent-causal phenomenon for another as the target of reduction, but to get the process of reduction going, by breaking agent-causation into its components. And surely, the principal component of agent-causation is the agent himself. Instead of looking for mental events and states to play the role of the agent's identifying with a motive, then, we should look for events and states to play the role of the agent.

Something to play the role of agent is precisely what I earlier judged to be lacking from the standard story of human action. I pointed out that the agent intermediates in various ways between his reasons and intentions, or between his intentions and bodily movements; and I argued that the standard story omits the agent, not because it fails to mention him by name, but rather because it fails to mention anything that plays his intermediating role.

What plays the agent's role in a reductionist account of agent-causation will of course be events or states—most likely, events or states in the agent's mind. We must therefore look for mental events and states that are functionally identical to the agent, in the sense that they play the causal role that ordinary parlance attributes to him.

Looking for a mental event or state that's functionally identical to the agent is not as bizarre as it sounds. Of course, the agent is a whole person, who is

---

[36] See nn. 26 and 28, above.

not strictly identical with any subset of the mental states and events that occur within him. But a complete person qualifies as an agent by virtue of performing some rather specific functions, and he can still lay claim to those functions even if they are performed, strictly speaking, by some proper part of him. When we say that a person digests his dinner or fights an infection, we don't mean to deny that these functions actually belong to some of his parts. A person is a fighter of infections and a digester of food in the sense that his parts include infection-fighting and food-digesting systems. Similarly, a person may be an initiator of actions—and hence an agent—in the sense that there is an action-initiating system within him, a system that performs the functions in virtue of which he qualifies as an agent and which are ordinarily attributed to him in that capacity. A reductionist philosophy of action must therefore locate a system of mental events and states that perform the functional role definitive of an agent.

I sometimes suspect that Frankfurt sees the necessity of this approach and may even think that he's taking it. My suspicion is based on the potential confusions that lurk in Frankfurt's talk of "identifying oneself" with a motive and thereby "making it one's own."[37] The reader, and perhaps the writer, of these phrases may think that when a person identifies himself with motives, they become functionally identical to him, or that when motives become his, they do so by becoming him, in the sense that they occupy his functional role. But the psychological items that are functionally identical to the agent, in the sense that they play the causal role attributed to him in his capacity as agent, cannot be items with which he identifies in Frankfurt's sense, because identifying with something, in that sense, is a relation that one bears to something functionally distinct from oneself. The agent's identifying with an attitude requires, not only something to play the role of the attitude identified with, but also something else to play the role of the agent identifying with it; and the latter item, rather than the former, will be what plays the functional role of the agent and is therefore functionally identical to him.

What, then, is the causal role that mental states and events must play if they are to perform the agent's function? I have already outlined what I take to be the causal role of an agent; but for the remainder of this paper, I want to confine my attention to that aspect of the role which interests Frankfurt, since my approach is simply a modification of his. Frankfurt doesn't think of the agent as having a function to play in implementing his own decisions, nor does he think of the agent as interacting with reasons *per se*. Frankfurt focuses instead on the agent's interactions with the motives in which his reasons for acting are ordinarily thought to consist. The agent's role, according to Frankfurt, is to

---

[37] Frankfurt, *The Importance of What We Care About*, 18.

reflect on the motives competing for governance of his behavior, and to determine the outcome of the competition, by taking sides with some of his motives rather than others. For the moment, then, I shall adopt Frankfurt's assumption that the agent's role is to adjudicate conflicts of motives (though I shall subsequently argue that such adjudication is best understood as taking place among reasons instead).

Which mental items might play this role? Here, too, I want to begin by following Frankfurt. Frankfurt says that adjudicating the contest among one's motives entails occupying an "identity apart" from them (p. 18); and he says this, I assume, because a contest cannot be adjudicated by the contestants themselves. When an agent reflects on the motives vying to govern his behavior, he occupies a position of critical detachment from those motives; and when he takes sides with some of those motives, he bolsters them with a force additional to, and hence other than, their own. His role must therefore be played by something other than the motives on which he reflects and with which he takes sides.

Indeed, the agent's role is closed, not only to the actual objects of his critical reflection, but to all potential objects of it as well. Even when the agent's reflections are confined to his first-order motives, for example, his second-order attitudes toward them cannot be what play his role; for he can sustain his role as agent while turning a critical eye on those second-order attitudes, whereas they cannot execute such a critical turn upon themselves. The functional role of agent is that of a single party prepared to reflect on, and take sides with, potential determinants of behavior at any level in the hierarchy of attitudes; and this party cannot be identical with any of the items on which it must be prepared to reflect or with which it must be prepared to take sides.

Thus, the agent's role cannot be played by any mental states or events whose behavioral influence might come up for review in practical thought at any level. And the reason why it cannot be played by anything that might undergo the process of critical review is precisely that it must be played by whatever directs that process. The agent, in his capacity *as* agent, is that party who is always behind, and never solely in front of, the lens of critical reflection, no matter where in the hierarchy of motives it turns.

What mental event or state might play this role of always directing and never merely undergoing such scrutiny? It can only be a motive that drives practical thought itself. That is, there must be a motive that drives the agent's critical reflection on, and endorsement or rejection of, the potential determinants of his behavior, always doing so from a position of independence from the objects of review. Only such a motive would occupy the agent's functional role, and only its contribution to his behavior would constitute his own contribution.

What I'm positing here is an attitude that embodies the concerns of practical thought *per se*, concerns distinct from those embodied in any of the attitudes that practical thought might evaluate as possible springs of action. Frankfurt seems to assume that the concerns animating the agent's critical reflection on his first-order motives are embodied in his second-order desires about whether to be governed by those motives—such as the desire not to act out of anger, for example, or the desire to be actuated by compassion instead. Yet these second-order desires figure in critical reflection only with respect to a particular conflict of motives, and they can themselves become the objects of critical reflection one step further up the attitudinal hierarchy. Hence the concerns that they embody cannot qualify as the concerns directing practical thought as such, concerns that must be distinct from the objects of critical reflection and that must figure in such reflection whenever it occurs. If we want to find the concerns of practical thought *per se*, we must find motives that are at work not only when the agent steps back and asks whether to act out of anger but also when he steps back further and asks whether to restrain himself out of shame about his anger, and so on. Only attitudes that are at work in all such instances of reflection will be eligible to play the role of agent, who himself is at work whenever critical reflection takes place.

One is likely to balk at this proposal if one isn't accustomed to the idea that practical thought is propelled by a distinctive motive of its own. Agency is traditionally conceived as a neutral capacity for appraising and exercising motives—a capacity that's neutral just in the sense that it is not essentially animated by any motive in particular. This traditional conception is not hospitable to the idea that the deliberative processes constitutive of agency require a distinctive motive of their own. My point, however, is that anyone who wants to save our ordinary concept of full-blooded action, as involving behavior caused by the agent, had better grow accustomed to this idea, because the problem of agent-causation cannot be solved without it. Some motive must be behind the processes of practical thought—from the initial reflection on motives, to the eventual taking of sides; and from second-order reflection to reflection at any higher level—since only something that was always behind such processes would play the causal role that's ordinarily attributed to the agent.

Is there in fact such a motive? I believe so, though it is not evident in Frankfurt's account. Frankfurt's conception of critical reflection strikes me as omitting a concern that's common to reflection in all instances and at all levels.

The agent's concern in reflecting on his motives, I believe, is not just to see which ones he likes better; it's to see which ones provide stronger reasons for acting, and then to ensure that they prevail over those whose rational force is weaker. What animates practical thought is a concern for acting in accordance with reasons. And I suggest that we think of this concern as embodied in a desire that drives practical thought.

When I speak of a desire to act in accordance with reasons, I don't have a particular desire in mind; any one of several different desires would fill the bill. On the one hand, it could be a desire to act in accordance with reasons so described; that is, the *de dicto* content of the desire might include the concept of reasons.[38] On the other hand, it could be a desire to act in accordance with considerations of some particular kind, which happened to be the kind of consideration that constituted a reason for acting. For example, I have argued elsewhere[39] that rational agents have a desire to do what makes sense, or what's intelligible to them, in the sense that they could explain it; and I have argued that reasons for a particular action are considerations by which the action could be explained and in light of which it would therefore make sense. Thus, if someone wants to do what makes sense, then in my view he wants to act in accordance with reasons, though not under that description. In any of its forms, the desire to act in accordance with reasons can perform the functions that are attributed to its subject in his capacity as agent. We say that the agent turns his thoughts to the various motives that give him reason to act; but in fact, the agent's thoughts are turned in this direction by the desire to act in accordance with reasons. We say that the agent calculates the relative strengths of the reasons before him; but in fact, these calculations are driven by his desire to act in accordance with reasons. We say that the agent throws his weight behind the motives that provide the strongest reasons; but what is thrown behind those motives, in fact, is the additional motivating force of the desire to act in accordance with reasons. For when a desire appears to provide the strongest reason for acting, then the desire to act in accordance with reasons becomes a motive to act on that desire, and the desire's motivational influence is consequently reinforced. The agent is moved to his action, not only by his original motive for it, but also by his desire to act on that original motive, because of its superior rational force. This latter contribution to the agent's behavior is the contribution of an attitude that performs the functions definitive of agency; it is therefore, functionally speaking, the agent's contribution to the causal order.

What really produces the bodily movements that you are said to produce, then, is a part of you that performs the characteristic functions of agency. That part, I claim, is your desire to act in accordance with reasons, a desire that produces behavior, in your name, by adding its motivational force to that of whichever motives appear to provide the strongest reasons for acting, just as you are said to throw your weight behind them.

Note that the desire to act in accordance with reasons cannot be disowned

---

[38] This possibility may be ruled out by an argument in Bernard Williams' paper 'Internal and External Reasons' in his *Moral Luck* (Cambridge: Cambridge Univ. Press, 1981), 101–13. In any case, Williams' argument does not rule out the alternative possibility, which is the one that I favour. I discuss Williams' argument in Chap. 8.

[39] *Practical Reflection* (Princeton: Princeton Univ. Press, 1989).

by an agent, although it can be disowned by the person in whom agency is embodied. A person can perhaps suppress his desire to act in accordance with reasons; but in doing so, he will have to execute a psychic manoeuvre quite different from suppressing his anger or his addiction to drugs or his other substantive motives for acting. In suppressing his anger, the person operates in his capacity as agent, rejecting anger as a reason for acting; whereas in suppressing his desire to act in accordance with reasons, he cannot reject it as a reason for acting, or he will in fact be manifesting his concern for reasons rather than suppressing it, after all. The only way for a person truly to suppress his concern for reasons is to stop making rational assessments of his motives, including this one, thus suspending the processes of practical thought. And in suspending the processes of practical thought, he will suspend the functions in virtue of which he qualifies as an agent. Thus, the sense in which an agent cannot disown his desire to act in accordance with reasons is that he cannot disown it while remaining an agent.

Conversely, a person's desire to act in accordance with reasons cannot operate in him without its operation's being constitutive of his agency. What it is for this motive to operate is just this: for potential determinants of behavior to be critically reviewed, to be embraced or rejected, and to be consequently reinforced or suppressed. Whatever intervenes in these ways between motives and behavior is thereby playing the role of the agent and consequently *is* the agent, functionally speaking. Although the agent must possess an identity apart from the substantive motives competing for influence over his behavior, he needn't possess an identity apart from the attitude that animates the activity of judging such competitions. If there is such an attitude, then its contribution to the competition's outcome can qualify as his—not because he identifies with it but rather because it is functionally identical to him.

Note, finally, that this reduction of agent-causation allows us to preserve some aspects of commonsense psychology about which we may have had philosophical qualms. What we would like to think, pre-philosophically, is that a person sometimes intervenes among his motives because the best reason for acting is associated with the intrinsically weaker motive, and he must therefore intervene in order to ensure that the weaker motive prevails. What inhibits us from saying this, however, is the philosophical realization that the weaker motive can never prevail, since an incapacity to prevail over other motives is precisely what constitutes motivational weakness. Every action, we are inclined to say, is the result of the strongest motive or the strongest combination of motives, by definition.

But my reduction of agent-causation enables us to say both that the agent makes the weaker motive prevail and that the contest always goes to the strongest combination of motives. The agent can make the weaker motive prevail, according to my story, in the sense that he can throw his weight behind the weaker of those motives which are vying to animate his behavior and are therefore objects of his practical thought. But the agent's throwing his weight behind the weaker of these motives actually consists in its being reinforced by another motive, so that the two now form the strongest combination of motives. Thus, the weaker motive can prevail with the help of the agent simply because it can prevail with the help of another motive and because the agent *is* another motive, functionally speaking.

Come to think of it, what else could an agent be?

7

The Story of Rational Action[1]

Decision theory comprises, first, a mathematical formalization of the relations among value, belief, and preference; and second, a set of prescriptions for rational preference. Both aspects of the theory are embodied in a single mathematical proof. The problem in the foundations of decision theory is to explain how elements of one and the same proof can serve both functions.

I hope to solve this problem in a way that anchors the decision-theoretic norms of rational preference in fundamental intuitions about rationality in general. I will thus depart from the tradition of anchoring those norms in intuitions about gambling strategies or preference structures of the sort that are the special concern of the theory itself. Although my interpretation is meant to capture what is right about the decision-theoretic conception of rational preference, it will lead me to argue that there is also something fundamentally wrong about that conception. In my view, decision theory tells us how to be rational in our preferences because it tells us how to have preferences that make sense; but there are ways of making sense that outrun, and may in fact conflict with, the prescriptions of decision theory.

The mathematical proof at the heart of decision theory concerns an agent and a set of *options*, some of which are chancy, in the sense that they can yield various possible *outcomes*, depending on whether particular *contingencies* obtain. The agent is imagined to have binary *preferences* among these options—that is, preferences for one option over another in the situation that only those two options are available. What the proof demonstrates is that if the agent's binary preferences satisfy various formal requirements, then we can construct a pair of functions assigning quantities called *utilities* to the possible outcomes of his taking an option, and quantities called *probabilities* to the contingencies on which those outcomes depend, in such a way that he always prefers the option

[1] This chapter originally appeared in *Philosophical Topics* 21 (1993) 229–54 and is reprinted by permission of the Board of Trustees of the University of Arkansas. I am indebted to Jim Joyce for extensive comments on several drafts of this chapter; I also received valuable suggestions from John Broome, Jean Hampton, and John Devlin. Some of the material in this chapter was presented in the "Philosopher's Holiday" lecture series at Vassar College, thanks to Stephanie Spalding, Tim Horvath, and Jennifer Church. Work on this chapter was supported by the Edna Balz Lacy Faculty Fellowship at the Institute for the Humanities, University of Michigan.

with the higher *expected utility*—that is, the higher sum of possible utilities, after each has been discounted by its probability.

This proof is called a representation theorem, because it demonstrates the possibility of representing the agent's preferences in a particular way—namely, as maximizing the actuarial product of two functions. The formal requirements that an agent's preferences must satisfy, in order to be assured of such a representation, serve as the axioms of the theory.[2] The axioms state that the agent's preferences satisfy conditions such as transitivity, independence, monotonicity, and the like.

The transitivity axiom states that, for any A, B, and C, if the agent prefers A to B and B to C, then he prefers A to C. The independence axiom states that if he prefers A to B, and his preference for A is unaffected by whether p is true, then he prefers the chancy option [A if p, C if not-p] to the option [B if p, C if not-p]—that is, he prefers a chance of getting A to an equal chance of getting B, provided that the "consolation prize" is the same in either case.

The monotonicity axiom states that if the agent prefers betting for the truth of p to betting against it with a given pair of payoffs, then he will prefer betting for p to betting against it with any other pair of payoffs. Here a bet for the truth of p is a chancy option in which the preferred payoff is obtained if p is true. Thus, preferring to bet for the truth of p with the payoffs A and B consists in preferring the option [A if p, B if not-p] to [B if p, A if not-p], given that A is also preferred to B. The axiom states that under these circumstances, the agent prefers [C if p, D if not-p] to [D if p, C if not-p] for any C and D where C is preferred to D.

A fourth axiom, the axiom of continuity, states that if the agent prefers A to B, and B to C, then there will be some contingency p such that the agent is indifferent between B and the gamble [A if p, C if not-p]. That is, there will be some contingency on which the agent is willing to risk losing B for the chance of winning A instead.

Even without rehearsing the proof of the representation theorem, we can see intuitively how preferences obedient to these requirements (among others, perhaps) provide the basis for constructing utility and probability functions. If the agent prefers A to B, then we infer that his expected utility for A is greater than that for B. If the agent prefers betting for p to betting against it, then we infer that his probability for p is greater than that for not-p. And suppose that the agent prefers A to B, and B to C, but is indifferent between B and a bet for p with payoffs A and C. In that case, we infer that he regards the gain he

---

[2] My summary of the theorem omits axioms that are required to guarantee the uniqueness of the utility and probability functions constructed from an agent's preferences. I have chosen to focus on the axioms that are required to guarantee the existence of such functions.

stands to realize if he gets A instead of B, and the loss he stands to suffer if he gets C instead of B, as canceling each other out in the expected value of the gamble, so that the gamble is equivalent in value to B itself. These gains and losses will cancel each other out in the gamble's expected value only if the probabilities by which they're discounted succeed in erasing any difference in size between them. We therefore infer that the proportion between the agent's gain for getting A instead of B, and his loss for getting C instead of B, is the inverse of the proportion between his probability for p and that for not-p.[3] By following these and similar principles, we can reason from the agent's preferences to assignments of utility and probability that represent those preferences as maximizing expected utility.

These axioms express conditions that are not only jointly sufficient (when appropriately supplemented) but also individually necessary for the agent's preferences to be representable in this fashion. Thus, for example, if the agent prefers A to B, and B to C, then we shall have to infer a higher value for A than for B, and a higher value for B than for C—in which case we shall already have inferred a higher value for A than for C. The resulting values won't represent the agent's preferences unless he obeys the requirement of transitivity, by preferring A to C. Secondly, if the agent prefers A to B, we shall have to infer a higher value for A than for B, which will cause the expected value of [A if p, C if not-p] to be higher than that of [B if p, C if not-p], since these gambles are similar in every other respect. These values won't represent the agent's preferences, then, unless he obeys the requirement of independence, by preferring the former gamble to the latter. Thirdly, if the agent prefers to bet for p with payoffs A and B, but prefers to bet against p with payoffs C and D—thereby violating the requirement of monotonicity—then there will be no probability that we can infer for p in such a way as to represent both preferences. And, finally, if the agent prefers A to B, and B to C, then we shall have to infer utilities such that the utility of A minus that of B stands in some determinate proportion to that of B minus that of C. But these utilities will represent the agent's preferences only if he obeys the requirement of continuity, by being indifferent between B and any gamble that links the payoffs A and C to a contingency whose probability is the inverse of this proportion.

The representation theorem of decision theory is irrefutable. Like any mathematical theorem, however, it is a formal structure that needs to be interpreted. And the interpretation of this particular theorem is highly problematic.

One might think that the utility and probability functions constructed in the theorem could be interpreted as representing how much value the agent places on the various possible outcomes and how much credence he places in the

---

[3] That is, we infer that $Pr(p)/Pr(\neg p) = U(B)–U(C)/U(A)–U(B)$.

contingencies on which those outcomes depend. In that case, they would represent what we ordinarily call the agent's values and beliefs. Yet if the utility and probability functions constructed in the theorem are to represent the agent's values and beliefs, we shall have to define the term "preference" in such a way as to denote a phenomenon from which an agent's values and beliefs can be so constructed. How, then, shall we define the term?

A preference might simply be a behavior or behavioral disposition; that is, preferring A to B might consist in taking or being disposed to take A when choosing between A and B.[4] Alternatively, preferring A to B might be a kind of affect, such as liking or wanting A more than B. Or this preference might be a rudimentary value judgment to the effect that A is preferable, more desirable, or simply better than B. Will any of these phenomena yield utilities and probabilities that actually represent the agent's state of mind?

Inferences about the agent's state of mind are especially questionable when preference is defined behavioristically. From an agent's taking or being disposed to take A instead of B, we cannot necessarily infer that he values A more, since his behavior might also manifest weakness of will with respect to a contrary evaluation, or might be compatible with his inability or refusal to make any comparative evaluation at all; and yet the representation theorem instructs us to assign him a higher expected value for A, if his behavior or behavioral disposition qualifies as a preference.

The mentalistic conceptions of preference are not necessarily more conducive to inferences about the agent's values and beliefs. Even an agent's rudimentary value judgments, such as regarding A as preferable to B, may not provide a basis for such inferences. For if the agent prefers A to B, the theorem instructs us to infer, not just that he places a higher value on A—something that might indeed be entailed in his regarding A as preferable—but that he places a higher *expected* value on it, a value decomposable into values placed on its possible outcomes, and probabilities placed on the relevant contingencies. Yet an agent's regarding A as preferable to B may not in fact indicate that the higher value he thereby places on A is decomposable into values and probabilities that he places on its constituents.[5]

This problem becomes clearest when the agent has a preference for or

[4] Actually, taking or being disposed to take A instead of B is more likely to constitute the disjunctive state of preferring A *or* being indifferent, since our ordinary notion of someone's being indifferent between A and B still allows room for his picking one at random so as to avoid the fate of Buridan's ass. Decision theorists who favor a behaviorist interpretation of preference are therefore inclined to state the theory in terms of the disjunctive state of preference-or-indifference. I shall henceforth ignore this complication.

[5] The possibility that a person's preferences might represent judgments of value but not judgments of expected value is discussed by John Broome in ' "Utility",' *Economics and Philosophy* 7 (1991) 1–12.

against taking risks.[6] Consider an agent who prefers A to B, and B to C, but is indifferent between B and the gamble [A if p, C if not-p]. As we have seen, the representation theorem will instruct us to infer that the agent regards his potential gain for getting A instead of B, and his potential loss for getting C instead of B, as canceling each other out once they have been discounted by the probabilities of p and not-p, respectively. But if B is not itself a chancy option and the agent is averse to risk, then he wouldn't have accepted the chancy alternative unless his expected value for the gain was more than would be required to cancel that for the loss, since his aversion to risk leads him to avoid even fair gambles. Conversely, if the agent enjoys risky ventures, then his accepting the gamble may be consistent with his assigning the gain an expected value too small to cancel that of the loss, since the value of risk itself makes even unfair gambles worth his while. In either case, the inference mandated by the theorem—that the agent's expected values for gain and loss are equally balanced—will not result in an accurate representation of his attitudes.[7]

Thus, the representation theorem does not show how an agent's preferences indicate what values and beliefs he actually holds. At most, it shows how an agent's preferences indicate values and beliefs that he appears to hold, in the sense that he behaves *as if* he holds them. Even a risk-averse agent behaves as if he holds values and beliefs corresponding to the utilities and probabilities that the representation theorem constructs for him: specifically, he behaves *as* he would *if* he held those attitudes *and* he wasn't risk-averse.[8] These "as if" attitudes can still be attributed to the agent, provided that they are conceived as having no reality beyond the patterns of preferences from which we construct them. That is, we can think of these values and beliefs as attitudes that are emergent in the agent's preferences—as complicated ways of preferring.

By sticking with the technical vocabulary of subjective utility and probability, we can remind ourselves that the decision-theoretic constructs are not values and beliefs in the ordinary sense. And having interpreted subjective utility and probability as ways of preferring, we can construct them from preferences of any kind—behavioral dispositions, feelings, or value judgments, all of which can display the patterns in question.

---

[6] See Bengt Hansson, 'Risk Aversion as a Problem of Conjoint Measurement,' in *Decision, Probability, and Utility; Selected Readings*, ed. Peter Gärdenfors and Nils-Eric Sahlin (Cambridge: Cambridge Univ. Press, 1988), 136–58.

[7] Here I am considering a case in which the agent's aversion to risk does not lead him to violate the axioms. Some economists will insist that the theory can represent such cases of risk-aversity, in the form of a "concavity" in the agent's utility function. Intuitively, however, we think there is a difference between how an agent feels about various outcomes and how he feels about their depending on chancy contingencies; whereas the theory represents the latter, if at all, only in terms of the former.   [8] *Or* weak-willed, or. . . .

A second challenge for the interpreter of decision theory is to find within it some norm of rational preference. Decision theory is generally assumed to involve, not just a method for representing the preferences that you actually have, but a norm prescribing which preferences or patterns of preference you ought to have. The interpretive problem is to say what the relevant norm of rational preference is and where it appears in the formal theory.

The relevant norm is often assumed to be the one that tells you to prefer the option with the higher expected utility. To be sure, the prescription to maximize your expected utility may well be the norm implicit in the theory; but in the context of formal decision theory, this norm has a force somewhat different from that which it is ordinarily thought to have.[9]

As ordinarily understood, the prescription to maximize your expected utility presupposes that there is some measure of expected utility that applies to you and that your preferences are therefore obliged to maximize. But in the context of decision theory, the utility and probability functions that apply to you are constructed out of your preferences, and so your expected utility is not an independent measure that your preferences can be obliged to maximize; rather, your expected utility is whatever your preferences *do* maximize, if they obey the axioms. Hence, the injunction to maximize your expected utility can at most mean that you should have preferences that can be represented as maximizing some measure (or measures) of expected utility, which will then apply to you by virtue of being maximized by your preferences.

The only cases in which this injunction yields any criticism of your preferences are those in which you violate the axioms. In such cases, the theory implies that your preferences do not maximize your expected utility. But this criticism doesn't mean that there is some antecedent measure of your expected utility that your preferences fail to maximize: according to the fundamental theorem, your violating the axioms entails that no measure of expected utility can be assigned to you. The only criticism that can be directed at your preferences when they violate the axioms is precisely that there is no measure of expected utility that can be assigned to you, because there is none that they maximize. And no matter how you bring your preferences into conformity with the axioms, you will thereby silence this criticism, since you will maximize some measure (or measures) of expected utility, which will consequently turn out to be yours.

In the context of traditional decision theory, then, the injunction "Maximize your expected utility" means no more than "Obey the axioms, and you

---

[9] Several of the points made in this and the following sections are summarized by John Broome in 'Should a Rational Agent Maximize Expected Utility?', in *The Limits of Rationality*, ed. Karen Schweers Cook and Margaret Levi (Chicago: Univ. of Chicago Press, 1990), 134.

will have maximized any measure of expected utility that might be yours." Put more simply, the injunction says, "Obey the axioms, and expected utility will take care of itself."

The problem with the latter injunctions is that they lack the intuitive appeal of the prescription to maximize expected utility, as that prescription is ordinarily understood. The prescription to maximize expected utility has intuitive appeal if interpreted as presupposing that you already place different values on different outcomes, and that you therefore have reason to prefer those things which are most likely to promote whatever you already value most. But in the context of decision theory, the values that you place on outcomes are "as if" values constructed out of your preferences; and so those values aren't antecedently available to generate reasons for having preferences. To be sure, the theory guarantees that if your preferences conform to the axioms, then you will systematically prefer options that promote what you value, in some sense of the word; but you will systematically prefer options that promote what you value, in this sense, only because you will turn out, by definition, to value whatever your preferred options systematically promote. And the question is why you ought to prefer things that promote what you value in this *post facto* sense.

Exponents of decision theory claim that they needn't derive normative force from the notion of maximizing utility, because the axioms have normative force of their own. Thus, Savage writes:[10]

> [W]hen it is explicitly brought to my attention that I have shown a preference for **f** as compared with **g**, for **g** as compared with **h**, and for **h** as compared with **f**, I feel uncomfortable in much the same way that I do when it is brought to my attention that some of my beliefs are logically contradictory. Whenever I examine such a triple of preferences on my own part, I find that it is not at all difficult to reverse one of them. In fact, I find on contemplating the three alleged preferences side by side that at least one among them is not a preference at all, at any rate not any more.

Here Savage is saying that the transitivity requirement has a normative force for him in its own right, as a requirement that he feels obliged to obey in his preferences, just as he feels obliged to obey the requirements of consistency in his beliefs.[11] Savage is therefore content with the suggestion that the only norm implicit in the theory is an injunction to obey the axioms.

But why exactly does Savage feel "uncomfortable" when he finds himself with intransitive preferences? Are intransitive preferences really like inconsistent beliefs?

What makes a triad of intransitive preferences seem inconsistent is that they

---

[10] L. J. Savage, *The Foundations of Statistics* (New York: John Wiley and Sons, 1954), 19–21.
[11] That Savage defines preference as a disposition to choose can be confirmed on p. 17.

tend to conflict, in the sense that acting on any two of them would entail frustrating the third. That is, if someone with Savage's intransitive preferences is offered a choice between H and G, his preference between these options commits him to taking G; and if he is then offered a choice between keeping G and getting F instead, his preference between them commits him to taking F; but his rejecting H in favor of G, and G in favor of F, would add up, in effect, to his rejecting H in favor of F, which would be contrary to his own preference between these two options.

Some theorists prefer to demonstrate the conflict among intransitive preferences by showing that the agent who holds them can be turned into a "money pump." Granted H, the agent should be willing to trade it plus a small sum of money in exchange for G, which he prefers to H; whereupon he should be willing to trade G plus a small sum for F, which he prefers to G; whereupon he should be willing to trade F plus a small sum for H, which he prefers to F; whereupon he will be back where he started but substantially poorer. What this argument shows is that the agent's intransitive preferences commit him to giving up something that he prefers—namely, having more money rather than less—without gaining any preferred option in compensation. Similar arguments can be constructed to show that preferences violating other axioms commit the agent to contravening his own preferences in the same way, by accepting the frustration of preferences that were previously satisfied without gaining the satisfaction of any preferences that were previously frustrated.[12]

Note, however, that all of these arguments depend on the assumption that an agent's preferences can be satisfied or frustrated by transactions other than the binary choice over which they are defined.[13] The preference for H over F, for example, is defined in the context of a choice between these two options. Yet in arguing that intransitive preferences are mutually conflicting, we assumed that the agent committed to rejecting H for G and G for F was thereby committed to a course of action that would frustrate his preference for H over F, since it would in effect (as we put it) entail his rejecting the preferred alternative. But rejecting H for F *in effect*, by choosing first between H and G and then between G and F, is not strictly the same as rejecting H for F in a choice between H and F themselves—the choice over which the preference for H over F is defined. Similarly, sacrificing wealth for poverty in the course of buying and selling F, G, and H is not strictly the same as sacrificing wealth for poverty when these two financial conditions are the only alternatives on offer.

Thus, the axioms of decision theory express conditions of consistency for

---

[12] No such argument can be constructed for the continuity axiom. And arguments constructed for the other axioms may depend on the agent's willingness to engage in an infinite series of transactions.

[13] This claim is equivalent to the thesis of Frederic Schick's 'Dutch Bookies and Money Pumps,' *The Journal of Philosophy* 83 (1986) 112–19.

preferences only if each preference is to be regarded as transcending its context—that is, as satisfied or frustrated not only in the context of the choice over which it is defined but also in the context of other choices that somehow add up to that choice in effect. Otherwise, violations of the axioms cannot be characterized as committing the agent to accepting losses in preference satisfaction.

Unfortunately, preferences needn't be context transcendent. Indeed, we can explicitly restrict each preference to its context by incorporating a description of that context into our specification of the options involved. And the effect of this redescription will be to short-circuit the normative force of the axioms, by making them impossible to violate.[14]

The apparent intransitivity of Savage's preferences, for example, can be eliminated if he claims to be holding preferences—not for F over G, G over H, and H over F—but rather for F-rather-than-G over G-rather-than-F, for G-rather-than-H over H-rather-than-G, and for H-rather-than-F over F-rather-than-H. Under these contextualized descriptions, no alternative is repeated across any two of the agent's preferences: each of his preferences ranges over its own unique pair of options. Hence the fundamental conditions for transitivity or intransitivity are lacking from these preferences, and any opportunity to violate the transitivity axiom with these preferences has vanished.

The contextualization strategy works by spreading out the agent's inconsistent preferences, so to speak, over an expanded range of options. It refracts each option through the prism of other options, so that F is split into F-not-G and F-not-H, G is split into G-not-F and G-not-H, and so on. Each of his initially inconsistent preferences can then be insulated from possible conflict with the others by being reassigned to its own, distinct pair of options. Because the agent's preferences over F, G, and H violated the axioms to begin with, his preferences over the expanded range of options may be uncoordinated, in the sense that preferences involving F-not-G will bear no systematic relation to preferences involving F-not-H (or to preferences involving F simpliciter, if any such preferences remain). Though uncoordinated in this sense, however, the agent's preferences will no longer violate the axioms, and they will no longer be inconsistent, strictly speaking.

One might think that redescribing the options doesn't save the agent from conflicts of the sort we have already considered.[15] For if he already has H but prefers G-not-H to H-not-G, then he should be willing to trade H plus a sum

---

[14] For a recent discussion of this issue, see John Broome, 'Can a Humean be Moderate?', in *Value, Welfare, and Morality*, ed. R. G. Frey and Chris Morris (Cambridge: Cambridge Univ. Press, 1992), 51–73.

[15] This response is discussed by Broome in 'Can a Humean be Moderate?' Broome gives a slightly different rejoinder (which I describe in n. 17, below).

of money in exchange for G; whereupon, if he prefers F-not-G to G-not-F, he should be willing to trade G plus a sum of money for F; whereupon, if he prefers H-not-F to F-not-H, he should be willing to exchange F plus a sum of money for H—whereupon he'll be back where he started but substantially poorer.[16] Hence, the agent's preferences still seem to conflict with his preference for more money rather than less.

The problem with this version of the money-pump argument is that it depends on the agent to be less than thorough in implementing the contextualization strategy. For it assumes that the agent can still be led around a circle that returns him, with less money in his pocket, to an earlier state of play. But an agent who is sufficiently thorough in contextualizing his preferences can avoid ever having to return to the same state of play. Having exchanged H-not-G for G-not-H, he can describe the next pair of options—not as G-not-F and F-not-G—but as (G-not-H)-not-F and F-not-(G-not-H); moreover, if he takes the latter option, he can describe the succeeding pair as [F-not-(G-not-H)]-not-H and H-not-[F-not-(G-not-H)]; and so on, indefinitely. The agent can thereby avoid ever revisiting the same state, and so he can avoid the discomfiture of having shelled out money to do so. Contextualized descriptions can thus eliminate the conditions necessary for being described as a money pump, just as they can eliminate the conditions necessary for violating the axioms.[17]

A sufficiently thorough implementation of the contextualization strategy can similarly undermine any attempt to criticize that strategy as leading to losses in preference satisfaction. This criticism always depends on a judgment that some sequence of transactions fails to satisfy any previously unsatisfied preferences while frustrating some preference that wasn't previously frustrated. But the contextualization strategy ensures that every transaction in a sequence will satisfy a preference that *couldn't* previously have been satisfied, precisely because its satisfaction requires the prior occurrence of all the preceding transactions.

The axioms of decision theory cannot rule out this evasive maneuver. For

[16] Strictly speaking, the agent is not back where he started: he started with H-not-G and ended up with H-not-F, and he prefers the latter of these outcomes to the former. From his perspective, then, he has been compensated for the outlay of money by the satisfaction of an additional preference. Nonetheless, if he is once again offered G in exchange for H, then his preference for G-not-H over H-not-G commits him to accept, and he will indeed return to an earlier state of play with less money in his pocket.

[17] John Broome offers a different objection to this version of the money-pump argument. Being offered G a second time in exchange for H (as described in the preceding note) will have forced the agent to choose between H-not-G and G-not-H, thereby depriving him of the preferred outcome that he had managed to buy—namely, H-not-F. The fact that someone can then sell H-not-F back to him doesn't show that he can be exploited. All it shows, as Broome puts it, is that someone can steal his shirt and then get him to buy it back. (See 'Can a Humean be Moderate?')

although the axioms stipulate that the agent's response to an outcome F as it appears in one choice must be coordinated with his response to F as it appears in other choices, the axioms do not require that these choices be described, to begin with, as involving one and the same outcome F rather than as involving different outcomes, consisting of F-in-different-contexts. Nevertheless, the maneuver of eliminating inconsistencies by contextualizing the options strikes us as violating the spirit, if not the letter, of the theory. It strikes us, in a word, as cheating.

An account of the theory's normative force must be able to explain why contextualization is illegitimate. The threat posed by this strategy is not merely that it will prevent the axioms from requiring any adjustments in our preferences, so long as we're willing to adjust our descriptions of them. A more fundamental threat is that the axioms won't count as requirements on preference, to begin with, if preferences are confined to their contexts, whether by description or otherwise.

Even if we don't describe our preferences contextually, our sense that they are subject to the axioms as requirement of consistency depends on the assumption that they transcend the choices over which they are defined. We cannot say what's inconsistent about preferring F to G, G to H, and H to F without assuming that each of these preferences can be satisfied or fulfilled outside of the associated choice, in a sequence of the other two choices. Our sense that these *un*contextualized preferences are inconsistent thus depends on the sense that they are such as *shouldn't* be described contextually. Unless we can explain why contextualization seems wrong in this sense, we cannot defend our conception of the axioms as requiring anything.

As John Broome has noted, contextual descriptions can be appropriate in particular cases, because they highlight evaluatively significant features of the choice at hand. Broome's example of this possibility is an agent who feels better about staying home when the alternative is sightseeing than he does about staying home when the alternative is mountaineering, because staying at home would be cowardly in the latter instance but not in the former.[18] This agent can justifiedly think of himself as choosing between sightseeing-rather-than-staying-home and staying-home-rather-than-sightseeing, or between mountaineering-rather-than-staying-home and staying-home-rather-than-mountaineering.

Contextualization is problematic only in other cases, Broome suggests, in which it entails drawing distinctions that make no significant difference. For many instances of F, G, and H, the alternative F-rather-than-G won't differ from F-rather-than-H in any respect that one might rationally care about. Con-

---

[18] *Weighing Goods* (Oxford: Blackwell, 1991), ch. 5. See also 'Can a Humean be Moderate?', 58.

textualizing the descriptions of these alternatives will entail drawing senseless distinctions, according to Broome, thereby violating what he calls principles of rational indifference.

I agree that contextualized descriptions can draw sensible distinctions in some cases and not in others. But I don't think that we can explain what's wrong with contextualization by saying that it sometimes entails drawing senseless distinctions among the options, since we aren't currently considering it as a way of drawing such distinctions, in the first place. We are considering contextualization as a way of formalizing a conception of preference—namely, the conception that each preference is specific to the choice over which it is defined. We are therefore considering descriptions such as "staying-home-rather-than-sightseeing" and "staying-home-rather-than-mountaineering," not to indicate supposed differences between the options so described, but rather to express the notion that staying home can be an object of preference only in the context of binary choices involving specific alternatives. And when contextualized descriptions are used to express this conception of preference, they cannot be rejected on the grounds that they indicate no significant difference between the options, since they don't purport to indicate such differences, anyway.

What's more, rejecting contextualized descriptions on grounds of their misrepresenting the options won't rule out the conception of preferences that they were in fact meant to express. For even if the agent agrees to describe his options simply as staying home, sightseeing, and mountaineering, he can still conceive of his preferences among them as capable of being satisfied or frustrated only in the choices over which they are defined; and he will then have no reason to see the axioms as requirements of consistency for these preferences. In that case, we shall still have to tell him why his preferences shouldn't be conceived as context-bound, whether or not he expresses this conception in how he describes the options.

The question therefore remains why we shouldn't contextualize preferences in general, irrespective of how we describe particular cases. The normative force of the axioms has yet to be explained in a way that answers this question. I hope to offer such an explanation.

Let me develop my explanation by returning to our intuitive dissatisfaction with contextualization as a means of obeying the axioms. We initially expressed this dissatisfaction by saying that contextualizing one's preferences satisfies the letter of the axioms while violating their spirit. Surely, the "spirit" of the axioms is what we're trying to understand when we try to understand their normative force. The way to understand the normative force of the axioms may therefore be to figure out what exactly is violated by the strategy of contextualization. What are we talking about when we say that contextualizing one's preferences violates the spirit of the axioms?

What we're saying, I think, is that contextualizing one's preferences satisfies the axioms while somehow defeating the point of doing so. That is, there must be some ulterior point or purpose to having preferences that are transitive, monotonic, and so on; and it must be a point or purpose that could somehow be defeated when transitivity, monotonicity, and the rest are achieved by contextualization rather than by straightforward means. But what is the point or purpose that obedience to the axioms is meant to serve?

Well, a purpose that we know to be served by obedience to the axioms is representability. The proof of the representation theorem demonstrates that obeying the axioms enables us to represent our preferences in terms of utility and probability functions. Of course, the same proof applies to any preferences that obey the axioms, including those whose obedience has been achieved by contextualization rather than straightforwardly. Hence, representability alone cannot be the point that's defeated by contextualization.

There is this difference, however. If an intransitivity in one's preferences among F, G, and H is eliminated by the straightforward reversal of a preference, then the resulting preferences can be represented by assignments of utility to the three options F, G, and H.[19] But if the intransitivity is eliminated by means of contextualization, the resulting preferences must be represented by assignments of utility to the six distinct options that contextualization has produced: F-not-G, G-not-F, G-not-H, H-not-G, H-not-F, and F-not-H. In the former case, one's preferences are represented by pairs of utilities drawn from the same three values; in the latter case, one's preferences are represented by pairs of utilities that are entirely disjoint, six different values in all.

Although contextualization succeeds in making preferences representable, then, an important virtue is lacking from the resulting representation. The representation made possible by contextualization doesn't reduce three preferences to alternative pairings of the same three values; rather, it elaborates them into unrelated pairings of six different values. Contextualization makes one's preferences representable, but only in more complex terms, each of which carries less descriptive power.

Thus, a purpose that obedience to the axioms generally serves, but contextualization defeats, is the purpose of representing one's preferences in concise and powerful terms. So let's reflect, for a moment, on the descriptive power of the representation whose possibility is asserted by the representation theorem.

An agent's options can include not only every possible outcome but also

---

[19] Of course, if F, G, or H represents chancy options, then the utilities assigned to it will be expected utilities. I shall ignore this complication.

every possible permutation of outcomes and contingencies, combined to form gambles. Since the agent can have preferences over every possible pairing of these multifarious options, his preferences can be exponentially multifarious.[20] Yet the representation theorem guarantees that so long as his preferences obey the axioms, they will be fully characterizable in concise and systematic terms— specifically, in terms of a single number for each basic outcome, a single number for each basic contingency, and a simple formula for computing the actuarial products of these numbers. This characterization of the agent's preferences will be concise because it will attach numbers only to basic outcomes and contingencies rather than to permutations of their permutations, which is what pairs of options are. And the characterization will be systematic because it will relate every preference to these numbers by means of a single mathematical formula.

Suppose that the world can be in any one of ten states, and that each state can result in the agent's receiving any one of ten different payoffs. These outcomes and contingencies can be combined to form 10^{10} gambles, which can be paired in $(10^{10})!$ possible binary choices. Yet, even if the agent has a preference over each of these choices, his preferences can be represented by ten utilities, ten probabilities, and a single formula for computing expected utility—provided, of course, that his preferences obey the axioms. Obedience to the axioms thus guarantees truly impressive economies in the agent's self-description.

What the representation theorem tells us, then, is that preferences obedient to the axioms will be synoptically describable. And to my way of thinking, this is the ultimate basis of the axioms' normative force.

After all, to guarantee that something will be synoptically describable is to guarantee that it will make a certain kind of sense. When we have managed to comprehend manifold items under a simple but informative description, a description that subsumes their multiplicity under some uniformity, we have then made sense of those items—that is, rendered them intelligible—in the most fundamental way. Representable preferences will make sense in this way, by being subsumable under the uniformity of maximizing expected utility, as calculated from a common set of values. What I claim is that making sense is the point of having representable preferences, and hence the ultimate point of conforming one's preferences to the axioms of decision theory.

Indeed, I think that for preferences to make sense, by being synoptically describable, just is for them to be formally rational. I therefore interpret the

---

[20] Some versions of the theory actually require an agent to have preferences over all of these choices; others do not. My point is simply that the agent *can* have preferences over all of these choices and still represent them in the same concise and powerful terms spelled out by the representation theorem.

representation theorem as asserting, and the proof of that theorem as proving, that obedience to the axioms yields formally rational preferences.

This brief statement of my view contains what may strike the reader as an equivocation. I say that formally rational preferences are the preferences that make sense; and the reader may think that what I say is true enough, but only if "making sense" is understood as a normative expression synonymous with "being rational." When I say that rational preferences are the ones that make sense, however, I am not propounding the tautology that rational preferences are the ones that are rational. Rather, I'm saying that formally rational preferences are the ones that are accessible to a particular mental act, an act of synoptic characterization or comprehension. How can I assume that this purely psychological conception of making sense can be substituted for the normative conception?

Well, I'm not exactly assuming this; I've argued for it elsewhere,[21] and I'm arguing for it again here. My argument is partly an inference to the best explanation: for as I shall show in a moment, the identification of rationality with intelligibility helps to explain our dissatisfaction with the strategy of contextualization.

But my argument is also partly an appeal to brute intuition. I am asking the reader to reflect on the felt authority of the requirements expressed in the axioms of decision theory, and to consider the following hypothesis. When you feel obliged to make your preferences transitive (for example), isn't it because you feel obliged to align them into some coherent posture toward the options? And isn't the point of such a posture simply that it will lend your preferences an intelligible order, a unifying thread, a common orientation—in short, a *rationale*? What it is for preferences to have a rationale—some rationale or other, whether it be good or bad—is simply for them to follow some organizing principle under which they can be comprehended. The felt obligation to have transitive preferences, I am claiming, is an obligation to have preferences that cohere around a rationale in this manner. It's thus an obligation to have preferences that make sense.

In the past I have argued that practical rationality consists in intelligibility of a more robust kind. I have argued, for example, that a rational thing to do is a thing that would make sense, or be intelligible, in that one would be able to explain doing it. And I have assumed that explaining what one does entails citing its causes. I have therefore argued, for example, that desires and beliefs are reasons for acting insofar as they are causes by reference to which an action might be explained.

Yet to represent one's preferences in terms of utilities and probabilities is not to explain them causally. Remember, the utilities and probabilities that help

---

[21] *Practical Reflection* (Princeton: Princeton Univ. Press, 1989).

to represent consistent preferences are emergent in, or supervenient on, the preferences that they help to represent: they are complex ways of preferring. And ways of preferring cannot cause the very preferences in which they emerge, or on which they supervene.

The utilities and probabilities that represent consistent preferences make them susceptible, not to causal explanation, but merely to perspicuous summarization. I do not find it helpful to describe this rudimentary vehicle of understanding as an explanation of any sort. To subsume something under a synoptic characterization is not really to explain it. But some philosophers have analyzed explanation as a kind of synoptic description, and their analyses can help me to clarify what I have in mind.

One such analysis is an account of scientific explanation offered by Michael Friedman in the 1970s.[22] Friedman's paradigm of scientific explanation is the derivation of one natural law from a more general law or theory—for instance, the derivation of the Boyle-Charles law of gases from the kinetic theory of molecular behavior. Friedman asks:

> How does this make us understand the behavior of gases? I submit that if this were all the kinetic theory did we would have added nothing to our understanding. We would have simply replaced one brute fact with another. But this is not all the kinetic theory does—it also permits us to derive other phenomena involving the behavior of gases, such as the fact that they obey Graham's law of diffusion and (within certain limits) that they have the specific-heat capacities that they do have, from the same laws of mechanics. The kinetic theory effects a significant *unification* in what we have to accept. Where we once had three independent brute facts— that gases approximately obey the Boyle-Charles law, that they obey Graham's law, and that they have the specific-heat capacities they do have—we now have only one—that molecules obey the laws of mechanics.[23]

Friedman thus arrives at the following account of scientific explanation:

> [S]cience increases our understanding of the world by reducing the total number of independent phenomena that we have to accept as ultimate or given. A world with fewer independent phenomena is, other things equal, more comprehensible than one with more.[24]

Now, I suspect that Friedman's account neglects one aspect of his example that is partly responsible for its being truly explanatory. The derivation of the Boyle-Charles law doesn't just unify one fact with two other facts under the cover of a single, more comprehensive fact; it unifies one law with two other laws under the cover of a single, more comprehensive law. Friedman seems to obscure

---

[22] 'Explanation and Scientific Understanding,' *The Journal of Philosophy* 71 (1974) 15–19.
[23] *Ibid.*, 14–15.
[24] *Ibid.*, 15. For a critique of Friedman's theory, see Wesley C. Salmon, 'Four Decades of Scientific Explanation,' *Minnesota Studies in the Philosophy of Science* 13 (1989) 94–101. The debate here is primarily about whether Friedman's notion of "the total number of independent phenomena" can be satisfactorily formalized.

this distinction with the ambiguous word "phenomenon," which can refer to either accidental or lawlike regularities. But I doubt whether unifying purely accidental regularities under more comprehensive but equally accidental regularities would look like scientific explanation, even though it would indeed yield a world that was more comprehensible by virtue of having "fewer independent phenomena." Scientific explanation has to provide something more.[25]

Still, Friedman has identified one element of scientific explanation, and it's the element that interests me at present. Whatever else scientific explanations may provide, Friedman is right that they provide greater comprehension—a synoptic grasp of several phenomena that were previously grasped independently. And this sort of comprehension is what I am claiming that we attain when we can apply the methods of the representation theorem to a congeries of preferences. If someone's preferences obey the axioms of decision theory, we can grasp them as falling into the coherent pattern of promoting constant utilities in light of constant probabilities. Thus comprehended, the preferences make more sense.

Another source for the relevant concept of comprehension is Louis Mink's account of narrative explanation in history. Dissatisfied with the suggestion that historical narratives render events intelligible by revealing their causes,[26] Mink characterized narrative understanding as comprehension in the literal sense of a "grasping together"—"a characteristic kind of understanding which consists in thinking together in a single act . . . the complicated relationships of parts which can be experienced only *seriatim*."[27] When history is presented in a coherent narrative, Mink argued, "actions and events, although represented as occurring in the order of time, can be surveyed as it were in a single glance as bound together in an order of significance, a representation of a *totum simul*."[28]

Mink presented this account of historical understanding as a variation on the views of W. B. Gallie, which he summarized as follows:[29]

---

[25] The distinction between brute facts and laws is more carefully observed in a passage that Friedman quotes from William Kneale: "[T]he explanation of laws by showing that they follow from other laws is a simplification of what we have to accept because it reduces the number of untransparent necessitations we need to assume," *Probability and Induction* (New York: Oxford Univ. Press, 1949), 91–92.

[26] See Mink's critique of Morton White's *Foundations of Historical Knowledge*, in 'Philosophical Analysis and Historical Understanding,' in *Historical Understanding*, ed. Brain Fay, Eugene O. Golob, and Richard T. Vann (Ithaca: Cornell Univ. Press, 1987), 118–46. For another review of philosophical work in this area, see W. H. Dray, 'On the Nature and Role of Narrative in Historiography,' *History and Theory* 10 (1971) 153–71.

[27] 'History and Fiction as Modes of Comprehension,' in *Historical Understanding*, 50.

[28] *Ibid.*, 56.

[29] *Ibid.*, 46. The view being summarized here is set forth by W. B. Gallie in *Philosophy and the Historical Understanding* (New York: Schocken Books, 1968).

In following a story, as in being a spectator at a [cricket] match, there must be a quickly established sense of a promised although unpredictable outcome: the county team will win, lose, or draw, the separated lovers will be reunited or will not. Surprises and contingencies are the stuff of stories, as of games, yet by virtue of the promised yet open outcome we are enabled to follow a series of events across their contingent relations and to understand them as leading to an as yet unrevealed conclusion without however necessitating that conclusion.

Mink did not share Gallie's concern with unpredictability and its role in drawing us along through a story; indeed, he was not interested in how we follow a story when reading or hearing it for the first time, since historians often tell us stories whose outcomes we already know. Rather, Mink was interested in how the characterization of events in terms of their relations to an outcome enables us to comprehend them as a completed whole after the story is finished.

Consider, for example, the story of *Treasure Island*, whose very title already hints at the "promised although unpredictable outcome" in light of which the story's various episodes are to be comprehended. Every major event in the story has some intrinsic description of its own, but it also has some description in relation to the outcome in question. Each major event can be regarded as either motivating or furthering or hindering or somehow bearing on the pursuit of Flint's treasure. And within the story, other promised outcomes serve a similar organizing role. As soon as the word "mutiny" is uttered in the confrontation between the Captain and the Squire, subsequent events can be comprehended as revelations of, responses to, actions upon, or deviations from the sailors' plan to revolt (which can itself be comprehended as an obstacle to recovering the treasure). The mutiny and the recovery of the treasure are thus common points of reference towards which we can orient our conception of the other events in the story; and having thus aligned our conception of the events, we can grasp them together rather than merely review them in succession.[30]

Although we thereby gain comprehension, which might be called a kind of understanding, this mode of understanding doesn't necessarily rest on an explanation of the events understood. Of course, the narrators of *Treasure Island* offer explanations of many events, but these explanations are self-contained digressions from the narrative and do not contribute to the sort of comprehension that interests Gallie or Mink. Again, many of the events that are comprehensible by virtue of their relation to the mutiny, or to the recovery of the treasure, are related to these outcomes as individually necessary or jointly sufficient conditions for them, and so they provide a partial explanation of why the mutiny occurred or why the treasure was recovered.

---

[30] These retrospective characterizations of events are what Arthur C. Danto calls "narrative sentences," *Narration and Knowledge* (New York: Columbia Univ. Press, 1985), ch. 15.

But equally many events may be comprehensible by virtue of being related to these outcomes as hindrances, inhibitions, or obstacles; and the comprehensibility of the story does not depend on its making clear why the favorable conditions won out over the unfavorable. In short, how comprehensible the story is does not depend on how well it explains *why* the treasure was found. Rather, it depends on how well the events in the story can be grasped together as bearing on this outcome in some way or other, favorably or unfavorably.[31]

The orientation of events toward a foreshadowed outcome is only one of many ways in which narrative form renders events comprehensible. Philosophers of history, literary theorists, and cognitive scientists offer many other examples of, and criteria for, the intelligibility of stories. For my purposes, however, this one illustration of narrative intelligibility will do, since it serves as a convenient analog for the way in which preferences make sense when they obey the decision-theoretic axioms.

The completed analogy is this. Preferences that obey the axioms can be represented as jointly oriented towards the outcome of maximal expected utility, and so they are intelligible in the same way as disparate events that point toward the foreshadowed outcome of a narrative. Consistent preferences make sense because they hang together, like the episodes in a coherent story.[32]

I can summarize these digressions into the philosophy of science as follows. Whereas the principle of intelligibility in a story is called the plot, and the principle of intelligibility in natural phenomena is called a law, the principle of intelligibility in an agent's preferences, I am claiming, is called a rationale. And having a rationale, I claim, is the condition of formal rationality in preferences.

This interpretation of the norm embodied in decision theory enables me to explain why contextualizing your preferences seems like cheating. For I interpret the axioms of decision theory as directing you to coordinate your preferences in such a way that they will make sense; and when so interpreted, the axioms have a point that is indeed defeated by the strategy of contextualization.

[31] Conversely, the complete explanation of an outcome may convey more than an understanding of its explanandum, since it may also convey comprehension of the events mentioned in its explanans. An historical explanation of why the Civil War occurred, for example, may help us not only to understand the outbreak of the Civil War but also to grasp together many otherwise disparate conditions and events, by unifying them under the concept "causes of the Civil War."

[32] Alasdair MacInytre also combines the concepts of rational action, intelligibility, and narrative. See, e.g., 'The Intelligibility of Action,' in *Rationality, Relativism and the Human Sciences*, ed. J. Margolis, M. Krausz, and R. M. Burian (Dordrecht: Martinus Nijhoff, 1986), 63–80. Other than the fact that we both combine these three concepts, however, I can find very little in common between us.

The point of having transitive preferences among three options, according to my interpretation, is to have preferences that can be easily comprehended as pairwise comparisons of the same three values. But if your preferences must be redescribed in terms of six different options, none of which is repeated, then they can no longer be unified in the same fashion. To be sure, utilities will still be assignable in such a way that the option with the higher utility is always preferred; but the utilities thus assigned won't serve as unifying threads among these preferences, aligning them into a coherent posture toward the options, since each utility will help to represent only one of the preferences, and each preference will be represented by different utilities. These utilities may also unify the preferences in question with yet further preferences over the expanded range of options that contextualization has generated; but the unification thus achieved will not provide a common rationale for the three preferences with which you began—the preferences whose intransitivity drove you to contextualize. It will therefore fail to resolve the problem that the intransitivity initially posed, and so it will defeat the point of removing that intransitivity

The point, as I have suggested, is to comprehend the preferences you have as forming a coherent posture toward the choices you face. And this point requires not only that you coordinate your responses to the same outcome or contingency as it appears in different choices, but also that you conceive of your choices, in the first place, as containing the same repeatable outcomes and contingencies. Insofar as you redescribe each of your choices as unique, as sharing no components with other choices, you ensure that your responses to them will resist synopsis; and so you ensure that your responses to these choices will elude any synoptic grasp. You therefore violate the spirit of the axioms when you redescribe your existing options as having nothing in common with one another, even if you simultaneously invent a larger range of choices for them to have something in common with. Multiplying your options and preferences in this manner yields less intelligibility, not more, and so it violates the underlying norm of decision theory, which is the injunction to have preferences that make sense.

Note that this critique is aimed, not at contextual descriptions of particular options, but rather at the conception of preferences that's expressed by contextualization as a general strategy. It explains why there is a rational pressure against confining preferences to their own contexts. The reason is that making sense of your preferences requires you to see them as manifesting some constant, underlying posture toward the options, and hence as bearing upon one another as expressions of the same rationale. To regard your preferences for F over G and for G over H as having nothing to do with your preference between F and H would run directly contrary to the goal of having preferences that hang together so as to make sense.

Of course, merely making sense can render preferences rational only in a very weak understanding of the word. All sorts of bizarre, perverse, and otherwise unsavory sets of preferences are organized around some principle of intelligibility or other. Surely I don't intend to claim that all such preferences are rational?

My reply is that I am trying to identify the norm of rationality that's embodied in decision theory, and decision theory can claim to embody only one such norm, and a weak one at that. As many have noted, all sorts of bizarre, perverse, and otherwise unsavory sets of preferences can satisfy the axioms of decision theory, too, if they are consistently bizarre, consistently perverse, or consistently unsavory.[33] All that decision theory can claim to formalize is rational consistency—a virtue possessed by many agents whom we would still like to criticize. In looking for the norm that's formalized in decision theory, then, we should expect to find a norm that's very weak when compared with the other norms that we wish to apply.

These other norms, whatever they are, can be described in one of two ways. On the one hand, we might think that norms other than that of rational consistency can still be norms of rationality, expressing substantive demands that rationality makes over and above merely formal demands of the sort that are embodied in decision theory. We might think that substantive rationality requires us, for example, to prefer pleasure over pain, or not to prefer present pleasure over future pleasure, and so on.

On the other hand, we might think that consistency is the only requirement of rationality, and that all other requirements are expressive of other virtues. Consistent preferences may still be criticized on many grounds, we might think—e.g., as insensitive, short-sighted, masochistic—but not on the grounds of being irrational.

My interpretation of decision theory lends support to the former view. For if the rational consistency of our preferences consists in their having an intelligible structure, as I have claimed, then a coordinate, substantive mode of rationality can be discerned in their having an intelligible content. Some sets of preferences that make formal sense, in that they can be perspicuously summarized, may still be at odds with what we know about human nature in general, for example, or about ourselves in particular; and so they may still fail to make sense, substantively speaking. Synoptically describable preferences may still be inexplicable or inscrutable in their content, because we cannot understand or explain why we, or anyone, would have preferences with that content, no matter how internally coherent they may be. As we have seen, the mode of understanding that's provided by coherent narratives, according to

---

[33] See, e.g., Sen, 'Rationality and Uncertainty,' in *Recent Developments in the Foundations of Utility and Risk Theory*, ed. L. Daboni et al. (Dordrecht: D. Reidel, 1986), 4.

Mink, or by overarching generalizations, according to Friedman, is not all of the understanding we might want of the phenomena that they summarize. Similarly, summarizing our preferences in terms of utilities and probabilities may still leave us quite baffled by those preferences in many respects.

If so, our preferences will lack a virtue that's clearly of a piece with synoptic describability, and hence with rational consistency, as I conceive it. Indeed, this virtue is related to rational consistency in precisely the way that one would expect substantive and formal rationality to be related, since it is a substantive form of intelligibility distinct from, but coordinate with, the purely formal intelligibility found in preferences that can be synoptically described.

Note, however, that under my interpretation the relation between formal and substantive rationality is not as it is ordinarily imagined to be. Ordinarily, rational consistency is imagined to be a necessary (but not sufficient) condition for substantive rationality in one's preferences. All rational preferences are assumed to be at least rationally consistent; substantively rational preferences are assumed to be rationally consistent and more. A theory of substantive rationality is therefore expected to tell us which among the rationally consistent sets of preferences one ought to have.

Yet if formal and substantive rationality are related as formal and substantive intelligibility, then they have the potential to conflict. The preferences that make the most sense substantively, in light of human or individual natures, may not be the ones that are most perspicuously summarized when considered alone. Conversely, the preferences that can be summarized most perspicuously may be quite inexplicable or inscrutable as expressions of our personality, or of any human personality at all.

In order to understand this point, keep in mind that I interpret formal rationality as a matter of degree. Rational consistency, conceived as intelligibility, is not an all-or-nothing affair, and so it is unlike consistency as understood in other contexts.

Consider a set of preferences that depart only slightly from the requirements of maximizing expected utility. Suppose that you prefer two million dollars to one million dollars and yet prefer one million dollars to any gamble with payoffs of two million dollars and zero dollars. In that case, there are no utilities and probabilities whose actuarial products you are maximizing. Any assignment of utilities to these monetary sums will yield a determinate proportion between your potential gain, in getting two million dollars instead of one million, and your potential loss in getting no dollars; and there will therefore be a determinate probability of winning at which your discounted gain from the gamble is greater than your discounted loss. But there is no probability of winning at which you prefer to take the gamble, and so there is no assignment of values for which your preferences maximize expected utility.

Because your preferences in this example maximize no measure of expected utility, they do not add up to a coherent posture toward the outcomes as being simply better or worse. There are assignments of utility and probability that will represent your response to any choice in which your financial security is not at stake—that is, any choice that doesn't set a certainty of having enough money against a risk of having less. But the same utilities and probabilities, by themselves, will not represent your responses to the remaining choices, in which you are invited to place financial sufficiency at risk for further gain. Indeed, no assignment of utilities and probabilities can unify these two subsets of your preferences.

The discontinuity in your preferences makes them less unifiable, less synoptically describable, and consequently less intelligible in the sense that I have defined. Formally speaking, then, these preferences are less rational, not only according to traditional decision theory but also according to my interpretation of it.[34]

Although discontinuous preferences lack the highest degree of formal rationality, they still possess such rationality to some degree. For although they do not add up to a coherent posture toward the outcomes as being simply better or worse, they still add up to a somewhat subtler posture toward the outcomes, as being better or worse but also, in some cases, good enough.[35]

In my example you behave as if you value one million dollars less than two million and yet value one million as being enough, in the sense that you refuse to put it at risk for the sake of a chance to gain more. One thing that we sometimes mean in saying that we have enough is precisely that we would rather

---

[34] This loss of intelligibility is reflected, by the way, in the diminished degree to which your preferences can transcend their contexts. Suppose that you are offered, first, a choice between $1 million and a chance of getting $2.5 million if the toss of a coin comes up heads; and, second, a choice between $1 million and a chance of getting $2.5 million if the same toss comes up tails. In either choice considered alone, your threshold of sufficiency dictates preferring the certainty of $1 million to the mere chance of getting more; but when both choices are considered together, they offer the prospect of getting $2.5 million for sure, which you prefer to $1 million. Acting on the former preferences will lead you to frustrate the latter, and vice versa.

The only way to avoid this conflict is to contextualize your preferences. What your underlying values should lead you to say is that, although you prefer $1 million to a chance of $2.5 million when choosing only between these options, you prefer the chance of $2.5 million if you'll be getting another choice, in which you'll have the opportunity to raise that chance to the level of certainty. The discontinuity in your other preferences thus forces you, in this case, to frame two different preferences addressed to two different contexts in which the choice between these outcomes might arise.

This inability to generalize your preferences goes hand in hand with your inability to represent them as maximally unified. It therefore goes hand in hand with their falling short of maximal rationality in the formal dimension.

[35] Although I use the language of satisficing to describe your strategy in this example, it is not quite the same as the strategies of satisficing defined by Simon (e.g., 'A Behavioral Model of Rational Choice,' *Quarterly Journal of Economics* 69 (1955) 99–118) or Slote, *Beyond Optimizing; a Study of Rational Choice* (Cambridge, Mass.: Harvard Univ. Press, 1989).

pocket what we have than risk losing it, even if that risk is paired with a chance of further gain. A refusal to trade one million dollars in the hand for two million in the bush can thus be understood as expressing the attitude that one million dollars is sufficient.

Your behavior in my example can be summarized, then, by a value function for money and a threshold designating some amount of money as sufficient. When such a threshold is added to a value function, the result is still a coherent scheme for unifying disparate preferences.[36] And when represented by this scheme, the preferences still make sense. Hence your preferences in this example are rational in the same sense as preferences obedient to the axioms: they can be perspicuously unified by a general framework of values, which provide their rationale. They're just slightly less unifiable—and hence slightly less rational, formally speaking—than preferences that obey the axiom of continuity.

Must we avoid even this slight loss of formal rationality? I think not. For I think that this loss in formal rationality yields a considerable gain in rationality on the substantive dimension. Evaluating everything as continuously better or worse than everything else makes less sense, for creatures like us, than evaluating things not only as better or worse but also, at times, as sufficient or insufficient. Hence continuous preferences, though easier to formulate in themselves, are harder to understand as preferences of ours.

Fully defending this claim about what makes sense for human beings is not the business of the present paper. I think that there are many different aspects of human nature that make discontinuous preferences especially intelligible; here I shall mention just one. Human beings are subject not just to desires but also to needs; and while we often have desires to satisfy our needs in some ways rather than others (say, by gaining two million dollars rather than one million dollars), the satisfaction of those desires is of no importance to us when the relevant needs are at risk.[37] Thus, a creature whose preferences are intelligible in terms of an undifferentiated continuum of values may make less sense as a

---

[36] Provided, of course, that your other preferences are in keeping with the threshold of sufficiency. If you refuse to trade a certainty of $1 million for any chance of $2 million but willingly trade it for a chance of $3 million, then you aren't consistently treating $1 million as sufficient.

[37] Another relevant aspect of human nature, I think, is that we experience our lives from different perspectives, including not only a succession of momentary present-tense perspectives but also a perspective of tenseless reflection on our lives as a whole. I have argued elsewhere that discontinuities between these perspectives yield discontinuities in the kinds of value to which we are subject. What is good for us at a particular moment is not necessarily the same, I think, as what is good for us in life; and what is good for us in life is not simply a function of what is good for us at the various moments during which we're alive. (See my 'Well-Being and Time,' Chap. 3, above.) This view yields a scheme of values that may best be expressed in discontinuous preferences.

person than a creature whose preferences are intelligible in terms of values intersected by various thresholds of sufficiency.

I therefore think that fully continuous preferences—in which any loss will be risked for the chance of a large enough gain—can be so coherent in themselves as to be incoherent with our understanding of the people who have them. And if the formal rationality of preferences is a matter of their internal coherence, I don't see how it can be required of them to a degree that undermines their coherence more broadly construed. The virtue that we have found in obeying the decision-theoretic axioms is the virtue of being formally intelligible, which is of a piece with the virtue of being intelligible as a person, in general, and as one sort of person, in particular. How can we owe the former virtue an allegiance so strong that it requires us to forsake the latter?

My interpretation of decision theory thus suggests that preferences can have too much formal rationality. Substantively rational preferences aren't maximally consistent and more, according to my view: they may be *less* than maximally consistent, so as to make more sense in substantive respects.

Actually, a corresponding point may well be true of consistency in beliefs as well. That is, rational beliefs may not be consistent and more; substantive rationality in theoretical matters may sometimes favor sacrificing the consistency of our beliefs, for heuristic or other epistemic purposes. Sometimes consistency really is the hobgoblin of little minds.

Courtesy inhibits me from using this aphorism to sum up my assessment of decision theory as an account of rational preference. I'll sum up my assessment like this. Preferences that obey the axioms of decision theory may indeed possess the ultimate degree of formal consistency, but the ultimate degree of formal consistency is sometimes too much.

Of course, there are differences between consistency in belief and consistency in preference; but these differences only militate against demanding the latter to the same degree as the former. The primary difference, I think, is that belief constitutively aims at the truth, and the body of true beliefs must be fully consistent; whereas preference has no constitutive aim for which consistency is required.[38] Inconsistency in our beliefs entails that some of them are false; and so it is an unmistakable sign of failure, even if it isn't necessarily irrational in some epistemic circumstances. But the reason why obeying the axioms of decision theory is rational, if it is rational, is not that it's a necessary condition for attaining some goal that's essential to preference. Insofar as obeying the axioms of decision theory is rational, it's rational because it makes our preferences formally coherent, thus ensuring that they are intelligible. And sacrificing some degree of formal intelligibility may enable our preferences to

---

[38] On this contrast, see my 'The Guise of the Good,' Chap. 5, above.

make more sense substantively and may consequently better serve the spirit of practical rationality.

Insisting on decision-theoretic consistency in our preferences may amount to insisting on preferences that make perfect sense in themselves but no sense at all *for us*. Once we understand the point of obeying the axioms of decision theory, we can see that the same point, appreciated more broadly, may be better served by violating them instead.

8

The Possibility of Practical Reason

Suppose that reasons for someone to do something must be considerations that would sway him toward doing it if he entertained them rationally.[1] And suppose that the only considerations capable of swaying someone toward an action are those which represent it as a way of attaining something he wants, or would want once apprised of its attainability.[2] These assumptions, taken together, seem to imply that the only considerations that can qualify as reasons

This chapter originally appeared in *Ethics* 106 (1996) 694–726 and is reprinted by permission of the University of Chicago. I am grateful to Sonja Al-Sofi, Stephen Darwall, Jennifer Church, Paul Boghossian, Alfred Mele, Elijah Millgram, Derek Parfit, Peter Railton, Sigrun Svavarsdottir, Nicholas White, Bernard Williams, Stephen Yablo, and several anonymous referees for helpful discussions of the issues raised in this chapter. Earlier versions of the chapter were presented to the philosophy departments at New York University, Stanford University, the University of Illinois at Urbana-Champaign, and the University of Houston; and to the philosophy faculty colloquium at the University of Michigan. Some of the material was also presented to Michael Bratman's 1993 National Endowment for the Humanities seminar on intention. I have benefited from comments received on all of these occasions, especially the comments of Frances Kamm, Fred Dretske, Rachel Cohon, Allan Gibbard, Sally Haslanger, David Hills, Tomis Kapitan, Jeff McMahan, Patrick Hays, and David Phillips. Finally, I received many helpful comments from participants in a graduate seminar taught at the University of Michigan in the winter of 1993. Work on this chapter was supported by the Edna Balz Lacy Faculty Fellowship at the Institute for the Humanities, University of Michigan.

[1] This principle is meant to apply only to complete sets of reasons, not to reasons taken individually. That is, if a particular consideration counts as a reason only in the context of a larger set or series of considerations, then it need not be capable of swaying the agent unless it is considered in that context. The assumption that 'reasons' denotes complete sets of reasons will be in force throughout the following discussion. I shall also rely on the success-grammar of the word 'considerations': considerations are, by implication, true considerations—or, as I shall sometimes call them, facts.

[2] The last clause is meant to account for cases like this: "It may be true of me that were the aroma of fresh apple pie to waft past my nose I would be moved to discover its source and perhaps to try to wangle a piece. It does not follow from this, however, that before I smell the pie I desire to eat it or to eat anything at all" (Stephen L. Darwall, *Impartial Reason*, Ithaca: Cornell Univ. Press, 1983, 40). Here apple pie is something that the agent doesn't yet want but will want once he considers its attainability, and so considerations about how to obtain it are capable of influencing him in the requisite way. I take it that this mechanism is what David Hume regarded as the first of the two ways in which reason can influence action: "Reason . . . can have an influence on our conduct only after two ways: Either when it excites a passion by informing us of the existence of something which is a proper object of it; or when it discovers the connexion of causes and effects, so as to afford us means of exerting any passion" (*A Treatise of Human Nature*, ed. L. A. Selby-Bigge, Oxford: Clarendon, 1978, 459).

for someone to act are considerations appealing to his antecedent inclina-tions[3]—that is, his desires or dispositions to desire.[4]

This conclusion amounts to an admission that reason really is, as Hume put it, the slave of the passions,[5] and Hume's conclusion is one that many philoso-phers hope to avoid. Some try to avoid the conclusion by rejecting one of the premises from which it appears to follow.[6] Others prefer to keep the premises while arguing that the conclusion doesn't actually follow from them.[7]

In my view, the question whether reasons do or do not depend on an agent's inclinations should simply be rejected, because it embodies a false dichotomy. This dichotomy has recently come to be formulated in terms introduced by Bernard Williams.[8] In Williams's terminology, "internal" reasons are those which count as reasons for someone only by virtue of his antecedent inclina-tions; "external" reasons are those which count as reasons for someone inde-pendently of his inclinations.[9] The Humean conclusion implies that all reasons

---

[3] Note that I am not using the word 'inclination' in its Kantian sense. I am using it as the generic term for conative or motivational states of all kinds.

[4] The argument presented here is discussed at length in Darwall, *Impartial Reason*, esp. chs. 2 and 5.

[5] Hume, 415. I do not claim that the argument offered above for Hume's conclusion should necessarily be attributed to Hume.

[6] The most frequent target has been the second assumption, which is sometimes called the Humean theory of motivation. See, e.g., Thomas Nagel, *The Possibility of Altruism* (Princeton, N. J.: Princeton Univ. Press, 1970); John McDowell, 'Are Moral Requirements Hypothetical Imperatives?', in *Proceedings of the Aristotelian Society*, suppl. ser., 52 (1978) 13–29; Darwall, *Impartial Reason*, ch. 5; Rachel Cohon, 'Are External Reasons Impossible?' *Ethics* 96 (1986) 545–56. For arguments defending this assumption, see Michael Smith, 'The Humean Theory of Motivation,' *Mind* 96 (1987) 36–61; and Alfred Mele, 'Motivational Internalism: The Powers and Limits of Practical Reasoning,' *Philosophia* 19 (1989) 417–36. Arguments against the first assump-tion are rare, although some philosophers have argued against a related assumption applied to moral requirements rather than reasons for acting. See, e.g., William Frankena, 'Obligation and Motivation in Recent Moral Philosophy,' in *Essays on Moral Philosophy*, ed. A. I. Melden (Seattle: Univ. of Washington Press, 1958), 40–81; and David Brink, *Moral Realism and the Foundations of Ethics* (Cambridge: Cambridge Univ. Press, 1989), ch. 3.

[7] See Christine Korsgaard, 'Skepticism about Practical Reason,' *Journal of Philosophy* 83 (1986) 5–25.

[8] Bernard Williams, 'Internal and External Reasons,' in *Moral Luck* (Cambridge: Cambridge Univ. Press, 1981), 101–13; 'Internal Reasons and the Obscurity of Blame,' in *Making Sense of Humanity and Other Philosophical Papers* (Cambridge: Cambridge Univ. Press, 1995), 35–45; 'Replies,' in *World, Mind, and Ethics; Essays on the Ethical Philosophy of Bernard Williams*, ed. J. E. J. Altham and Ross Harrison (Cambridge: Cambridge Univ. Press, 1995), 185–224.

[9] Here I am choosing one of two possible readings that have occasioned considerable con-fusion in the literature. The confusion can be traced to the casual manner in which Williams introduces the term 'internal reason'. Williams carefully defines what he calls the "internal inter-pretation" of the statement "A has reason to φ." Interpreted internally, the statement implies that A has some motive that can be served by his φ-ing. Williams then says "I shall also for conve-nience refer sometimes to 'internal reasons' and 'external reasons'" ('Internal and External Reasons,' 101). But Williams never explains how a scheme for interpreting reason-attributions can be transformed into a scheme for classifying reasons themselves.

Two different schemes of classification have suggested themselves to philosophers writing in

are internal, in this sense, and it is therefore called internalism; its denial is called externalism.[10] My thesis is that we do not in fact have to choose between the two.

Christine Korsgaard has pointed out that the foregoing argument doesn't necessarily yield any constraint on what counts as a reason for acting.[11] It may instead yield a constraint on who counts as a rational agent.

The first premise of our argument doesn't entail that if a consideration fails to influence someone, then it isn't a reason for him to act; it entails that if a consideration fails to influence someone, then either it isn't a reason for him to act or he hasn't entertained it rationally. The inclinations that would make an agent susceptible to the influence of some consideration may therefore be necessary—not to the consideration's being a reason for him—but rather to his being rational in entertaining that reason. And our premises may consequently imply that an agent's inclinations determine, not what he has reason for doing, but whether he is rational in his response to the reasons he has.

Korsgaard favors the latter conclusion over the former.[12] In denying the

this area. One scheme classifies as internal any reason that can engage one of the agent's motives so as to sway him toward doing that for which it is a reason. The other scheme classifies as internal only those reasons whose status as reasons depends on their capacity to engage the agent's motives in this way. An internal reason, on this latter scheme, is one that wouldn't be a reason if the agent didn't have a motive that it could engage. The difference between these schemes of classification can be illustrated by the case of an agent who has both a reason and a corresponding motive. According to the first scheme, this reason is definitely internal, since the agent has a motive corresponding to it. According to the second scheme, however, this reason could still be external, if it would remain a reason for the agent whether or not he had the motive.

Only the latter scheme captures the entailment that distinguishes Williams's "internal interpretation" of reason-attributions. For on the former scheme, the agent's having a reason doesn't require him to have a motive. If he lacks a corresponding motive, then his reason doesn't necessarily cease to be a reason, on this scheme; it simply ceases to be internal. Yet under the internal interpretation of reason-attributions, the agent must have the motive in order for it to be true that he has a reason at all. I therefore prefer the latter scheme of classification.

[10] Note that this usage differs somewhat from that of other philosophers, for whom the term 'internalism' refers to our first premise, requiring reasons to have the capacity of exerting an influence.

[11] Korsgaard, 'Skepticism about Practical Reason.' For other discussions of Williams, see Cohon, 'Are External Reasons Impossible?', and Rachel Cohon, 'Internalism about Reasons for Action,' *Pacific Philosophical Quarterly* 74 (1993) 265–88; Martin Hollis, *The Cunning of Reason* (Cambridge: Cambridge Univ. Press, 1987), ch. 6; Brad Hooker, 'Williams' Argument against External Reasons,' *Analysis* 47 (1987) 42–4; John McDowell, 'Might There Be External Reasons?', in Altham and Harrison (eds.), 68–85; Elijah Millgram, 'Williams' Argument against External Reasons,' *Noûs* 30 (1996) 197–220.

[12] See also Michael Smith, 'Reason and Desire,' *Proceedings of the Aristotelian Society* 88 (1988) 243–58. Smith seems to think (248–52) that he and Korsgaard disagree, but I think that they don't. In particular, Smith believes that Korsgaard rejects the second premise, that considerations can influence an agent only in conjunction with his conative attitudes. But I don't interpret Korsgaard as rejecting this premise. Korsgaard never claims that a consideration, or belief, can move an agent without the help of a conation or motive; what she claims, I think, is that the desires and values mediating the influence of a consideration need not be ordinary motives, of the sort that are directed at the agent's ends, since they can instead constitute his virtue of rationality. Williams

dependence of reasons on inclinations, she qualifies as an externalist, in Williams's terminology.[13]

Korsgaard's critique of Williams suggests a version of externalism that goes something like this.[14] Being a rational agent entails having various motives, including a preference for one's own greater good[15] and an acceptance of moral principles.[16] A rational agent is influenced by a reason for doing something when, for example, he considers some respect in which doing it is morally required; and this consideration can influence him because an inclination to abide by moral requirements is partly constitutive of his rationality. If an agent lacks this inclination, its absence won't prevent him from having moral reasons for acting: moral requirements will still count as reasons for him to act. Rather, lacking an inclination to abide by moral requirements will render the agent irrational, by making him insensitive to this particular kind of reason.

The Externalist's Burden of Justification

One liability of this model is that it must identify particular features of an action as constitutive of reasons for taking it, whether an agent cares about them or not, and it must then criticize an agent as irrational if he should fail

responds to this argument but seems to misunderstand it. He seems to think that if all rational agents have, say, a motive for doing what's right, then the fact that an action is right will turn out to be an internal reason for them, after all: "If this is so, then the constraints of morality are part of everybody's [motivational set], and every correct moral reason *will be* an internal reason" ('Internal Reasons and the Obscurity of Blame,' 37). But here Williams adopts a sense of the phrase 'internal reason' that fails to capture his own "internal interpretation" of reason-attributions, as I have explained in n. 9, above. In this sense, an internal reason is one with the capacity to engage an agent's motives, but not necessarily one whose very status as a reason depends upon that capacity.

I believe that Korsgaard is working with the alternative (and, to my mind, preferable) sense of 'internal reason', according to which an internal reason is one whose status as a reason depends on its capacity to engage the agent's motives. And what Korsgaard envisions is that reasons for behaving morally will qualify as reasons whether or not people have motives that such reasons can engage. Even if people happen to have the relevant motives, reasons for behaving morally will still be independent of them, in Korsgaard's view, and such reasons should be classified as external.

For a misinterpretation similar to Williams's, see John Rawls, *Political Liberalism* (New York: Columbia Univ. Press, 1993), 85, n. 33.

[13] I do not mean that Korsgaard would call herself an externalist, since she uses the term in a somewhat different sense. See n. 10 above.

[14] I don't mean to claim that Korsgaard holds this version of externalism. Korsgaard's 'Skepticism about Practical Reason' seems designed to be independent, in many respects, of her larger metaethical project. It therefore leaves open various versions of externalism that Korsgaard herself would not necessarily endorse. Indeed, I suspect that the version of externalism discussed here in the text corresponds to what Korsgaard rejects under the label "dogmatic rationalism" in 'The Normativity of Instrumental Reason,' in *Value and Practical Reason*, ed. Garrett Cullity and Berys Gaut (Oxford: Oxford Univ. Press, 1997).

[15] Korsgaard, 'Skepticism about Practical Reason,' 18.   [16] *Ibid.*, 22.

to care about those features. The model thus incorporates specific normative judgments, to the effect that one ought to be inclined toward courses of action with the features in question.

What entitles the externalist to build these normative judgments into his model of practical reason? As Williams puts it, "Someone who claims the constraints of morality are themselves built into the notion of what it is to be a rational deliberator cannot get that conclusion for nothing."[17]

Korsgaard does not try to get this conclusion for nothing, however. On the contrary, she insists that the normative judgments built into her conception of practical reason will require an "ultimate justification," which the externalist hopes to provide.[18] Indeed, the possibility of such a justification is the centerpiece of her paper.

Korsgaard's quarrel with Williams, after all, is that he prematurely discounts the possibility of justifying externalism. In assuming that an agent's imperviousness to a consideration impugns its status as a reason, rather than the agent's rationality, Williams assumes that its status as a reason cannot be established independently. For if a consideration could be certified as a reason for someone irrespective of whether he's susceptible to it, then his lack of susceptibility would thereby come to impugn his rationality instead. Yet certifying something as a reason for someone irrespective of his susceptibilities would amount to showing that it is an external reason, and hence that externalism is true. When Williams presupposes the impossibility of such a showing, he is presupposing the impossibility of justifying externalism. His case for internalism thus rests on antecedent skepticism about the alternative.

So Korsgaard argues—cogently, I believe. Yet even if she is right that the case for internalism rests on skepticism about externalism, the question remains whether we aren't entitled to be skeptical. What are the prospects for showing that something is a reason for someone whether or not he has the inclinations to which it would appeal? How will the externalist demonstrate that there are considerations by which any agent ought to be moved?

One might think that an externalist could avoid this burden of justification by avoiding the identification of any particular considerations as reasons, or of any particular inclinations as rational. But I doubt whether this strategy can work.

The version of externalism outlined above incurs a burden of justification because it judges an agent to be irrational unless he is inclined to be swayed by particular, substantive features of actions, whose value or importance may be open to question. All that externalism needs to say, however, is that the incli-

[17] Williams, 'Internal Reasons and the Obscurity of Blame,' 37.
[18] Korsgaard, 'Skepticism about Practical Reason,' 22.

nation responsible for the influence of reasons is one that's essential for the agent's rationality. Does this inclination have to be an inclination to be swayed by particular considerations, specified by their substance? Maybe it can be an inclination to do whatever is supported by reasons as such, or whatever is rational as such.

The inclination that's now being proposed isn't an inclination to do things with any particular features, other than the feature of being favored by reasons (whatever they may consist in) or the feature of being rational (whatever that is). Hence the claim that this inclination is essential to an agent's rationality doesn't call for any justification. For how could rationality fail to require an inclination to do what's rational, or what's favored by reasons?

Unfortunately, this version of externalism doesn't ultimately succeed in shedding the burden of justification, since it doesn't avoid the need to specify what counts as a reason or a rational action. To be sure, all it requires of a rational agent is that he be inclined to act in accordance with reasons or rationality as such. But in order for reasons to influence an agent by way of this inclination, he must recognize them as reasons, or as evidence of rationality, and so he needs some criterion of what counts as a reason or as a rational action. And until such a criterion is supplied, the proposed version of externalism will be nothing but the trivial assertion that rationality is a disposition to be influenced by reasons.

What's needed to save this version of externalism from triviality is a criterion specifying what it is about an action that makes it rational or constitutes a reason for taking it. And this criterion will once again require justification.

At this point, the externalist may attempt to repeat his earlier evasive maneuver. He is committed to the existence of a criterion by which an agent can recognize reasons or rational actions; but is he committed to its being a substantive criterion, which would have to be justified? Maybe an agent can recognize reasons or rational actions by their satisfying the generic concepts of what it is to be a reason or a rational action as such.[19]

Yet this strategy of continually postponing controversy is unlikely to help. Asking the agent to identify a rational action under the guise of rationality as such, or to identify a reason for acting under the guise of a reason as such, would be somewhat like asking him to hunt for something described only as "the quarry," or to play a game with an eye to something described only as

[19] I believe that Korsgaard proposes this very strategy ('Skepticism about Practical Reason,' 30–31). And I believe that there may be a way—a distinctively Kantian way—of making the strategy work. I discuss this Kantian version of the strategy briefly in n. 25, below. Note, then, that the present argument does not purport to prove that the strategy in question is unworkable. It's meant to justify doubts about the strategy, by showing just how difficult it will be to carry out.

"winning." It would be to assign him a task with a formal object but no substantive object—and hence with no object at all.

The Object of Practical Reasoning

The formal object of an enterprise is a goal stated solely in terms of, or in terms that depend on, the very concept of being the object of that enterprise.[20] Thus, for example, winning is the formal object of a competitive game, since "winning" just is the concept of succeeding in competition. Similarly, the formal object of a search or hunt is the quarry, and the formal object of a question is the answer.

Any enterprise that has a formal object must have a substantive object as well—that is, a goal that is not stated solely in terms that depend on the concept of being the object of that enterprise.[21] In the case of a competitive game, there must be a substantive object of the game, something that constitutes winning but cannot simply consist in winning, so described. A game whose object was specifiable only as "winning" wouldn't have an object—that is, wouldn't have any object in particular. And if a game had no particular object, then there would be no such thing as winning it, and so it wouldn't be a fully constituted competitive game. Similarly, a hunt whose object was specifiable only as "the quarry" wouldn't be a fully constituted search, and the question "What is the answer?" isn't by itself a fully constituted question.

Since practical reasoning is an enterprise at which one can succeed or fail, it must have an object against which success or failure can be measured. What, then, is the object of practical reasoning?

One might suggest that practical reasoning has the object of figuring out what to do, or answering the question "What shall I do?" But this suggestion either misstates the object of practical reasoning or states it in merely formal terms.

The statement that practical reasoning has the object of figuring out what to do may simply mean that it has the object of arriving at something to do or of issuing in an action. So interpreted, however, the statement is mistaken,

---

[20] I suspect that the argument offered in this section is related to the argument offered by Williams on pp. 109–10 of 'Internal and External Reasons.' Because I don't fully understand the relevant passage, however, I hesitate to attribute the argument to Williams.

[21] The distinction between the formal and substantive aims of practical reason is discussed by Derek Parfit in *Reasons and Persons* (Oxford: Clarendon, 1984), 3, 9, 37. As David Gauthier has pointed out ('Rationality and the Rational Aim,' in *Reading Parfit*, ed. Jonathan Dancy (Oxford: Blackwell, 1997), 24–41), Parfit is less than clear on the relation between these aims; in particular, Parfit doesn't appear to believe that the substantive aim of practical reason, as identified by a particular theory, is a specification of the formal aim. Like Gauthier, I prefer to use the phrase 'substantive aim' for that which specifies what it is to achieve the formal aim.

since issuing in an action—some action or other—is not the object of practical reasoning. Issuing in an action may be what makes reasoning practical, but the object of such reasoning is, not to issue in just any action, but to issue in some actions rather than others.

The object of practical reasoning must therefore be to arrive at a privileged action or an action in some privileged class. And when "figuring out what to do" is interpreted as expressing this object, it turns out to be a merely formal specification, since "what to do," so interpreted, simply means the correct or privileged thing to do, the thing whose discovery is being attempted. Hence there must be a further, substantive specification of the action or kind of action that practical reasoning aims to identify. A mode of reasoning whose goal was specified solely as "figuring out what to do" would be like a search whose object was specified solely as "figuring out where to look," or a question whose object was specified solely as "figuring out how to reply."

Similar remarks apply to the notion that practical reasoning aims at figuring out the best thing to do.[22] This notion is correct if 'the best thing to do' means "the privileged action"—that is, the action that uniquely satisfies the standard of success for this very reasoning. But in that case, it merely expresses the formal object of the enterprise. There can be an enterprise of figuring out the best thing to do, in this sense, only if that enterprise also has a substantive standard of success, just as there can be an enterprise of figuring out the best way to reply only if there is a substantive question, and there can be an enterprise of figuring out the best place to look only if there is a substantive quarry.

Of course, 'the best thing to do' might be interpreted, alternatively, as already expressing a substantive value: it might mean, for example, "the action that's optimific," in the sense that it contributes most to the agent's welfare or to the welfare of everyone. But in that case, the notion that practical reasoning aims to figure out the best thing to do will once again express a value judgment that calls for justification.

What, then, about rational action or reasons for acting? Can the object of practical reasoning be to identify a rational thing to do, or a thing that one has reason for doing?

The concepts of rational action and reasons for acting are potentially confusing in that they can have both generic and specific uses. If we specify a substantive kind of action as the object of practical reasoning, then we can grant it the honorific "rational," so that the phrase 'rational action' names actions of the specified kind. Similarly, if we specify substantive features that practical

---

[22] This notion is, for example, the basis of Donald Davidson's conception of practical reasoning. See his *Essays on Actions and Events* (Oxford: Clarendon, 1980). The problems mentioned here are discussed further in the text accompanying n. 45 below.

reasoning looks for in an action, we can grant the honorific "reasons for acting" to those features. Practical reasoning will then turn out to aim at the rational thing to do, or at what there is reason for doing, but only because 'rational' and 'reasons' are names for substantive objects.

What cannot be the aim of practical reasoning is rational action merely as such—that is, action conceived as rational in the generic sense, rather than in a sense defined by a specific standard. The generic concept of rational action is just the concept of action that would issue from competent practical reasoning. Until there is something that counts as competence in practical reasoning, nothing counts as a rational action in the generic sense. And competence in practical reasoning can be defined only in relation to the object of the enterprise, since competence is a disposition toward success. To be indicative of competent practical reasoning is to be indicative of practical reasoning that's well suited to achieving its object. Defining the object of practical reasoning as action that's rational in this sense would thus be to string definitions in a circle, leaving the object of practical reasoning still undefined. It would be like trying to teach someone a game by telling him that the object was to make a competent showing; whereas what counts as a competent showing always depends on the substantive object of the game.[23]

Similarly, the sole aim of practical reasoning cannot be action supported by reasons merely as such—that is, reasons conceived under the generic concept expressing what it is to be a reason. The generic concept of a reason for acting is the concept of something that warrants or justifies action. And to justify something is to show or indicate it to be just—that is, in accordance with a *jus*, or rule of correctness. Until there is something that constitutes a correct conclusion or a correct inference, there can be nothing that constitutes justifying a conclusion or an inference, and so there can be nothing that constitutes a reason for a conclusion or an inference, in the generic sense. So, too, until there is something that constitutes correctness in actions, or in outcomes of practical reasoning, there can be nothing that satisfies the generic concept of a justification for action, or a justification in practical reasoning; and so there can be nothing that satisfies the generic concept of a reason for acting.

Justifying a Substantive Conception of Reasons

This argument suggests that the externalist cannot indefinitely postpone giving substantive characterizations of rationality or reasons. The externalist must at

---

[23] Of course, we could introduce a substantive conception of competent practical reasoning— a substantively specified procedure, adherence to which constitutes good reasoning. In that case, however, the definition of rational action as that which would issue from competent practical reasoning will become a substantive concept, which once again requires justification.

some point provide practical reasoning with a substantive standard of success, which will either consist in or give rise to a substantive account of the features that constitute reasons for an action. The externalist will then have to justify his normative judgment that an agent ought to be swayed by consideration of the specified features.[24]

What's more, the requisite justification is unlikely to emerge from an analysis of concepts such as "reason" or "rational action." As we have seen, these are formal concepts that have no application except in relation to a substantive object or standard of success. Because these concepts implicitly require such a standard to be supplied, we can hardly expect to deduce it from them, any more than we should expect to deduce the object of a game from the mere concept of winning, or the object of a hunt from the mere concept of a quarry.[25]

I cannot prove that the task of justifying an externalist conception of reasons is impossible, but I think it's going to be awfully hard. I'm just a fainthearted externalist, I guess. Being fainthearted, however, I want to consider whether the benefits of externalism can be obtained without the burdens. I shall therefore turn to an alternative conception of practical reason, which straddles the line between internalism and externalism.

Outline of an Alternative View

Suppose that we want to frame a conception of reasons that isn't relativized to the inclinations of particular agents. That is, we want to identify particular things that count as reasons for acting *simpliciter* and not merely as reasons for some agents rather than others, depending on their inclinations.

One way to frame such a conception is to name some features that an action can have and to say that they count as reasons for someone whether or not he is inclined to care about them. The problem with the resulting conception, as we have seen, is that it entails the normative judgment that one ought to be inclined to care about the specified features, on pain of irrationality, and this normative judgment requires justification.

The advantage of internalism is that it avoids these normative

---

[24] The notion that practical reasoning is framed by a criterion of success for actions is discussed by David Gauthier in 'Assure and Threaten,' *Ethics* 104 (1994) 690–721. I discuss Gauthier's treatment of this notion in Chap. 10, below.

[25] Kant's conception of practical reason, as I understand it, is an attempt to circumvent this problem, by using the concept of a reason, not to identify which features are reasons, but rather to identify which features aren't, and by replacing the rule of acting for reasons with a rule of not acting for nonreasons. On Kant's conception, as I understand it, the object of practical reasoning is to act on any consideration but one whose being a reason would entail a contradiction. It's like a hunt whose object is to locate anything but that which could not possibly be a quarry. Perhaps the generic concepts of a quarry or a reason can indeed serve this modest role.

commitments.[26] It says that things count as reasons for someone only if he is inclined to care about them, and so it leaves the normative question of whether to care about them entirely open. Yet if we try to leave this question open, by defining things as reasons only for those inclined to care about them, we'll end up with a definition that's relativized to the inclinations of particular agents— won't we?

Not necessarily. For suppose that all reasons for acting are features of a single kind, whose influence depends on a single inclination. And suppose that the inclination on which the influence of reasons depends is, not an inclination that distinguishes some agents from others, but rather an inclination that distinguishes agents from nonagents. In that case, to say that these features count as reasons only for those who are inclined to care about them will be to say that they count as reasons only for agents—which will be to say no less than that they are reasons for acting, period, since applying only to agents is already part of the concept of reasons for acting. The restriction on the application of reasons will drop away from our definition, since it restricts their application, not to some proper subset of agents, but rather to the set of all agents, which is simply the universe of application for reasons to act.

The foregoing paragraph is an outline for a conception of reasons for acting— a bare outline that needs filling in. The remainder of this article will be devoted to filling it in, at least to some extent, though not, I admit, to the extent that's needed. I shall begin by making a digression into the subject of theoretical reasoning. My hope is that we can understand reasons for acting by analogy with reasons for belief.[27]

The nature of reasons for belief, and the inclination that mediates their influence, are fairly clear. The object of theoretical reasoning is to arrive at true belief;[28] and since true belief needn't be defined in terms of success in theo-

---

[26] I don't mean to imply that internalism avoids all normative commitments. In 'Skepticism about Practical Reason,' Korsgaard suggests that the instrumental principle of adopting the means to one's ends is a substantive norm; she defends this point at length in 'The Normativity of Instrumental Reason.' But even if internalism has to justify requiring us to care about the means to what we already care about, it avoids the further and heavier burden of justifying any requirements to care about particular things.

[27] The analogy between theoretical and practical reason is being pursued independently by my colleague Peter Railton, with somewhat different results. See his 'What the Noncognitivist Helps Us to See the Naturalist Must Help Us to Explain,' in *Reality, Representation, and Projection*, ed. John Haldane and Crispin Wright (New York: Oxford Univ. Press, 1993), 279–300, at 292 ff.; 'A Kind of Nonsubjective Reason?', in *Reason, Ethics, and Society*, ed. J. Schneewind (New York: Open Court, 1997), 117–43; and 'On the Hypothetical and Non-hypothetical in Reasoning about Action,' in Cullity and Gaut (eds.). David Gauthier also discusses the analogy, but he ultimately rejects it ('Assure and Threaten,' 699–702).

[28] Some may be inclined to think that the object of theoretical reasoning is not true belief but empirically adequate and explanatorily fruitful belief, or belief of some other kind. My argument doesn't depend on the outcome of this disagreement. What matters for my purposes is that theo-

retical reasoning, it constitutes a substantive rather than formal standard of success.[29] Reasons for a particular belief are recognized by their perceived relevance to this substantive standard of success, as considerations that appear to guarantee or probabilify the truth of the belief.[30] And these considerations influence a person's beliefs by virtue of an inclination to believe what seems true. Here, then, are considerations of a single kind and a single inclination to mediate their influence.

Perhaps we should ask whether the absence of this inclination would undermine the existence of reasons for belief or would alternatively undermine the believer's claim to rationality.[31] The answer to this question would determine whether reasons for belief were internal or external reasons. If someone weren't inclined to believe what seemed true, would signs of truth in a proposition no longer count as reasons for him to believe it? Or would he no longer qualify as a rational believer?

Both, I think—which goes to show that the question incorporates a false dichotomy. I shall argue that the dichotomy should be replaced with a subtler account of theoretical reasoning, along the following lines.

If someone isn't inclined to believe what seems true on a topic, he is no longer subject to reasons for believing things about it; but he is no longer subject to reasons for belief about it, I shall argue, because he is no longer a believer about it at all, and a fortiori no longer a rational believer.[32] He isn't in the business of forming beliefs on the topic, to begin with, unless he is inclined to believe what seems true about it.

Thus, reasons for believing something apply only to those who are inclined to believe what seems true on the topic, and so they are like internal reasons;

---

retical reasoning aims at some outcome specified substantively (i.e., not in terms of its being the object of theoretical reasoning or belief).

[29] The claim that truth isn't defined in terms of success in theoretical reasoning is potentially controversial. It must be rejected by those who hold a pragmatist conception of truth as the eventual deliverance of rational inquiry. In my view, however, the pragmatist conception renders theoretical reasoning vacuous, like a game whose only object is winning.

[30] In the case of inductive reasoning, of course, we may have trouble saying what relevance reasons have to the truth of a belief. Nevertheless, such reasons count as reasons for a belief because they make it seem true, even if we cannot say how or why. (An alternative way of handling this case would be to point out that inductive reasons satisfy a substantive procedural criterion of correctness in inductive inference. See n. 23, above.)

[31] Williams raises this question and seems to suggest that the absence of an inclination toward the truth would undermine the existence of reasons for belief ('Internal Reasons and the Obscurity of Blame,' 37). This is, of course, the internalist answer to the question.

[32] I believe that Korsgaard makes a similar point ('The Normativity of Instrumental Reason,' 42). In passages such as this, where Korsgaard seems to be pursuing a strategy like the one I am developing here, I begin to doubt whether she really is an externalist, in Williams's sense of the term. My reasons for this doubt will be explained in the text, below, when I explain why I do not regard the present strategy as a version of externalism.

but to say that they are reasons only for those who are so inclined is just to say that they are reasons only for potential believers on the topic—which is to say no less than that they are reasons for believing, period. Reasons for belief can therefore be identified independently of the inclinations of individuals, and so they are like external reasons, too.

The foregoing paragraph is a bare outline for an account of theoretical reasoning, and this outline also needs filling in. In order to fill it in, I shall have to explore the sense in which being inclined toward the truth is essential to being a subject of belief. I therefore turn to a different thesis associated with the name of Bernard Williams, the thesis that belief is an attitude that "aims at the truth."[33]

The Constitutive Aim of Belief

The grounds for this thesis emerge when we try to distinguish belief from the other propositional attitudes. One difference between belief and other attitudes is that it entails regarding its propositional object as true.

The difference between believing that *P* and desiring that *P*, for example, is that the former attitude treats *P* as a report of how things are, whereas the latter treats *P* as a mandate for how things are to become.[34] Desire takes its propositional object as representing *facienda*—things that aren't the case but are to be brought about. By contrast, belief takes its propositional object as representing *facta*—things that are the case and in virtue of which the proposition is true.[35]

---

[33] Bernard Williams, 'Deciding to Believe,' in *Problems of the Self* (Cambridge: Cambridge Univ. Press, 1973), 136–51.

[34] This difference between belief and desire can be obscured by the fact that desiring that *P* entails desiring *P* to be true, just as believing that *P* entails believing it to be true. These locutions obscure the difference between belief and desire because they use the infinitive 'to be', which is required for indirect discourse, to replace what would be different moods of the copula in direct speech. In believing *P* to be true, one believes in its completed truth, as would be expressed by the indicative statement that *P* is true; whereas in desiring *P* to be true, one desires its to-be-completed truth, as would be expressed by the optative that it *be* true. Thus, although we can speak either of believing or of desiring *P* to be true, transposing these statements from *oratio obliqua* to *oratio recta* reveals an underlying difference in the relation that *P* is taken as bearing to the world.

[35] The language used in this contrast should not be overinterpreted. To say that belief involves regarding a proposition as true, or that desire involves regarding it as to be made true, is simply to articulate our concepts of belief and desire as propositional attitudes. We express the fundamental similarity among these content-bearing mental states by describing them as ways of regarding propositional contents, and we express the differences among them by differentiating among the ways in which those contents can be regarded. The resulting locutions should not be understood as positing any particular mental architecture, least of all an inner eye that squints at propositions or raises its eyebrow at them so as to regard them in different ways. Rather, these locutions simply translate our terms for propositional attitudes into a common vocabulary, in

This conception of belief is correct as far as it goes, but it doesn't go far enough. It's incomplete because regarding a proposition as true is involved in many cognitive attitudes, including not only belief but also other attitudes from which belief must still be distinguished. Assuming a proposition—say, for the sake of argument—entails regarding it as a report rather than a mandate, as a truth rather than something to be made true. Even imagining that *P* entails regarding it as a completed rather than a to-be-completed truth. One hasn't imagined that *P* unless one has regarded *P* as reflecting how things are, and hence as true. Yet to assume that *P* or imagine that *P* is not to believe it, and so regarding a proposition as true must not be sufficient for belief.[36]

Of course, there is a sense in which things that are merely assumed or imagined are not regarded as really true. But the relevant sense is not that they aren't regarded as true at all; it's rather that they are regarded as true but not really—regarded as true, that is, but not seriously or in earnest. What distinguishes a proposition's being believed from its being assumed or imagined is the spirit in which it is regarded as true, whether tentatively or hypothetically, as in the case of assumption; fancifully, as in the case of imagination; or seriously, as in the case of belief.

What's the difference between seriously regarding a proposition as true and doing so in some other spirit? Here is the point at which belief is distinguished from other attitudes by its aim.

The sense in which fantasies and assumptions aren't serious is that they entail regarding a proposition as true—or accepting the proposition, as I shall put it—without sensitivity to whether one is thereby accepting the truth. We assume a proposition when we regard it as true for the sake of thereby framing a possibility to be entertained in argument or inquiry and when we can therefore be said to accept it for polemical or heuristic purposes. We imagine a proposition when we regard it as true for the sake of thereby stimulating or vicariously satisfying our desires and when we can therefore be said to accept it for recreational or motivational purposes. But we believe a proposition when

which their similarities and differences can be clearly expressed. To say that belief entails regarding a proposition as true is therefore not to commit ourselves to any particular theory about which physical, neurological, or otherwise subdoxastic states make up the mental state of belief. It commits us only to a view about what such states must amount to if they are to constitute belief—namely, that they must amount to the state of regarding a proposition as true. For recent discussions of this phenomenon, commonly called "direction of fit," see Lloyd Humberstone, 'Direction of Fit,' *Mind* 101 (1992) 59–83; and G. F. Schueler, 'Pro-attitudes and Direction of Fit,' *Mind* 100 (1991) 277–81. Note that I understand direction of fit somewhat differently from these and other authors. For a fuller treatment of the differences, see my 'The Guise of the Good,' *Noûs* 26 (1992) 3–26; and n. 55, below.

[36] For related discussions of the similarities and differences among these cognitive states, see Jennifer Church, 'Judgment, Self-Consciousness, and Object Independence,' *American Philosophical Quarterly* 27 (1990) 51–60; and Mark Leon, 'Rationalising Belief, *Philosophical Papers* 21 (1992) 299–314.

we regard it as true for the sake of thereby getting the truth right with respect to that proposition: to believe something is to accept it with the aim of doing so only if it really is true.

Thus, the purpose or aim with which a proposition is regarded as true is partly constitutive of the resulting attitude toward the proposition. It determines whether the proposition is being accepted hypothetically, as in assumption; playfully, as in imagination; or seriously, as in belief. These attitudes can therefore be conceived as having two tiers. The first tier, which they share and by virtue of which they differ as a group from the conative attitudes, is the attitude of regarding a proposition as true—the attitude of bare acceptance. The second tier, in which the various cognitive attitudes differ among themselves, encompasses the different aims with which a proposition can be accepted.[37]

To say that our attitude toward a proposition is partly constituted by the aim or purpose with which we accept the proposition is not to say that the aim is itself an attitude of ours, or that acceptance is an action. This point cannot be overemphasized.[38] Acceptance is a mental state whose aim may be emergent in the cognitive mechanisms by which that state is induced, sustained, and revised. For example, if our acceptance of a proposition is regulated by mechanisms performing their function of therein framing a possibility to be tested, then our acceptance may have a heuristic aim whether or not we have heuristic motives or take any action toward heuristic ends. Similarly, if our acceptance of a proposition is regulated by mechanisms performing their function of therein tracking the truth of the proposition, then it may have an epistemic aim whether or not we have or act on such an aim.[39] In short, our acceptance

---

[37] An example that can help to illustrate this conception of the propositional attitudes appears in Bernard Williams's discussion of 'Imagination and the Self' (in *Problems of the Self*, 29–31). Williams compares two men who imagine assassinating the Prime Minister in the person of Lord Salisbury. One man imagines assassinating the Prime Minister but falsely believes that Lord Salisbury occupies that position; the other man, who knows that Lord Salisbury isn't Prime Minister, nevertheless imagines him to be, while also imagining a similar assassination. "On the purely psychological level," Williams remarks, "the same visualisings, the same images, could surely occur in both cases. The difference lies rather in how the story is meant" (31). According to my account, "how the story is meant" should be understood in terms of the aim with which it is regarded as true that Lord Salisbury is Prime Minister. Each subject includes this identification in his "story," and thereby regards it as true. But one subject regards it as true for the sake of correctly identifying the Prime Minister, whereas the other regards it as true for the sake of his own entertainment.

[38] The point will be lost on those who believe that any goal-directed movement, mental or physical, automatically qualifies as an intentional action. I reject this view, as will become clear on p. 189 ff. My reasons for rejecting it are developed more fully in Chaps. 5 and 6, above. In any case, the present account of belief will be misunderstood if aims are assumed to be necessarily agential.

[39] As David Phillips has pointed out to me, the mechanisms whose function is to track the truth may employ assumptions or even fantasies along the way. Thus, whether a particular instance of acceptance is an hypothesis, fantasy, or belief cannot depend on the ultimate aim

of a proposition may be aimed at the truth by our cognitive faculties rather than ourselves.

This possibility suggests that one can have beliefs—aimed, as required, at the truth—while also being indifferent, at another level, to the truth of those beliefs. There are two ways of being indifferent to the truth, of which only one is an obstacle to believing.

To begin with, I can accept a proposition in a manner indifferent to its truth, thereby forming an assumption or fantasy rather than a belief. I am not then proceeding with indifference to the truth of a belief; I'm proceeding with indifference to the truth of what I accept, thereby falling short of belief altogether.

In another sense, however, I can be indifferent to the truth of something conceived as a belief. I cannot believe something without accepting it seriously—in an attempt, by me or my cognitive faculties, to arrive at acceptance of the truth—but I can still have further, second-order goals with respect to this attempt. For example, I can try to ensure that an attempt to accept what's true with respect to a proposition will lead to acceptance of that proposition whether it's true or not. This second-order attempt, to manipulate the outcome of a first-order attempt to accept what's true, is precisely what I undertake when I try to get myself to hold a particular belief irrespective of its truth. And in this case I am indifferent to the truth specifically of a belief, because my indifference is directed at the success of something conceived as an attempt at accepting the truth.[40]

I can thus fail to care about the truth of my beliefs. Yet if indicators of truth in a proposition are reasons for believing it, then indifference to the truth of my beliefs would seem to leave me insensitive to reasons, and hence irrational. My conception of theoretical reason would thus seem to resemble externalist conceptions of practical reason, in mandating a particular concern or inclination as required for rationality.

---

toward which it is directed. Rather, the nature of each acceptance must depend on its immediate aim, as I have tried to indicate with the words 'therein' and 'thereby': to assume that P is to accept P for the sake of thereby formulating a possibility to be tested, whereas to believe that P is to accept P for the sake of thereby accepting the truth with respect to P. (Peter Railton raises the same problem in his 'Truth, Reason, and the Regulation of Belief,' *Philosophical Issues* 5 (1994) 71–93.)

[40] As Williams noted in 'Deciding to Believe,' this account of indifference to the truth of a belief explains the difficulty of acting on that indifference. In order to end up believing the proposition that I want to believe, I must accept it in the course of an attempt to accept what is true, not an attempt merely to accept this proposition. Indifference to the truth must not seep into my first-order attempt from my second-order attitude toward its success or failure. Some psychological partitioning is therefore necessary. On the difficulty of manipulating beliefs, see also Leon.

But this appearance is misleading. The conception of reasons for belief as indicators of truth doesn't imply that indifference to the truth of my beliefs would be irrational. Indifference to the truth of my beliefs would not in fact make me insensitive to the associated reasons for believing.

Of course, evidence for the truth of some belief may not sway me toward wanting or getting myself to hold that belief, if I'm indifferent to its truth. But we don't necessarily think that indicators of truth are reasons for such second-order measures as wanting or getting myself to hold beliefs. We identify them as reasons for *believing*, which are simply reasons for accepting something in the course of an attempt to arrive at acceptance of what's true. And insofar as I or my cognitive faculties attempt to arrive at the truth on a topic, that attempt will already make me potentially sensitive to indicators of the truth; whereas if no such attempt is in the works, the topic will be one on which I am not in the business of holding beliefs, in the first place.

What provides my sensitivity to reasons for believing, then, is not a second-order aim of having true beliefs but rather the first-order aim that makes my acceptance of something into a belief. And if this first-order aim is lacking from my approach to some topic, then I am not irrationally insensitive to reasons for belief about it; I am out of the business of having beliefs about it altogether, and so I am no longer subject to reasons for belief about it at all. Thus, my conception of theoretical reason doesn't condemn this form of indifference as irrational, either.

In identifying something as a reason to believe a proposition, we are implicitly identifying it as a reason for a potential believer, someone who is in a position to believe or disbelieve the proposition at issue. Now, someone can be in a position to form a belief even though he lacks an interest in the truth of that belief—the second-order interest in the success of this attempt at accepting what's true. But he is not prepared to believe or disbelieve a proposition if he isn't prepared for an attempt to accept what's true with respect to it. Thus, he is not a potential believer with respect to a proposition—and hence not subject to reasons for believing it—in the absence of an inclination that would cause him to be swayed by indicators of its truth.

So when we say that indicators of truth are reasons for belief, we aren't making a normative judgment about whether to be inclined toward the truth; we're saying that they're reasons for someone only if he is inclined toward the truth, since we're identifying them as reasons of a kind whose universe of application is the set of potential believers, who are constitutively truth inclined. The question whether to be inclined toward the truth on some topic—and hence whether to be subject to reasons for belief about it—is left entirely open.

In some sense, theoretical reasoning now seems to fit the model of internalism. Indicators of truth count as reasons for someone to believe only if he has a cognitive inclination that makes him susceptible to their influence. And reasons that apply to someone only if he's susceptible to their influence are supposed to be internal reasons.

At this point, however, the distinction between internal and external reasons is out of its depth, so to speak. Reasons for belief are dependent on a particular inclination, all right, but they're dependent on that inclination which makes one a believer. They don't depend on one's peculiar inclinations *as* a believer—on one's second-order attitudes toward or preferences among beliefs.

Indeed, the dependence of theoretical reasons on a cognitive inclination does not justify relativizing them to particular believers at all. The inclination on which these reasons depend is constitutive of belief itself, and to that extent they are reasons simply *for belief* rather than for any particular person to believe.[41] If something counts in a particular epistemic context as a reason to believe that P, then it counts in that context as a reason simply to believe that P, and not just for this or that believer to do so, since all potential believers of P are alike in the cognitive inclination that gives application to such a reason.

The question of whether reasons for belief are internal or external reasons thus presents a false dichotomy. Reasons for belief are like internal reasons in that they exist and exert an influence only in relation to a particular inclination; but they are like external reasons in that the inclination on which they depend is embedded in the attitude of belief, so that they can count as reasons for belief per se, in abstraction from motivational differences among individual believers.

Maybe the way to understand the status of reasons for belief is to consider an analogy between belief and another enterprise that's partly constituted by a substantive aim. Consider reasons for sacrificing a pawn in the game of chess.

Reasons for sacrificing a pawn depend for their existence on a goal or aim, and in this respect they look like internal reasons. But the goal on which reasons for this move depend is partly constitutive of the move itself, because sacrificing a pawn is by definition a move in the game of chess, which is partly defined by its object; and because the move is by definition a sacrifice, which it can be only in relation to the object of the game. Reasons for sacrificing a pawn therefore exist in abstraction from the temperament of any particular player: they are reasons simply for the move itself, and in this respect they look like external reasons, too.

---

[41] Of course, reasons for belief are also relative to an informational context, and insofar as different people are in possession of different information, they will be subject to different reasons. But if the informational context is held constant, the relativity of reasons to persons disappears.

A player may have second-order aims with respect to his success or failure in a particular game of chess. He may even have the goal of losing a game—if his opponent is a sensitive eight-year-old, for example. But in order to lose a game of chess, he must stay in the game, by continuing to pursue its object, however insincerely or ineffectually. And so long as he is pursuing that object, he will have the inclination that answers to reasons for sacrificing a pawn.

A player can lose his susceptibility to those reasons only by giving up the associated object—moving his pieces around aimlessly, for example. In that case, he will in effect have quit the game: his opponent will say, not just "You're letting me win," but "You're not playing any more." Once the player has quit the game of chess, however, he has quit the only game in which pawns can be sacrificed, and his resulting insensitivity to reasons for sacrificing a pawn will not make him irrational. To someone who isn't playing chess, reasons for sacrificing a pawn simply don't apply.

In sum, reasons for sacrificing a pawn apply to anyone with the capacity to do so, irrespective of his inclinations about how to exercise that capacity. They apply to him only because he has an inclination that lends them an influence, of course, but the requisite inclination is the one that makes him a chess player, not one that determines his individual style of play.

Applying the Analogy to Practical Reasoning

I think that practical reasoning occupies the same middle ground between internalism and externalism. That is, reasons for acting apply to someone only because he has an inclination that lends them an influence, but the requisite inclination is the one that makes him an agent, not one that determines his individual course of action.

This account of practical reason simply follows the structure of theoretical reason, as analyzed above. That analysis began with the claim that belief is distinguished from other cognitive states by a substantive goal, and then it claimed that an inclination toward this goal creates the susceptibility necessary to the application of reasons for believing. Perhaps, then, action can be distinguished from other forms of behavior by a substantive goal, and an inclination toward this goal can create the susceptibility necessary to the application of reasons for acting. In that case, reasons for acting would be considerations relevant to the constitutive aim of action, just as reasons for believing are indicators of truth, which is the constitutive aim of belief. And anyone who wasn't susceptible to reasons for acting, because he had no inclination toward the relevant aim, wouldn't be in a position to act, anyway, and therefore wouldn't be subject to reasons for acting; just as anyone who has no inclination toward the truth isn't in a position to believe and isn't subject to reasons for belief.

The account rests, of course, on the initial claim that behaviors qualify as actions by virtue of having a particular aim. Let me say a word about the philosophical point of such a claim.

The point of specifying which behaviors qualify as actions is not, I think, to delineate the extension of 'action' or 'to act' as used in ordinary language. These terms are used quite loosely, in application not only to paradigm cases of action, in which human agency is exercised to its fullest, but also to marginal cases, in which agency is exercised only partially or imperfectly. The fundamental question in the philosophy of action is not how imperfect an exercise of agency can be while still qualifying as an action. The question is the nature of agency itself, and agency, like any capacity, fully reveals its nature only when fully exercised. We therefore want to know what makes for a paradigm case of action, a full-blooded action, an action par excellence.

I claim that what makes for an action, in this sense, is a constitutive aim. This claim sounds odd, to say the least. We may think that a full-blooded action must have some goal or other;[42] but we tend to think that its status as an action doesn't depend on what goal it has. Action, we tend to think, is just behavior aimed at some goal, any goal.

In my opinion, however, we are mistaken in assuming that behavior approaches full-blooded action by having a goal of the sort that varies from one action to another. Simply being goal directed is not a mark of action.

Consider a case of unintentional behavior. An old friend unexpectedly walks into your office, and surprise lights up your face: your eyes widen, a smile flashes, an exclamation escapes your lips. These reactions just happen to you, and they may even hit you with an aftershock of surprise. Now suppose, instead, that you encounter your friend on the quad, recognizing him as he approaches. You are moved to the same reactions, but you now have a chance to modulate them or compose them into an intentional expression of surprise.

Take another case of unintentional behavior. Say, a child accidentally brushes a glass off of the table, and your hand shoots out to catch it. Everything happens so fast that you see your hand catching the glass before you fully realize that the glass is falling. Now suppose, finally, that another child—an older and sassier child—hefts the glass with a smirk and calls, "Here, catch!" You then undertake the same behavior, but as a fully intentional action.

The first instance in which you catch the glass is an instance of behavior

---

[42] See, e.g., Jay Wallace, 'How to Argue about Practical Reason,' *Mind* 99 (1990) 355–85, at 359: "To act intentionally . . . is necessarily to be in a goal-directed state"; see also Smith, 'The Humean Theory of Motivation.'

directed at a goal, but it isn't a full-blooded exercise of your agency. Unlike your reflexive expression of surprise, which springs *out of* the emotion of surprise but not *toward* any purpose or goal, the reflexive extension of your hand is aimed at something—namely, preventing the glass from smashing on the floor.[43] Despite being goal directed, however, this behavior still lacks some element that's necessary to full-blooded action. So what makes for action is not simply being goal directed.

The question is what's missing from this goal-directed behavior. In my view, what's missing is some additional goal that every action shares, no matter what its other, contingent goals may be.

There is an ancient thesis along these lines, to the effect that action, no matter where it aims, must thereby aim at the good.[44] This thesis identifies a constitutive goal of action—the good—and it thus implements the strategy of analysis that I favor. But in this implementation, the strategy fails to achieve its purpose, since it doesn't avoid the twin pitfalls of internalism and externalism.[45]

The thesis that action constitutively aims at the good can be interpreted in at least two ways. It may simply mean that an action must aim at something, which consequently counts as good in the sense of being that whose attainment will make the action a success. But this sense of the word 'good' is a formal sense, denoting whatever is the aim of an action. It identifies no particular thing at which every action must aim, and hence no particular kind of consideration as capable of influencing anyone insofar as he is an agent. If the thesis uses this formal sense of the word 'good', then the considerations that it classifies as reasons will vary along with the good being aimed at. Reasons will then depend for their application on one's inclinations as an agent, as they do under internalism.

In order to avoid this consequence of internalism, the ancient thesis would have to identify a substantive goal for action, by saying that every action aims at something conceived as good in a sense independent of its being the aim. But when the thesis uses a substantive sense of the word 'good' in this manner, it characterizes action as necessarily well-intentioned, thus ruling out various kinds of perversity. To those who believe, as I do, that behavior can still qualify as action even if its end-in-view is conceived as bad, the thesis will now appear to be burdened with controversial normative commitments, like the version of externalism considered above.[46]

---

[43] The idea that some actions spring out of motives without being directed toward any ends or goals is defended by Michael Stocker, 'Values and Purposes: The Limits of Teleology and the Ends of Friendship,' *Journal of Philosophy* 78 (1981) 747–65.

[44] This view is echoed by Donald Davidson in 'How Is Weakness of the Will Possible?' in *Essays on Actions and Events*, 21–42, at 22.

[45] This problem was foreshadowed in the text accompanying n. 22, above.

[46] In adopting an evil end, the perverse agent may of course be said to make evil his good, as Satan does in *Paradise Lost* (bk. 4, line 110). But Satan makes evil his good only in the formal

The ancient thesis goes wrong, I think, in treating the constitutive aim of action as something shared or jointly promoted by all of an agent's other ends-in-view, as if it were an ultimate or all-encompassing end. If action is to be constituted by an aim, however, that aim cannot be an end at all.

An end is something conceived by an agent as a potential object of his actions. It is therefore something that one cannot have unless one already is an agent, in a position to act, and so it cannot be something that one must already have in order to occupy that position. If action is to be constituted by an aim, that aim must be, so to speak, subactional or subagential—something that a subject of mere behavior can have, and by having which he can become an agent, as his behavior becomes an action.

This subactional aim can be discerned, I think, in our contrasting pairs of behaviors. It is that which the unintentional behaviors are missing in comparison with the corresponding full-blooded actions.

Intuitively speaking, what these behaviors lack is that, while directed *at* various things, they are not directed *by* you. When the glass is brushed off the table, for example, behavior aimed at arresting its fall is initiated and completed before you know it, and so you have no chance to take control of that behavior. In the intentional instance, the same goal-directed behavior occurs, but it occurs under your control.

The kind of control at issue here is not the sensorimotor process that adjusts ongoing behavior in light of perceived progress toward a desired outcome. That process of real-time adjustment is simply eye-hand coordination, which occurs in both the intentional and the reflexive cases. What's missing from the reflexive case is conscious direction on your part, which is something other than eye-hand coordination. When goal-directed behavior proceeds under this conscious control, it becomes a full-blooded action, rather than a well-coordinated reflex.[47] And behavior that isn't directed at a goal can become an action in the same fashion. The smile that springs spontaneously from your emotion of surprise isn't aimed at any result, but it, too, can be transformed into a full-blooded action if it is brought under your conscious control.

Now, if an action comprises behavior of which you take control, then taking control of your behavior cannot itself be an action; otherwise, a vicious regress will ensue. Yet controlling your behavior is indeed an activity: it's something that you do. The reason why the falling glass leaves you no time to perform

sense that its attainment will be the criterion of his success. The fact that even Satan's actions aim at the good in this formal sense doesn't help us to identify a substantive aim that constitutes them as actions. G. E. M. Anscombe discusses this passage (*Intention* (Ithaca: Cornell Univ. Press, 1963), 75), and I have elsewhere criticized her discussion (Chap. 5, above).

[47] I do not mean that every part or aspect of the behavior must come under your conscious control in order for the behavior to constitute a full-blooded action. How you execute the catch may still be left to those reflexes which make up your skill as a catcher; that you execute a catch, however, must come under your control, or the catch won't be an action in the fullest sense.

a full-blooded action is that, although it leaves you time to stick out your hand, it doesn't leave you time to do something else that's essential to a full-blooded action—that is, to exercise conscious control of your catch. Hence when you catch the glass intentionally, you must be doing two things: extending your hand in order to avert a mishap and exercising control over that behavior.

Let me reiterate that I am using the noun 'activity' and the verb 'to do' in senses that do not imply the performance of a full-blooded action. To suggest that an action comprises behavior on which you perform the action of exercising control would be absurd. But you do many things that aren't actions— such as when you reflexively stick out your hand to catch a falling glass or smile out of surprise. And exercising conscious control over your behavior is indeed something that you do, in this thin sense of the verb.

I therefore suggest that our ordinary concept of a full-blooded action is in fact the concept of two, hierarchically related activities. Action is like the corporate enterprise of work performed under management: it's behavior executed under conscious control. And just as the corporate enterprise includes both a basic work activity and the higher-order activity of managing that work (neither of which is itself a corporate enterprise), so full-blooded action comprises both a basic activity and the higher-order activity of controlling it (neither of which is itself an action).

This analysis of action suggests how action might have a constitutive goal. According to the analysis, various actions involve various behaviors—directed, in many cases, at various goals—but they also share an additional, higher-order activity, the activity of consciously directing these behaviors. This activity is constitutive of action, in the sense that its addition is what makes a full-blooded action out of a merely reflexive or unintentional movement. If this higher-order activity entails the pursuit of a goal, then there may indeed be a constitutive goal of action.[48]

What I have in mind here is not an ulterior goal or aim toward which behavior is consciously directed, as a corporation's work activity might be managed toward the end of maximizing profits. The executive officers can still manage the work of a corporation without having the goal of profit maximization, in particular, and so this goal is not itself essential to work's being performed under management. Similarly, a goal toward which behavior is consciously directed may not be essential to the behavior's being consciously directed, insofar as behavior might be consciously directed at other goals or no goal in particular.

---

[48] I have elsewhere presented an independent argument for this thesis (Chap. 6, above). The idea that practical reason has motives of its own, directed at the control of one's behavior, is contained in the theory of motivation attributed to Plato by John Cooper, 'Plato's Theory of Human Motivation,' *History of Philosophy Quarterly* 1 (1984) 3–21.

What I have in mind is a goal that must be pursued if behavior is to be consciously directed at all. This goal will not be one of the agent's ends-in-view, nor will it be something on which those ends converge. Rather, it will be something whose pursuit is ancillary to theirs—something whose pursuit transforms them, from outcomes sought unconsciously or reflexively, into ends at which action is consciously directed.

The Constitutive Goal of Action

What is this goal? A hint lies in the fact that consciously controlling one's behavior is not something that one can do without aiming to.[49] Maybe, then, the aim without which there is no conscious control of behavior is simply the aim of being in conscious control of one's behavior. If so, then the constitutive aim of action will turn out, in Kantian fashion, to be autonomy.[50] And considerations will turn out to qualify as reasons—also in Kantian fashion—by virtue of their relevance to our autonomy rather than their relevance to our interests or our good.[51]

These remarks are merely suggestive at best, and this is not the place to develop them into a full account of autonomy or its role as the constitutive goal of action.[52] I can only sketch how they might be developed.

My sketch begins with the conception of autonomy as conscious control over one's behavior. Consciously controlling one's behavior involves two elements: being conscious of one's behavior and controlling it. How are these elements connected?

One possibility is that they aren't connected at all. Conscious control might just be the sum of two independent elements, control over what one is doing and consciousness of what one is doing. Another possibility is that

---

[49] Bernard Williams has pointed out to me that one can consciously control one's behavior while aiming not to—as, for example, when one unsuccessfully tries to let one's reflexes or instincts take over. But this point strikes me as compatible with my claim that one cannot consciously control one's behavior without aiming to. Trying not to control one's behavior involves a second-order goal, of relaxing one's first-order efforts at control. If one continues to control one's behavior while trying not to, the reason is that one continues to aim at controlling it while trying not to persist in that aim. (Remember that the aims under discussion here may be sub-agential. See p. 191, above).

[50] Thanks to Chris Korsgaard for publicly daring me to express this thought.

[51] Stephen Darwall has proposed a similar conception of reasons, under the name "autonomist internalism" ('Autonomist Internalism and the Justification of Morals,' *Nous* 24 (1990) 257–68). Of course, considerations may be relevant to our autonomy because of their relevance to our interests. The point is that their relevance to autonomy will be what makes them reasons for acting.

[52] See my *Practical Reflection* (Princeton, N.J.: Princeton Univ. Press, 1989); and Chap. 7.

exercising control over one's behavior is what brings it to consciousness. One might control what one is doing and thereby become conscious of that behavior.

The problem with these possibilities is that they would leave an agent's knowledge of his behavior dependent on the usual inbound channels, such as perception of the behavior itself or introspection on the process by which it is directed. And as many philosophers have noted, an agent's knowledge of his behavior is not receptive knowledge: an agent knows what he is doing, as they say, without observation.[53]

The work of these philosophers points to a third possibility for the relation between self-control and self-awareness. Maybe consciousness of what one is doing is that by which one exerts control. Consciously controlling one's behavior would then be—not just controlling it and also, or thereby, becoming conscious of it—but rather having a *controlling consciousness* of one's behavior, a guiding awareness of what one is doing. This possibility would account not only for an agent's self-control but also for the quality of his self-awareness, since his knowledge of what he was doing would be, so to speak, directive rather than receptive knowledge.[54]

But how can knowledge be directive? For the answer, let me return to my earlier account of cognition. (I'll give the answer in this section and then illustrate it in the next.)

Consciousness or knowledge must be a cognitive state, and so it must involve regarding propositions as true rather than as to be made true. It must also be a serious cognitive state, regarding propositions as true in an attempt thereby to get the truth right. Indeed, the success that's implied in the concept of consciousness or knowledge is success in this very attempt, to regard as true what really is true.

But there are two ways of attempting to regard as true, or accept, what really is true. One way is to accept a proposition in response to its being true; the other is to accept a proposition in such a way as to make it true. Note that the latter method does not entail regarding the proposition as *to be made* true. It

---

[53] See Anscombe, *Intention*; Stuart Hampshire, *Freedom of the Individual* (Princeton, N.J.: Princeton Univ. Press, 1975), ch. 3; Brian O'Shaughnessy, *The Will: A Dual Aspect Theory* (Cambridge: Cambridge Univ. Press, 1980), ch. 8. See also Ludwig Wittgenstein, *Philosophical Investigations*, trans. G. E. M. Anscombe (Oxford: Blackwell, 1967), secs. 627 ff.

[54] Compare the ancient and medieval notion of "practical knowledge," which is "the cause of what it understands" (Aquinas, *Summa Theologica*, Ia IIae, Q3, art. 5, obj. 1). Anscombe discusses this notion in the last two paragraphs of her paper 'Thought and Action in Aristotle' (in *New Essays on Plato and Aristotle*, ed. R. Bambrough (London: Routledge & Kegan Paul, 1965), 143–58), thereby picking up a theme that was left undeveloped in *Intention*, 1–5, 56–58, 87. See also David Pears, *Motivated Irrationality* (Oxford: Clarendon, 1984), ch. 8; and Arthur Danto, 'Action, Knowledge, and Representation,' in *Action Theory*, ed. Myles Brand and Douglas Walton (Dordrecht: Reidel, 1976), 11–25.

entails attempting to make the proposition true by regarding it as such, but attempting to make a proposition true by regarding it as true is quite different from regarding it as to be made true. The proposition is regarded as fact, not *faciendum*, and so it is accepted, in a cognitive rather than conative attitude. What's more, the proposition is accepted seriously, not hypothetically or frivolously. For in attempting to accept something so as to make it true, one attempts to reach the position of accepting a genuine truth, no less than when one attempts to accept something in response to its being true. In either case, one's acceptance aims at correspondence between what's regarded as true and what is true, and so it is a serious cognitive attitude, whose success deserves to be called knowledge.[55]

How can one regard a proposition as true in such a way as to make it true? Well, when one accepts a proposition in response to its truth, one registers the influence of evidence and other reasons for belief, thereby manifesting an inclination to conform one's acceptance to the facts. Accepting a proposition in such a way as to make it true would simply require a converse inclination, to conform the facts to one's acceptance. And one can indeed be inclined to conform the facts to one's acceptance, if the proposition accepted is about one's own behavior. One need only be inclined to do what one accepts that one will do. If one has this inclination, then accepting that one will do something can be a way of making this proposition true, and it can therefore be an attempt at accepting the truth.

This admittedly convoluted proposal can be applied to the contrast between your reflexively and intentionally catching that glass. In both cases, your desire to save the glass causes your hand to extend. In both cases, you're aware of this causal sequence, since you're aware of extending your hand in order to save the glass. But in only one of the cases is your knowledge directive, or your behavior autonomous.

---

[55] Here I am expanding on two themes that I have discussed elsewhere. First, I am expanding an earlier critique of the traditional notion of direction of fit (in Chap. 5, above). In my view, this notion conflates two different distinctions. One is the distinction between the cognitive and the conative—the distinction between accepting, or regarding as true, and approving, or regarding as to be made true. The other is a distinction between the receptive and the directive, which are two different ways of attempting to accept what's true—namely, by accepting so as to reflect the truth, and by accepting so as to create the truth. If these distinctions are conflated under the heading "direction of fit," then one and the same mental state can appear to have two different directions of fit, since a subject can attempt to accept what's true by accepting something so as to make it true. The resulting state is cognitive rather than conative, but directive rather than receptive: it's directive cognition. I would claim that this state of directive cognition is the state of intending to act. This is the second theme on which I am currently expanding. In the past, I have said that an intention is a self-fulfilling and self-referring belief (*Practical Reflection*, ch. 4; see also Chap. 9, below). The present discussion explains why I call it a belief, but also why I can dispense with that label. What matters is that intention is a state of directive cognition, not whether that state should be called belief.

When you extend your hand reflexively, you react before you know it, but then you observe your reaction. Extending your hand in order to save the glass causes you to accept the proposition that you're doing so. When you react intentionally, however, acceptance precedes behavior: you accept that you'll extend your hand to save the glass, and this acceptance is what prompts you to do so.

In the latter case as well as the former, your acceptance is an attempt to accept something true. You're not just hypothesizing or fantasizing that you'll extend your hand; you're seriously regarding it as true that you will extend it. Of course, your acceptance of this proposition is not an attempt to accept something that's true antecedently; it's an attempt to accept something whose truth will follow as a result. But it is not therefore less serious as an attempt to accept a truth. If the proposition accepted comes true, then its acceptance is a cognitive success—an instance of directive knowledge.

In sum, instead of reacting before you know it, you react after and because you know it, and that's what makes your behavior an autonomous action. You act autonomously because you extend your hand in, and out of, a knowledge of what you're doing.

But why would your extending a hand to save the glass result from your accepting that you would do so?

Suppose that you have an inclination toward being in conscious control of your next move. This inclination will inhibit you from doing anything out of other motives until you've accepted that you're going to—precisely so that you'll do it only after and because you know it, and hence under conscious control. Once you accept that you're going to do something, however, the inclination toward being in conscious control will reinforce your other motives for doing it, since doing what you've accepted you'll do is what puts consciousness in control. Your inclination toward conscious control is thus converted, from an inhibition against doing something into a motive in favor of doing it, by your accepting that you'll do it. Accepting that you'll extend your hand to save the glass can therefore prompt you to do so.

Here, then, is how autonomy can serve as the constitutive goal of action. The goal-directed movement of your hand comes under your conscious control because it is prompted by your accepting that you will perform such a movement. And it is prompted by that acceptance because of your inclination toward conscious control of what you're doing—which is just an inclination toward autonomy. Your movement thus becomes autonomous precisely by manifesting your inclination toward autonomy; and in becoming autonomous, it becomes a full-blooded action. A full-blooded action is therefore behavior that manifests your inclination toward autonomy, just as a belief is a cognitive attitude that manifests your inclination toward the truth.

My view is that your inclination toward the constitutive goal of action also mediates the influence of your reasons for acting, just as your inclination toward the truth mediates the influence of your reasons for belief. Your reasons for acting can be displayed as the premises of a practical inference:

> I want to save that glass.
> I could save the glass by extending my hand.
> So I'll extend my hand.

Since the premises of this inference are about how to fulfill a desire of yours, they sound like reasons that Williams would call internal. But in my view, they don't influence you in quite the way that internal reasons are supposed to.

Here is how internal reasons are supposed to work. The first premise of your inference is about a desire of yours: "I want to save that glass." The second premise is about the means to the object of that desire: "I could save the glass by extending my hand." The desire mentioned in the first premise and the belief expressed in the second combine to motivate the action mentioned in your conclusion: "So I'll extend my hand." According to the internalist tradition, this process of motivation is the very process whereby reasons for acting exert their influence as reasons.

This conception of how reasons exert their influence encourages a particular reading of the statements displayed above. Since the influence of reasons is conceived as the motivational influence of desire and belief, and since the second premise expresses the operative belief, the first premise is read as expressing the associated desire.[56] Similarly, the conclusion is sometimes read as expressing—or standing in for—the action itself, which is said to be the real conclusion of your inference.[57] The three displayed statements are thus interpreted as expressions of your reasons and of the action that they influence you to perform.

I don't dispute the traditional account of how desire and belief motivate behavior. My quarrel is with the claim that when desire and belief motivate behavior, they exert the influence of reasons.[58] You extend your hand, I agree, out of a desire for something and a belief about how to attain it. But you can extend your hand out of a desire and belief even when you do so reflexively, without knowing what you're doing or why, and hence without the benefit of practical reasoning.

In my view, extending your hand out of a desire and belief is the underlying behavior over which you may or may not exercise conscious control—the

---

[56] See Davidson, 'Intending,' In *Essays on Actions and Events*, 83–102, at 86. Because Davidson thinks that this premise should express your desire, he would reformulate it, from "I want to save that glass" to "Saving that glass would be desirable."

[57] Davidson, 'How Is Weakness of the Will Possible?', 32; and 'Intending,' 98–99.

[58] This quarrel is a continuation of Chaps. 5 and 6, above.

underlying work that may or may not come under your executive management. And practical reasoning is the process by which you exercise conscious control over this activity in some cases but not others. If you extend your hand without any guiding knowledge of what you're doing, then even though your behavior is motivated by a desire and belief, it isn't under your conscious control, and so it isn't a full-blooded action. Your behavior amounts to a full-blooded action only when it is performed in, and out of, a knowledge of what you're doing— or, as I have said, after and because you know it.[59]

This view of practical reasoning encourages a different interpretation of the statements displayed above. The first premise expresses a desire-based reason, in my view, but the reason expressed is not the desire itself. The reason expressed by "I want to save that glass" is your recognition of the desire.

This recognition is a reason because, together with the belief expressed in your second premise, it forms a potentially guiding awareness of what you would be doing in extending your hand. The awareness that you want to save the glass, and that extending your hand would save it, puts you in a position to frame a piece of directive knowledge—"I'm extending my hand in order to save the glass"—a proposition that you can now make true by accepting it. Your awareness of the desire thus presents the behavior of extending your hand in a form prepared for your conscious control, as a potential object of your directive grasp. It presents the behavior, if you will, as fit for (en)action, given the constitutive aim of action, just as theoretical reasons present a proposition as fit for belief, given the constitutive aim of belief.

This view of practical reasoning requires far more elaboration and defense than I can offer here. Its only relevance to this article is that it implements the compromise that I favor between internalism and externalism. For according to this view, even desire-based reasons for acting derive their influence from an inclination other than the desires on which they are based.

The reasons displayed above are desire based in the sense that they mention your desire to save the glass and the means to fulfilling that desire. Yet their influence as reasons is not mediated by the desire that they mention.

Your desire to save the glass does exert a motivational influence in this example. But its influence as a motive contributes to the underlying activity of

---

[59] Note that in my account, your autonomy isn't an ability to control the motions of your hand; it's an ability to control your behavior, which is bodily motion psychologically understood, in terms of its motivation. Even a robot can control whether its hand moves. It takes an autonomous agent to control whether he moves his hand out of a desire to save a glass. The object of autonomous control is thus the entire behavior, comprising motivation as well as movement. The same point can be put in (somewhat) Kantian terms, as follows. Acting autonomously isn't just moving in accordance with one's idea of a movement; it's acting in accordance with one's idea of a law—in this case, the law of motivation.

extending your hand in order to save the glass—the activity that comes under the control of your practical reasoning. And the contribution of your reasons to the control of this activity is distinct from the contribution of your motives to the activity itself.

What exerts the influence of a reason in this example is the recognition that you want to save the glass. And this recognition doesn't influence you by engaging your desire to save the glass. Wanting to save the glass is a motive that can be engaged by considerations about how to save it, not by the recognition that you want to. The recognition that you want to save the glass engages a different inclination, your inclination toward autonomy—toward behaving in, and out of, a knowledge of what you're doing. And it thereby exerts a rational influence distinct from the motivational influence of the desire that it's about.

Now, if desire-based reasons derive their influence from something other than the desires on which they are based, then perhaps the same influence is available to considerations that aren't based on desires at all. Perhaps considerations that aren't about your inclinations can still provide potentially directive knowledge.

Such considerations would still have the influence of reasons, by virtue of their capacity to engage your inclination toward autonomy. But they wouldn't depend for their influence on the inclinations that differentiate you from any other agent, and they wouldn't be about such inclinations, either. They might therefore be reasons that Williams would call external.

My thesis, in any case, is that reasons for acting shouldn't be classified as external or internal, since they don't conform to the assumptions underwriting the use of these terms. A reason applies only to those whom it can influence, but its application is not therefore limited to agents of a particular temperament. The inclination that makes one susceptible to a reason for acting is just the inclination that makes one an agent.

9

How to Share an Intention[1]

Literally sharing a single intention is easier than it seems—and fortunately so, since it seems quite impossible, at least to some philosophers.

Philosophical puzzlement about how to share an intention doesn't inhibit us from speaking of shared intention in daily life. When the Dean asks what the Philosophy Department intends to do about a vacancy in its ranks, she seems to be asking seventeen people to participate in a single intention. She is certainly not envisioning that the seventeen members of the department will arrive at seventeen individual intentions that somehow converge. And what rules out this possibility is not just that convergence among these particular people is unlikely; it's that none of them is in a position to have an individual intention, rather than an individual preference, about how the vacancy is to be filled. How to fill the vacancy is up to the department, and so any intention on the subject must be formed and held by the group as a whole. The trick of sharing a single intention is thus essential to what the Dean has in mind.

The question is how an intention can subsist in a subject so motley as seventeen philosophers—or even two reasonable people. An intention, after all, is the state in virtue of which someone is said to have made up his mind. How can several different minds submit themselves to a single making up?

One way to answer this question would be to spell out necessary and sufficient conditions for the sharing of an intention, but my ambitions are more modest. I will be satisfied with finding a single instance that can convincingly be characterized as one in which an intention is shared. How the features of

[1] This chapter was originally published in *Philosophy and Phenomenological Research* 57 (1997) 29–50 and is reprinted by permission of the International Phenomenological Society. Portions of this chapter were contained in a response to Michael Bratman's 'Shared Intention,' which was delivered at a conference at the University of Chicago in memory of Alan Donagan. I am grateful to Bratman and other participants at the conference for valuable comments and suggestions. (Bratman's paper appeared in *Ethics* 104 (1993) 97–113.) An early draft of this chapter was presented at the 1993 meetings of the APA, Pacific Division, in a symposium with Bratman and Margaret Gilbert. On that occasion I received helpful comments not only from Bratman and Gilbert but also from: Kent Bach, Annette Baier, Rachel Cohon, Eric Gampel, Ron Laymon, Al Mele, and Harry Silverstein. Thanks also to Jennifer Church, Roger Squires, and an anonymous referee for comments and discussion.

such an instance are to be generalized into an analysis of shared intention will not be my concern.

What has made some philosophers skeptical about literally sharing an intention is that intention is a mental state or event, and minds belong to individual persons. As John Searle puts it, "[T]alk of group minds . . . [is] at best mysterious and at worst incoherent. Most empirically minded philosophers think that such phenomena must reduce to individual intentionality."[2] Similarly, Michael Bratman says, "[A] shared intention is not an attitude in the mind of some superagent."[3]

An apparent voice of dissent comes from Margaret Gilbert, who is willing to speak of a "plural subject," produced by a "pool of wills."[4] Surely, a truly "plural subject" ought to be a single subject that isn't singular—or, if you like, a plural subject that isn't just a plurality of subjects. That is, it ought to involve two or more subjects who combine in such a way as to constitute one subject, just as two or more referents combine to constitute one referent when subsumed under a plural pronoun. Talk of plural subjects therefore sounds perilously close to talk of group minds or superagents.

Although Gilbert explains how two or more subjects combine to form what she calls a plural subject, she doesn't fully explain how the combination qualifies, in its own right, as a subject. The possibility therefore remains that Gilbert, too, is using talk of a plural subject as a mere *façon de parler*, a convenient way of summarizing facts about a collection of subjects who never actually meld.

Gilbert says that a plural subject comes into being when "each person expresses a form of *conditional commitment* such that (as is understood) only when *everyone* has done similarly is *anyone* committed."[5] Yet if this arrangement is just a collection of well coordinated commitments, then it would seem to yield nothing more than a collection of well coordinated subjects. A pool of

---

[2] 'Collective Intentions and Actions,' in *Intentions in Communication*, ed. Philip R. Cohen, Jerry Morgan, and Martha E. Pollack (Cambridge, Mass.: MIT Press, 1990), 404.

[3] 'Shared Intention,' 99.

[4] 'Walking Together; a Paradigmatic Social Phenomenon,' *Midwest Studies in Philosophy* 15 (1990) 1–14, 7. See also Gilbert's *On Social Facts* (Princeton: Princeton Univ. Press, 1992). Note that Gilbert thinks of shared intention as requiring more than a "pool of wills." For Gilbert, the pooling of wills is the general condition for producing a "plural subject," which can be the subject of shared intention, shared belief, or various other shared states and activities. A shared intention, according to Gilbert, requires not just the pooling of wills but the pooling of wills that are embodied, specifically, in commitments *to intend*; whereas a shared belief requires the pooling of commitments to believe; and so on.

Although I sympathize with Gilbert's desire to explain the sharing of intentional states in general, I think that her interest in generality has led to an account of shared intention that is, in a sense, redundant. Anything that qualifies as a pool of wills, I think, already *is* a shared intention, without those wills' having to be commitments to intend. I shall therefore be defending Gilbert's conception of the pooling of wills rather than her conception of shared intention.

[5] *Ibid.*, 7.

wills can hardly produce a composite subject if it fails to constitute, in itself, a composite will. And Gilbert doesn't explain how a single will can be forged from the wills of different individuals.

I want to fill in this gap in Gilbert's view, by showing how distinct intentions held by different people can add up to a single token of intention, jointly held. Surprisingly, perhaps, the materials with which to demonstrate this possibility are to be found in Searle's conception of intention. I believe that Searle's account of shared intention is not entirely faithful to his own conception of what an intention is. A more faithful application of Searle's fundamental conception yields the conclusion that talk of literally shared intention is neither mysterious nor incoherent.

Before applying Searle's conception, however, I want to examine a different and, in my view, more difficult challenge to the notion of sharing an intention. For I believe that the discussion of shared intention has not yet pinpointed what is problematic about this notion. What's problematic, I think, is not the idea of sharing a mental item but rather the idea of sharing the particular kind of item that intention is.

As Michael Bratman pointed out in his ingenious paper 'Two Faces of Intention,'[6] there must be a difference between the mental state of having a plan and that of having a goal, although either state can be called an intention, in one or another sense of the term.[7] Bratman argues that an agent can rationally have two goals that he knows to be mutually incompatible, in the sense that they cannot both be attained; for he can aim at both and "let the world decide" which one he attains in fact. But an agent cannot rationally plan to produce two outcomes that he knows to be incompatible, since rationality forbids him to have inconsistent plans.

Thus, for example, you can rationally aim to win a research fellowship while also aiming to receive a visiting professorship in the same year, even though you know that you cannot in fact receive both at once; for you can simply let the relevant institutions decide which, if either, you are to receive. But you cannot rationally plan to get a fellowship while also planning to get a visiting appointment, given your knowledge of their incompatibility.

As you update your *curriculum vitae*, you can be described as acting both with the intention of getting a fellowship and with the intention of getting a visiting professorship, in a broad sense of the word 'intention' that applies to any goal or purpose with which you act. But Bratman points out that there is a narrow sense of 'intention' that's confined to plans and other, plan-like com-

---

[6] *The Philosophical Review* 93 (1984) 375–405.

[7] On the ambiguity of 'intention' see Gilbert Harman, 'Willing and Intending,' in *Philosophical Grounds of Rationality: Intentions, Categories, Ends*, ed. Richard E. Grandy and Richard Warner (Oxford: Oxford Univ. Press, 1986), 363–80; and *Change in View: Principles of Reasoning* (Cambridge, Mass.: MIT Press, 1986), ch. 8.

mitments to act. In this sense, you cannot intend to get both awards if you know that you can't get both. Indeed, you probably cannot intend, in this sense, to get either, since you're well aware that whether you get them isn't up to you.

This last observation helps to explain why intentions thus narrowly defined are subject to more exacting rational constraints than goals.[8] (I shall follow Bratman in adopting the narrower definition as the default for the word 'intention.')

Your intentions, so defined, are the attitudes that resolve deliberative questions, thereby settling issues that are up to you. If an issue isn't up to you, then you are not in a position to settle it, and so you face no deliberative question about it. But if an issue is up to you, then you are in a position to settle it, and there is consequently a deliberative question for you as to how it will turn out.[9] In resolving this deliberative question, you will arrive at an attitude that settles the issue both actually and notionally. That is, the presence of this attitude will cause the issue to turn out one way rather than another, thus resolving it in fact; while the attitude will also represent the issue as turning out one way rather than another, thereby resolving it in your mind. This issue-resolving attitude is an intention, in the usage that I have now adopted.

Having a goal doesn't resolve anything, in either sense. Your having the goal of getting a fellowship doesn't settle whether you will in fact get it, nor does it constitute your viewing this issue as settled. Your having a goal merely motivates you to undertake various measures believed conducive to the goal— including measures of deliberation and planning. (Of course, if you have the goal of getting the fellowship, then you can also form the intention of *trying* to get it, since whether you try is still up to you; but intending to make an attempt at doing something is not the same as intending to do it.)[10]

---

[8] I discuss this issue in my review of Bratman's first book, *Philosophical Review* 100 (1991) 277–84, 282–4. Note that the distinction I draw here between goal and intention corresponds to that between *boulesis* ("wish") and *prohairesis* ("choice"), as they are contrasted by Aristotle in *Nicomachean Ethics* III.ii. 7–11. Aristotle says that choice is confined to matters that are "up to us" (*ta eph' hemin*), such as which means to adopt toward an end; whereas wish is often directed at the end itself, whose attainment is not within our control. As Aristotle puts it, we wish to be happy, and we choose means to happiness, but we cannot choose to be happy; we can only wish it. Note, again, that the English word 'intention' is often used for both phenomena. We would say not only that we intend (i.e., choose) to adopt the means but also that we adopt them with the intention (i.e., in the hope or wish) of attaining the end. Hence we use 'intention' and its cognates for both *prohairesis* and *boulesis*.

[9] For the idea that an agent can form intentions only on issues that are (or at least appear to be) up to him, see Annette Baier, 'Act and Intent,' *Journal of Philosophy* 67 (1970) 648–58. Baier has recently applied this idea to the problem of shared intention in much the same way as I do: 'Doing Things with Others: the Mental Commons' (MS).

[10] David Pears argues that the intention of trying to do something cannot be distinguished from the intention of doing it, since "if I were asked whether I had done what I had intended to do when I had tried and failed, I would give a negative answer" ('Intention and Belief,' in *Essays on Davidson*, ed. Bruce Vermazen and Merrill B. Hintikka (Oxford: Clarendon Press, 1985), 86). (See also Hugh McCann, 'Rationality and the Range of Intention,' *Midwest Studies in Philosophy* 10 (1986) 191–211.) I think that Pears is falling prey here to the ambiguity of

The reason why you cannot rationally intend to do things that you regard as incompatible is that you cannot actually settle matters, or rationally regard them as having been settled, in ways that aren't compatible. The reason why you can rationally have incompatible goals is that having a goal settles nothing. So long as practical issues remain unresolved, they can be pushed toward incompatible resolutions; they just can't be resolved incompatibly, or rationally regarded as having been so resolved. That's why intentions and goals are subject to different rational constraints.

These reflections cast doubt, in my opinion, on one attractive strategy for explaining how intentions can be shared. This strategy is to imagine two or more agents as individually holding different token intentions of the same type, by holding intentions formulated in the first-person plural. The idea is that you and I can partake in the same intention if there is something that each of us individually intends that "we" are going to do.[11] The problem with this

the word 'intention.' If someone tries to do something, then success is ordinarily his goal, and so it is what he intends, in one sense of the word. But it isn't what he intends in the sense of his being settled upon it; for if he could simply have settled upon succeeding, then he wouldn't have needed to think of himself as engaged in a mere attempt. The question to which Pears envisions giving a negative answer is the question whether he has attained his goal. If asked, by a more subtle questioner, whether he has done what he was *settled on* doing, he might answer in the affirmative: "All that I was in a position to settle on was an attempt, and *that* I have done."

[11] This strategy is incorporated into the views of Searle and Bratman. In response to the objection that I raise here (and to similar objections raised by others), Bratman has written a paper demonstrating that an intention about what "we" will do, if held by each agent conditionally on being held by the other, can indeed allocate discretion appropriately, so that each agent's intention settles matters that are up to him (Bratman, 'I Intend that We *J*,' in G. Holmstron-Hintikka and R. Tuomela (eds.), *Contemporary Action Theory*, vol. ii (Dordrecht: Kluwer, 1997), 49–63; reprinted in Bratman, *Faces of Intention: Selected Essays on Intention and Agency* (Cambridge: Cambridge Univ. Press, 1999), 142–61). Because Bratman quotes and discusses my objection, I have let it stand, despite being convinced that he has successfully answered it. In light of his paper, I would now be inclined to frame a less ambitious objection, to the effect that attributing unconditional "we" intentions does not solve the problem of shared discretion but merely presents it in a new form—albeit a form in which, as Bratman has now shown, it can be solved, by making the intentions mutually conditional. I would add that Bratman's solution, which relies on making the tokens of a "we" intention mutually dependent, is consistent with the solution (due to Margaret Gilbert) that I defend below. I discuss these issues further in a review of Bratman's *Faces of Intention*, to appear in *The Philosophical Quarterly*.

Tuomela also speaks of "we-intentions," but he does not conceive of them as intentions framed in the first-person plural. As conceived by Tuomela, we-intentions arise when each individual in a group intends to do his share in some common activity, and various conditions of belief and common knowledge are satisfied. Although Tuomela sometimes characterizes the intentions in such a case as having the form 'We will do it,' they would seem instead to have the form "I will do my part in it." Tuomela, 'What are Joint Intentions?', in *Philosophy and the Cognitive Sciences*, ed. R. Casati and G. White (Austrian Ludwig Wittgenstein Association, 1993), 543–7; 'We Will Do It: An Analysis of Group Intentions,' *Philosophy and Phenomenological Research* 51 (1991) 249–77; 'Actions by Collectives,' *Philosophical Perspectives* 3 (1989) 471–96; Tuomela and Miller, 'We-Intentions,' *Philosophical Studies* 53 (1988) 115–37.

analysis of shared intention is that it yields, so to speak, too many chiefs and too few braves, or too many cooks and too little broth.

There is nothing problematic about first-person-plural intentions in themselves. One person can decide or plan the behavior of a group, for example, if he holds authority or control over the behavior of people other than himself. If you will do whatever I tell you to do, then what you'll do is up to me, and I am in a position to make decisions about it. As your boss or commanding officer or master, then, I am in a position to decide what you and I will do together, and so I am in a position to form intentions about what "we" will do.

But shared intention is not supposed to be a matter of one person's deciding or planning the activities of a group; it's supposed to be a matter of shared *intending*, in which each member of the group participates equally in forming and maintaining the intention, fully recognizing the others as equal participants. What we are going to do is supposed to be determined by you and me jointly, in this case; and each of us is supposed to regard the issue as being thus jointly determined.

The problem about sharing this role is that one person's exercise of discretion over some issue would seem to exclude any other person from exercising discretion over the same issue. That is, if I decide that you are going to do something, then I cannot think that whether you're going to do it remains up to you; whereas if I want to leave it up to you, I cannot simultaneously regard myself as having decided it. If I am to settle the matter, I cannot think of you as having settled it first or as being in a position to settle it later; whereas if I am to leave you to settle it, I must not preempt you by settling it myself.

Yet framing an intention as to what "we" are going to do together would seem to entail settling what you are going to do with me as well as what I am going to do with you. And insofar as either participant thus purports to settle what both will do, he would seem to leave no discretion to the other. The model of first-person-plural intentions requires each of us to intend that we will do something, as if he were in fact settling the issue for both of us. Yet how can I frame the intention that "we" are going to act, if I simultaneously regard the matter as being partly up to you? And how can I continue to regard the matter as partly up to you, if I have already decided that we really *are* going to act? The model seems to require the exercise of more discretion than there is to go around.

What makes shared intention a puzzling phenomenon, then, is that the logical space of decisionmaking is open only to those who are in a position to resolve an issue, and it admits only one resolution per issue. Shared intention therefore involves the sharing of something that ordinarily seems indivisible.

Suppose that we jointly decide to lift a heavy sofa together. We thereby exercise a kind of joint discretion over the issue of whether the sofa will leave the ground. The interesting question is precisely how two people can jointly exercise discretion over a single issue. The answer cannot be that each of us exercises full discretion over the issue individually, as we would have to do if each of us were to intend that "we" will lift the sofa. Discretion cannot be shared by being multiplied in this way, since no issue can be settled by each of two people at once.

Of course, each of us can exercise discretion over a part of the sofa-moving operation, I deciding whether to lift my end of the sofa, and you deciding whether to lift yours. But in that case, we wouldn't really be sharing an intention; we would be holding different intentions that yielded a single result. This result might in fact be intended in the broad sense that encompasses goals. For I might lift my end of the sofa in the hope that you would lift yours, and you might lift your end in the hope that I would lift mine—in which case, the sofa's leaving the ground would be a goal for each of us. But neither of us would have settled whether the sofa would leave the ground, that outcome being up to neither of us individually; and so neither of us would have intended that outcome in the stricter sense of the word.[12]

Holding different, coordinated intentions in the pursuit of a common goal may turn out to be the closest that people can come to sharing an intention. If so, then the phenomenon holds no mystery, since the logical space of goals is less exclusive than that of intentions. Even if two people cannot individually settle one and the same issue, they can easily have one and the same outcome as their individual goals. Settling different issues in the pursuit of one goal is thus unproblematic.

Precisely because it's unproblematic, however, the sharing of goals is of little philosophical interest. What's interesting is the possibility that two or more people can somehow share, not the goal of producing a particular outcome, but rather discretion as to whether the outcome will occur.

Gilbert's account of pooled wills is the only one, to my knowledge, that doesn't portray the participants either as holding similar intentions that preempt one another or as holding disparate intentions with nothing in common but a goal. It's the only account in which the participants manage to exercise shared discretion over a single issue.[13]

The way they accomplish this feat, in Gilbert's account, is by individually exercising conditional discretion over the issue, in such a way that their conditionally settling the issue separately adds up to their categorically settling it together. As I have said, I think that Gilbert is correct about how this pooling

[12] Of course, I can settle whether the sofa will leave the ground if (or given that) you will lift your end; and you can settle whether the sofa will leave the ground if (or given that) I will lift mine. But the question is precisely how our individually settling these slightly different issues can involve a shared intention by which we jointly settle one and the same issue.

[13] But see n. 11, above.

of wills occurs. But she doesn't fully explain how individual exercises of conditional discretion add up to something that qualifies as a joint exercise of categorical discretion—how a collection of wills becomes one collective will. I want to clarify this feature of Gilbert's account, by applying Searle's theory of intention.

Searle's theory of intention is appropriate to the task because it picks out the features that make intention an exercise of discretion, which is what seems so difficult to share. According to Searle, an effective intention is a mental representation that causes behavior by representing itself as causing it.[14] That is, when I effectively intend to take a walk, I represent this very representation as causing me to take a walk, and this self-referring representation causes me to take a walk.[15]

This representation settles the question whether I am going to take a walk, and it settles the question, as an intention should, both actually and notionally. It settles the question notionally because it represents my taking a walk as resulting from this very representation; and it settles the question in fact by causing me to take a walk, just as it represents.

My power to settle an issue in this fashion is what we're talking about, I believe, when we say that the issue is up to me. For I am entitled, by virtue of this power, to think of myself either as taking a walk or not, insofar as either thought would cause me to behave accordingly. From my perspective, then, there is no antecedently right answer to the question whether I am going to take a walk—nothing that I must think on pain of being wrong—since the right answer will be whatever I think. And that's just what it is, I believe, for an issue to be up to me.[16]

Searle's analysis thus lays bare how an intention constitutes an exercise of discretion—that is, an agent's settling of an issue that is up to him. And if the phenomenon described in this analysis can somehow straddle the boundaries between people, then the problem of shared discretion will have been solved.

Searle regards intentions as belonging essentially to individuals because he regards the representations involved as essentially mental and hence as being essentially lodged in minds, which belong to individuals. But I do not think

---

[14] *Intentionality* (Cambridge: Cambridge Univ. Press, 1983), ch. 3, 408–9. Actually, Searle draws a distinction between representations and "presentations," and he identifies intentions with the latter. Insofar as I omit this detail, my application of Searle's analysis may conflict with its intended interpretation.

[15] I do not think that this account of intention is adequate as it stands. In particular, I think that an adequate account of intention must specify not only the effects of an intention-constituting representation but also its causes. An intention, in my view, is a self-described self-fulfilling representation that is partly caused by a desire for its fulfillment. As for *how* such a representation can be so caused, see p. 210, below.

This conception of intention cannot be defended within the confines of the present paper. A defense of it is offered in ch. 4 of my *Practical Reflection* (Princeton: Princeton Univ. Press, 1989).

[16] I argue at length for this view in Chap. 2, above, and in *Practical Reflection*, ch. 5.

that we can rule out the possibility of literally shared intentions on the grounds that there are no collective minds.

To begin with, I am not sure that intention is essentially mental. There are of course mental intentions, but perhaps there can also be oral or written intentions—just as there are not only mental but also oral or written assertions. Of course, talk of oral or written intentions sounds odd, but talk of oral or written decisions sounds less odd, and talk of oral or written commitments is not odd at all. If I can commit myself to a course of action by speaking or writing, then there would seem to be a sense in which I am thereby making an oral or written decision; and if I can make a decision by speaking or writing, then there would seem to be a sense in which I can frame an oral or written intention.[17] Indeed, the possibility of such intentions appears to be a consequence of Searle's theory. All that's essential to intention, in Searle's theory, is a representation with a particular content and causal role. Why shouldn't the relevant content and causal role attach to representations that aren't in the mind?

One may want to insist on intention's being a mental state, of course. But then I would be inclined to say that the existence of collective minds remains an open question. Whether there are collective minds depends on whether there are collective mental states. And if we insist on the proposition that any state constituting an intention is *ipso facto* mental, then whether there are collective mental states will depend, in part, on whether there are collective intentions. Hence we cannot rule out the possibility of collective intentions on the grounds that there are no collective minds: the direction of logical dependence goes the other way.

I propose to suspend judgment on whether intentions are essentially mental and whether minds are necessarily lodged in the heads of individuals. What I want to do is to examine whether there can be an item that is literally shared between two or more people while bearing the content and playing the functional role identified by Searle as characteristic of intention. Such an item would be a representation that caused action by representing itself as causing it, but it would be a token representation that was in some sense jointly held by two or more people.

In order to be jointly held, this representation will have to be public. That is, it will have to be an utterance, inscription, or depiction of some kind.[18] And it will have to belong to more than one agent, in some sense of the word "belong."

---

[17] For the idea that intentions are essentially commitments, see Bratman, *Intention, Plans, and Practical Reason* (Cambridge, Mass.: Harvard Univ. Press, 1987), 4 ff.

[18] As Jennifer Church has pointed out to me, I am ignoring the possibility (if it is indeed a possibility) that two or more people might jointly occupy a state that has representational content and yet constitutes neither a mental state of one of them nor a public representation between them. Such a state would truly belong to a "collective mind," and it is no doubt what Searle and Bratman were thinking of when they disparaged the idea of literally sharing intentions.

The most obvious candidate is a verbal representation that consists partly in the speech of one agent and partly in the speech of the other, like the statements or anecdotes that one person starts and another finishes.

I think that the conditional commitments described by Gilbert may in fact combine to form such a jointly held representation. Speaking only roughly for a moment, I would put it like this. When one agent says, "I will if you will," and the other says, "Well, *I* will if *you* will," their speech-acts combine to produce a single story, just as when you start telling an anecdote and your spouse finishes it for you.[19] Speaking only roughly, I would say that these two utterances combine to form a verbal representation that's equivalent in content to "We will." If this representation plays the right causal role, by prompting the behavior that it represents, and if it also represents itself as playing that role, then it will just *be* an intention—or, at least, it will be everything that an intention is except mental, if anyone still wants to quibble about that term.

Now, an exchange of commitments with the form "I will if you will" seems problematic, because each agent seems to make his action conditional upon the action of the other agent, with the result that neither will act unless the other does, and hence with the result that action will never get started. But Gilbert cuts through this problem, by understanding this commitment as making the speaker's action conditional upon the other agent's commitment rather than his action. "I will if you will," as interpreted by Gilbert, means something like "I'm willing if you're willing"; and as I shall explain, each of these statements can constitute the very willing that is required by the other.

Rather than scrutinize these statements further, however, let me try to construct the right sort of statement from scratch. I'll start by illustrating how a statement can play the role of an individual's intention; then I'll consider how two people's statements can form an intention that is shared between them.

I think that the statement "I'm going out for a walk" can sometimes be causally responsible for the speaker's going out for a walk. Before making the statement, the person's motives for taking a walk may not outweigh his motives against taking a walk, or may not outweigh them enough to produce the kind of exertion required to get him out of the house. But they may be sufficient to produce the statement "I'm going out for a walk," and this statement may then bring into play an additional motive for taking a walk. The speaker's love of the outdoors and his desire for exercise may now be significantly reinforced by a further motive—for example, the desire not to have spoken falsely.[20] Having

---

[19] One might think that I am begging the question here, since jointly telling a story is a collective action, requiring a collective intention. I discuss this issue below, at pp. 219–20.

[20] Actually, an agent may have many different standing motives that would be engaged by his announcing a future action and would consequently reinforce his preexisting motives for acting as announced. The desire not to have spoken falsely is only one example of such a motive. But

said that he's going out for a walk, the agent faces two alternatives: either go out for a walk or be in the position of having asserted a falsehood. And taking a walk may well be preferable to having said what turns out to be untrue. The agent may thus have a new motive that tips the balance enough to get the projected walk underway.

Of course, the announcement "I'm going out for a walk" often plays no role in causing the walk that it announces. If someone speaks these words on his way out the door, chances are that he was already going out for a walk, without any further prompting. But the case that I'm imagining, in which the statement helps to cause its own fulfillment, is a case in which the statement is made from the armchair, by an agent who would have preferred to sit still if he hadn't raised the price of doing so, by saying that he was going for a walk.

It's precisely because an agent expects such a statement to raise the price of inaction that his desire to act can move him to make it. Lethargy may prevent his initial motives from setting his legs in motion, but it won't prevent them from setting his mouth in motion so as to bring additional motives to bear on his legs. It sounds odd, I know, to speak of getting one's legs to move by moving one's mouth. Yet I venture to say that everyone—or at least, anyone who has struggled with lethargy—knows what it's like to announce his departure in order to counteract the temptations of further delay.

When the agent says "I'm going out for a walk" in such a case, his utterance isn't meant or understood as a mere report or prediction of his behavior. One might want to distinguish his utterance from a report or a prediction by saying precisely that it expresses an intention to take a walk; and I would agree. But one might then want to question whether this utterance aims or purports to be true, and hence whether it provides a basis on which the speaker might be guilty of asserting a falsehood.

Yet I think that we can pinpoint the features in virtue of which this utterance expresses an intention rather than a report or prediction, and these features are compatible with—and, in fact, depend on—its purporting to be true. The utterance expresses an intention because it is meant to be understood as not only playing but also implicitly claiming the role of causing its own fulfillment. That is, when the agent says from his armchair, "I'm going out for a walk," his utterance not only causes him to go out for a walk but also implicitly describes itself as doing so. It is meant to be understood as "I am hereby causing myself to go out for a walk"—a statement that will be false if the agent doesn't go for a walk, but will be true if the agent is moved to go for a walk in order to make the statement true.[21]

one example is enough—enough, that is, to show that a person's announcements of his future actions can sometimes be self-fulfilling.

[21] For a full account of how self-described self-fulfilling predictions can constitute intentions, see ch. 4 of my *Practical Reflection* and Chap. 2, above.

What distinguishes this statement from a prediction or report is that it doesn't purport to represent a fact that's independent of itself. To report or predict a walk would be to represent the walk as something that was already happening or destined to happen, whether it was announced or not. A report or prediction would thus purport to convey an independent fact. By contrast, the agent who expresses an intention by saying "I'm going out for a walk" does not represent the projected walk as something that was going to happen anyway, whether or not he had said so; he represents it as something that is now going to happen precisely because of his hereby saying so. His statement thus differs from a report or prediction in that it doesn't purport to convey a truth independent of itself.[22] But it still purports to convey a truth.

When we say that this statement expresses an intention, we might mean that there is some inner state of intention to which it gives vent. But we might alternatively mean—and in this case, I think we should mean—that the statement expresses an intention that consists in the statement itself, much as the utterance "I promise" both expresses and is a promise. The former statement is an intention because it causes its own fulfillment by representing itself as doing so. In its own right, then, it possesses the features that Searle has identified as characteristic of the will.

But how can a statement be an intention? We ordinarily think of an intention as something that an agent not only forms but also maintains, from the time at which he forms it to the time at which he executes it. We therefore think that someone who once intended to do something in the future can sensibly be asked whether he still has that intention. But what I have been calling a statement, in my example, is a speech-act, and hence an occurrence: it's made at a particular time, and it certainly isn't still being made throughout the interval between utterance and action. How, then, can we regard a statement as constituting an intention?

The solution is to recognize that Searle's analysis naturally encompasses more than intentions conceived as states. Searle analyzes intentions as representations with a particular content and a particular causal role. And representations can be either representational states (like mental images or beliefs) or representational acts (like gestures or assertions), either of which can bear the appropriate content and play the appropriate role. The analysis gives us no grounds for distinguishing between the two, so long as they are representations of the self-describedly self-fulfilling kind.

Searle's analysis is therefore best deployed to encompass both states and acts of the will: states of intending, which are what we ordinarily mean by "intentions," and acts of intending, which we usually call "decisions" instead. So interpreted, the analysis yields a more complicated—but, to my mind, more

---

[22] Could this be the distinction that Searle intends to mark with the terms "representation" and "presentation"?

life-like—picture than one might previously have had of the relation between decisions and intentions.

One might have thought that all intentions are states, some of which are, though others are not, produced by mental acts on the part of the agent. In this simple picture, decisions are acts of the will only by virtue of having states of the will as their products: the act of producing an intention is not an instance of intention in its own right.

In the picture that I am suggesting, however, some acts of deciding are intentions in their own right, because they are representational acts with the content and role characteristic of the will.[23] When someone says "I'm going out for a walk," he may be *deciding aloud* to go for a walk: his speech-act may in itself be an occurrent intention.

Having carried Searle's account this far, however, we should probably carry it one step further. For we can see that representational acts with the content and causal role of intentions may fulfill their role at a temporal distance, by initiating causal processes that will come to fruition long after the acts themselves are complete. Someone's saying "I'm going out for a walk" may bring into being various conditions that will cause him to go for a walk at a later moment, after his words have faded. These conditions may include, for example, his memory of having recently said that he would go for a walk, and his conception of how much time he has in which to make the statement true.

These persisting conditions, which secure the causal efficacy of a spoken decision, amount to the agent's *remaining decided*, since his decision remains in force so long as they persist. And if someone has decided to go for a walk and remains decided, in the sense that his decision is still in force, then surely he still intends to go for a walk. Extending Searle's analysis to acts of intending should therefore lead us to extend it even further, to persisting states in the aftermath of such acts.

Note that these states may not in themselves satisfy Searle's analysis, since they may not involve representations with the precise content and role that the analysis requires. (The memory that one has announced a forthcoming walk is a mental representation, and it may cause one to go for a walk, but its causing one to go for a walk may not be part of what it represents.) These states may therefore have to qualify as intentions in a secondary sense, by virtue of embodying the causal force of past decisions, which qualified as intentions in the primary sense defined by Searle.

---

[23] The difference between these pictures is analogous to that between two ways of picturing the cognitive act of judgment. A judgment might simply be the mental act of forming a belief— an act that qualifies as cognitive only by virtue of a having a cognitive state as its product. Alternatively, however, some judgments might be intrinsically cognitive acts, acts of mentally representing the world in the manner characteristic of cognition.

We thus arrive at a picture in which there are three distinct ways of intending to go for a walk. The intention to go for a walk can consist in a state representing one's going for a walk (partly because of this state); in an act of representing oneself as going for a walk (partly because of this act); or in the persisting causal force of such an act of deciding.

I find this picture especially life-like because it corresponds to what I find upon introspection when asked whether I still intend to do something. When asked this question, I sometimes find myself with a standing conception of the action as forthcoming (partly because of this very conception)—a state of mind that I might describe by saying that I was still intent, resolved, or determined to act. Sometimes, however, I find no more than a memory of having said I would act, and a desire to bear myself out—in which case, I might say that I had decided and hadn't changed my mind. These are two, phenomenologically distinct ways of "still intending."

Let us return to the statement "I'm going out for a walk." I have now suggested that this statement can simultaneously express an intention and constitute the intention expressed, much as a statement can express and constitute a promise. This statement can be made to resemble a promise even more closely; for it can be reworded so as to constitute an intention partly by virtue of *calling* itself one. Just as a statement can be a promise partly because it begins "I hereby promise . . . ," so a statement can be an intention partly because it begins "I hereby intend. . . ."

An effective intention, remember, is a representation that causes behavior by representing itself as causing it. To call something an effective intention to take a walk is therefore to represent it as something that causes the taking of a walk. Consequently, something can have the content of an intention to take a walk by calling itself an effective intention to take a walk. Someone can say, "This statement is an effective intention to take a walk," and his statement will have represented itself as causing him to take a walk—which is just what an intention to take a walk needs to represent. He can therefore say, "I hereby effectively intend to take a walk," and his utterance will have the content of an intention to take a walk, just as "I hereby effectively promise to take a walk" has the content of a promise.

The agent can omit the word "effectively" from this announcement, because announcing an intention carries the conversational implicature that it is effective. Announcing an intention that's ineffective could mislead, and announcing an intention *as* ineffective would be pointless. The tacit assumption that an utterance is neither misleading nor pointless thus supplies what the agent omits if he fails to say that his intention is effective. The agent can similarly drop the word "hereby," as being implicitly understood in the context. He can then issue an intention to take a walk simply by saying "I intend to take a walk."

One might question the analogy between "I intend" and "I promise" in light of how these utterances differ when spoken insincerely. An insincere utterance of "I promise" still constitutes a promise, whereas an insincere utterance of "I intend" is insincere precisely because the speaker has no corresponding intention. Doesn't this difference undermine the claim that "I intend" constitutes the intention that it expresses?

I think not. To be sure, an insincere utterance of "I intend" is insincere because there is no intention corresponding to it. But the intention that's missing in this case need not be one that, if it existed, would exist independently of the utterance. The intention that's missing can be one that would consist in the utterance—an intention that the utterance falsely purports to be.

Keep in mind that Searle's analysis requires an intention to have both a particular content and a particular causal role. The statement "I intend to take a walk" has the content of an intention, but it may still lack the causal role, of prompting the speaker to take a walk. If the utterance has no tendency to cause this action, then it is false; and if the speaker knows that it hasn't, then he is lying. His lie consists in saying "I (hereby) intend" while consciously failing to satisfy the causal condition for intending.[24] The insincerity of his utterance—its reporting an intention that he doesn't have—consists in its purporting to be an intention that it is not.

Thus, the difference between "I promise" and "I intend" is not that an utterance of "I intend" isn't an intention; the difference is rather than an utterance of "I intend" is an intention only if it has a tendency to prompt the intended action. An utterance of "I promise" can qualify as a promise whether or not it can prompt the promised result.

The explanation of this difference is that promises, unlike intentions, are constituted as commitments by social convention, independently of their causal role. The utterance of "I promise" commits the speaker by placing him under a socially defined obligation. But intentions are psychological rather than social commitments. An utterance of "I intend" must commit the speaker in

---

[24] The causal condition on intending is difficult to state precisely. We do not want to say that an intention must actually cause the intended action, since there are genuine intentions that are revoked, overridden, or forgotten. In the text I have weakened this condition by saying that an intention must have a tendency to cause the intended action, but talk of tendencies is notoriously imprecise.

My suspicion is that we cannot give precise conditions that are necessary and sufficient for intending. What we can give, I think, is a precise description of the paradigm case, with a commentary on some of the ways in which actual cases fall short of the paradigm. How short can a case fall while still counting as an intention will then vary with the context. Of course, the paradigm case of intention is one that actually causes the intended action.

As I have mentioned in n. 15, above, I do not think that the paradigm case of intention can be characterized solely in terms of its content and effects. The paradigm case of intention not only causes the intended action, I think, but is itself caused by the agent's motives for acting.

the sense of making him psychologically committed to action.[25] This utterance must therefore play the appropriate role in the speaker's psychology in order to qualify as a commitment, and hence as an intention.

This difference between "I intend" and "I promise" does not undermine the broader similarity between them. "I intend," like "I promise," can still constitute the intention that it expresses, and it can still constitute that intention partly in virtue of describing itself as such.

A statement can describe itself as an intention without beginning with the words "I intend. . . ." An agent can intend to take a walk by saying "I *will* take a walk," in a sense that means "I hereby effectively *will* it." The emphatic use of "will" in the first person can constitute a self-described willing, whose emphatic tone both acts out and connotes its effectiveness.

I suggest that the statement "I will if you will" should be understood in this sense. It means, "I hereby frame an effective intention that's conditional on your framing an effective intention as well"—that is, "I hereby *will* it, conditional on your willing likewise."[26] And this statement just is the conditional willing that it describes itself as being.

This analysis helps us to understand why it seems mildly uncooperative to

---

[25] Of course, an utterance of "I intend" can sometimes constitute a promise as well as an intention—in which case, it still commits the speaker even if it is insincere.

[26] It is an interesting question whether this statement or intention can be adequately specified. When I intend to act on the condition that you intend likewise, what I intend depends on what would count as a "like" intention on your part; and yet what counts as a "like" intention depends on what exactly I intend. My intention is thus self-referential in a way that leaves its content ungrounded.

The same problem arises in discussions of cooperative strategies for overcoming prisoner's dilemmas. In that context, some philosophers have proposed a syntactic solution. (See Peter Danielson, 'Closing the Compliance Dilemma: how it's rational to be moral in a Lamarckian world,' in *Contractarianism and Rational Choice; Essays on David Gauthier's Morals by Agreement*, ed. Peter Vallentyne (New York: Cambridge Univ. Press, 1991), 291–322; and J. V. Howard, 'Cooperation in the Prisoner's Dilemma,' *Theory and Decision* 24 (1988) 203–13.) According to this solution, my intention is conditional on your framing an intention that is syntactically similar—that is, framed in the same words. But this solution is clearly unsatisfactory, since it interprets my intention as committing me to act so long as you say "I will," even if you're speaking an idiolect in which "will" means "won't" and "likewise" means "differently."

I think that the solution to the problem of ungroundedness, in this instance, is to recognize that "intending likewise" can mean "framing an intention with the same determinate *or indeterminate* content." Suppose that I frame the conditional intention of taking a walk if you frame a particular intention; but that I risk failing to specify the latter intention because I attempt to specify it as similar in content to mine. And suppose that you frame the conditional intention of taking a walk if I frame a particular intention; but that you risk failing to specify the latter intention because you attempt to specify it as similar in content to yours. In that case, you and I have intentions that really are similar, precisely because they share the same potential indeterminacies of content. And in that case, their content isn't indeterminate, after all, since it is perfectly determinate whether either person's intention has the same potential indeterminacies as the other's.

I discuss the form of these intentions further in the Appendix to 'Deciding How to Decide,' (Chap. 10, below).

answer "I will if you will" with "Well, *I* will if *you* will." If I say "I will if you will," then I *have* thereby willed it and said that I've willed it—indeed, I've willed it precisely by saying so—and your saying "I will if you will" therefore sounds as if you haven't been listening. Your responding with "Well, I will if you will" perversely calls into question whether I have in fact willed; and so it doesn't bring the exchange to a satisfactory close.

The proper response to "I will if you will" is "Then I will." The word "then" indicates that your intention is conditional on mine, in the same way that mine is conditional on yours, but that the condition has already been satisfied. What you're saying is, "Given that you have willed likewise, I will it, too."

Suppose that I say, "I'll go for a walk if you will," and you answer, "Then I will." According to my analysis, each statement describes itself as an effective conditional willing, or intention, to take a walk; and each statement thereby ascribes to itself a conditional causal power—namely, the power of prompting the speaker to take a walk if (or given that) the hearer is found to have willed likewise.

I now suggest that these statements have the conditional causal powers that they ascribe to themselves, and hence that they qualify as the effective conditional intentions that they claim to be. Each statement will indeed prompt the speaker to take a walk if he finds that the only alternative is to have spoken falsely. Of course, avoiding this alternative won't entail taking a walk if the condition placed on the statement's self-ascribed causal power has not been fulfilled. If you haven't issued an effective conditional intention corresponding to mine, then I can stay home and still have spoken the truth in saying "I'll take a walk if you will." But if I find that you have willed accordingly, then I shall be prompted take a walk, since my statement claimed that it would prompt me to take a walk under these conditions, and I don't want to falsify it. Hence my statement is an effective conditional intention, and so is yours, for the corresponding reasons.

Note here that the conditional causal power of my statement won't be activated merely by your issuing the relevant intention; I must recognize that you have issued it. Thus, if my statement "I will if you will" had been fully precise and explicit, it would have carried an additional condition: "I will, if you will and if I recognize you as willing."[27] But then, if your intention is truly like

---

[27] Davidson thinks that only some intentions containing an "if" clause are genuinely conditional. "[B]ona fide conditions are ones that are reasons for acting that are contemporary with the intention," he says; other "if" clauses he dismisses as "bogus conditions" ('Intending,' in *Essays on Actions and Events* (Oxford: Clarendon Press, 1980), 83–102, at 94). He would therefore accept as genuine the condition "if you will" while rejecting as bogus the addition "if I recognize you as willing," since the latter doesn't allude to a reason.

I think that Davidson's discussion of conditional intentions is deeply confused. There is of course a difference between requiring the presence of a particular reason for one's intended

mine, it will be such as I can hardly help but recognize, since it will explicitly claim to be the effective conditional intention that it is. Your "Then I will" leaves me no way to deny that you have fulfilled my stipulation "if you will," except by failing to understand or to credit what you say. And since we are engaged in conversation, there is a tacit assumption of mutual understanding and credence.

The assumption of mutual understanding and credence amounts, on my part, to the concession that, if you issue an intention like mine—that is, a self-proclaimed intention—then I will indeed recognize it for what it claims to be. Hence the further condition on my intention is conceded in advance and can be omitted. I can say "I will if you will" without adding "and if I recognize you as willing," because if you do will as I have hereby willed, then (I tacitly concede) I shall recognize you as willing, since (we tacitly assume) I'll understand and credit what you say.

Your response "Then I will" thus satisfies the only condition that hasn't been tacitly conceded in my statement; it therefore leaves the truth of that statement to depend, in my eyes, on whether I take a walk; and so it activates the statement's self-ascribed power to get me walking. And of course, my statement has already satisfied the only condition not tacitly conceded in your statement, thus activating its causal power as well. Together the statements therefore prompt us to take a walk.

What's more, these statements jointly imply that they will prompt us to take a walk. Each statement not only fulfills the other's only remaining condition in fact but also discharges it in logic.

When you say "I will," you not only do as I stipulated when I said "if you will"; you also say that you're doing it; and so your statement licenses the detachment of my stipulation. My statement claims that it will prompt me to take a walk if you will likewise; your statement claims that you are willing likewise; and these statements imply that I shall now be prompted to take a walk. *Mutatis mutandis* they imply that you will be prompted to take a walk as well. And these very implications, rendered undeniable by the conventions of conversation, are precisely what will prompt you and me to take a walk, on pain of having said things that turn out to be false by virtue of implying falsehoods. Our statements therefore combine to form a joint statement saying, in effect, that they will jointly prompt us to take a walk; and they jointly prompt us to

---

action, as in "I'll do it if I like," and acknowledging a limitation on one's ability to perform the intended action, as in "I'll do it if I can." But Davidson offers no grounds for calling the former "if" clause a "genuine" condition while dismissing the latter as "bogus." Each clause helps to specify what one is settling in framing one's intention, which is precisely what the content of an intention serves to specify. Hence both intentions are conditional in content. For further discussion of Davidson on conditional intentions, see my *Practical Reflection*, 117–21.

take a walk, as they jointly say. They consequently add up to a single representation that causes our actions by representing itself as causing them—a single token intention that is literally shared between us.

This case of collective intention is designed to show that Gilbert's talk of "pooling our wills" can be taken quite literally without becoming either mysterious or incoherent, as Searle might suggest. Indeed, it shows that Searle's own analysis of intention can account for the possibility of literally pooling our wills, since it implies that two individual intentions, belonging to two different agents, can combine to form a single intention governing the behavior of both. This joining of intentions occurs when two spoken decisions, each of which is logically and causally conditional on the other, combine to form one spoken decision in which the conditions have been discharged.

The main virtue of this account is that it explains how several exercises of individual discretion can add up to a single exercise of collective discretion. The best way to formulate the explanation is by contrasting the case of shared intention with a case of disparate but parallel intentions.

Suppose that I say, "I'm going out for a walk," and you say, "I'm going out for a walk, too." In that case, our statements combine, in the sense invoked above, to form a story to the effect that both of us are going out for walks; and this story can in fact cause its own fulfillment. Why, then, do we not qualify as sharing an intention in this case?

The answer is that each half of the story settles only half of the story. The first half determines, and represents itself as determining, that I am going for a walk; the second half determines and represents itself as determining that you are. Hence I do not help to settle your behavior, actually or notionally, and you do not help to settle mine. We do not exercise discretion over any of the same issues.

The situation is different when I say, "I'll go for a walk if you will," and you say, "Then I will." If these statements have the meaning that I have attributed to them, then each of them determines the speaker's behavior, and represents itself as determining it, only in conjunction with the other's statement. My statement represents itself as causing my walk only in the presence of your statement; your statement represents itself as causing your walk only in the presence of my statement; and the causal powers of these statements are in fact interdependent, as the statements themselves represent. Hence the behavior of each of us is settled—and is represented as being settled—only by both of us together.

An interesting feature of this arrangement is that I do not *take* discretion over your behavior, nor you over mine; rather, you *give* me conditional discretion over your behavior, and vice versa. Each of us places his behavior under the joint control of both, by issuing an intention that's conditional on the other's intention. And each of us exercises the partial discretion that he's been granted over the other's behavior by exercising the partial discretion that he has retained over his own. The result is that each of us conditionally settles, and is represented as conditionally settling, one and same set of issues—namely, how both of us will behave—and we thereby categorically settle those issues together.

This case thus instantiates the phenomenon that initially puzzled us: a single making up of two minds. To make up one's mind, in practical matters, is to become committed to a course of action. Yet each of us becomes committed to taking a walk only by the combination of our utterances, and not by his own utterance alone. Hence each of us has his mind made up by both of us; and we jointly make up both minds simultaneously.

This joint making-up of minds is not the making-up of a joint mind. And if a commitment's being oral or written entails that it isn't mental, our commitment to taking a walk may not be a mental act or state at all.

Of course, our commitment may have mental consequences—must have them, in fact, if it is to be effective. Each of us must remember what has been said, must be somehow motivated to make it true, and must have some idea of how much time he has in which to do so. As I have suggested, this persisting mental state, which constitutes the persisting force of our decision, is entitled to be called an intention, since remaining decided is a way of intending.

If one of us has his share of the requisite memories and motives, then he will individually occupy the state of remaining decided to take a walk. But the decision that remains in force with him will be the joint decision, since only the joint decision has the force of a categorical commitment. If both of us have the requisite memories and motives, then both will be under the force of the joint decision.

This state, in which each of us is individually under the force of a joint decision, deserves to be called a shared intention, but I don't want to insist on calling it a single intention that is literally shared. In this case, each of us has his own private piece of the intention—maybe even his own private intention. What can be said is that our private intentions in this case consist in the lingering force of a single, shared intention. Although it is our individual minds that remain made up, they were initially made up jointly. Our minds individually remain as they were jointly made up: it's *that* kind of shared intention.

My analysis of this case may seem to be circular, however. What I claim to be a single token of intention, in the making-up of our minds, is formed out of two individual speech acts. Don't these acts need to combine into a joint speech act before they can combine into a joint intention? And doesn't their forming a joint act depend on their arising from some antecedently shared intention?

Well, I am committed to the proposition that when we exchange our mutually dependent decisions, it becomes appropriate to say of us that we have jointly decided to go for a walk. But this joint act of deciding is not a shared activity of the sort that requires an antecedently shared intention. It does require that we jointly tell a story to the effect that we will go for a walk (partly because of this story); but we can jointly tell this story without having shared an intention to tell it. We can jointly tell the story by acting with distinct, individual intentions: I, an intention to start a story and leave you to finish it; you, an intention to finish the story that I've started. Thus, the shared intention that we produce in telling our story doesn't require any antecedently shared intentions.

More importantly, the intentions that lie behind our stories are not intentions in the same sense of the word as the stories themselves.[28] That is, they are not practical conclusions, or exercises of discretion; they are rather aims or goals. If I decide aloud to take a walk, by saying "I'm going to take a walk," I must utter these words with the intention of making a particular assertion—in fact, a self-fulfilling assertion that will count as a decision—and I may also utter them with the intention of starting a self-fulfilling story that you will finish. But the intention with which I utter these words is not a prior decision to utter them, much less a prior decision, by uttering them, to make a decision. For if I'm going to decide aloud to take a walk, then I don't have to decide to make that decision; indeed, I had better not decide to make that decision, lest I leave too little remaining to be decided. (Deciding to decide to take a walk is almost already deciding to take it.)

Rather, deciding aloud to take a walk requires that I utter words for the purpose—that is, with the aim or goal—of making a particular assertion and thereby making a decision. The intention with which I utter these words is simply the purpose, aim, or goal with which I utter them. Hence there is no circularity or regress of intentions: there is simply an act carried out with an intention in one sense of the word, while constituting an intention in a different sense.

Sharing an intention in the latter sense is what looked difficult, if not impossible. But it's not difficult at all. Sharing an intention can be as easy as saying "I will."

---

[28] On the ambiguity of the word 'intention,' see n. 8, above, and the accompanying text.

10

Deciding How to Decide

By "deciding how to decide," I mean using practical reasoning to regulate one's principles of practical reasoning. David Gauthier has suggested that deciding how to decide is something that every rational agent does.[1] Whether or not we agree with Gauthier about agents in general, we might think that his suggestion applies well enough to many of us moral philosophers. We assess rival principles of practical reasoning, which tell us how to choose among actions; and assessing how to choose among actions certainly sounds like deciding how to decide.

One of my goals in this essay is to argue, in opposition to Gauthier, that assessing rival principles of practical reasoning is a job for theoretical rather than practical reasoning. How to decide is something that we discover rather than decide.

The idea that our principles of practical reasoning can be regulated by practical reasoning is essential to Gauthier's defense of his own, somewhat unorthodox conception of those principles. And although I do not endorse the specifics of Gauthier's conception, I do endorse its spirit. There is a flaw in the orthodox conception of practical reasoning, and Gauthier has put his finger on it. Unfortunately, Gauthier's account of why it is a flaw, and how it should be fixed, ultimately rests on practical considerations, whose relevance is open to question if, as I believe, practical reasoning cannot regulate itself.

This essay therefore has a second goal, which complicates matters considerably. Although I want to reject Gauthier's notion that we decide how to decide, I also want to preserve what rests upon that notion, in Gauthier's view: I want to resettle Gauthier's critique of the orthodoxy on a new foundation. I

This chapter originally appeared in *Ethics and Practical Reason*, edited by Garrett Cullity and Berys Gaut (Oxford: Oxford Univ. Press, 1997), 29–52. I received valuable comments on this chapter from Elizabeth Anderson, Jim Joyce, John Broome, and Stephen Darwall. It also had the benefit of an excellent commentary by Piers Rawling at the St. Andrews conference, as well as comments from participants, including Christine Korsgaard, Peter Railton, Joseph Raz, Michael Smith, Garrett Cullity, and Berys Gaut.

[1] Gauthier suggests that the capacity to choose one's conception of practical reason is essential to one's rational autonomy as an agent. See 'Reason and Maximization,' in *Moral Dealing: Contract, Ethics, and Reason* (Ithaca: Cornell Univ. Press, 1990), 209–33, at 231. See also *Morals By Agreement* (Oxford: Clarendon Press, 1986), 183–4.

shall try to carry out this delicate operation as follows. First I'll summarize Gauthier's critique of the orthodoxy about practical reasoning. Then I'll introduce Gauthier's alternative conception of practical reasoning and his practical argument for deciding upon it. After explaining why I think that practical reasoning cannot be self-regulated in this manner, I'll explain how I think that it must be regulated instead. Finally, I'll return to Gauthier's critique of the orthodox conception in order to reformulate it in theoretical terms.

Gauthier's Critique of Straightforward Maximization

The target of Gauthier's critique is what he calls the theory of straightforward maximization. The theory of straightforward maximization says that an agent should choose, from among the discrete actions currently available to him, the one that yields the greatest expectation of benefit for him.[2] Gauthier argues that the theory of straightforward maximization must be modified so as to enable rational agents to avoid falling into prisoner's dilemmas.

Prisoner's dilemmas get their name from a philosophical fiction in which two people—say, you and I—are arrested on suspicion of having committed a crime together. The police separate us for interrogation and offer us similar plea bargains: if either gives evidence against the other, his sentence (whatever it otherwise would have been) will be shortened by one year, and the other's sentence will be lengthened by two. In light of the expected benefits, maximizing rationality instructs each of us to give evidence against the other. The unfortunate result is that each sees his sentence shortened by one year in payment for his own testimony, but lengthened by two because of the other's testimony; and so we both spend one more year in jail than we would have if both had kept silent.

The moral of this story might appear to be, not just that crime doesn't pay, but that the pursuit of self-interest doesn't pay, either. But of course the individual pursuit of self-interest does pay in this story, since each of us does better by testifying than he would have by keeping silent, irrespective of what the other does. What fails to pay, in this story, is self-interested action on the part of two agents, when compared with self-sacrifice by both. Joint sacrifice would have yielded greater benefits for each of us than joint selfishness.

---

[2] Note that this theory does not spell out specific procedures for applying this principle of choice; it simply states the principle that ought to be implemented in one's deliberative procedures. All of the conceptions of rationality discussed below are articulated at the same level of generality, as principles of choice that will no doubt require more specific procedures for their implementation. To argue, as I do, that practical reasoning cannot regulate our principles of choice is not to argue that it cannot regulate the specific procedures in which those principles are implemented.

In order to illustrate Gauthier's complaint against the maximizing conception of practical reasoning, we must imagine that you and I have an opportunity to confer before being separated for interrogation. Since we expect to be offered incentives to betray one another, we try to attain solidarity by means of an agreement. "I'm willing to keep silent if you are," I say, and you say, "I am, too."[3] We thus appear to have agreed on joint sacrifice, to our mutual advantage.

Yet once we are led into our separate interrogation rooms and offered our separate plea bargains, the expected benefits of the alternatives are unaffected by our attempt at collaboration.[4] Each still stands to gain by testifying against the other, irrespective of what the other does; and so the principle of maximization still instructs each of us to testify, in violation of our supposed agreement.

What's more, each of us could have predicted that the other would violate the agreement if only he had known that the other was a maximizer. And neither of us would have been willing to forgo his plea bargain in order to reach an agreement that the other was in any case going to violate. When I said "I'm willing to keep silent if you are," I meant to express a willingness that would take effect in my behavior, but only on the condition that you express a willingness that would be equally effective in yours. Had I known that any willingness you might express was likely to be overridden by maximizing calculations, I would have realized that your expressed willingness to keep silent would be of no value to me, and so I would never have offered mine. Hence if either party's allegiance to maximization had been known, no agreement would ever have been offered to him. Straightforward maximizers thus find themselves excluded from co-operative agreements.

Being excluded from co-operative agreements is a cost that counts against the maximizing conception of practical reasoning, in Gauthier's eyes. Who, he asks, would want to have deliberative principles that would exclude him from the co-operative agreements by which prisoner's dilemmas are avoided? In Gauthier's view, one is better off adopting deliberative principles that favor the fulfilment of mutually beneficial agreements, so that one will be offered an opportunity to enter them.

Gauthier therefore proposes an alternative to the maximizing conception of practical reasoning. The alternative conception instructs an agent to maximize except when he is deciding whether to fulfil a commitment, in which case it

[3] Note that I say, "I'm willing to keep silent if you are," not "I'm willing to keep silent if you *do*." For a discussion of how this commitment is formulated, see the Appendix to this chapter.

[4] We can of course imagine mechanisms by which our agreement would have altered the expected benefits. For example, we might belong to a gang that exacts revenge on liars but not on stool-pigeons. But the argument depends on the assumption that no such mechanisms are in place.

compares the benefits, not of fulfilling or violating the commitment, but rather of two overall courses of action, one being that of making and fulfilling the commitment, the other being that of never having made the commitment at all.[5] The agent is instructed to fulfil his commitment if the package deal of making and fulfilling the commitment promises greater benefits than the package in which he never made it and so never had to consider fulfilling it.

But why should an agent base his decision on a comparison between these package deals? After all, an agent evaluates whether to fulfil a commitment at a juncture where never having made the commitment is no longer an option: the commitment has already been made. Why should he care whether, in fulfilling the commitment, he will complete a course of action whose consequences are better than those of an alternative that is no longer available? And why should his evaluation at this juncture ignore a course of action that still is available—namely, that of making the commitment and then violating it?[6]

Gauthier's answer to these questions is that the conception of practical reasoning that applies this comparison is superior to the straightforwardly maximizing conception, which compares all and only the discrete steps that are currently available.[7] What makes the alternative conception superior, Gauthier says, is that it enables the agent to make commitments that he can be counted on to fulfil, thus making him eligible as a partner in co-operative agreements. The benefits to be expected from co-operation give the agent reason for abandoning maximization and adopting Gauthier's alternative conception instead.

Here is where the notion of deciding how to decide first enters Gauthier's argument. His conception of practical reasoning is commended to the agent by practical considerations about the benefits of holding it. The deliberative principles that Gauthier favors are thus arrived at by deliberation.

The deliberations by which an agent arrives at these principles are articulated most fully in Gauthier's recent paper 'Assure and Threaten.'[8] There

---

[5] This proposal appears, in very different forms, in 'In the Neighborhood of the Newcomb-Predictor (Reflections on Rationality),' *Proceedings of the Aristotelian Society* 89 (1988–9) 179–94, esp. 186–94; and 'Assure and Threaten,' *Ethics* 104 (1994) 690–721, esp. 704–7. I am glossing over differences in these two formulations of the proposal.

[6] As Michael Bratman puts it, Gauthier's conception of practical reasoning recommends "ranking . . . courses of action that typically include elements no longer in the agent's causal control." Bratman remarks, "This seems to me not to do justice to the significance of temporal and causal location to our agency" ('Toxin, Temptation, and the Stability of Intention,' in Jules Coleman and Christopher Morris (eds.), *Rational Commitment and Social Justice: Essays for Gregory Kavka* (Cambridge: Cambridge Univ. Press, 1998, 58–90; reprinted in Bratman, *Faces of Intention: Selected Essays on Intention and Agency* (Cambridge: Cambridge Univ. Press, 1999), 58–90.)

[7] 'In the Neighborhood of the Newcomb-Predictor,' 192; 'Assure and Threaten,' 700–2.

[8] pp. 691–702.

Gauthier explains that these deliberations are framed by an ultimate or overall goal of the agent's—say, the goal of having as good a life as possible. In furtherance of this master-goal, Gauthier argues, straightforward maximization recommends its own replacement by the alternative conception, which will afford the agent a better life by affording him access to the benefits of co-operation.

At this point, however, we might suspect that an earlier problem has re-emerged. Suppose that an agent adopts Gauthier's conception of practical reasoning and is consequently offered a co-operative agreement, which he accepts. Holding Gauthier's conception will potentially have furthered the agent's master-goal by making the agreement available to him, since nobody would have offered to co-operate with a straightforward maximizer. But when the time for fulfilling the agreement arrives, Gauthier's conception of practical reasoning will no longer further the agent's goal, since his goal would he better served by reasoning that permitted him to violate the agreement.[9] If the agent's conception of practical reasoning were an object of choice in the sense that it was continually open to revision, then the agent would now find himself changing conceptions in midstream.

Of course, if the agent had been expected to change conceptions in midstream, then the co-operative agreement would never have been offered to him, in the first place, since his conception of practical reasoning, being thus revisable, would have offered no guarantee of his future co-operation. Hence Gauthier's conception of practical reasoning can create beneficial opportunities only if the agent appears unlikely to abandon that conception at a later date.

Gauthier has never explicitly addressed this problem, to my knowledge, but a solution to it is implicit in his discussions of the choice between conceptions of practical reasoning. The solution rests on the claim that Gauthier's conception, unlike straightforward maximization, is self-supporting.[10]

We have envisioned that an agent, having adopted Gauthier's conception of practical reasoning, might subsequently abandon it, at least temporarily, when he no longer benefits from holding it. But to abandon Gauthier's conception of practical reasoning on the grounds that it is no longer beneficial would be to apply the principle of straightforward maximization; whereas the agent, having adopted Gauthier's conception, is no longer a straightforward maximizer.

The question before the agent, at this juncture, is whether to retain a

---

[9] For this point, see Derek Parfit, *Reasons and Persons* (Oxford: Clarendon Press, 1984), 505, n. 8.

[10] For a similar interpretation of Gauthier, see Stephen L. Darwall, *Impartial Reason* (Ithaca: Cornell Univ. Press, 1983), 195–8.

conception of practical reasoning, and this conception can be regarded as a commitment to deliberate according to particular principles on practical questions. The question before the agent therefore belongs to the very class of questions on which his current conception of practical reasoning differs from straightforward maximization—questions, that is, about whether to abide by a previously adopted commitment. The agent's current conception of practical reasoning recommends that he answer such a question in accordance with a comparison between the consequences of making and abiding by his commitment, on the one hand, and the consequences of never having made it, on the other, each considered as a package deal. Reasoning in this manner, the agent will find that the advantages of being offered a co-operative agreement outweigh the disadvantages of fulfilling it; and so he will decide to abide by his commitment, and hence to retain Gauthier's conception of practical reasoning.

Thus, Gauthier's conception is stable in a way that straightforward maximization is not. If a straightforward maximizer applies his deliberative principle to a comparison between itself and Gauthier's principle, it will lead him to adopt Gauthier's instead; but if he then applies his new deliberative principle to the same comparison again, it will lead him to stick with Gauthier's. Indeed, the benefits that attracted him to Gauthier's principle will have depended on the fact that it wouldn't lead to its own abandonment, since its stability in this respect is what made him eligible as a partner in co-operative agreements.

The notion of deciding how to decide has now entered Gauthier's argument at two distinct points. A straightforward maximizer will replace his conception of practical reasoning, according to the argument, because an alternative conception is more conducive to his master-goal and is thus recommended by practical reasoning as he now conceives it. And the alternative conception of practical reasoning will better serve the agent's master-goal only because, once adopted, it will be retained at the recommendation of practical reasoning as he *then* conceives it.

Gauthier's Argument for Deciding How to Decide

At both points the argument depends on the assumption that how to conceive of practical reasoning is a question to be settled by practical reason. Yet evaluating conceptions of practical reasoning need not be a practical matter.

What if there is an objectively correct way to deliberate—one principle, or set of principles, whose application is valid independently of its pragmatic advantages or disadvantages.[11] In that case, the way to deliberate will be the correct way to deliberate, and the correct way to deliberate will not depend on how we would choose to deliberate, if choosing on pragmatic grounds. It will rather be a theoretical matter, which depends on which conception is right.

Now, if evaluating conceptions of practical reasoning is not a practical but a theoretical inquiry, which seeks principles that are right independently of what we would prefer, then it won't be an inquiry of the sort to which a conception of practical reasoning would apply. And if it is not an inquiry to which such a conception would apply, then no conception of practical reasoning will militate either for or against itself as the conclusion of that inquiry. A conception of practical reasoning cannot lay down principles that would lead to its own adoption or rejection if its adoption or rejection doesn't depend on practical reasoning.[12]

In short, conceptions of practical reasoning cannot be self-supporting or self-defeating unless evaluating such conceptions is an instance of practical reasoning. And why should we think of it that way?

Gauthier answers this question by contrasting two pictures of how conceptions of practical reasoning should be evaluated. He first considers a picture in which actions are subject to an independent criterion of success, and deliberative principles can therefore be evaluated by their tendency to yield actions that meet this criterion. As Gauthier points out, this picture portrays the practical sphere as analogous to the theoretical, in which beliefs are subject to the independent standard of truth, and principles of theoretical reasoning can be evaluated by their tendency to yield true beliefs.

What Gauthier might have added is that this picture portrays the evaluation of deliberative principles as a theoretical matter, since the objective criterion of success for actions entails a criterion of correctness for deliberation. In this picture, the correct way to deliberate is whichever way best tracks the criterion of success for actions, just as the correct way to theorize is whichever way best tracks the truth. The criterion of success for actions isn't up to us, in this picture; the tendency of deliberative principles to track that criterion isn't up to us; and so the way to deliberate isn't up to us, either. Hence evaluating conceptions of practical reasoning isn't an instance of practical reasoning.

Gauthier considers a specific version of this picture, in which the independent criterion of success for actions is conduciveness to the agent's master-goal. According to this criterion of success, of course, Gauthier's deliberative principle takes second place to straightforward maximization, since it often

---

[11] Of course, there may be more than one specific procedure by which these principles can be applied. But multiple procedures, in this sense, will all count as one way of deliberating, according to the scheme of individuation that was adopted in n. 2, above.

[12] The point made in this paragraph is made by Parfit on pp. 19–23 of *Reasons and Persons*.

recommends goal-defeating actions, such as the fulfilment of co-operative agreements. Not unsurprisingly, then, Gauthier prefers a different picture of how the agent's master-goal bears on his conception of practical reasoning.

In Gauthier's picture, the agent's master-goal sets a standard of success for deliberative principles, not for actions, and it bears on actions only indirectly: the rationality of actions depends on their issuing from the principles that best promote the goal. Deliberative principles can promote the master-goal not only through the actions that they recommend but also through collateral effects such as creating opportunities for action—for example, by making the agent eligible as a partner in co-operative agreements. On this standard, Gauthier's conception of practical reasoning surpasses straightforward maximization.

This picture favors Gauthier's conception of practical reasoning precisely because it portrays the evaluation of such conceptions as a practical matter. In this picture, there is nothing about actions that deliberative principles attempt to track in their recommendations, and so there is nothing to make them objectively correct or incorrect. Conceptions of practical reasoning must therefore be evaluated, not by whether they get the principles of deliberation right, but rather by the pragmatic pros and cons of holding them.

What reason does Gauthier offer for favoring the latter picture? He says that he favors it because it doesn't lead us to choose a conception of rationality that's self-defeating, as straightforward maximization appears to be. "[I]t is surely mistaken," he says, "to treat rational deliberation as self-defeating, if a non-self-defeating account is available."[13]

But now Gauthier has argued in a circle. He is currently comparing, not just rival conceptions of practical reasoning, but rival pictures of how conceptions of practical reasoning should be evaluated. In one picture, conceptions of practical reasoning are evaluated by whether their deliberative principles track actions that meet the relevant criterion of success, which (Gauthier envisions) is conduciveness to the agent's master-goal; and this evaluation militates against Gauthier's conception. In the other picture, conceptions of practical reasoning are evaluated by whether holding them is conducive to the agent's master-goal, and this evaluation militates in favor of Gauthier.

The question is which picture to adopt. Gauthier's answer is that we should adopt the latter picture, since the former recommends a self-defeating conception of practical reasoning. But as we have seen, a conception of practical reasoning cannot be self-defeating or self-supporting unless it is self-applicable—that is, unless its own evaluation is an inquiry of the sort to which the conception itself applies. And in the picture that Gauthier rejects,

---

[13] 'Assure and Threaten,' 702.

evaluating conceptions of practical reasoning is not a practical but a theoretical inquiry, which seeks to ascertain which principles of deliberation are correct. How can Gauthier reject this picture on the grounds that it favors a self-defeating conception of practical reasoning? The picture itself portrays conceptions of practical reasoning as incapable of defeating themselves, because they do not apply to their own evaluation. Only in the picture adopted by Gauthier do conceptions of practical reasoning apply to their own evaluation and thereby qualify as self-supporting or -defeating.

We have to join Gauthier in adopting this picture, then, before we can see it as saving us from a self-defeating conception of practical reasoning. Gauthier's reasons for adopting the picture are therefore visible only after we have already adopted it.

What's worse, Gauthier's picture severely limits the normative force that's available to conceptions of practical reasoning. Of course, any conception of practical reasoning will be normative in content, simply by virtue of applying terms like 'reason' and 'rational': any conception of practical reasoning will tell us how to deliberate and, by extension, what to do. But precisely because any conception will tell us how to deliberate, and hence what to do, we need to find a conception whose injunctions are authoritative or valid or genuinely binding.

One problem is that Gauthier's picture seems to rule out the possibility of our recognizing a conception as authoritative in this sense. If how to conceive of practical reasoning is itself a practical question, as Gauthier claims, then we shall have no conception of how to answer it until we have a conception of practical reasoning; and so we shall have no conception of how to answer the question until we have already answered it. We shall therefore find ourselves either unable to answer the question at all or forced to answer it arbitrarily. Having chosen a conception arbitrarily, we shall be equipped to reconsider our choice, of course, but only in an arbitrarily chosen manner. The results of such a procedure are unlikely to inspire confidence.[14]

---

[14] Christine Korsgaard suggests that Kant's purely formal conception of practical reason is a solution to this problem. Imagine that an agent is free to choose his conception of a reason for acting. The current problem is that, in order to avoid adopting a conception arbitrarily, the agent would seem to need a reason for adopting one conception rather than another; and yet he has as yet no conception—or only an arbitrarily chosen conception—of what would count as a reason for doing so. But perhaps the agent can adopt, as his conception of a reason for acting, the mere *form* of a reason for acting. Or rather, he *already has* this much of a conception, insofar as he is already committed to adopting something that will qualify as a conception of a reason. Since nothing that failed to respect the form of a reason would qualify as a conception thereof, the agent who sets out to choose his conception of a reason already has this much of a conception, and he therefore needs no reason for choosing it. He can end up with this purely formal conception of a reason without any circularity or arbitrariness. So, at least, says Korsgaard's version of Kant. ('Morality as Freedom,' in Y. Yovel (ed.), *Kant's Practical Philosophy Reconsidered* (Dordrecht: Kluwer, 1989), 23–48, at 30–1.)

This methodological problem may be tolerable by itself. Inquiry has to start somewhere, usually with received opinions, and it often relies on these opinions even in the process of criticizing and revising them. The principle of straightforward maximization may simply be the received opinion with which inquiry into practical reasoning is obliged to begin.

Yet Gauthier's picture portrays more than a methodology for answering the question how to conceive of practical reasoning; it portrays the very nature of that question, as one to which no one answer is better than another except in so far as it is favored by practical reasoning. The picture consequently undermines, not just the possibility of our recognizing a conception as authoritative, but the very possibility of a conception's being authoritative, in the first place. The only authority available to a conception of practical reasoning, in Gauthier's picture, lies in the fact that the conception is supported by itself or by another conception that cannot boast even that much authority.[15] Why should we feel bound by principles whose only claim on us is that they are recommended by themselves or by other principles that have even less to recommend them?

For these reasons, I am inclined to prefer the picture that Gauthier rejects, in which conceptions of practical reasoning are evaluable in relation to an independent criterion of success for actions. The philosophy of rational choice must therefore begin by finding the criterion of success for actions, in relation to which conceptions of rationality can be evaluated.

One might think that this task will draw us into reasoning just as circular as that involved in Gauthier's picture. A criterion of success for actions would seem to embody a normative judgment about how one ought to act. Finding a criterion of success for actions would therefore seem to be a practical inquiry about how to act, an inquiry that requires us to deliberate and hence to have deliberative principles already in hand. How, then, can we expect our criterion of success for actions to guide us in choosing deliberative principles?

A Theoretical Foundation for Deliberative Principles

The answer to this question is provided, I think, by the analogy between theoretical and practical reasoning—the analogy that Gauthier declines to apply.[16]

---

[15] This is the point that Parfit makes on pp. 19–20 of *Reasons and Persons*.

[16] This analogy is also being pursued by Peter Railton, with somewhat different results. See his 'On the Hypothetical and Non-Hypothetical in Reasoning about Belief and Action,' in Cullity and Gaut (eds.), *Ethics and Practical Reason*, 53–79; 'What the Non-Cognitivist Helps us to See the Naturalist Must Help us to Explain,' in John Haldane and Crispin Wright (eds.), *Reality, Representation, and Projection* (Oxford: Oxford Univ. Press, 1994), 292–4; and 'In Search of Non-subjective Reasons,' in J. B. Schneewind (ed.), *Reason, Ethics, and Society; Themes from Kurt Baier with his Responses* (Chicago: Open Court, 1996), 117–43.

In the case of theoretical reasoning, our criterion of success for beliefs doesn't embody a normative judgment on our part; rather, the criterion of success for beliefs is determined by the internal goal of beliefs themselves.

As Gauthier observes, it is in the very nature of beliefs to aim at being true.[17] Propositional attitudes that do not aim at the truth simply don't constitute beliefs, whereas attitudes that constitute beliefs do so partly in virtue of having that aim. Hence being true is simply what would be required for beliefs to succeed in their own terms. That beliefs must be true in order to succeed is a fact about them, given their goal-directed nature; it's not a normative judgment at which we arrive by practical reasoning. What is to count as success for belief is not for us to decide, because it's determined by an aim that's internal to belief itself.

Similarly, we can avoid circularity in our account of practical reasoning by finding an internal aim in relation to which actions can be seen as succeeding or failing in their own terms. If actions have a constitutive aim, then they will be subject to a criterion of success that's determined by their nature rather than our practical reasoning; and so that criterion will be available in advance of deliberation, as a basis for evaluating deliberative principles.

Some deliberative principles will then bear objective authority as norms of practical reasoning. There will be an objective fact as to what makes action successful as action, just as there is a fact as to what makes belief successful as belief. And in so far as deliberative principles tend to issue in action that succeeds *as* action, they will qualify as objectively correct ways to regulate action; just as theoretical principles qualify as correct ways to regulate belief in so far as they tend to issue in true belief, which succeeds *as* belief. The normative authority of deliberative principles will thus rest in the nature of action as constitutively directed at a particular aim.

Now, there are two possible views on the relation of aims to actions. One view is that there is no single aim that's constitutive of action in general, as aiming to be true is constitutive of belief. Actions are utterly heterogeneous as to their goals, according to this view: what's constitutive of action is simply having some goal or other.

This view yields a thoroughgoing instrumentalism about practical reason— an instrumentalism far more thorough, in fact, than that expressed in the norm of maximizing utility or value. For if the only goal internal to an action is the peculiar goal at which it is expressly directed by its agent, then each action will

---

[17] 'Assure and Threaten,' 699. Actually, what Gauthier says is that '[t]o believe is to believe true.' But this remark fails to pick out a distinctive feature of belief, since to desire is to desire true, to intend is to intend true, and so on, for all propositional attitudes. I assume, however, that Gauthier means to pick out the distinctive relation that belief bears to the truth, which is that to believe is to believe true *with the aim of thereby getting the truth right*. On this point, see Chap. 5, above, at pp. 10–14; and Chap. 8, above, at pp. 182–8; and Chap. 11, below.

have to be judged a success or failure solely on the basis of its conduciveness to its peculiar goal. And very few actions are expressly directed by their agents at maximizing some overall measure of value. Most actions are directed at less ambitious aims, which would be the only aims in relation to which they could be said to succeed or fail in their own terms. A conception of practical reasoning would therefore have to be evaluated by its tendency to recommend actions that succeeded in promoting whatever they were severally intended to promote.

The alternative view is that there is a common goal that's constitutive of action—something at which behavior must aim in order to qualify as an action, just as a propositional attitude must aim at being true in order to qualify as a belief. According to a tradition that stretches from Aristotle to Davidson, action has a constitutive aim of this sort—namely, the good.[18] Whatever an action aims at, according to this tradition, it aims at *sub specie boni*: in the guise of a good. In aiming at different things, actions are still aiming at things under the same description—as good—and so they share a constitutive aim.

This tradition might seem to offer a foundation for the maximizing conception of practical reasoning. If every action aims at something conceived as good, then conduciveness to the good would appear to be an internal criterion of success for actions—the criterion that actions must meet in order to succeed in their own terms. Since the most successful actions, by this criterion, are the ones that are most conducive to the good, the way to reach the truth about the success of actions will be to apply the method of maximization.

I believe that there are several errors in this foundational argument for the maximizing conception of practical reasoning. To begin with, aiming at things conceived individually as goods does not necessarily entail aiming to maximize a unified measure of goodness, since it doesn't necessarily entail regarding one's various ends as good in commensurable ways. More importantly, however, I doubt whether actions necessarily aim at things in the guise of goods.[19]

Yet the thesis that actions constitutively aim at the good is not the most plausible implementation of the view that they share a constitutive aim. This thesis assigns a constitutive aim to actions by claiming that they converge in their aims, in the sense that their various ends-in-view are all sought as means to, or components of, a single ulterior end. But the claim that actions converge in their aims is not necessary to the view that they share a constitutive aim.

[18] See e.g. Davidson, 'How is Weakness of the Will Possible?', in *Essays on Actions and Events* (Oxford: Clarendon Press, 1980), 21–42, at 22: "[I]n so far as a person acts intentionally he acts, as Aquinas puts it, in the light of some imagined good."

[19] This doubt is the theme of Chap. 5, above.

The relation between the shared, constitutive aim of actions and their differing ends-in-view need not be that they aim to attain the former by attaining the latter; it may instead be that they aim to attain the former in the course of pursuing the latter. The constitutive aim of action, in other words, may be a goal with respect to the manner in which other goals are pursued, rather than a composite or expected consequence of those other goals.

Consider, for example, the goal of efficiency. You cannot pursue efficiency by itself, in a vacuum: you must have other goals in the pursuit of which you seek to be efficient. But then you can seek to be efficient at everything you do in the pursuit of those other goals. And in that case, efficiency is a goal of all your actions, not because you hope to attain it by attaining the various goals peculiar to those actions, but rather because you hope to attain it in the course of pursuing them.

I'm not claiming that efficiency is the constitutive goal of action: Lord, no. I'm just pointing out that actions can share a common aim even though their ends-in-view do not in any sense converge. Your actions can be aimed in as many different directions as you like and yet share the common aim of efficiency. My view is that there is a goal that is similar to efficiency in just this structural respect and that is shared by all your actions as such.

Identifying the relevant aim is not on my agenda for the present essay.[20] My reason for introducing the possibility of such an aim is simply to fill out the methodological picture that I am opposing to Gauthier's. In Gauthier's picture, how to decide between actions is a practical matter, which we decide by weighing the practical advantages and disadvantages of various deliberative principles. In my picture, the principles for deciding between actions are not for us to decide, because they are determined for us by the point of action itself.

Gauthier's picture suggests that we can hope for a pure theory of practical reasoning. Nothing underwrites our principles of practical reasoning, in his picture, other than the principles themselves. But my picture suggests that the philosophy of practical reasoning cannot be purified, in particular, of considerations from the philosophy of action. The correct principles of practical reasoning are determined by the constitutive aim of action—the thing at which behavior must aim in order to qualify as action, in the way that propositional attitudes must aim at the truth in order to qualify as belief. What makes an action rational, then, must depend on what makes something an action, to begin with. The philosophy of action must provide a foundation for the philosophy of practical reasoning.

---

[20] I defend the view that action has a constitutive aim in Chap. 6, above. I offer one account of this aim in *Practical Reflection* (Princeton: Princeton Univ. Press, 1989); and Chap. 7, above. I offer a different (though, I believe, compatible) account in Chap. 8, above.

Of course, the order of logical dependence need not dictate the order of dis-covery. Rival conceptions of practical reasoning can be taken as proposals for what the underlying aim of action might be. In any deliberative principle, we can look for the implicit criterion of success that it tends to track, and we can ask whether satisfaction of that criterion might be the aim in virtue of which behavior qualifies as action.

Indeed, I think that Gauthier's critique of straightforward maximization can be reformulated along these very lines. What the maximizer's approach to prisoner's dilemmas reveals is, not that his conception of practical reasoning is disadvantageous, but rather that the criterion of success that it tracks in actions—namely, maximizing value for the agent—doesn't express a shared aim in which their status as actions could possibly consist.

Gauthier's Critique Reformulated

In order to reformulate Gauthier's critique of maximization along these lines, I must return to our initial story, in which you and I expect to be offered incen-tives to testify against one another about a jointly committed crime. Gauthier's complaint against maximization is that it prevents us from reaching a mutu-ally beneficial agreement to keep silent, since each of us would expect the other, as a maximizer, to violate such an agreement. Let me begin by re-examining this complaint.

The costs of being a maximizer are, in fact, less than obvious. Some philoso-phers have pointed out, for example, that the costs identified by Gauthier are primarily due, not to one's being a maximizer, but to one's being perceived as a maximizer; and they have argued against Gauthier's assumption that others can tell what one's conception of practical reasoning is.[21] But I want to grant Gauthier's assumption of translucency, as he calls it.[22] What is of greater inter-est for my purposes is that even translucent maximizers will not be excluded from co-operative agreements so long as they are capable of making commit-ments that are truly effective.

Suppose that when each of us says "I'm willing to keep silent if you are," what he thereby makes translucent to the other agent is a disposition that will withstand any subsequent calculations—an irrevocable disposition to keep silent, under the specified conditions. In that case, forming and expressing a willingness to keep silent will be tantamount to making an effective commit-

---

[21] See, e.g., Geoffrey Sayre-McCord, 'Deception and Reasons to be Moral,' in Peter Vallen-tyne (ed.), *Contractarianism and Rational Choice: Essays on David Gauthier's Morals by Agreement* (Cambridge: Cambridge Univ. Press, 1991), 181–95.

[22] *Morals By Agreement*, 174.

ment, which one's practical reasoning cannot overturn.[23] And the maximizing conception of practical reasoning will direct us to exchange such commitments, each conditional upon the other, since a conditional commitment will irrevocably dispose the issuer to keep silent only if the other agent has issued a reciprocal commitment, whose condition it will satisfy, so that the other will be irrevocably disposed to keep silent as well. Since each commitment will irrevocably lead to silence upon being reciprocated, silence will reign, and the harms of mutual betrayal will be avoided.

Rational maximizers seem to be capable of reaching co-operative agreements, then, provided that they can commit themselves effectively. So where are the costs of being a maximizer? And where is the need for a conception of practical reasoning that favors fulfilling co-operative agreements?

How, in fact, can there ever be a need for such a conception? The only commitment that either of us has an interest in making is one that is not only conditional on receipt of an effective commitment from the other but also sufficient to satisfy the condition on that reciprocal commitment, so that the other's silence will be ensured. And since each commitment will be conditional upon the efficacy of the other, each will have to be effective in order to satisfy the other's condition. Hence neither of us has any interest in making a commitment unless it is effective.[24]

So why do we need a conception of practical reasoning that will direct us to fulfil our commitments? The only commitments that we have any interest in making are effective commitments, sufficient to ensure their own fulfilment. A conception of practical reasoning that enjoined us to fulfil these commitments would thereby enjoin what is already guaranteed by the very existence of the commitments themselves. What would be the point?[25]

One might respond, on Gauthier's behalf, that commitments of such efficacy are beyond the capacity of human agents. But surely human agents are capable of devising mechanisms for predetermining their future behavior; and in so far as they aren't, this lack of ingenuity cannot be held against the maximizing conception of practical reasoning. A more plausible objection is that human agents do not ordinarily commit themselves by the brute predetermination of

---

[23] Here I seem to imply that the disposition to keep silent is first formed and then expressed. I am inclined to believe, instead, that the disposition in question is formed precisely by being expressed. (See Chap. 9, above.)

[24] Here, as elsewhere, the argument relies on Gauthier's assumption of translucency.

[25] Versions of this point are considered by Derek Parfit, *Reasons and Persons*, 35–7; Holly Smith, 'Deriving Morality from Rationality,' in Vallentyne (ed.), *Contractarianism and Rational Choice*, 229–53, n. 13; and Richmond Campbell, 'Gauthier's Theory of Morals by Agreement,' *Philosophical Quarterly* 38 (1988) 243–64, at 254, and 'Moral Justification and Freedom,' *Journal of Philosophy* 85 (1988) 192–213.

their behavior. The exchange of such mechanistic commitments wouldn't add up to a co-operative agreement in any ordinary sense of the phrase.

Each of these commitments would be effective, we said, in the sense that it would govern the agent's behavior irrespective of his subsequent deliberations about whether to fulfil it. Its efficacy would therefore consist in the fact that it left the agent no choice on that score. Yet if the agent would have no choice whether to fulfil his commitment, then his fulfilling it wouldn't qualify as an autonomous action on his part. And co-operative agreements are ordinarily understood as leading, not just to co-ordinated behavior, but to co-operative action—that is, behavior whose co-ordination is wittingly and willingly sustained by the agents involved. The envisioned commitments wouldn't enable rational maximizers to arrive at anything that would deserve to be called co-operative agreements in this sense.

Note that Gauthier's objection to maximizing rationality has now quietly been transformed from the practical to the theoretical mode. The objection is no longer that someone who holds the maximizing conception thereby sacrifices the benefits of co-operative agreements. As we have seen, a rational maximizer can obtain those benefits so long as he can determine his future behavior by means of an effective commitment. The objection is now that although an effective commitment can help to produce the benefits of a co-operative agreement, it can't help to constitute an agreement that would yield genuine co-operative action.

What's wrong with the maximizing conception, then, is that, in so far as it can account for co-operation, it gets the nature of co-operative action wrong. And getting the nature of co-operative action wrong is not a practical but a theoretical failing—in particular, a failing in the philosophy of action.

Although Gauthier doesn't charge the maximizing conception with a theoretical flaw of this kind, it is the very flaw that his conception of practical reasoning is suited to remedy. The need that's filled by a conception favoring the fulfilment of co-operative agreements is the need to explain how we can rationally exchange commitments that will leave us autonomous in carrying them out.[26]

The commitments envisioned thus far threaten the agent's autonomy because their efficacy depends on their power to withstand the agent's own deliberations about whether to fulfil them; and their efficacy depends on this power because the agent is assumed to be a maximizer, whose deliberations will direct him to violate his commitments. But suppose that the agent held

---

[26] Note the similarity to Rousseau's formulation of "the fundamental problem" to be solved by the social contract: "How to find a form of association which will defend the person and goods of each member with the collective force of all, and under which each individual, while uniting himself with the others, obeys no one but himself, and remains as free as before" (*The Social Contract*, trans. Maurice Cranston (Harmondsworth: Penguin, 1968), I. vi, p. 60).

Gauthier's alternative conception of rationality, which posits reasons for fulfilling mutually beneficial agreements. Then he could make commitments whose efficacy would consist precisely in the fact that he would subsequently be determined to fulfil them by his appreciation of reasons for doing so. And the agent's being determined to act by an appreciation of reasons wouldn't undermine his autonomy, since being determined by reasons is just what constitutes autonomy, according to compatibilism.[27] Rationally effective commitments wouldn't have to withstand the agent's subsequent deliberations about whether to fulfil them, thus leaving him no choice; rather, they would take effect through the agent's deliberations and consequently through his choice.

In sum, a theory like Gauthier's isn't needed to provide rational agents with the benefits of co-operation; it's needed to explain how rational agents can co-operate freely. The problem that Gauthier's theory solves, but the orthodox theory doesn't, is not the practical problem of how to achieve co-operation but the theoretical problem of how co-operating agents can be autonomous. This problem, I now suggest, is just an instance of a larger problem in characterizing the autonomy that rational agents enjoy over their future actions. The larger problem has nothing essentially to do with prisoner's dilemmas or co-operation or, for that matter, morality in general. It simply has to do with our nature as agents who exercise the power of choice over future actions.[28]

Our autonomy over future actions requires, on the one hand, that we have the power of making future-directed decisions that are effective, so that we can determine today what will get done by us tomorrow. On the other hand, our future-directed decisions must not simply cause future movements of our bodies. If they did, our later selves would lack autonomy of their own, since they would find their limbs being moved by the decisions of earlier selves, as if through remote volitional control. We must exercise agential control over our own future behavior, but in a way that doesn't impair our own future agential control.

The only way to control our future behavior without losing future control, I believe, is by making decisions that our future selves will be determined to execute of their own volition; and the only way to determine our future selves to do something of their own volition is by giving them reason to do it.[29] Hence

---

[27] This point is made by Holly Smith, 'Deriving Morality from Rationality,' n. 13.

[28] For a related discussion of this problem, see Elizabeth Anderson, 'Reasons, Attitudes, and Values: Replies to Sturgeon and Piper,' *Ethics* 106 (1996) 538–54, at 542.

[29] This claim does not commit me to sharing Gauthier's view on the so-called toxin puzzle. In the toxin puzzle, an agent is offered a large reward merely for forming a future-directed intention to do something mildly harmful to himself, such as drinking a toxin. The puzzle was originally offered by Gregory Kavka as a *reductio ad absurdum* of Gauthier's theory, which implies that after the agent has collected the reward for intending to drink the toxin, he should follow through on his intention, even though he has something to lose by doing so and nothing more to gain (see Kavka, 'The Toxin Puzzle,' *Analysis* 43 (1983) 33–6). Gauthier has simply bitten the

future-directed intentions or commitments must be capable of providing reasons to our future selves. Unless we can commit ourselves today in a way that will generate reasons for us to act tomorrow, we shall have to regard our day-older selves either as beyond the control of today's decisions or as passive instruments of them.

Yet the maximizing conception of rationality does not guarantee, or even make probable, that decisions made today will provide reasons tomorrow. According to that conception, the reasons available to our day-older selves will be generated by our day-older interests and day-older circumstances, which may or may not militate in favor of carrying out decisions made today. The maximizing conception of rationality therefore fails to account for the diachronic autonomy that we exercise in our future-directed decisions.

One might wonder whether there is really a problem here. If an agent forms an intention to do something in the future, and if he doesn't change his mind, then the intention will remain in place and eventually come into the hands of his future self. When the intention subsequently produces an action, the agent's future self will be acting of his own volition, since the intention producing the action will now be his.

Yet whether an agent acts of his own volition, when governed by an intention remaining from the past, depends on the manner in which it remains and governs. If the intention is simply a lit fuse leading to action by some self-sustaining causal mechanism that's insensitive or resistant to the agent's ongoing deliberations, then it is not really a volition of his current self; it's just a slow-acting volition from his past. In order for the volition to become his own, the agent must buy into—or, at least, not be shut out of—its governance over his behavior.

bullet in this case, arguing that the agent should indeed drink the toxin ('Assure and Threaten,' 707–9).

Yet I needn't endorse this course of action in order to hold that future-directed intentions provide reasons for following through. For one thing, my view may not require that the reasons provided by future-directed intentions outweigh all countervailing reasons; perhaps they should be required only to carry some rational weight. On this version of the view, the agent in the toxin puzzle may form an intention to drink the toxin, and thereby give his future self some reason to drink it, without giving him sufficient reason.

Of course, an intention that doesn't provide sufficient reason for following through will be inefficacious, according to my view. The question therefore arises whether the reward is being offered only for an efficacious intention, or whether an inefficacious intention would do. A reasonable answer might be that an inefficacious intention wouldn't be much of an intention and, in fact, might not be an intention at all. It that case, an agent's intending to drink the toxin would require giving his future self sufficient reason for drinking it. Even so, I needn't conclude that a rational agent will find himself with sufficient reason for drinking the toxin; I can conclude instead that a rational agent will be unable to muster an intention to drink the toxin, precisely because he'll be unable to give his future self sufficient reason for drinking it. (This treatment of the toxin puzzle corresponds to Dan Farrell's in 'Intention, Reason, and Action,' *American Philosophical Quarterly* 26 (1989) 283–95.)

Unfortunately, the practical reasoning of a straightforward maximizer will direct him to discard an intention whenever he stands to increase his expected benefits by doing so. An intention that doesn't continue to serve his interests can remain to govern his behavior only by avoiding or resisting interference from his practical reasoning; and such an intention won't qualify as his own volition. The only intention whose fulfilment will be attributable to the maximizer himself, and not to some mechanism within him, is an intention whose fulfilment serves his interests.

A capacity for such fair-weather intentions simply isn't enough, in my opinion. Of course, we could circumvent the practical drawbacks of this capacity by adopting an axiology that guaranteed compatibility between the interests of our present and future selves.[30] In that case, commitments undertaken rationally would always be seconded by the rational deliberations of later selves, whose interests would necessarily harmonize with those which made the commitments rational to undertake. But this axiology wouldn't help to explain our actual capacity for future-directed commitments; it would merely wish away the real conflicts of interest in which the true nature of that capacity is revealed.

There are cases in which we have an interest in committing ourselves to future courses of action whose relation to our future interests is unknown, or even known to be adverse.[31] And experience tells us that we can often make rationally effective commitments in these cases. We can form resolutions that a future self will find rationally binding, whether or not they are seconded by his interests at the time.

Thus, our future-directed autonomy is not just a capacity to choose now what our future selves will in any case find reason for choosing then; nor is it a capacity to bind them to something else against their better judgment. It's a capacity to make choices that our future selves will buy into but wouldn't otherwise have made. And the straightforwardly maximizing conception of rationality cannot accommodate rational efficacy of this sort.

To be sure, the maximizing conception of rationality doesn't rule out the possibility of giving our future selves reason to act. An agent may find or put in place arrangements whereby the interests that he will have tomorrow are somehow altered by the commitments he makes today. He can take out bets on his own constancy, for example, or he can train himself to feel costly pangs of self-reproach whenever he violates a past commitment. Making a commitment will then give his future self reason to follow through.

---

[30] This point was made in discussion at the St Andrews Conference by Joseph Raz and Michael Smith.

[31] Potential prisoner's dilemmas are not the only such cases. For additional examples, see Edward F. McClennan, *Rationality and Dynamic Choice: Foundational Explorations* (Cambridge: Cambridge Univ. Press, 1990).

But these devices for conveying reasons to one's future selves would be external to rational agency, as the maximizing conception portrays it. One could be a fully-fledged and perfectly rational agent without having any of these devices in place, and hence without having autonomous control over one's future behavior. What's more, employing these devices would entail treating one's future selves as one treats separate people, since it would entail influencing their behavior indirectly, by modifying their incentives. If I offer you a large enough reward for following my directions, or threaten a large enough penalty for disregarding them, I put myself in a position to give you directions that will take effect without overriding your autonomy, but I do not thereby put myself in a position to decide what you are going to do. The ability to influence you by manipulating your expected pay-offs does not give me agential control over your behavior. Yet the control I would enjoy over my own future behavior via the devices under consideration would be no different.

Finally, some of these devices—indeed, the ones best able to resist being characterized as external manipulation—would depend on thoughts or feelings that the maximizing conception itself must regard as baseless. Training oneself to feel bad about violating commitments might enable one to undertake commitments that give one's future selves reasons to act; but it would entail training oneself to feel bad about something that one has no reason to feel bad about, according to the maximizing conception, since that conception treats violating commitments as a perfectly rational thing to do.

For all of these reasons, the devices at the disposal of the maximizing conception of rationality provide at most a simulation of diachronic autonomy. They enable an agent to induce his future selves to act, but not in a way that amounts to deciding on future actions.

I believe that in failing to accommodate this form of autonomy, the maximizing conception misrepresents what action is. The criterion of success that maximizing principles are designed to track doesn't express a constitutive aim for action, since behavior oriented toward satisfying that criterion wouldn't amount to action, as we know it.

If an action were the sort of thing whose success or failure could be judged solely by utility-maximizing considerations, then it wouldn't be the sort of thing that we could decide on today in a way that would necessarily give us reason to perform it tomorrow, and so it wouldn't be behavior over which rational agents had diachronic autonomy. But action *is* that sort of thing—it *is* behavior over which rational agents have diachronic autonomy—and so it can't be the sort of thing whose success or failure can be judged solely by utility-maximizing considerations.

My view is that the constitutive aim of action—the aim in virtue of which behavior becomes action, and against which it can be judged a success or failure as action—is autonomy itself.[32] How behavior can aim at autonomy, and why it thereby qualifies as action, are questions beyond the scope of this paper.[33] Here I can merely point out that if autonomy is the constitutive goal of action, and hence the internal criterion of success for action, then reasons for acting will be considerations relevant to autonomy, rather than considerations relevant to utility or the good. And we can at least hope that reasons of this kind will be generated by future-directed decisions. An analysis of action as behavior aimed at autonomy may therefore explain how future-directed decisions can govern future behavior rationally; and so it may explain how the nature of action makes diachronic autonomy possible.

The notion of autonomy as the constitutive goal of action isn't essential to my present argument, however. Maybe other proposals for the constitutive goal of action would explain how considerations relevant to that goal forge an autonomy-preserving link between past decisions and future actions. My present argument invokes autonomy—specifically, diachronic autonomy—simply as a feature of action that cannot be explained by the orthodox conception of practical reason, because it gives no rational weight, and hence no autonomy-preserving influence, to past decisions.

There are of course those whose normative intuitions oppose giving rational weight to past decisions: they think that abiding by a commitment for its own sake is foolish. Then there are those whose normative intuitions demand rational weight for past decisions: they think that abandoning a commitment is fickle. But I am joining neither of these camps, since I cannot see how to settle the issue on normative grounds. What settles the issue, in my mind, is not an intuition to the effect that we ought or ought not to give weight to past commitments. What settles the issue for me is that simply being rational agents enables us to exercise autonomy over our futures without impairing our future autonomy—something that we couldn't do unless past commitments had rational weight.

Gauthier's critique of straightforward maximization has now been removed from its foundation in practical reasoning and resettled on a new foundation in the philosophy of action. I believe that the philosophy of action can provide a foundation, not just for criticizing inadequate conceptions of practical reasoning, but also for constructing an adequate conception. What it will thereby provide, of course, is not a foundation for deciding how to decide. How to decide is something that we will discover, by discovering what it is to act.

---

[32] Thanks to Christine Korsgaard for daring me to confess this view, in the discussion at St Andrews. [33] See Chap. 8, above. But see also Chap. 1, p. 30.

APPENDIX

Co-operative Agreements

Why do I formulate each commitment as making the agent's action conditional on the other agent's commitment rather than on the other agent's action? Consider.

A condition that an agent places on his action won't be enforceable unless he can test for its satisfaction before he has to act. Of course, Alphonse can refuse to act unless Gaston acts first; but then Gaston mustn't do likewise, or action will never get started. And Gaston cannot refuse to act unless Alphonse acts *afterwards*, since Gaston can't test for the satisfaction of this condition before he has to act. At best, Gaston can refuse to act unless something is present that will subsequently guarantee action from Alphonse. A transparently effective commitment on the part of Alphonse provides such an assurance.

Now, Alphonse shouldn't just commit himself to act on the condition that Gaston acts first. For suppose that Gaston would act first anyway, whether or not Alphonse was committed to reciprocate. In that case, Alphonse would unnecessarily have encumbered himself in advance with the costs of reciprocating, since he didn't have to do so in order to gain the benefits of Gaston's action. Alphonse should therefore commit himself to act on the condition that his being so committed is necessary to elicit action from Gaston.

But how can Alphonse test whether this condition is satisfied? If Gaston is to act first, what will make it the case that Alphonse's commitment was necessary to elicit his action? And how will Alphonse tell whether it was the case? The only way for it to be the case that Alphonse's commitment was necessary, and for Alphonse to tell that it was, will be for Gaston to have previously framed a transparent commitment making his action (bi)conditional on Alphonse's commitment. If Alphonse wants to lay down an enforceable condition, then, he should commit himself to act on the condition that Gaston frame a commitment that's conditional on his, Alphonse's, being so committed.

Of course, if Gaston is to fulfil this condition, by framing a commitment, he will want to avoid thereby encumbering himself with the costs of acting unless his doing so is necessary in order to elicit action from Alphonse. So he will want to commit himself to act on the condition that Alphonse's commitment is conditional on his, Gaston's, being so committed. The agents will thus issue mirror-image commitments, each conditional upon the other.

Yet neither agent needs to spell out his commitment at such length. Each wants his commitment to be conditional on its being required to satisfy the condition on a commitment framed by other. And this condition can be imposed by a commitment to act simply on the condition that the other agent frame a similar commitment, since a similar commitment from the other agent will be one whose condition this commitment is required to satisfy.

A further problem arises, however, as to whether this commitment is sufficiently determinate in content. When Alphonse says "I'll act if you frame a similar commitment," what he is undertaking depends on what would count as a similar commitment from Gaston; and yet what would count as a similar commitment depends on what exactly Alphonse is undertaking. Alphonse's commitment is thus self-referential in a way that leaves its content ungrounded.[a]

Some philosophers have proposed a syntactic solution to this problem.[b] According to this solution, Alphonse's commitment is conditional on Gaston's framing a commitment that is syntactically similar—that is, framed in the same words. But this solution is clearly unsatisfactory, since it interprets Alphonse's commitment as requiring him to co-operate so long as Gaston says "I'll act if you undertake a similar commitment," even if Gaston is speaking an idiolect in which 'act' means "refrain" or 'similar' means "different."

I think that the solution to the problem of ungroundedness, in this instance, is to recognize that a similar commitment can be defined as a commitment with the same determinate *or potentially indeterminate* content. Suppose that Alphonse frames the conditional commitment to act if and only if Gaston issues a particular commitment; but that he risks failing to specify the requisite commitment because he attempts to specify it as similar in content to his own. And suppose that Gaston frames the conditional commitment to act if and only if Alphonse issues a particular commitment; but that he risks failing to specify the requisite commitment because he attempts to specify it as similar in content to his own. In that case, Alphonse and Gaston have issued commitments that really are similar, precisely because they share the same potential indeterminacies of content in addition to the determinate aspects of content that they share. The upshot is that the risk of indeterminacy in their commitments has been avoided, after all, since it is perfectly determinate whether either person's commitment has the same potential indeterminacies as the other's.

---

[a] Versions of this problem—or of a problem similar to it—are discussed by Holly Smith, 'Deriving Morality from Rationality,' 240–2, esp. n. 18; Peter Danielson, 'Closing the Compliance Dilemma: How it's Rational to be Moral in a Lamarckian World,' in Vallentyne (ed.), *Contractarianism and Rational Choice*, 307–15; and Richmond Campbell, 'Gauthier's Theory of Morals by Agreement,' 250–1. Some of these authors formulate the relevant commitments as making each agent's action conditional on the other's action. For them, the problem is how Alphonse tells whether he should act, given that he has made his action conditional on Gaston's, which is in turn conditional on his, Alphonse's. This problem disappears if the agents make their actions conditional on one another's commitments. But the problem of each action's being conditional on the other action is then replaced by the problem of each commitment's being dependent for its content on the other's content.

[b] See Danielson, loc. cit., and J. V. Howard, 'Co-operation in the Prisoner's Dilemma,' *Theory and Decision* 24 (1988) 203–13.

On the Aim of Belief

Introduction

There are several reasons for being interested in the fact—if it is a fact—that belief aims at the truth. I am going to argue that it's a fact. But first, the reasons for taking an interest in it.

Reasons for studying truth-directedness

One reason, first pointed out by Bernard Williams, is that belief's aiming at the truth enables us to explain the difficulty of believing at will.[1] The explanation is that believing a proposition at will would entail believing it without regard to whether it was true, and hence without the aim requisite to its being a belief.

Another reason for taking an interest in the truth-directedness of belief is that it may explain the phenomenon that has generally come to be known as the normativity of content. It may even explain the phenomenon away.

The phenomenon to be explained in this case is that the attribution of propositional content to a thought seems to yield normative consequences, on

In writing this chapter I have benefited from conversations with Linda Brakel and Nishiten Shah. I have also received helpful comments and suggestions from Paul Boghossian, Michael Bratman, John Broome, Jennifer Church, Stephen Everson, Tamar Gendler, John Gibbons, David Hills, Paul Horwich, Jim Joyce, Mike Martin, Ruth Garrett Millikan, Richard Moran, Jerome Neu, Lucy O'Brien, David Papineau, Georges Rey, Gideon Rosen, Zoltan Szabo, Stephen Schiffer, Peter Vranas, and Ken Walton. The chapter was presented to the 1998 Chapel Hill Colloquium, with comments by Gideon Rosen; to a conference at University College London, with comments by Lucy O'Brien; to a Philosophy of Mind seminar at New York University conducted by Paul Boghossian and Stephen Schiffer; and to the Philosophy Departments of Stanford University, Washington University, the University of Missouri, Columbia, and Cornell University. Work on this chapter was supported by a fellowship from the John Simon Guggenheim Memorial Foundation, together with matching grants from the Department of Philosophy and the College of Literature, Science, and the Arts, University of Michigan.

[1] 'Deciding to Believe,' in *Problems of the Self* (Cambridge: Cambridge Univ. Press, 1973), 136–51. I have argued elsewhere that belief's aiming at the truth does not prevent us from adopting a belief at will if our adopting it can be expected to make it true (*Practical Reflection* (Princeton: Princeton Univ. Press, 1989), 127 ff.); see also Chap. 8, above, pp. 194–6.

purely conceptual grounds. To say of a thought that it has the content that snow is white, for example, seems to imply that one ought to have the thought only if snow is white; and this normative consequence seems to follow immediately from the very concept of a thought's possessing such a content. The normative force inherent in content attributions has struck some philosophers as evidence against their being analyzable in naturalistic terms or assimilable into the natural sciences.[2]

But the normative implications claimed here for content attributions are not quite right. It isn't true that one ought to have the thought that snow is white only if snow is white; or, at least, it isn't true on the most inclusive interpretation of the phrase "to have a thought." If one can have a thought merely by entertaining it, without belief, then having the thought that snow is white would be perfectly in order even if one were up to one's neck in black snow. What one would be obliged to avoid, if snow weren't white, is not the mere thought of snow's being white but rather the belief with that content. And one would be obliged to avoid the belief because, given its nature as a belief, it would aim at being true but, given its content, would fall short of this aim on account of snow's not being white. The belief would be wrong or incorrect in the sense that it would be a failure in relation to its own aim.

The normativity previously attributed to content thus turns out to arise from the combination of content plus belief. We may even be tempted to say that the normativity is due entirely to the truth-directedness of belief and not at all to the nature of content. All that follows from a thought's having the content "snow is white" is that the thought is true if and only if snow is white. Whether the thought ought or ought not to be held in a world containing black snow depends on whether it is to be held in a way that aims at the truth—that is, as an object of belief.

The result appears to be that in order to naturalize the normativity associated with content, we need only naturalize the truth-directedness of belief. If it can be a natural or scientific fact that belief aims to be true, then it can also be a natural or scientific fact that false beliefs are wrong or incorrect, which is the fact underlying the normativity generally attributed to content.[3] The hope of naturalizing that normativity is thus a reason for being interested in how belief aims at the truth.

A third reason for taking an interest in the truth-directedness of belief is that it may help us to understand theoretical reasoning and perhaps, by analogy,

[2] See Saul A. Kripke, *Wittgenstein on Rules and Private Language* (Cambridge, Mass.: Harvard Univ. Press, 1982).

[3] Naturalizing the aim of belief is not on my agenda for this paper. For an attempt to naturalize the normativity of content via the nature of belief, see Ruth Millikan, 'Truth Rules, Hoverflies, and the Kripke-Wittgenstein Paradox,' in *White Queen Psychology and other Essays for*

practical reasoning as well. Theoretical reasoning justifies a belief by adducing considerations that indicate it to be true. And a belief can be justified by indications of its truth because being true is what would make it successful or correct, given that being true is its aim as a belief. Hence the truth-directedness of belief is what accounts for the justificatory force of theoretical reasoning.

I have argued on other occasions that practical reasoning must be understood along similar lines.[4] If there is to be a mode of reasoning that justifies action, as theoretical reasoning justifies belief, then there must be a criterion of correctness or success in relation to which action can be justified, just as there is a criterion of correctness or success for belief. If there's nothing that constitutes success for action as such, in the way that truth constitutes success for belief, then practical conclusions will not be supported by considerations with the normative force of justification or reasoning.

I am not going to defend this argument here—nor either of the preceding arguments, for that matter. My goal in this chapter is not to prove that the truth-directedness of belief can help us to understand the difficulty of believing at will, or the normativity generally attributed to content, or the form of practical reasoning. I have introduced these topics only as ulterior reasons for being interested in the phenomenon that I want to discuss.

Summary

I'll begin the next section by teasing apart the multiple relations that belief bears to the truth, setting aside those relations which do not amount to belief's having the truth as its aim. I will argue that the sense in which belief aims at the truth is not that it involves believing a proposition to be true; nor that it involves regarding a proposition *as* true; but rather that it involves so regarding a proposition with a particular aim. Just as a proposition is assumed by being regarded as true for the sake of argument or testing, so a proposition is believed by being regarded as true for the sake of something else. That "something else"—the aim with which a proposition must be regarded as true in order to be believed—is the aim of getting its truth-value right, by regarding it as true only if it really is. However, I will briefly postpone defining what it is to regard a proposition as true. Instead, I'll close the section by identifying various ways in which this subdoxastic attitude of acceptance, as I'll call it, can satisfy the concept of having an aim, or how its aim can be realized in the subject's psychology.

At the start of the third section, I'll define regarding-as-true as the attitude that plays a particular motivational role—indeed, the role that is traditionally

---

Alice (Cambridge, Mass.: MIT Press, 1993), 211–39. I would favor a strategy that is only slightly different in emphasis from Millikan's: see n. 18, below.   [4] See Chaps. 5, 8, and 10, above.

thought to be definitive of belief. I will thus commit myself to the claim that this motivational role, far from being definitive of belief, is definitive instead of the subdoxastic attitude of acceptance, which is involved in assuming, as I've just mentioned, as well as other cognitive attitudes, such as imagining. I'll devote most of this section to arguing that the attitude of imagining does indeed play this motivational role. My conclusion will be that belief must be characterized, not just as the attitude having the motivational role, but rather as a truth-directed species of that attitude: to believe a proposition is to regard it as true with the aim of thereby accepting a truth. The final section will deal with a few objections to this conclusion.

What is Truth-directedness?

The statement that belief aims at the truth is supposed to reveal something about the nature belief, something that distinguishes it from other propositional attitudes. So if we want to define truth-directedness, perhaps we should start by asking what is distinctive about the nature of belief. Not all relations between belief and the truth are sufficiently revealing.

What truth-directedness isn't: believing-true

For example, every instance of believing is an instance of believing something to be true, and this relation to the truth is sometimes confused with truth-directedness.[5] But in bearing this particular relation to the truth, belief is just like any other propositional attitude, since wishing entails wishing something to be true, hoping entails hoping something to be true, desiring entails desiring something to be true, and so on. Hence the fact that believing entails believing-true doesn't set belief apart from other attitudes, as truth-directedness is supposed to do.[6]

---

[5] For this confusion see, e.g., David Gauthier, 'Assure and Threaten,' *Ethics* 104 (1994) 699. Zoltan Szabo has persuaded me that there may be a species of believing that doesn't entail believing-true. If there were, my discussion in this section would have to be modified, but its overall point wouldn't be undermined.

[6] Steve Schiffer has pointed out that, although every propositional attitude ϕ is such that it entails ϕing-true, belief is the only attitude ϕ that entails believing-true. (Or, more precisely, it's the only non-composite attitude that entails believing true. Some composite attitudes also entail believing-true—for example, regretting.) Although the property of being a non-composite attitude that entails believing-true does distinguish belief from other attitudes, it does so without conveying much about the nature of belief. My working assumption in this paper is that truth-directedness is not just distinctive of belief but informatively so. (See also n. 8, below.) What would be most informative, of course, is a fully reductive account of belief, in terms of uncontroversially naturalistic concepts. I do not claim to have a fully reductive account (but see n. 16, below).

One might take exception to the last item on the foregoing list: maybe we can simply desire an object, without desiring anything to be true. Similarly, one might claim that we can simply imagine an object, without imagining anything to be true.[7] One might then draw a contrast with belief by pointing out that, although there are objects that we believe without believing *them* to be true (as when we believe a person, for example), we still cannot believe them unless there is *something* that we believe to be true (such as something the person has told us).

Yet the contrast that one would have drawn, in that case, is a contrast between belief and attitudes that are thought to have non-propositional instances. That is, one would have claimed that there are instances of desiring and imagining that don't entail desiring or imagining that *p*, for some proposition *p*, whereas there cannot be non-propositional instances of believing. In saying that believing entails believing-true, one would have said no more than that belief must have a propositional object, and so one still wouldn't have said anything that distinguished believing from propositional instances of desiring and imagining. For in cases of desiring or imagining that *p*, the proposition *p* is desired or imagined to be true, just as a proposition is believed to be true whenever it is believed.

The point is that truth-directedness is supposed to distinguish belief from other attitudes generally, and not just from their non-propositional instances. That believing entails believing-true cannot be what is meant, then, by the observation that belief aims at the truth.

What truth-directedness isn't: regarding-as-true

We can make some progress toward distinguishing belief from other attitudes by noting that the similarity between the expressions 'believing to be true' and 'desiring to be true' conceals an underlying difference. Believing a proposition to be true entails regarding it as something that is true, as a truth already *in*

---

[7] Sebastian Gardner claims that the unconscious phantasies cited in psychoanalytic explanations are non-propositional (*Irrationality and the Philosophy of Psychoanalysis* (Cambridge: Cambridge Univ. Press, 1993), 104, 122, 155–6, 189–91). The object of such phantasies wouldn't be a truth-bearer, and so they wouldn't entail imagining-true. Although I believe that some imagining doesn't entail imagining-true, I don't believe that the reason is necessarily that it is non-propositional. Such imagining may simply consist in picturing a state of affairs without engaging in the mental fiction *that* it obtains. (See n. 11, below.) I agree that some imagining may not even be propositional—for example, imagining a particular color without imagining any state of affairs involving it. But such rudimentary cases of imagining wouldn't do the work required of the phantasies discussed by Gardner. I suspect that Gardner confuses the question whether unconscious phantasies are propositional with the question whether they are sentential, in the sense of being represented in a language of thought, or readily expressible in ordinary language. They may be non-sentential, in this sense, while also having truth-conditions and hence being propositional.

being; whereas desiring a proposition to be true entails regarding it as something to be made true, as a truth-*to-be*. So in 'believing to be true', the infinitive 'to be true' takes the place of what would be, in direct speech, a predication of truth in the indicative mood; whereas in 'desiring to be true', the infinitive takes the place of what would be a predication of truth in the optative or gerundive.

This distinction is so subtle as to seem like a quirk of grammar rather than evidence of a genuine difference between desire and belief. We must therefore try to flesh out the distinction.

One way *not* to flesh it out is by incorporating indicative and optative predications of truth into the propositional objects of these attitudes. Believing that *p* entails believing *p* to be true, but it does not involve an attitude toward the proposition '*p* is true'; it involves only an attitude toward the proposition *p*. If it did involve an attitude toward the proposition '*p* is true', then the latter attitude would have to be a belief: what other attitude toward '*p* is true' could constitute believing *p* to be true? The result would be a problematic regress.[8] The belief that *p* would involve a belief that *p* is true, which would have to involve a belief that '*p* is true' is true, and so on, *ad infinitum*. Surely, we should say that believing *p* to be true involves, not an attitude toward the proposition '*p* is true', but only an attitude toward *p* itself, albeit an attitude toward it *as* true.

From the fact that believing entails believing-true, we have now derived two features of belief: belief always takes a propositional object, and it regards that object as true. Unfortunately, these two features do not take us very far toward distinguishing belief from the other attitudes.

One respect in which they fall short is that talk of regarding a proposition as true is no more informative the other expressions with which we're already dissatisfied. What is it to regard a proposition as true?

In past discussions, I have refused to answer this question, or I have given a non-answer.[9] My non-answer has been that a complete theory of belief will owe us an account of what it is to regard a proposition as true, but that

---

[8] What's problematic about the regress would depend on how belief-attributions were interpreted. If the truth of "*S* believes that *p*" required *S* to have a mental representation with the content *p*, then the regress would be vicious, since it would require the subject to have an infinite number of mental representations in order to have even one belief. If "*S* believes that *p*" wasn't interpreted as crediting *S* with a distinct representation, then the regress would be benign, but the resulting account of belief would be uninformative. In that case, "*S* believes that *p*," "*S* believes that *p* is true," "*S* believes that '*p* is true' is true," and so on, would be logically redundant attributions of one and the same attitude; and the fact that the first attribution entails all the rest would just be the trivial fact of their redundancy rather than a substantive fact about the nature of belief. (See also n. 6, above.)

[9] See above, Chap. 8, p. 182, n. 35.

different theories will discharge this obligation differently, offering alternative accounts among which I can reasonably wish to be neutral. I have simply insisted that believing, whatever it turns out to be, will have to involve regarding a proposition as true, whatever *that* turns out to be.

Yet there is another respect in which we have fallen short of distinguishing belief from the other attitudes. Whatever regarding-as-true turns out to be, it will still be involved in more than believing, since it will be involved, for example, in supposing or assuming, and in propositional imagining as well.[10] These attitudes are cognitive, like belief, rather than conative, like desire. To imagine that *p* is to regard *p* as describing how things are, not as prescribing how they should be.[11] Imagining is therefore a way of regarding a proposition as true— or, to introduce a term, a way of accepting a proposition.[12] The question remains how belief differs from imagining and the other cognitive attitudes.

What truth-directedness is

But here, at last, is the payoff to our strategy of asking what is distinctive about belief: we have found the role of truth-directedness. Differences among the cognitive attitudes appear to consist in the aim with which they accept a propo-

---

[10] For discussions that support this claim, see Robert C. Stalnaker, *Inquiry* (Cambridge, Mass.: MIT Press, 1984), 79 ff.; and Michael Bratman, 'Practical Reasoning and Acceptance in a Context,' *Mind* 101 (1992) 1–15, reprinted in Bratman, *Faces of Intention: Selected Essays on Intention and Agency* (Cambridge: Cambridge Univ. Press, 1999), 15–34.

[11] This issue is complicated by an ambiguity in the verb 'to imagine', which can be used to describe a thought either as imagistic in its intrinsic character or as fictional in its intent. In the former sense, imagining may entail no more than entertaining a thought; only in the latter sense does imagining entail regarding the thought as true. The differences between these senses can be marked by a difference in the grammatical form of the complement phrase. To imagine *the moon's being made of green cheese* may simply be to entertain a thought in the form of a mental image, an image of a green-cheesey moon. But to imagine that *the moon is made of green cheese* is to engage in a mental fiction, which may or may not involve imagery. I shall be using the verb 'to imagine' exclusively in the latter sense. (See Kendall Walton's discussion of imagining in *Mimesis as Make-Believe; on the Foundations of the Representational Arts* (Cambridge, Mass.: Harvard Univ. Press, 1990), 19–21.)

[12] The distinction I am drawing here is, in my view, the distinction that philosophers have generally been trying to pinpoint with the term 'direction of fit'. Unfortunately, many discussions of direction of fit tend to conflate regarding-as-true with aiming at the truth. See, e.g., Humberstone, 'Direction of Fit,' *Mind* 101 (1992) 59–83. Because of this confusion, I will avoid the term 'direction of fit' in this paper. I discuss the issue in Chap. 5.

Note also that my use of the term 'acceptance' is stipulative and idiosyncratic. The distinction that I draw between belief and acceptance is very different from distinctions drawn by Keith Lehrer in 'The Gettier Problem and the Analysis of Knowledge,' in *Justification and Knowledge*, ed. George S. Pappas (Dordrecht: D. Reidel, 1979), 65–78; John Perry, 'Belief and Acceptance,' *Midwest Studies in Philosophy* 5 (1980) 533–542; Bas C. Van Fraassen, *The Scientific Image* (Oxford: Clarendon Press, 1980); and L. Jonathan Cohen, *An Essay on Belief and Acceptance* (Oxford: Clarendon Press, 1992). My distinction is slightly different from those drawn by Stalnaker, *Inquiry*, 79 ff.; and Bratman, 'Practical Reasoning and Acceptance in a Context.'

sition, or regard it as true. Assuming, for example, involves accepting a proposition for the sake of argument, or for some similar purpose, but it doesn't involve believing the proposition. When a mathematician says, "Suppose that $\sqrt{2}$ is rational," he is not inviting us to believe it, but he is inviting us to take an attitude that's more like a belief than it is like a desire. I suggest that this attitude is like a belief because it is an acceptance, and that it is unlike a belief because it is acceptance for the sake of argument, whereas belief is acceptance for the sake of something else.

What else could we accept a proposition for? What purposes or aims could acceptance have? Well, imagining involves regarding a proposition *as* true irrespective of whether it *is* true—regarding it as true, that is, without trying to get its truth-value right. Perhaps, then, believing involves regarding a proposition as true with the aim of so regarding it only if it really is.[13] Thus, to believe a proposition is to accept it with the aim of thereby accepting a truth.[14]

The result is a fairly modest conception of how belief aims at the truth. This conception is modest, to begin with, because it avoids burdening belief with some of the more ambitious aims that might be suggested by talk of truth-directedness.

Perhaps the most ambitious aim suggested by such talk would be the aim of believing as many truths as possible. This aim would be irrational, of course, since the world is teeming with truths, most of which are too trivial to be worth believing. But there are qualified versions of this aim that might not be irrational, such as the aim of believing as many as possible of those truths which are useful or interesting. Also rational, perhaps, would be the aim of maximizing the proportion of truths to falsehoods among one's beliefs.

Yet none of these aims would answer to what I have in mind when postulating an aim that distinguishes belief from other cognitive attitudes. What I have in mind is an aim that differentiates believing a particular proposition

[13] Walton has argued that imagining, though not constrained by the truth, is not entirely unconstrained, either (39 ff.). Various imaginative games and projects may lay down rules for what is appropriate to imagine—for example, a game in which the participants agree to imagine that the tree-stumps in the forest are bears. What is appropriate to imagine in such a context, Walton describes as being "fictional" in that context. And he therefore concludes, "Imagining aims at the fictional as belief aims at the true" (41).

I don't think that this statement is meant to imply that aiming at the fictional is constitutive of imagining. At most, I think, it is meant to imply, conversely, that being aimed at by some form of imagining is constitutive of the fictional. Thus, Walton does not mean to rule out the possibility of aimless imaginings, as I would rule out the possibility of non–truth-directed beliefs. He simply means to define the fictional as that at which some form of imagining aims, in the way that belief aims at the truth. So interpreted, Walton's statement is compatible with my view.

[14] Here and throughout this paper, I deal exclusively with full belief—i.e., belief of the all-or-nothing kind. For the sense in which partial belief aims at the truth, see James M. Joyce, 'A Non-pragmatic Vindication of Probabilism,' *Philosophy of Science* 65 (1998) 573–603.

from other ways of regarding that proposition as true, such as imagining or supposing it. I thus have in mind an aim with which a particular proposition can be accepted, such that its being accepted with that aim constitutes its being believed. And one's acceptance of a proposition can amount to a belief without being part of any global epistemological project of accumulating true beliefs.[15]

What distinguishes believing a proposition from imagining or supposing it is a more narrow and immediate aim—the aim of getting the truth-value of that particular proposition right, by regarding the proposition as true only if it really is. Belief is the attitude of accepting a proposition with the aim of thereby accepting *a* truth, but not necessarily with any designs on truths in general, or Truth in the abstract.

How is the aim realized?

A further note of modesty in this conception of belief is that it leaves open how the aim of belief is realized. It allows but does not require the aim of belief to be an aim on the part of the believer; and it allows but does not require the aim of belief to admit of a naturalistic reduction. The conception merely requires that belief aim at the truth in some way or other, there being a broad spectrum of ways in which it might do so.[16]

At one end of the spectrum is the case in which a person intentionally aims a belief at the truth, by forming it in an act of judgment. He entertains a question of the form '*p* or not *p*?', wanting to accept whichever disjunct is true; to that end he accepts one or the other proposition, as indicated by evidence or argument; and he continues to accept it only so long as he receives no evidence or argument impugning its truth. The resulting cognition qualifies as a belief because of the intention with which it is formed and subsequently maintained by the believer, and because of the way in which that intention regulates its formation and maintenance.[17]

---

[15] This issue is discussed by Peter Railton in 'Truth, Reason, and the Regulation of Belief,' *Philosophical Issues* 5 (1994) 73–4.

[16] The following discussion may give the false impression that I hope to reduce the concept of truth-directedness to other concepts that are not teleological. Although I do think that truth-directedness is reducible to some extent, I do not think that its reduction can dispense with teleology. Any reduction will have to allude either to the subject's aims or to the design of his cognitive systems, both of which are teleological notions. I do not regard the ineliminability of teleology to be a flaw in my account of belief; on the contrary, I think of it as a virtue. For I think that the concept of belief just is a teleological concept, of a mental state constituted in part by its point or constitutive aim.

[17] Note that this belief may consist in a cognition that is *mis*directed at the truth. When the subject intentionally sets out to accept whichever proposition is true, he will be guided by methodological beliefs about how to discriminate truth from falsehood. Even if he is wrong about how to arrive at the truth, he is still aiming to arrive at it; his acceptance of a proposition is still regulated in ways that he regards as truth-conducive; and so it will still qualify as a belief, whether or not it is regulated in a manner that is truth-conducive in fact.

A person can also aim cognitions at the truth without necessarily framing intentions about them. Suppose that one part of the person—call it a cognitive system—regulates some of his cognitions in ways designed to ensure that they are true, by forming, revising, and extinguishing them in response to evidence and argument. Regulating these cognitions for truth may be a function for which the system was designed by natural selection, or by education and training, or by a combination of the two.[18] In any case, the system carries out this function more or less automatically, without relying on the subject's intentions for initiative or guidance. Even so, the subject may identify with this system, by endorsing it or fostering it or doing something else that makes its operations attributable to him, in the manner made familiar by Harry Frankfurt.[19] Its workings may then count as his doings, so that he can be said to have regulated the resulting cognitions, and thus to have aimed them at the truth.

At the far end of the spectrum, we can imagine a subject who is dissociated from the workings of this cognitive system, also in Frankfurt's sense: he is oblivious to it, or he disapproves of it, wishes it would stop, hopes it will fail, either in general or on a particular occasion. In that case, the resulting cognitions may not qualify as having been regulated by him. But they will still have been regulated for truth, and hence aimed at the truth, albeit by a part of him with which he doesn't identify. They will still be attempts at accepting truths, even though they will be attempts on the part of a cognitive system rather than the person as a whole. As cognitions aimed at the truth, they will still qualify as beliefs, according to my conception.[20]

---

[18] This sentence suggests one strategy for naturalizing the truth-directedness of belief. The strategy suggested is slighted different from that pursued by Ruth Millikan in her 'Truth Rules' paper; and it would apply to only some of the mechanisms that regulate beliefs.

The difference in strategy this. On the one hand, beliefs guide the subject's behavior in a manner that benefits him only—or, at least, most reliably—when they are true. Their guiding the subject when true is what confers advantages on him, and so it appears to be what beliefs were selected for, in the course of evolution. Beliefs were thus, metaphorically speaking, designed to be true. On the other hand, beliefs are regulated by psychological mechanisms designed to ensure that they are true. These mechanisms dispose the subject to form and revise his beliefs in response to indicators of their truth—that is, in response to reasons. Thus, beliefs perform their function best when true, just as various bodily systems perform best at 98.6 degrees; and beliefs are regulated so as to be true, just as the body's temperature is regulated so as to be 98.6. I would emphasize the latter explanation as conveying the sense in which belief aims at the truth; Millikan would emphasize the former.

In any case, an evolutionary explanation can apply only to some but not all of the mechanisms that regulate beliefs. Although some of our cognitive mechanisms are designed by evolution, others consist in acquired habits of mind or learned methodologies. The aim of the latter mechanisms may be implicit in the way they are acquired and refined, or explicit in the instruction from which they are learned. As I have said before, naturalizing the aim of belief, or the proper function of belief-regulating mechanisms, is not the purpose of this paper.

[19] *The Importance of What We Care About* (Cambridge: Cambridge Univ. Press, 1988), especially chs. 2, 5, 7, and 12.

[20] I discuss this issue at greater length in Chap. 8, pp. 184–8, above.

All of the cases in this spectrum can be described as follows. An acceptance has the aim of being the acceptance of a truth when it is regulated, either by the subject's intentions or by some other mechanisms in ways designed to ensure that it is true.[21]

Finally, my conception of belief is modest in that it doesn't require belief to be governed by truth-seeking mechanisms alone. There are probably psychological mechanisms that cause, and are designed to cause, beliefs that happen to diverge from the truth. Evolution or education may have given us dispositions to err on the side of caution in perceiving predators, to overestimate our own popularity, and so on.[22] But my thesis is not that belief is completely shielded from mechanisms that tend to make it false; my thesis is that belief is necessarily subject to mechanisms designed to make it true.

In most cases, the latter mechanisms retain some influence, despite interference from the former. Arguments can dispel our belief that there is a predator in the shadows, though they may not dispel the visual appearance. Evidence can undermine our belief in our own popularity, though perhaps not an egotistical phantasy to the same effect. Unlike an optical illusion or a phantasy, a biased belief usually responds to indications of the truth, however imperfectly.

Even when a belief is prevented from responding to corrective influences, the fact remains that its regulative mechanisms are being prevented from doing what they were designed to do. A phantasy and a biased belief are alike in that

---

[21] If belief can be aimed at the truth by the subject's cognitive mechanisms, rather than by the subject himself, then Davidson may well be wrong when he says that "someone cannot have a belief unless he understands the possibility of being mistaken, and this requires grasping the contrast between truth and error—true belief and false belief" ('Thought and Talk,' in *Inquiries into Truth and Interpretation* (New York: Oxford Univ. Press, 1984), 170). The subject himself would be required to grasp or understand the possibility of false belief only if he was himself required to aim at avoiding it. If he can have beliefs by virtue of cognitive mechanisms designed to avoid that possibility, then he needn't be able to grasp or understand it.

Paul Boghossian has objected that the resulting account of truth-directedness is disjunctive and therefore seems *ad hoc*. I think, on the one hand, that the account's being disjunctive would not necessarily make it *ad hoc*. There is a marked difference between beliefs that are formed by deliberate acts of judgment and beliefs that are formed sub-personally. An account of belief should not be faulted for marking this difference. On the other hand, I don't think that the resulting account of belief really is disjunctive. Rather, it is an account of a functional state that has multiple realizations. On the difference between disjunctiveness and multiple realizability, see Jerry Fodor's 'Special Sciences: Still Autonomous after All These Years (A Reply to Jaegwon Kim's "Multiple Realization and the Metaphysics of Reduction"),' *In Critical Condition: Polemical Essays on Cognitive Science and the Philosophy of Mind* (Cambridge, Mass.: MIT Press, 1998), 9–24.

[22] Relevant here is Jerry Fodor's, 'Is Science Biologically Possible? Comments on Some Arguments of Patricia Churchland and of Alvin Plantinga,' *In Critical Condition*, 189–202. Note that some apparent cases of adaptively biased belief may not be cases of belief at all. For example, one may benefit from a bias toward the view that a prospective opponent in iterated prisoner's dilemmas will play the strategy of tit-for-tat. But one needn't believe that he will; one need only assume it. (I owe this point to Michael Bratman.)

they fail to track the truth; but the phantasy has no tendency to track the truth at all, whereas a biased belief is diverted from the truth; and something can be diverted from the truth only against the background of a tendency to track it. To say that belief aims at the truth isn't to say that it can never be misled; on the contrary, it's to say that belief *can* be misled: what can't be misled are phantasies.

Can't Belief be Defined by its Motivational Role?

Modest as this claim may be, it is ambitious enough to rule out a purely motivational conception of belief. According to the latter conception, all that's necessary for an attitude to qualify as a belief is that it dispose the subject to behave in ways that would promote the satisfaction of his desires if its content were true. An attitude's tendency to cause behavioral output is thus conceived as sufficient to make it a belief.[23] According to my conception, however, an attitude doesn't qualify as a belief unless it also has a tendency to be constrained by input in ways designed to ensure that it is true. I thus conceive of belief as constituted both by its power to cause behavioral output and by its responsiveness to epistemic input.

The claim that belief cannot be characterized solely by its motivational role is similar in form to my earlier claim that it cannot be characterized solely as a matter of acceptance, or regarding-as-true: both claims point to truth-directedness as necessary to complete the characterization. And this similarity suggests a solution to my earlier problem of explaining the nature of acceptance. For in the motivational role of belief we find a plausible account of what it is to regard a proposition as true. We can say that belief involves regarding a proposition as true in the sense that it involves a disposition to behave as would be desirable if the proposition *were* true, by doing things that would promote the satisfaction of one's desires in that case. We can thus interpret the locution 'regarding *as* . . .' to mean "representing in a way that disposes one to behave *as would be desirable if* . . ."—or just ". . . *as if* . . . ," for short.[24]

---

[23] A classic exposition of this view is R. B. Braithwaite's 'The Nature of Believing,' *Proceedings of the Aristotelian Society* 33 (1932–33) 129–46, reprinted in *Knowledge and Belief*, ed. A. Phillips Griffiths (Oxford: Oxford Univ. Press, 1967), 28–40. See also D. M. Armstrong, *Belief, Truth, and Knowledge* (Cambridge; Cambridge Univ. Press, 1973), 3–6; W. V. Quine and J. S. Ullian, *The Web of Belief* (New York: Random House, 1978), 9–19; Robert C. Stalnaker, *Inquiry* (Cambridge, Mass.: MIT Press, 1984), 4; Lynn Rudder Baker, *Explaining Attitudes; a Practical Approach to the Mind* (Cambridge: Cambridge Univ. Press, 1995), 154 ff; Daniel C. Dennett, 'Do Animals Have Beliefs?' in *Brainchildren: Essays on Designing Minds* (Cambridge, Mass.: MIT Press, 1998), 323–31.

[24] On this sense of "behaving as if . . . ," see Braithwaite, 31–32. Ruth Millikan has suggested to me that the output dispositions relevant to the characterization of a cognitive state are, not its

Under this interpretation, saying that belief cannot be characterized solely by its motivational role is just the same as saying that it cannot be characterized solely as a matter of acceptance, since its being a matter of acceptance just consists in its having that role. But then the same reasons should apply to both claims. The reason why belief cannot be characterized solely as a matter of acceptance, I said, is that acceptance is also involved in other attitudes, such as hypothesizing and imagining. Having identified acceptance with the motivational role of belief, I am now committed to saying that the other attitudes sharing the element of acceptance must also share the motivational role. But does imagining that *p*, for example, typically dispose the subject to behave as would be desirable if *p* were true?

Well, it does in at least one context: the context of child's play, in which imagining disposes the child to pretend. When a child imagines that he is a nurse, for example, he is disposed to behave as would be desirable if he were a nurse; when he imagines that he is an elephant, he is disposed to behave as if he were an elephant; and so on.

Here I depart from the received version of folk psychology, which frames all motivational explanations in terms of desires and beliefs. A desire-belief explanation of pretending would go something like this: the child wants to behave like an elephant, he knows how to behave like an elephant—or, at least, he knows some behaviors that are recognized as elephant-like under the conventions of the nursery—and he is consequently moved to engage in those behaviors. I reject this explanation, in favor of one that invokes the motivational force of the imagination.

In order to defend this departure, I will have to turn from discussing how belief aims at the truth to a discussion of how the imagination motivates. The one discussion depends on the other, however, since the necessity of truth-directedness to the characterization of belief depends on the insufficiency of a purely motivational characterization. I'll return to truth-directedness shortly.

Behavior motivated by imagining: make-believe

As I see it, the desire-belief explanation of pretending makes the child out to be depressingly unchildlike. According to this explanation, the child keeps a firm grip on reality while mounting an appearance conceived as such. He puts on an act—an elephant-act—conceived by him as a means of impersonating

actual dispositions, but rather the dispositions that it was designed to have. Just as belief need only be regulated in ways *designed* to track the truth, so it need only be *designed* to produce behavior that would be desirable if the belief were true. Whether it actually tends to produce that behavior is no more relevant to its being a belief than whether it actually tends to track the truth. I like this suggestion, and yet I'm not sure whether to adopt it. My own linguistic intuitions inclined me to question whether a state without the appropriate motivational force would count as a belief.

something that he is not. His subsequent pretending is a case of purposeful simulation, no different from an adult's pretense.[25]

I call this explanation depressing because it denies that the child ever enters into the fiction of being something other than he is. In order to enter *into* the fiction, the child would have to act it *out*; and in order to act it out, I think, he would have to act *out of* imagining it, not out of a desire to represent it in action.[26] A child who was motivated by such a desire would remain securely outside the fiction, thinking about it as such—that is, as a fiction to be enacted. I'll expand on this claim below; but first, let me mention some further drawbacks of the desire-belief explanation of pretending.

One further drawback is that the desire-belief explanation fails to account for children's ability to invent and to understand novel ways of pretending. An especially imaginative child may come up with his own way of pretending to be an elephant, but not by considering which behaviors would be most suitable to an elephant-act, as if he were an impressionist honing some zoological schtick. Rather, the child's method is to imagine being an elephant—weighing a ton, walking on stumpy legs, carrying floppy ears—and then to wait and see how he is disposed to behave.[27]

Similarly, this child's playmates do not appreciate his inventions by recognizing that they are especially similar to the behavior of real elephants, and hence good choices for an aspiring elephant-impersonator. On the contrary, success at pretending to be an elephant need not involve behavior that is realistically elephant-like at all. What it requires is rather behavior that's expressive of elephant-mindedness—expressive, that is, of vividly imagining that one is an elephant.

Finally, I think that the present explanation is wrong developmentally, in that it credits the child with a precocious mastery of the distinction between fact and fiction. According to this explanation, pretending entails deliberately producing a false appearance. This explanation should lead us to expect adults to be even better than children at playing pretend: adults are better than

---

[25] I am going to argue that pretending is not purposeful simulation, but I do not mean to deny that one can enter into a game of pretend with a purpose, or that one may have a purpose in allowing oneself to continue the game. Getting oneself to pretend, and letting oneself go on pretending, may be things that one does for a purpose. But the pretending itself consists in behavior that isn't purposeful, I shall argue, because the particular things that one does in the course of pretending are motivated by wish and imagination rather than by desire and belief. (See the discussion on pp. 272–4 ff. below.)

[26] I am focussing here on one sense in which the child can be said to "enter into" his imaginary world. Walton discusses a broad range of senses in his chs. 6 and 7.

[27] Ian Rumfitt has suggested Peter Schaffer's play *Black Comedy* as an illustration of this point. During a large portion of this play, the actors must pretend to be in a pitch black room, though they are in fact playing on a fully lit stage. How is an actor in this play to approach his role? Hardly by mimicking what he has seen people do in the dark. The only answer seems to be: by imagining that he's in the dark.

children at acting—and lying—so why are they worse at pretending? The answer, I think, is that pretending isn't a matter of deliberately producing a false appearance; it's a matter of expressing one's imagination, an activity to which mastery of the distinction between fact and fiction is actually a hindrance, not a help.

I have said that a child's imagining that he is an elephant disposes him to behave as would be desirable if he were an elephant. Yet if imagining is to have a motivational force like that of belief, then it ought to work in concert with an attitude that has a motivational force like that of desire. The behavior to which someone is disposed by accepting p is behavior that, if p were true, would be desirable in the sense of promoting the satisfaction of his actual desires. Where does desire fit in to my account of pretending?

Note, to begin with, that imagining myself to be an elephant entails other, more specific bits of imagining: here is my trunk, there is my tail, and this— say, this chair—is a tree, or my elephant baby, or a pail of water, or whatever.[28] Within the fiction of being an elephant, I then have various desires with respect to my elephant-world—desires to rub my head against the tree, to drink out of the pail, to nurse my baby, or whatever. And my fictional behavior then expresses my fictional desires: I elephant-do as I elephant-want.

The question is what conation in the real world motivates the behavior that is fictionally motivated by these desires. What conative attitude in me, the child, makes me behave as if I'm an elephant who wants to drink from a pail with his trunk? The desire-belief explanation would be that the actual motive is a desire to simulate the fictional motive—in this case, a desire to act as if I'm an elephant who wants to drink from a pail. According to this explanation, I have no conations with respect to the fictional pail; I have only conations with

---

[28] The chair then becomes what Walton calls a "prop" (35 ff.). My discussion of this case seems to be at odds with the discussion of imagining that I am Napoleon in my paper 'Self to Self,' *Philosophical Review* 105 (1996) 39–76. Here I say that imagining that I am an elephant entails imagining, of my actual body, that it is an elephant's—that my arm is an elephant's trunk, and so on. In 'Self to Self' I argued that imagining that I am Napoleon need not involve imagining anything about my actual self, since it may involve only imagining the world as experienced by Napoleon.

These arguments are consistent, however. My claim in 'Self to Self' was not that I *cannot* imagine my actual self to be Napoleon; it was rather that I *need* not imagine this in order to imagine that I am Napoleon. There is a way of imagining that I am Napoleon such that the 'I' in this specification of what I'm imagining doesn't refer to me, the imaginer. My claim in the present paper is not that I must attribute elephanthood to my actual self in order to imagine that I am an elephant; it's rather that I must do so if my imagining is to subserve pretending or make-believe. The reason is that my imagining must refer to my actual body in order to motivate bodily behavior. If I imagined that I was an elephant in the manner described in 'Self to Self,' my imagining wouldn't have the content that I, David Velleman, was an elephant; and so it shouldn't move to me to behave as if that content were true—which is what it would do if it moved me to behave like an elephant. (I am grateful to Lucy O'Brien for raising this issue in her commentary on an earlier draft of this chapter.)

respect to the fiction as such, that it *be* a fiction in which there is a conation with respect to the pail.

As noted above, this explanation excludes me from my own imaginary world. It explains how I can be motivated to put things *into* my fiction, including fictional motives, but not how I can act *out* my fiction, in the sense of acting out of my fictional motives. I can't act out of my fictional motives at all, according to this explanation, because they are merely fictional: they don't exist.

An explanation that admitted me into my fictional world would have to allow me real motives toward objects and events in that world: it would have to allow me elephant-desires and elephant-beliefs. In such an explanation, my motivating cognition would not be the thought "Here is how to behave as if this chair were a pail of water"; my motivating cognition would be the thought "Here is a pail of water." And my motivating conation would be, not "Let me behave as if I wanted to drink," but rather "Let me drink." Only by acting out of such motives, framed from the elephant's point-of-view, could I enter into the fiction of being an elephant. So long as I acted out of motives framed from the child's point-of-view, I would remain on the outside of the fiction, looking in.

Consider again the motivating thought "Here is a pail of water," described above as an elephant-belief. This thought is not actually a belief: I cannot believe something to be a pail of water if I know that it is a chair. But the cognition can properly be described as an elephant-belief, because I imagine it to be a belief on my part as an elephant.[29]

Part of what I imagine in thinking "I am an elephant" is that I am an elephant reflecting on what he is rather than a child imagining himself to be what he isn't. Similarly, part of what I imagine with "Here is a pail of water" is that I am an elephant recognizing a pail of water rather than a child re-imagining a chair. I thus imagine my thought "Here is a pail of water" to be a belief.

My imagining this thought to be a belief helps explain how its motivational force enables me to enter into the fiction. When my imagining "Here is a pail of water" moves me to behave toward the chair as would be desirable toward a pail of water, it operates as it would if it were a belief, as I imagine it to be. I therefore act out of motives like the ones that I imagine myself to have. That's why acting out of my imaginings is a way of entering into them: I am motivated as if from within the point-of-view that I imagine occupying.

---

[29] Walton discusses this phenomenon at pp. 34 and 214–15. Imagining that one (hereby) believes something is analogous in many respects to pretending that one is (hereby) asserting it. On the latter phenomenon, see Walton, pp. 220–24. Also relevant here is the case in which a movie-goer experiences fear-like responses and imagines them to be real fear (241–49). In this case, Walton says that the viewer's responses become props in his imagining (247). Similarly, we might say of a participant in a game of make-believe that his imagining itself becomes a prop, because it is imagined to be a belief.

This phenomenon is summed up by the description of my activity as *make-believe*. I cannot *make* myself *believe* that a chair is a pail of water. But I can imagine that a chair is a pail of water, and that I am thereby believing it to be one; and my imagining can then motivationally simulate its own imagined role, so that it functions as a *mock-belief*. In the motivational grip of this mock-belief, I am gripped as if by the belief that I imagine having as an elephant, and so I am inside the fiction, acting it out.[30]

The previous question, about the role of conations, can now be rephrased as follows. If my imagining "Here is a pail of water" serves as a mock-belief, is there something that serves as the corresponding mock-desire? Could there be an actual state of mind that I imagine to be the desire "Let me drink"?

What serves as this mock-desire could not actually be a desire, for reasons similar to those for which my elephant-belief cannot actually be a belief. Just as I cannot believe something to be a pail of water if I know that it is a chair; so, too, I cannot desire to drink from what I know to be a chair. I usually cannot desire things that are patently unattainable, any more than I can believe things that are patently false. If I think that something cannot come about through efforts of mine, then the most I can do is hope for it; and if I think that it cannot come about at all, then the most I can do with respect to it is wish.[31]

In the present case, what is imagined to be an elephant's desire for an attainable drink must in reality be a child's conation toward a drink known to be unattainable. And if I am to have a conation toward an admittedly unattainable drink, then it must be a wish rather than a desire, just as my cognition of the drink must be an instance of imagining rather than belief. What is imagined to be my elephant-desire for a drink must therefore be a wish. Of course, it isn't an earnest or heartfelt wish; it's a faint and ephemeral wish of the sort that we might ordinarily call a whim. Imagining that I am an elephant, I am struck with the whim of taking a drink.[32]

A motivational explanation of make-believe has now emerged along the following lines. What moves me to dangle my arm between my nose and the seat of a chair is, on the one hand, imagining that this is the way to drink from a

---

[30] As David Hills has pointed out to me, another respect in which imagining functions as a mock-belief is suggested by Walton's thesis that imagining aims at the fictional. As the child finds his imaginings dictated by what is fictional in the context of the game, he imagines that they are beliefs being dictated by the facts around him.

[31] Of course, I may occasionally find myself desiring patently unattainable things, just as I sometimes find myself believing patent falsehoods; but such cases are exceptions to a rule that I cannot simply and straightforwardly break.

[32] One might think that I need only imagine wanting to take a drink, without necessarily wishing to take one, or even having a whim to that effect. But I do not see how I can be moved by a merely imagined conation. I do think, however, that a whim is the sort of conation that is easy to acquire. Indeed, a whim may be possible to *conjure up*—to form simply by imagining having the corresponding desire.

pail of water with my trunk; and, on the other hand, wishing to drink from a pail of water with my trunk. In the fiction that I am an elephant, my imagining and wishing are a belief and desire, moving me to drink from the pail. When my imagining and wishing move me to behave as if drinking, they fulfill the motivational role of the belief and desire that they are imagined to be, with the result that I enact my imagined role as an elephant.[33]

This motivational explanation of make-believe implies that the attitudes of imagining that p and believing that p are alike in disposing the subject to behave in ways that would satisfy his conations if they were true. It therefore supports my thesis that the motivational role of belief is not sufficient to distinguish it from other cognitive attitudes. To represent a proposition in a way that confers a disposition to behave as if it were true is simply to regard the proposition as true—which is to have a cognition of it, but not necessarily a belief.

One might think that my explanation of make-believe already suggests

---

[33] An anonymous referee has proposed an alternative account of make-believe. The referee proposes that imagining that p consists in making it the case that it is for oneself as if p. Pretending that p is a way of making it for oneself as if p. Hence pretending is itself a form of imagining, as the referee conceives it. This conception of imagining implies that the child's pretending to be an elephant constitutes—and hence cannot result from—his imagining that he is an elephant.

According to this conception, the child's imagining takes place, not in the medium of mental imagery or a language of thought, but in the outward medium of symbolic behavior, which is not to be explained by any antecedent, inner imagining. The problem with this conception is that, whereas the child has an innate ability to represent things in mental imagery or the language of thought, he must choose his behavioral symbols, and his choices would seem to require some psychological explanation. Why does the child use his arm to represent an elephant's trunk? Why doesn't he use his nose instead? And what makes it the case that he's using his arm to represent the elephant's trunk rather than its tusk, or nothing at all? Surely, the explanation is that the child *thinks* of his arm as somehow corresponding to a trunk. And now the question is how to characterize this thought. The answer cannot be that the child's outward movement plays the role of this thought, too—that he "thinks" of his arm as a trunk just by using it to represent a trunk. This answer would raise the same questions all over again. What would explain the child's "thinking" with his arm rather than his nose? And what would make it the case he was "thinking" of a trunk—or, indeed, that he was "thinking" at all, rather than just waving his arm around? The child's symbolic use of his arm must be explained by some thought lying behind it, and the question is how to characterize that thought. My answer is that the thought consists in the child's imagining his arm to be a trunk. The only alternative I can think of is to say that the thought is a belief, to the effect that his arm is a means of representing a trunk. But then the proposed explanation of make-believe would collapse into the belief-desire account that I criticize in the text.

A closely related problem is this. How does a particular way of moving his arm succeed in making it for the child as if he were an elephant? Does it somehow seem elephant-like to him? If so, then make-believe requires the child to find behavior that strikes him as elephant-like, and it therefore amounts to an elephant-impersonation that the child directs at himself. As I argue in the text, this conception of make-believe portrays the child as implausibly sophisticated and calculating. In my view, a particular way of moving succeeds in making it for the child as if he were an elephant because *it is the way he finds himself disposed to move when he imagines being an elephant.* This account has the virtue of not requiring the child to have any prior conception of how an elephant moves.

a simpler way of distinguishing belief from imagination. The explanation suggests that belief is the attitude that motivates in conjunction with desire, whereas imagining is the attitude that motivates in conjunction with wish. Perhaps, then, a belief disposes the subject to do what would satisfy his desires if it were true, whereas imagining disposes him to do what would satisfy his wishes.

A problem with this suggestion is that belief and imagining may not be so exclusive about the conations with which they combine to motivate behavior. I shall later be discussing cases in which imagining seems to motivate in conjunction with desire;[34] and there may also be cases in which belief motivates in conjunction with wish.[35] Furthermore, even if belief motivated solely in conjunction with desire, and imagining solely in conjunction with wish, the problem would remain how to distinguish the one kind of pair from the other. Attitude-pairs of both kinds dispose the subject to behave in ways that would promote the satisfaction of the one attitude under circumstances satisfying the other. Which pairs of such motives are the belief-desire pairs? If we try to fix the motivational characterization of belief by pairing belief and desire, we end up with an inadequate motivational characterization of belief-desire pairs.

My motivational explanation of make-believe gains support from the experience of adults who have difficulty joining wholeheartedly into this activity. Consider the adult who freezes when invited by a child to join the other elephants at the watering-hole. What this adult experiences is an inhibition, but it isn't at bottom an inhibition against the requisite outward behavior. He could force himself to go through the outward motions of participating in the make-believe while still being inhibited from actually participating. The reason is that he could still be inhibited from acting out his imaginings, which is what make-believe requires.

As I suggested earlier, this inhibition is acquired on the way to adulthood, in the process of mastering the distinction between fact and fiction, or between fantasy and reality. I can now explain further how I conceive of that process.

Mastering the distinction between fantasy and reality requires that we learn to seek what we can actually obtain, and to seek it in ways by which we can actually obtain it. It therefore requires that we come to suppress some of our behavioral dispositions. We have to suppress our dispositions toward trying to make thoughts true, if they cannot be made true, or not by us; and we have to

---

[34] Consider my variation on Hume's case of a man suspended in a cage (pp. 269–72, below). This man doesn't merely wish that he wouldn't fall; he wants not to fall. But he imagines that clinging to his cage will provide additional safety.

[35] Such cases seem harder to come by, because the distinction between desire and wish is less clear. Do you want to win the lottery, or do you merely wish that you would win? Certainly, you believe rather than merely imagine that buying a ticket is the only means of winning. Are you then moved to buy a ticket wishfully or desirously?

suppress our dispositions to behave as would be desirable if thoughts were true, if they aren't actually true. Both sets of dispositions lead to behavior that's unrealistic, either because it has unattainable ends in view or because it adopts ineffective means. We need a way of suppressing our dispositions toward such unrealistic behavior.

Our solution, I think, is first to segregate our realistic conations and cognitions from their unrealistic counterparts, and then to acquire an inhibition against the motivational force of the latter. Among the thoughts that we are disposed to make true—that is, among our conations—we delimit a subset whose members we are disposed to revise, discard, or at least reclassify if we cannot actually make them true. These reality-tested conations are our desires, which interact with one another in relative isolation from our mere hopes and wishes. Similarly, among the thoughts for which we have a disposition to behave as would be desirable if they were true—that is, among our cognitions—we delimit a subset whose members we are disposed to revise, discard, or at least reclassify if they aren't actually true. These reality-tested cognitions are our beliefs, which interact with one another in relative isolation from our mere imaginings. Setting our desires and beliefs apart from our wishes and imaginings is the first step toward mastering the distinction between fact and fiction.

The second step, I suggest, is to develop an inhibition against the motivational force of the unrealistic attitudes.[36] This inhibition tends to prevent us from manifesting the dispositions to make-true that are associated with thoughts unregulated for practicability; and it tends to prevent us from manifesting the dispositions to behave-as-would-be-desirable-if-true that are associated with thoughts unregulated for truth. It tends to prevent us, in other words, from manifesting the motivational force of wishes and imaginings, so that we tend to act only on desires and beliefs. We thus learn to behave realistically, out of conations that have been constrained by what is attainable, and cognitions that have been constrained by what is the case.

Behavior motivated by imagining: talking to oneself

Our inhibition against being motivated by unrealistic attitudes is perhaps clearest when it is less than fully effective. One such case is the behavior that is ordinarily called talking to ourselves.[37]

---

[36] I am now using the term 'realistic' to mean "tested against reality." Of course, we sometimes use the term to mean "properly and successfully tested against reality," so as to exclude attitudes that have failed reality-testing, or whose reality-testing has been inadequate. Thus, there is the sense in which wishes and fantasies are unrealistic attitudes, and then there is the sense in which some desires and beliefs are less realistic than others. From here on, I'll be using the term in the former sense.

[37] One of the "arational actions" discussed by Rosalind Hursthouse, in her paper by that title, is "muttering imprecations under one's breath" which can be an instance of talking to oneself in the sense that I have in mind ('Arational Actions,' *Journal of Philosophy* 88 (1991), 64). I am in

By "talking to ourselves," I don't mean literally addressing remarks to ourselves, as when we give ourselves a reminder or a scolding. The case that I have in mind is the one in which, though described as talking to ourselves, we are actually imagining ourselves in conversation with someone else, saying things that we wish we had said or could say. We walk down the street muttering at an invisible interlocutor, perhaps even shaking our head for emphasis; we sit at a red light and tick off our points on the steering wheel; or we sit at the computer alternately writing a sentence and reading it to an imagined audience.

This behavior eludes desire-belief explanation.[38] There is nothing that we both want to do and believe ourselves to be doing by talking to ourselves in this way. If someone stopped us on the street and asked "Why were you just muttering and shaking your head like that?" we could not offer an answer that began with the words "I wanted. . . ." What could we have wanted? To walk along muttering and shaking our heads? Hardly.

An explanation of our behavior would have to begin "I imagined . . ." or "I wished . . . ." Indeed, the explanation would have to include both. Merely wishing to say something to someone wouldn't have made us move our lips unless we had imagined ourselves in conversation with him. And merely imagining ourselves in conversation with someone wouldn't have made us move our lips if there hadn't been something that we wished to say.

---

agreement with Hursthouse's negative thesis about such actions—namely, that they cannot be explained as motivated by desire and belief. But Hursthouse thinks that they have no further explanation than that the agent, in the grip of an emotion, felt like performing them; whereas I believe that they can be explained as motivated by the imagination.

[38] Desire and belief can move us to initiate an imaginary conversation—for example, when we want to prepare for a real conversation in the future. But what desire and belief move us to initiate in that case is an adult form of make-believe (or role-playing, as we might call it), which then proceeds under the guidance of wish and imagination.

Thus, at the point in the imaginary conversation when we retort with "So's your old man," we aren't moved by a desire to prepare for a future utterance of this retort; we're moved by the wish to insult our imagined interlocutor. Our only reason for wanting to rehearse such a remark in the imaginary conversation would be that we foresaw wanting to deliver it in the real one; but our only way to foresee wanting to deliver it in the real conversation would be by finding ourselves moved to deliver it in the imaginary one; and at that point, we would already have rehearsed it, thus preempting any desire to do so. That's why role-playing, even if initiated by desire and belief, must still consist in behavior motivated by wish and imagination. Even when we talk to ourselves because we want to prepare for a future conversation, we have to say things that we wish we were saying to our prospective interlocutor, rather than things that we want to say to ourselves. (This argument bears some similarity to that at the end of n. 33, above.)

In any case, deliberately imagined conversations are not what I am discussing at this point in the text. I am discussing conversations that we have no reason for wanting to imagine, because they are already over or could never take place. Our only motive for imagining these conversations, to begin with, is wishing that we had or could say something that we didn't or can't. (The attribution of wishes in this note is subject to difficulties that I discuss in nn. 40 and 43, below.)

The normal inhibition against acting on such unrealistic motives slackens when we talk to ourselves, but it doesn't entirely let go. It is still evident in the fact that we talk under our breaths. If we entirely lost this inhibition, we would address our imagined interlocutors right out loud, and the sidewalks would be filled with a babble of half-conversations. The fact that we talk to ourselves under our breaths suggests that the inhibition against unrealistic motivation is selective: it prevents behavior that would be inconvenient or self-destructive, but it permits behavior that is harmless, despite being unrealistic.

Make-believe and talking to oneself differ in two circumstantial respects. The imagining involved in these activities is anchored differently in the surrounding conations and cognitions.

When I make believe that I am an elephant, my imagining is realistically motivated by a desire. I want to imagine that I am an elephant, and this desire moves me to imagine that I am an elephant, with the result that I do what I want.[39] My imagining is itself a mental action motivated by a desire for some result and a (trivial) belief about how to attain it. When I talk to myself, however, my imagining is motivated by the same wish that makes me move my lips. What moves me to imagine myself conversing with someone is, not wanting to *imagine* conversing with him, but rather wishing that I *were* conversing with him.[40] Hence my imagining is not a way of doing what I wish; indeed, it is a way of not doing what I wish, by imagining it instead. It is thus an unrealistic, wishful mental activity rather than a realistic, goal-pursuing action.[41]

Another difference between make-believe and talking to myself is that, in the former, my imagining is accompanied by beliefs about the same behavior. I imagine that I am dipping my trunk into a pail of water, but I also believe that I am dangling my arm over a chair. I know what I'm doing, even as I

---

[39] On deliberate imagining, see Walton, 13–16, and n. 25, above.

[40] Here my discussion encounters a difficulty in the attribution of wishes. (Until now I have avoided this difficulty by avoiding the construction "wishing that . . ." in favor of the construction "wishing to. . . . ") When we characterize a wish with a that-clause, we are sometimes unable to make our characterization as indefinite as the wish itself. "I wish that I were conversing with him" suggests a determinately present-tense wish—the wish to be conversing even now. Yet the wish itself may have no temporal aspect at all; its propositional content may simply be "I converse with him," representing a conversation without specifying its temporal relation to the present. Unfortunately, English usage does not permit us to say "I wish that I converse with him." It forces us to put the dependent verb in the subjunctive, where its tense is unavoidably interpreted as attributing a temporal aspect to the wish. (See also n. 43).

[41] In fact, I think that there are two different mechanisms by which imagining can be motivated. On the one hand, imagining that p can be directly motivated by the wish that p, through the mechanism of wishful thinking. On the other hand, imagining that p can be motivated by the wish that p combined with a further bit of imagining, to the effect that one is actually bringing p about by imagining it. In the latter case, imagining that p is itself a bit of make-believe, acting out the phantasy that Freud called "the omnipotence of thought." I discuss this phantasy further in n. 48, below.

imagine myself doing something else. When talking to myself, however, I may have no beliefs at all about my verbal behavior. If someone really did stop me to ask why I was muttering and shaking my head, I would probably respond "Was I?"—or perhaps even "I was not!" As I imagined speaking with someone, I was completely oblivious to the fact that I was speaking into thin air.

In these two respects, talking to myself resembles some further, less familiar cases of motivation by imagining. I therefore turn to a new category of examples.

Behavior motivated by imagining: psychoanalytic examples

Freud draws our attention to a passage in which Goethe recounts his earliest childhood memory, as follows: he was throwing crockery out a window and watching it smash in the street, to the wicked delight of older boys.[42] Freud tells us that he thought nothing of the passage until a patient, who was unacquainted with the works of Goethe, remembered doing precisely the same thing. What was significant for Freud was that the patient dated his memory to the age at which he had also attacked his baby brother in the cradle. Freud hypothesized that in casting out the crockery, the child phantasized that he was casting out his baby brother.[43] His behavior was thus motivated, according to

---

[42] 'A Childhood Recollection from *Dichtung und Wahrheit*,' *The Standard Edition of the Complete Psychological Works of Sigmund Freud*, ed. James Strachey et al. (London: Hogarth Press, 1958), xvii, 146–56.

[43] I will reserve the term 'fantasy' (and its homonym 'phantasy') for imaginings that are generated by wish rather than purposely formed by the subject, out of a desire to imagine. I use the spelling "fantasy" for those wishful imaginings which are self-consciously unrealistic, in that they are accompanied by an occurrent awareness of their being in tension with the truth. We sometimes allude to this awareness in specifying the fantasy's content. When we say, for example, that someone has a fantasy of being taller than he is, we do not mean that he has a fantasy with the content "I am taller than I am." We usually mean that he has a fantasy of being a particular height, colored by the knowledge that he isn't. For wishful imaginings that are not self-consciously unrealistic in this sense, I use the spelling "phantasy." Thus, a person cannot phantasize being taller than he is, in the sense just explained, because a phantasy (so spelled) would exclude any awareness of the contrast between his imagined and actual height.

The term 'wish', like the term 'fantasy', tends to be interpreted as denoting an attitude that is self-consciously unrealistic—in this case, a conation felt to be in tension with what is practicable. Here again, this awareness tends to be incorporated into our specification of the attitude's content. When we say that someone wishes that he could be six feet tall, we do not mean that the object of his wish is a mere ability, the ability to be six feet tall; we mean that he wishes he *were* six feet tall but realizes that he isn't and, more importantly, that he can't be. Saying "he wishes that he could be" is our way of highlighting the point at which the subject feels his wish to be in tension with what is practicable. Unfortunately, wishes that are not self-consciously unrealistic in this sense have no term of their own. I am tempted to coin the spelling "whish" for this purpose. Whishes would be unrealistic conations that are not accompanied by any thought as to the impracticability of their object.

The English language is not well equipped for the attribution of whishes. If someone has an unrealistic conation toward the proposition "I am six feet tall," we are forced to use the subjunctive in specifying the content of his attitude: we say "He wishes that he were six feet tall."

Freud, by a wish to be rid of his infant rival.[44] Freud then reads the same interpretation back into the passage quoted from Goethe, with the help of data about the birthdates of the poet's younger siblings.

Elsewhere Freud tells of an obsessive patient who "used to repeat an especially noticeable and senseless obsessive action":[45]

> She would run out of her room into another room in the middle of which there was a table. She would straighten the table-cloth on it in a particular manner and ring for the housemaid. The latter had to come up to the table, and the patient would then dismiss her on some indifferent errand. In the attempts to explain this compulsion, it occurred to her that at one place on the table-cloth there was a stain, and that she always arranged the cloth in such a way that the housemaid was bound to see the stain.

Freud explains this bizarre behavior as follows:

> The whole scene proved to be a reproduction of an experience in her married life which had later on given her thoughts a problem to solve. On the wedding-night her husband had met with a not unusual mishap. He found himself impotent, and 'many times in the course of the night he came hurrying from his room into hers' to try once more whether he could succeed. In the morning he said that he would feel ashamed in front of the hotel housemaid who made the beds, and he took a bottle of red ink and poured its contents over the sheet; but he did it so clumsily that the red stain came in a place that was very unsuitable for his purpose.

Freud concludes: "With her obsessive action, therefore, she was representing the wedding-night."

The "problem" posed by this patient's wedding night might just have been that her husband was impotent and that she wished he wasn't. But other symptoms attributed to this patient suggest that the problem was more complicated: she couldn't leave her husband without casting doubt on his potency, and she wished that she could. Her solution was to phantasize that the table-cloth was a bed-sheet, and that the stain on it enabled her to prove her husband's potency, as a previous stain had not.

Unfortunately, the subjective "were," which marks the contrast between content and reality, is normally interpreted as attributing an awareness of that contrast to the subject. "He wishes that he were six feet tall" is thus understood to describe a subject whose conation toward being six feet tall is accompanied by the awareness that he isn't and can't be. We have no way of saying that the subject has a conation toward being six feet tall without any thought as to how tall he could actually be.

These remarks on whish and phantasy are intended to be a gloss on some of Freud's views about primary process (as expressed, for example, in part V of 'The Unconscious,' *SE* xiv, 161–215, at 186 ff). For another difficulty in the attribution of wishes, see also n. 40, above. Putting these two notes together, I would be inclined to argue that whishes necessarily lack a temporal aspect, and that this phenomenon is what Freud had in mind in saying that unconscious processes are "timeless" (187).

[44] *Ibid.*, 152.   [45] 'Obsessive Actions and Religious Practices,' *SE* ix, 116–27, 121.

Freud's explanations for these behaviors make them seem somewhat like make-believe, and somewhat like talking to oneself, but also significantly different from both. They consequently provide us with a third set of circumstances in which imagining can motivate.

Freud's hypothesis is not that the jealous child was playing a game of Throwing Out the Baby, or that the dissatisfied wife was playing a game of Show the Stain, though this image of symptomatic behavior as make-believe can perhaps serve as a first approximation to Freudian theory. One difference is that the phantasies that motivate these behaviors are themselves motivated by the associated wishes rather than a desire to phantasize. What leads the child to phantasize that he is throwing out the baby is, not that he wants to *phantasize* doing this, but rather that he wishes to *do* it. Similarly, the wife wishes that she could prove her husband's potency; she doesn't want to phantasize proving it.[46]

In this respect, symptomatic behavior is more like talking to oneself than it is like make-believe. The wife is like someone who wishes that some fateful conversation had gone differently, and who is thereby moved repeatedly to imagine its going differently and to speak her part in the re-imagined conversation under her breath. In this case, she wishes that her honeymoon had gone differently, and she is thereby moved to phantasize its going differently, though she is moved to play her part, as it were, right out loud.

The wife's failure to mute her symptomatic behavior points to a respect in which it differs from talking to herself. In talking to herself, she would usually be aware of the conversation that she was imagining, though perhaps oblivious to moving her lips. In calling the housemaid to the table, however, she is aware of her overt behavior but oblivious to the phantasy that it enacts. Hence the pattern of awareness is reversed, and this reversal may explain why her behavior isn't muted, like speech under the breath. Because she is unaware of acting out a phantasy, she cannot be restrained by any inhibition against unrealistic motivation.[47] She is aware only of calling the housemaid to the table, a behavior against which she has no inhibition.[48]

---

[46] On the expression "she wishes that she could," see n. 43, above.

[47] As Jerry Neu has pointed out to me, I am oversimplifying the connection between the subject's overt behavior, on the one hand, and her ignorance of its motivation, on the other. I point out that the subject feels free to produce this behavior because she is unaware of the phantasy that it enacts. But there is another connection: she acts out her phantasy symbolically, in behavior that she feels free to produce, partly in order to protect herself from awareness of the phantasy. This latter connection belongs to the mechanisms of repression, which are beyond the scope of the present paper.

[48] My account of how phantasy figures in these instances of Freudian explanation differs from an account favored by other philosophers. (See, e.g., Richard Wollheim, 'Wish Fulfillment,' in *Rational Action*, ed. Ross Harrison (Cambridge: Cambridge Univ. Press, 1979), 47–60; Sebastian Gardner, *Irrationality and the Philosophy of Psychoanalysis* (Cambridge: Cambridge Univ. Press, 1993).) These philosophers emphasize the role of phantasy in placating or gratifying desire. They consequently conceive of phantasy as shorting the motivational circuit that connects conation with outward behavior: conation produces and is placated by phantasy instead. Wollheim's

Behavior motivated by imagining: expressive behavior

Another kind of behavior that is often motivated by phantasy is behavior that's expressive of emotion.[49] Hume points out that a person who is suspended at a great height in a metal cage may tremble with fear despite knowing that he is securely supported.[50] Hume's point is that, although the person doesn't believe that he's going to fall, he does imagine falling, and imagination can arouse the

account of this motivational short-circuit strikes me as question-begging. In order to explain how the imagination gratifies desire, he hypothesizes that it produces belief; and in order to explain how the imagination produces belief, he credits the subject with an underlying belief in the "omnipotence of thoughts"—that is, in his own ability to produce states of affairs by imagining them. But surely, the omnipotence of thoughts is a phantasy. The claim that this product of the imagination is actually believed would itself call for some explanation, which could hardly invoke the subject's belief in the omnipotence of thoughts.

A further question raised by the present interpretation is this. If phantasy shorts the motivational circuit connecting conation with behavior, then why does any behavior ensue? Why does young Goethe actually throw crockery out of the window, if his wish can be gratified internally, by phantasies of expelling his younger sibling? Gardner's answer is that the subject's behavior is expressive rather than instrumental: it doesn't aim at producing wished-for results; it merely expresses the phantasy that has gratified the subject's wish for them. (See pp. 169–72 of Gardner; see also J. Balmuth, 'Psychoanalytic Explanation,' *Mind* 74 (1965) 229–35.)

I think that Gardner is too quick to deny that the behavior in question is aimed at producing results. Of course, it isn't *realistically* aimed at producing them. That is, the wish for some results does not move the subject to do what he *believes* will produce them; but it does move him to do what he *phantasizes* as producing them. When Gardner denies that the subject's behavior is instrumental, he seems to mean that it isn't realistically instrumental, which is true, but he thereby seems to ignore the possibility of its being phantastically instrumental instead. The latter possibility shows that the instrumental and the expressive are not mutually exclusive categories of behavior: behavior often expresses phantasies precisely in the unrealistic way that it aims at producing wished-for results.

Even phantasies themselves can be instrumentally motivated in this fashion; and here the "omnipotence of thoughts" appears in its proper role, as a phantasy rather than a belief. What moves a subject to conjure up wished-for results in his imagination may be the phantasy that he is thereby producing them in reality. Imagining what he wishes for is then a piece of phantastically instrumental behavior, motivated by conation and cognition. The motivating conation is a wish for some results; the motivating cognition is the phantasy that he is producing those results, when he is in fact only imagining them. In such a case, the motivational circuit really is shorted. For if someone imagines that he is producing the wished-for results by imagining them, then he usually does not go on to imagine producing them by means of additional, outward behavior. I suspect, however, that most phantasies are motivated by wishes without any help from the phantasy of omnipotence: they are instances of directly wishful thinking. (See n. 41, above.)

[49] On this topic, see Rosalind Hursthouse, 'Arational Actions.' I share with Hursthouse the view that actions expressive of emotions are not to be explained as motivated by desire and belief. But Hursthouse believes that "[their] only explanation is that, in the grip of the relevant emotion, the agent just felt like doing them" (61). I think that we can often explain why the agent's emotion made him feel like doing these things rather than other things. The explanation involves phantasies that are naturally associated with the emotion's propositional content.

[50] *A Treatise of Human Nature*, ed. L. A. Selby-Bigge and P. H. Nidditch (Oxford: Clarendon Press, 1978), I.iii.13, p. 148. For other cases of emotional responses to what is merely imagined, see Richard Moran, 'The Expression of Feeling in Imagination,' *The Philosophical Review* 103 (1994) 75–106. See also Jerome Neu, 'A Tear is an Intellectual Thing,' *Representations* 19 (1987) 35–61.

same emotions as a belief.[51] Hume might have added that imagination can also motivate the same behavior as belief, since the person in this example may not only tremble but also cling to the bars of his cage, despite the knowledge that he is thereby gaining no additional safety.

When this person is lowered to the ground, he may rattle the bars of his cage in his impatience to get out. Does he believe that he can rattle his way out of the cage? Probably not. But his impatience will just consist in the wish that he could escape from the cage more quickly, and he will be imagining a quicker way out.

Why do you scratch your head when you're puzzled, hold your head when you're worried, or smack your head when you've made a dumb mistake?[52] Are these gestures a kind of sign-language? And then, if no one else is in the room, are you talking sign-language to yourself? No, you're acting out corporeal images of your own thinking—your mind's body-image, so to speak. You're acting out the phantasy of your memory as a balky machine (or a balky child), your curiosity as an itch, or your worries as raising the pressure inside your skull. You wish that you could jar your memory (or punish it), scratch your curiosity, or contain your worries. Your behavior is thus motivated by wish and imagination rather than desire and belief.

Why do you cower in fear, hide your face in shame, clench your fists in anger, shake your head in regret? There are fantasies at work here, fantasies of shrinking, disappearing, fighting someone, or undoing something.[53] These behaviors,

---

[51] Walton denies that we have real emotions toward merely imagined objects and events; what we have, he argues, are physiological and psychological reactions that we imagine to be emotions. According to Walton, then, we don't fear fictional characters but only imagine fearing them. I favor a somewhat different hypothesis, that our reactions to fictional characters should be understood on the model of mock-desires and mock-beliefs. I am inclined to think that emotions can be reality-tested, and that our terms for particular emotions properly refer only to their realistic instances. Thus, the term 'fear' is reserved for a response that is somehow regulated in a way designed to make it correlate with real dangers; but we also experience an unregulated version of the same response, which constitutes a kind of fantasy-fear. Unlike Walton, I do not conceive of fantasy-fear as a response that is merely imagined to be fear; I conceive of it as non–reality-tested fear, experienced in the unrealistic mode that is characteristic of the imagination. What we feel toward fictional characters, then, is a real emotion, but it is the real emotion of fantasy-fear. (These remarks are indebted to—though not ultimately in agreement with—views expressed by Jonathan Lear in 'Restlessness, Phantasy, and the Concept of Mind,' *Open Minded: Working Out the Logic of the Soul* (Cambridge, Mass.: Harvard Univ. Press, 1998), 80–122.)

[52] I owe this example to David Hills, who also suggested looking to Hume for other examples.

[53] Also relevant in this context is Jennifer Church's claim that the emotions are "internalized actions" ('Emotions and the Internalization of Actions,' (MS) (published in French as 'L'Emotion et L'interiorisation des actions,' in *La couleur des pensees*, s. dir. P. Paperman & R. Ogien (Paris: Editions de l'Ecole des Houstes Etudes en Sciences Sociales, 1995), 219–36).

Stuart Hampshire proposes a different explanation for expressive behaviors. When you clench your fists in anger, according to Hampshire, you are beginning and then cutting short the aggressive behavior to which anger necessarily disposes you. Similarly, "the man who cowers or shrinks, only sketching the action of flight, makes a gesture, or assumes a posture, that is the suggestion

like many of the others mentioned in this section, have an expressive or communicative role, but they are not motivated by desires to express or communicate anything: when you're afraid, you don't cower out of a desire to express or communicate your fear.[54] Rather, I would say, the expressive or communicative role of these behaviors is what wins them some reprieve from the normal inhibition on unrealistic motivation. As an adult, you allow yourself to act out your fantasies insofar as doing so is expressive of your emotions.

Acting out fantasies may go beyond mere gestures. Consider, for example, why setting your watch ahead by a few minutes helps to prevent you from being late.[55] You know that your watch is a few minutes fast, and so looking at your watch never leads you to believe that you are a few minutes later than you actually are. What, then, makes you hurry? Surely, the answer is that you are motivated by a cognition other than a belief.

When you're in the passenger seat of a speeding car, why do you press your foot to the floor? When you're behind the wheel, why do you yell at the drivers of the cars in front of you? And why do you yell at the referees of a sporting event that you're watching on television? I know of no satisfactory explanation of these behaviors in terms of desires and beliefs. I can of course concoct desire-belief explanations for them: desire-belief explanations are all too easy to concoct. But the resulting explanations aren't satisfactory, because they make your behavior look realistically purposive, when it is in fact utterly fantastic.

Motivational differences between imagining and belief

I have now introduced several categories of examples that feature motivation by imagining. These examples show that imagining that *p* and believing that *p* are alike in disposing the subject to do what would satisfy his conations if *p* were true, other things being equal. Admittedly, the examples have also

of the action, with the effective remainder of it removed" ('Feeling and Expression,' in *Freedom of Mind and Other Essays* (Princeton: Princeton Univ. Press, 1997), 143–59, at 145–46). Hampshire's hypothesis may be plausible in the case of anger, but it is quite implausible in most other cases. Cowering is not truncated or ineffective flight, nor does it sketch or suggest that action. What it suggests is a perfectly fantastic "action," to which Hampshire himself alludes with a figurative synonym: it suggests the action of *shrinking*. When you cower, you behave as if you could become small and inconspicuous at will; and this behavior would seem to be motivated by fantasy.

Of course, cowering may not have a motivational explanation: it may just be an innate, primitive behavior associated with fear. As Ruth Millikan has pointed out to me, even dogs and cats cower when they're afraid. I'm not sure that what this fact proves, however, since I'm not sure that dogs and cats don't have imaginations. They are certainly capable of *playing*, in a way that is strongly suggestive of make-believe; they are also capable of dreaming. In any case, I concede that these expressive gestures are among the more controversial of the examples that I discuss.

[54] Hursthouse makes the same point on pp. 60–61.

[55] I owe this example to a talk by the economist Robert Frank.

suggested that other things are rarely equal between cases of imagining and believing, and hence that the actual manifestations of these states are often different. But these differences do not undermine my thesis.

After all, belief itself cannot be characterized in terms of the behavior that it actually causes, since most beliefs cause no behavior at all, and the same belief will cause different behavior in different psychological contexts. Belief can be characterized only in terms of its disposition to produce behavior under various conditions, such as the presence of a relevant conation and the requisite motor skills, and the absence of conflicting motives and inhibitions. The examples suggest that imagining can be characterized as having the same conditional disposition as belief; the only differences have to do with the satisfaction of the associated conditions.

Thus, for example, most deliberate imagining is accompanied by countervailing beliefs, embodying the subject's knowledge of the facts that he is imagining to be otherwise, such as his knowledge that an imagined pail of water is really a chair. These beliefs exert their own motivational force, which can be expected to compete with that of the subject's imagination. Ordinary beliefs are not regularly accompanied by countervailing beliefs, and so their motivational force encounters less competition.[56] I have also hypothesized that the motivational force of imagining comes under an inhibition, whose effects can be detected, of example, in the way that we lower our voices when talking to ourselves. Both of these differences make imagining less likely to cause actual behavior.

Yet the conditional disposition to cause behavior is the same, and this disposition is all that figures in the nature of belief. The only essential difference between these states is that believing that p, unlike imagining that p, is regulated in ways designed to make it reflect the actual truth-value of p. That's why truth-directedness is essential to the characterization of belief.

Why motivational accounts seem right

Motivational characterizations of belief seem to dispense with reference to truth-directedness only because they tacitly restrict themselves to realistic motivation, whose cognitive component is necessarily truth-directed. For example, we might define belief as the state that determines the means by

---

[56] Paul Boghossian has pointed out to me that countervailing beliefs are present in the child who plays make-believe. Why don't they outweigh the motivational force of the child's imagining? The answer may be that the motives of a young child are less well integrated than those of an adult. A young child tends to act, not on the vector sum of all of his motives combined, but on whichever motive is at the front of his mind. That's why he is so impulsive and has difficulty making stable choices or postponing gratification. The child's ability to lose himself in a game of make-believe may thus be related to his tendency more generally to get lost in the salient motive of the moment.

which the subject is moved to pursue desired ends; and we might think that we had managed to distinguish beliefs from fantasies without alluding to whether they aimed at the truth. In fact, however, our definition would tacitly allude to truth-directedness under cover of other terms.

This definition would distinguish beliefs from fantasies only because the behaviors motivated by fantasies—make-believe, talking to oneself, yelling at the television—don't count as instances of pursuing desired ends. Yet the reason why yelling at the television isn't an instance of pursuing an end is, not that it doesn't have envisioned results, but only that it acts out a fanciful conception of how to produce them, whereas the pursuit of an end is essentially behavior whose conduciveness to its envisioned results is taken seriously. To pursue something is, by definition, to implement a serious rather than fanciful idea of how it can be attained; and so the very concept of pursuit already implies motivation by a truth-directed cognition. Defining belief by its role in the pursuit of desired ends would thus conceal but not eliminate reference to its truth-directedness.

I suspect that all motivational characterizations of belief tacitly rely on truth-directedness in similar fashion. Consider, for another example, the notion that belief can be defined in terms of its role in determining what the subject is willing to bet on.[57] This notion is familiar to students of formal decision theory, which is sometimes interpreted as showing how to deduce a person's relative degree of belief that p from his preferences among various possible gambles on p (among other propositions). This interpretation of the theory relies, I suspect, on the assumption that attaching payoffs to the truth or falsity of a proposition will induce the subject to get real about it, so to speak, in the sense that he will now respond with his best attempt at getting its truth-value right.[58] Hence the decision-theoretic characterization of belief conceals an assumption of truth-directedness.

Even as innocent a concept as 'action' can be used to smuggle truth-directedness into motivational characterizations of belief—in discussion among philosophers, at least. Philosophers tend to assume that every action involves the pursuit of some desired end, or that every action is performed for a purpose. This conception of action immediately excludes a behavior like yelling at the referees on television, which the agent does for no purpose. All the agent has in this case is a wish, which he only imagines that he is

---

[57] Thanks to Nishi Shah for suggesting this case.

[58] Not surprisingly, I doubt whether attaching payoffs to the truth or falsity of a proposition will necessarily have this effect. Money and chance are two subjects on which people tend to have powerful phantasies. Asking someone to wager large sums on the proposition that the next toss of a coin will turn up heads may not be a way of eliciting his degree of belief in that proposition; it may instead be a way of stirring up his fantasies of being punished by Fate or contaminated by lucre.

fulfilling; and a wish doesn't lend his behavior any purpose, because a purpose must be something that's realistically pursued.

If we conceive of action as necessarily having a purpose, then we can define belief by its role in motivating action, but only because our concept of action already requires it to be realistically motivated. Properly understood, then, motivational characterizations of belief tend to confirm rather than refute the thesis that belief aims at the truth.

How motivational accounts mislead

Ideally, conceiving of action as necessarily having a purpose should lead philosophers to withhold the term from unrealistically motivated behavior. In practice, however, it sometimes leads them to see, or to think they see, realistic purposes where none exist. Consider, for example, Donald Davidson's discussion of a case borrowed from Freud.

Davidson describes the case as follows:[59]

> A man walking in a park stumbles on a branch in the path. Thinking the branch may endanger others, he picks it up and throws it in a hedge beside the path. On his way home it occurs to him that the branch may be projecting from the hedge and so still be a threat to unwary walkers. He gets off the tram he is on, returns to the park, and restores the branch to its original position. Here everything the agent does (except stumble on the branch) is done for a reason, a reason in the light of which the corresponding action was reasonable. Given that the man believed the stick was a danger if left on the path, and desired to eliminate the danger, it was reasonable to remove the stick. Given that, on second thought, he believed the stick was a danger in the hedge, it was reasonable to extract the stick from the hedge and replace it on the path. Given that the man wanted to take the stick from the hedge, it was reasonable to dismount from the tram and return to the park. In each case the reasons for the action tell us what the agent saw in his action, they give the intention with which he acted, and they thereby give an explanation of the action. Such an explanation, as I have said, must exist if something a person does is to count as an action at all.

Davidson's explanation of this case contains a telling misstatement. He says that it was reasonable for the man, having removed the stick from the hedge, to return it to the path. Why was this reasonable? The man thought that the stick posed a danger in the hedge, but he had previously thought that it posed a danger in the path as well. Why did he remove the stick from one dangerous position only to place it in another position recognized as equally dangerous? Why didn't he throw it even further out of the way? The answer to this question is not available to Davidson, because it entails interpreting the behavior as unrealistically motivated.

[59] 'Paradoxes of Irrationality,' in. *Philosophical Essays on Freud*, ed. Richard Wollheim and James Hopkins (Cambridge: Cambridge Univ. Press, 1982), 289–305, at 292.

Freud introduces this example in a footnote to his case study of the patient known as the Rat Man.[60] The behavior described in the footnote belongs to a different patient, but it closely resembles behavior displayed by the Rat Man himself, which Freud describes as follows:[61]

> On the day of [his beloved's] departure he knocked his foot against a stone lying in the road, and was obliged to put it out of the way by the side of the road, because the idea struck him that her carriage would be driving along the same road in a few hours' time and might come to grief against this stone. But a few minutes later it occurred to him that this was absurd, and he was obliged to go back and replace the stone in its original position in the middle of the road.

Note that the Rat Man didn't even have the other patient's pretext for returning the object to its original position, since he didn't think that it posed any danger in the new position to which he had moved it; he simply thought that moving it had been absurd. But why, then, did he go back to replace it? Surely, taking the trouble to undo an absurd action is doubly absurd.[62]

Freud's explanation is that the Rat Man is deeply ambivalent toward his beloved and has difficulty coping with his ambivalence toward her, as with various other figures in his life. He has therefore repressed the hostile component of his ambivalence, remaining conscious only of unalloyed love. But his hostility occasionally breaks through the repression, moving him to obsessive actions, in which he enacts murderous phantasies of which he is completely unaware. In replacing the stone in the road, the Rat Man was unconsciously phantasizing that his beloved's carriage would, after all, come to grief against it.[63] Of course, the Rat Man's phantasy was quite unrealistic, as was the conscious thought that originally prompted him to move the stone. There is no reason to believe of a particular stone that it will upset a particular carriage, and so there is no reason for moving the stone in either direction, whether for the sake of protecting or of harming a future passenger on the road. But the Rat Man wasn't motivated, in either instance, by a belief that the stone would harm his beloved; he was motivated by a phantasy of its harming her, which in one instance was mistaken for a belief, and in the other instance was repressed entirely.

Freud explains the behavior of his other, unidentified patient along the

---

[60] 'Notes upon a Case of Obsessional Neurosis,' *SE* x: 192, n. 2.

[61] *Ibid.*, 190 (emphasis omitted).

[62] Tamar Gendler has suggested to me that the Rat Man may have wanted to escape responsibility for any mishap caused by the stone, by returning it to where it had been anyway, without his intervention. Of course, such an action would actually absolve him of responsibility only if it succeeded in literally undoing his first action, making it the case that he had never moved the stone at all. And the notion that his second action could change the past in this fashion is of course a phantasy, no less than the phantasy that Freud postulates.

[63] 'Notes upon a Case of Obsessional Neurosis,' *SE* x: 191.

same lines. Returning the branch to the path was, in Freud's view, a "hostile act," which wasn't really due to the public-spirited motives adduced by the agent.[64] This explanation cannot be filled out as Davidson recommends. We cannot say: "Given that he wanted to harm someone, it was reasonable to extract the stick from the hedge and replace it on the path." Even if harming someone had been a reasonable project, leaving a branch in the path would not have been a reasonable way of going about it. The correct interpretation of this behavior is therefore unavailable to Davidson, who insists on interpreting it as the realistic pursuit of an end.

The problem for Davidson's theory doesn't depend on the peculiarly pathological features of these cases, such as repressed hostility or obsessive repetitions. A perfectly normal agent may see a stick or stone in his path, imagine its causing a freak accident, and feel compelled to shift it out of the way, well knowing that it is not really a hazard. If we insist on explaining his action in terms of attitudes that would make it reasonable, we shall end up attributing to him a stronger belief in the occurrence of the envisioned accident than he actually had. He didn't believe that the accident would happen; he just imagined its happening, but his fantasy was enough to motivate him. How often have you felt for your wallet or purse after merely imagining a mugging? How often has a mere fantasy of disaster prompted you to check whether you turned off the stove or fastened your seatbelt?[65]

---

[64] 'Notes Upon a Case of Obsessional Neurosis,' 192, n. 2.

[65] Experimental psychologists have found that 4- to 6-year-old children, if asked to imagine a monster or bunny in a box, will profess to know that the box is empty but, if subsequently left alone with it, will get up from their seats to look (P. I. Harris et al., 'Monsters, Ghosts and Witches: Testing the limits of the fantasy-reality distinction in young children,' *British Journal of Experimental Psychology* 9 (1991) 105–123). Some interpret these experiments as indicating that the children "believe" in the products of their imaginations. Yet as others have pointed out, similar results have been obtained with adults, who clearly do not believe in what they have imagined (Jacqueline D. Woolley and Henry M. Wellman, 'Origin and Truth: Young Children's Understanding of Imaginary Mental Representations,' *Child Development* 64 (1993) 1–17). In the latter experiments, adults were instructed to prepare two containers of sugar water and to label one of them "Sugar" and the other "Cyanide." The subjects then showed reluctance to drink from the second container, though not from the first, despite knowing that the two were equally harmless. (See P. Rozin and C. Nemeroff, 'The Laws of Sympathetic Magic: A psychological analysis of similarity and contagion,' in J. W. Stigler, R. A. Schweder, and G. Herdt (eds.), *Cultural Psychology; Essays on Comparative Human Development* (Cambridge: Cambridge University Press, 1990).) Woolley and Wellman attribute this result to the "emotionally charged" nature of what the adults were invited to imagine; and they suggest that the same explanation may apply to the corresponding results with children. I would argue that the "emotional charge" in these cases simply ensured that the subjects had a conative attitude toward the imagined objects, without which their cognition of the objects would fail to motivate behavior. (See also Angeline Lillard, 'Making Sense of Pretence,' in *Children's Early Understanding of the Mind; Origins and Development*, ed. Charlie Lewis and Peter Mitchell (Hove: Lawrence Erlbaum, 1994), 211–34, at 220–21. For another relevant experiment, see D. M. Wegner, G. Coulton, and R. Wenzlaff, 'The Transparency of Denial: Briefing in the debriefing paradigm,' *Journal of Personality and Social Psychology* 32 (1985) 338–46.)

What these cases tell us, I think, is that tacitly incorporating truth-directedness into our conception of action can lead us to misinterpret people's behavior. Better to incorporate truth-directedness into our conception of belief, and to recognize that beliefs are not the only cognitions that can motivate.

Answers to Objections

I initially described my thesis as modest, but my arguments for it have now revealed two respects in which it could be even humbler. Let me explain these possible modifications to the thesis and my reasons for resisting them.

Must truth be the aim?

My thesis is that belief is an acceptance regulated in ways designed to ensure that its content is true. All that my primary arguments have shown, however, is that belief cannot be fully characterized in terms of its power to cause behavioral output. Even if the upshot of these arguments is that belief must also be characterized in terms of how it is constrained by input, the question remains whether it is constrained in ways designed to ensure that its content is true. Belief might be an acceptance regulated for empirical adequacy, or merely for consistency with other, similarly regulated acceptances. It would then have a constitutive aim other than the truth.[66]

I am less intent upon fending off this objection than some of the others that I have entertained. If I have managed to show that belief must be characterized by its responsiveness to input as well as its power to produce output, I will consider my arguments to have succeeded in some measure, at least. But I do think that the input constraints definitive of belief are designed to yield beliefs that are true, and I'd like to be able to say why I think so.

I take it to be a conceptual truth that beliefs are correct when true and incorrect when false: false beliefs are necessarily faulty or mistaken.[67] What's more, I don't think that the fault in false beliefs can consist in their tendency to misdirect our behavior, since many beliefs have little or no chance of directing behavior, and even some false beliefs can direct us well enough.[68] False beliefs

---

[66] John Gibbons has suggested to me that the aim of belief is knowledge. This suggestion subsumes my view. If belief is an acceptance that aims at being knowledge, then it aims at the truth *and more*—i.e., at truth plus proper justification. But I would like the aim of belief to account for our intuition that even an unjustified true belief is correct or right, whereas Gibbons's view would imply that such a belief was a failure as a belief.

[67] On this point, see A. Phillips Griffiths, 'On Belief,' in *Knowledge and Belief*, 127–43.

[68] Most if not all beliefs have some tendency to cause behavior, of course, since they tend to be expressed in assertions. But causing false assertions counts as a form of misdirection, I suspect,

are faulty in themselves, antecedently to and independently of any untoward practical consequences. In what sense are they faulty? The most plausible answer, I think, begins with the observation that we conceive of beliefs as constitutively regulated by input. Faulty or mistaken beliefs are the ones whose regulation has not succeeded in producing the kind of cognitions that it was designed to produce. The fact that beliefs are conceived to be faulty when false indicates that the regulation conceived to be constitutive of them is regulation for truth. Truth-directedness thus appears to be enshrined in our concept of belief.

Our conceiving of belief as truth-directed doesn't necessarily settle the issue, however. Perhaps we could discover that the attitudes we call beliefs are actually regulated in ways designed to promote something other than their being true. Would we conclude that these attitudes weren't really beliefs, after all? Or would we revise our conception of belief, to reflect its newly discovered aim?

I do not have an answer to this question. But I would like to point out, very briefly, the extreme improbability of its premise, that we might discover belief to be regulated for something other than truth.

I think that introspection argues against this possibility. When we discern a gap between a belief and the truth, the belief immediately becomes unsettled and begins to change. If it persists, we form another belief to close the gap, while reclassifying the recalcitrant cognition as an illusion or a bias. I cannot imagine evidence that would show this reclassification to be a mistake.

Some people claim that their cognitive efforts are aimed at something short of the truth, such as instrumental success or empirical adequacy. Under some interpretations, however, this claim is compatible with my thesis. For example, what people call aiming at empirical adequacy may in fact be only a willingness to settle for it. If a basketball player says "I'm just aiming to win by one point," we don't necessarily assume that he is engaged in point-shaving; we assume that he is aiming to score as many points as possible but willing to settle for any margin of victory. His willingness to settle for a small margin is a second-order aim with respect to his degree of success in the first-order aim of scoring points. I don't deny that we have a similar second-order aim with respect to our cognitive effort: we're willing to settle for empirical adequacy rather than truth. What I deny is that we are engaged in epistemic point-shaving, aiming for empirical adequacy in the first instance.

A basketball player may say, alternatively, that his ultimate aim is to raise his own salary, but we don't therefore assume that his every move on the court is

only because of the role that assertions play in forming the beliefs of others—and hence only because of the faultiness of false beliefs.

directed at that aim. The best way for him to raise his salary is to aim at victory for its own sake, without regard to monetary rewards. Money may be the goal for which he enters the game, but he enters the game by adopting its object as an intrinsic aim. Similarly, we may enter the game of having beliefs on a particular subject because we want our motivating cognitions on that subject to yield successful actions; but success in action does not thereby become the object of the game.

As these analogies suggest, the best way of achieving empirical adequacy or instrumental success may be to aim at the truth instead, just as the best way of raising one's salary may be to aim at winning, and the best way of winning may be to aim for the highest possible score. In each case, the former outcomes are much harder to aim at, and aiming at them can be counterproductive.

Must each belief have the aim?

Here is another respect in which my thesis could be more modest. I have claimed that our concept of belief is such that each instance of belief must aim at the truth in its own right. But I have also argued that truth-directed cognitions are psychologically segregated from their non–truth-directed counterparts, whose motivational force is generally inhibited; and this argument raises the possibility of defining belief as a cognition that is psychologically grouped with the truth-directed ones, whether or not it is truth-directed itself. Belief would then be defined as a cognition that is *treated as* aiming at the truth, either by the subject or by his psychological mechanisms, in that it is included among those cognitions whose motivational force is uninhibited because of their truth-directedness.[69]

We are all familiar with the experience of finding one of our own mental states on the wrong side of a psychological boundary, as when we find the residue of a dream mixed in with our experiential memories. Ronald Reagan was often reported to have retailed the plots of movies under the guise of historical anecdotes, as if the fantasies in which he had participated as an actor had become mixed in with his beliefs. Reagan, or his mind, treated these cognitions as if they were truth-directed, and yet they were permanently disconnected from the truth, since he went on repeating them, and thus behaving as

---

[69] In 'Truth, Reason, and the Regulation of Belief,' Peter Railton suggests that belief aims at the truth in the sense it "takes itself to be correct only if [its] content is true," or "presents itself" as "getting things right" (74). In another paper, he says: "It is part of the *price of admission* to belief as a propositional attitude that one not represent one's attitude as unaccountable to truth" ('On the Hypothetical and Non-Hypothetical in Reasoning about Belief and Action,' in *Ethics and Practical Reason*, ed. Garrett Cullity and Berys Gaut (Oxford: Clarendon Press, 1997), 53–79, at 57). These statements are similar to the view that I am currently considering, that an attitude qualifies as a belief partly by virtue of being *treated as* truth-directed.

if they were true, no matter how often he was told that they were false. Did the President believe what he was saying?

I am assuming that the President was not deliberately lying. I'm also assuming that he didn't find grounds, however spurious, for discounting the corrections that were offered to him. Finally, I am assuming that he wasn't engaged in any complex form of self-deception, unconsciously orchestrating the evidence that was allowed to enter his thinking. Rather, I assume that he was just as he seemed, blithely impervious to the facts. And on that assumption, I am inclined to think that he did not believe what he was saying. He may have believed *that* he believed what he was saying; but what he was saying conveyed the content of fantasies on his part rather than beliefs.

My reasons for favoring this description of the case derive partly from introspection. Sometimes I find myself wondering whether I really believe a proposition that I'm about to assert. What I ask myself on such occasions is not whether I have found a representation of the proposition among my beliefs. I *have* found it among my beliefs, witness my disposition to assert it. Of course, I may be asking whether I *ought* to believe the proposition—that is, whether it is true—but in at least some cases my question is descriptive with respect to my attitude, not prescriptive. I'm asking whether I even now believe the proposition, or whether it isn't instead the content of a fantasy or assumption that has fallen in among my beliefs. This question could never arise, however, if an attitude's falling in among my beliefs was sufficient for its being a belief. If my mental classification of the attitude determined its nature, then it couldn't be misclassified.

Furthermore, if an attitude's being treated as a belief were sufficient for its being a belief, then misclassified fantasies would tend to fall under epistemic norms. To describe the attitudes expressed in President Reagan's anecdotes as beliefs would imply that Reagan should have discarded them or revised them so as to conform with historical reality. All he should have done, however, was to reclassify them—to re-shelve them, mentally speaking. The President wasn't so much a bad historian as a sloppy mental housekeeper. If we want to cut him this much normative slack, however, we have to think of his anecdotes as reporting the contents of misplaced fantasies rather than irrational beliefs.

I am therefore inclined to resist the suggestion that the acceptance of a proposition can qualify as a belief merely by virtue of being mentally classified among the acceptances whose motivational force is uninhibited because they are regulated for truth. Whether an acceptance qualifies as a belief depends, I think, on whether it is so regulated in its own right.

I don't pretend that our colloquial use of terms like 'fantasy' and 'belief' will always follow my definition in classifying mixed or borderline cases. I am especially worried about cases of delusion. Aren't there people who believe that they are Napoleon? (People other than Napoleon, I mean.) Don't such people have a belief that isn't regulated for truth?[70]

I think the answer is that it isn't literally a belief. I suspect that we tend to apply the term 'belief' in a figurative sense to phantasies for which the subject doesn't or cannot have countervailing beliefs. When someone is said to believe that he is Napoleon, he actually has a phantasy to that effect; but on the question of who he is, a phantasy is all he has. He is somehow incapable of reality-tested cognitions of his identity. The phantasy of being Napoleon is thus what he has instead of a belief about his identity; and in this sense it is his belief on the topic, just as a cardboard box on the sidewalk may be his house by virtue of being what he has instead of a house.[71]

If you ask me, however, a cardboard box on the sidewalk isn't really a house. And a phantasy of being Napoleon isn't really a belief.

---

[70] Like President Reagan's historical anecdotes, someone's claiming to be Napoleon may be subject to many different explanations, which would yield different verdicts as to whether he believed what he was saying. Perhaps a person could get himself to think that he was Napoleon by orchestrating the evidence available to him, or by developing elaborate theories discrediting the counter-evidence. At some level, this person's cognition of being Napoleon might then remain under the control of truth-directed mechanisms, which were being diverted from their goal; and in that case, he would literally have deceived himself, by self-inducing a false belief. In the text, however, I am assuming that the subject is simply impervious to the facts of his real identity, and that his cognition of being Napoleon is therefore a phantasy. For a fascinating discussion of some extreme delusions, see Tony Stone and Andrew W. Young, 'Delusions and Brain Injury: The Philosophy and Psychology of Belief,' *Mind and Language* 12 (1997) 327–64. The explanations favored by Stone and Young are consistent with the thesis that belief aims at the truth. See also David Shapiro, 'The Loss of Reality,' in *Neurotic Styles* (New York: Basic Books, 1965), 48–53.

[71] The usage discussed in this paragraph may also apply to phantasies considered in the context of the Unconscious, where there are no reality-tested cognitions at all. Phantasies may qualify as unconscious beliefs, but not because they are beliefs that are inaccessible to consciousness. They may qualify as unconscious beliefs because they are what the Unconscious has instead of beliefs.

BIBLIOGRAPHY

Anderson, Elizabeth
   Value in Ethics and in Economics, Cambridge, Harvard University Press, 1993.
   'Reasons, Attitudes, and Values: Replies to Sturgeon and Piper,' *Ethics* 106 (1996)
      538–54.
   'The Source of Norms' (unpublished MS).
   'Pluralism, Deliberation, and Rational Choice' (MS).
Anscombe, G. E. M.
   Intention, Ithaca, Cornell University Press, 1963.
   'Thought and Action in Aristotle; What is "Practical Truth"?' in R. Bambrough
      (ed.), *New Essays on Plato and Aristotle*, London, Routledge and Kegan Paul, 1965,
      143–58.
Armstrong, D. M.
   Belief, Truth, and Knowledge, Cambridge, Cambridge University Press, 1973.
Baier, Annette
   'Act and Intent,' *Journal of Philosophy* 67 (1970) 648–58.
   'Doing Things with Others: the Mental Commons' (MS) (1993).
Baier, Kurt
   'Rationality, Reason, and the Good,' in D. Copp and D. Zimmerman (eds.), *Moral-
      ity, Reason and Truth*, Totowa, NJ, Rowan and Littlefield, 1984, 193–211.
Baker, Lynn Rudder
   Explaining Attitudes; a Practical Approach to the Mind, Cambridge, Cambridge Uni-
      versity Press, 1995.
Balmuth, J.
   'Psychoanalytic Explanation,' *Mind* 74 (1965) 229–35.
Bigelow, John, John Campbell, and Robert Pargetter
   'Death and Well-Being,' *Pacific Philosophical Quarterly* 71 (1990) 119–40.
Bishop, J.
   Natural Agency: An Essay on the Causal Theory of Action, Cambridge, Cambridge
      University Press, 1989.
Bittner, Rüdiger
   What Reason Demands, trans. Theodore Talbot, Cambridge, Cambridge University
      Press, 1989.
Black, Max (ed.)
   Philosophical Analysis, Ithaca, Cornell University Press, 1950.

Boghossian, Paul A., and Velleman, J. David
'Color as a Secondary Quality,' *Mind* 98 (1989) 81–103.
'Physicalist Theories of Color,' *Philosophical Review* 100 (1991) 67–106.
Bond, E. J.
Reason and Value, Cambridge, Cambridge University Press, 1983.
Braithwaite, R. B.
'The Nature of Believing,' *Proceedings of the Aristotelian Society* 33 (1932) 129–46, reprinted in *Knowledge and Belief*, ed. A. Phillips Griffiths, Oxford, Oxford University Press, 1967, 28–40.
Brandt, Richard
'Two Concepts of Utility,' in Harlan B. Miller and William H. Williams (eds.), *The Limits of Utilitarianism*, 1982, 169–85.
'Fairness to Happiness,' *Social Theory and Practice* 33 (1989) 33–58.
Bratman, Michael
'Two Faces of Intention,' *The Philosophical Review* 93 (1984) 375–405.
Intention, Plans, and Practical Reason, Cambridge, Mass., Harvard University Press, 1987.
'Practical Reasoning and Acceptance in a Context,' *Mind* 101 (1992) 1–15; reprinted in *Faces of Intention*, 15–34.
'Shared Intention,' *Ethics* 104 (1993) 97–113; reprinted in *Faces of Intention*, 109–29.
'Identification, Decision, and Treating as a Reason,' *Philosophical Topics* 24 (1996) 1–18; reprinted in *Faces of Intention*, 185–206.
'I Intend that We J,' in G. Holmstrom-Hintikka and R. Tuomela (eds.), *Contemporary Action Theory*, Vol. II, Dordrecht Kluwer, 1997, 49–63; reprinted in *Faces of Intention*, 142–61.
'Toxin, Temptation, and the Stability of Intention,' in Jules Coleman and Christopher Morris (eds.), *Rational Commitment and Social Justice: Essays for Gregory Kavka*, Cambridge, Cambridge University Press, 1998, 59–83; reprinted in *Faces of Intention*, 58–90.
Faces of Intention: Selected Essays on Intention and Agency, Cambridge, Cambridge University Press, 1999.
'Valuing and the Will' (MS).
Brink, David O.
Moral Realism and the Foundations of Ethics, Cambridge, Cambridge University Press, 1989.
Broad, C. D.
Ethics and the History of Philosophy, London, Routledge and Kegan Paul, 1952.
Broome, John
'Should a Rational Agent Maximize Expected Utility?' in Karen Schweers Cook and Margaret Levi (eds.), *The Limits of Rationality*, Chicago, University of Chicago Press, 1990, 132–45.
''Utility',' *Economics and Philosophy* 7 (1991) 1–12.
Weighing Goods, Oxford, Blackwell, 1991.
'Can a Humean be Moderate?', in R. G. Frey & Chris Morris (eds.), *Value, Welfare, and Morality*, Cambridge, Cambridge University Press, 1993, 51–73.

Campbell, C. A.
On Selfhood and Goodhood, London, Allen & Unwin, 1957.
Campbell, Richmond
'Gauthier's Theory of Morals by Agreement,' *Philosophical Quarterly* 38 (1988) 243–64.
'Moral Justification and Freedom,' *Journal of Philosophy* 85 (1988) 192–213.
Canfield, John
'Knowing about Future Decisions,' *Analysis* 22 (1962) 127–9.
Chisholm, Roderick M.
Person and Object: A Metaphysical Study, London, Allen & Unwin, 1976.
'Comments and Replies,' *Philosophia* 7 (1978) 597–636.
'Human Freedom and the Self,' in Gary Watson (ed.), *Free Will*, Oxford, Oxford University Press, 1982, 24–35.
Christman, J.
'Autonomy and Personal History,' *Canadian Journal of Philosophy* 21 (1991) 1–24.
Church, Jennifer
'Judgment, Self-Consciousness, and Object Independence,' *American Philosophical Quarterly* 27 (1990) 51–60.
'Emotions and the Internalization of Actions,' (published in French as 'L'Emotion et L'interiorisation des actions, ' in *La couleur des pensees*, s. dir. P. Paperman & R. Ogien (Paris: Editions de l'Ecole des Hautes Etudes en Sciences Sociales, 1995, 219–236).
Cohen, L. Jonathan
An Essay on Belief and Acceptance, Oxford, Clarendon Press, 1992.
Cohon, Rachel
'Are External Reasons Impossible?', *Ethics* 96 (1986) 545–56.
'Internalism about Reasons for Action,' *Pacific Philosophical Quarterly* 74 (1993) 265–88.
Combs, Arthur W., and Snygg, Donald
Individual Behavior: A Perceptual Approach to Behavior, New York, Harper & Brothers, 1959.
Cooper, John M.
'Plato's Theory of Human Motivation,' *History of Philosophy Quarterly* 1 (1984) 3–21.
Cox, J. W. Roxbee
'Can I Know Beforehand What I Am Going to Decide?' *Philosophical Review* 72 (1963) 88–92.
Cullity, Garrett, and Gaut, Berys (eds.)
Ethics and Practical Reason, Oxford, Oxford University Press, 1997.
Danielson, Peter
'Closing the Compliance Dilemma; How It's Rational to be Moral in a Lamarckian World,' in P. Vallentyne, *Contractarianism and Rational Choice*, 1991, 291–322.
Danto, Arthur C.
'Action, Knowledge, and Representation,' in Myles Brand and Douglas Walton (eds.), *Action Theory*, Dordrecht, D. Reidel, 1976, 11–25.
Narration and Knowledge, New York, Columbia University Press, 1985.

Darwall, Stephen L.
  Impartial Reason, Ithaca, N.Y., Cornell University Press 1983.
  'Autonomist Internalism and the Justification of Morals,' *Noûs* 24 (1990) 257–68.
Davidson, Donald
  'Actions, Reasons, and Causes,' in *Essays on Actions and Events*, 3–21.
  'How is Weakness of the Will Possible?' (1970), in *Essays on Actions and Events*,
    21–42.
  'Psychology as Philosophy,' (1974) in *Essays on Actions and Events*, 229–44.
  'Thought and Talk,' in *Inquires into Truth and Interpretation*, 155–70.
  'Intending,' in *Essays on Actions and Events*, 83–102.
  Essays on Actions and Events, Oxford, Oxford University Press, 1980.
  'Paradoxes of Irrationality,' in Richard Wollheim and James Hopkins (eds.),
    Philosophical Essays on Freud, Cambridge, Cambridge University Press, 1982,
    289–305.
  Inquiries into Truth and Interpretation, Oxford, Oxford University Press, 1984.
Dennett, Daniel C.
  'Do Animals Have Beliefs?' in *Brainchildren: Essays on Designing Minds*, Cambridge,
    Mass., MIT Press, 1998, 323–31.
Dent, N. J. H.
  The Moral Psychology of Virtues, Cambridge, Cambridge University Press, 1984.
DeSousa, Ronald B.
  'The Good and the True,' *Mind* 83 (1974) 534–51.
Dray, W. H.
  'On the Nature and Role of Narrative in Historiography,' *History and Theory* 10
    (1971) 153–71.
Elster, Jon
  Ulysses and the Sirens: Studies in Rationality and Irrationality, Cambridge, Cambridge
    University Press, 1979.
  Sour Grapes; Studies in the Subversion of Rationality, Cambridge, Cambridge Uni-
    versity Press, 1983.
Epstein, Seymour
  'The Self-Concept Revisited; Or a Theory of a Theory,' *American Psychologist* 28
    (1973) 404–16.
Falk, W. D.
  'Action-Guiding Reasons,' reprinted in *Ought, Reasons, and Morality*, 82–98.
  'On Learning About Reasons,' in *Ought, Reasons, and Morality*, 67–81.
  Ought, Reasons, and Morality, Ithaca, Cornell University Press, 1986.
Farrell, Dan
  'Intention, Reason, and Action,' *American Philosophical Quarterly* 26 (1989) 283–95.
Fay, Brian, Golob, Eugene O., and Vann, Richard T. (eds.)
  Historical Understanding, Ithaca, Cornell University Press, 1987.
Fehige, Christoph, Georg Meggle, and Ulla Wessels (eds.) *Preferences*, Berlin, de
    Gruyter, 1998.
Feinberg, Joel
  Harm to Others, New York, Oxford University Press, 1984.

Feldman, Fred
'Some Puzzles About the Evil of Death,' *Philosophical Review* 100 (1991) 205–27.
Fodor, Jerry
'Special Sciences: Still Autonomous after All These Years (A Reply to Jaegwon Kim's " Multiple Realization and the Metaphysics of Reduction"),' in *In Critical Condition*, 9–24.
'Is Science Biologically Possible? Comments on Some Arguments of Patricia Churchland and of Alvin Plantinga, in *In Critical Condition*, 189–202.
In Critical Condition; Polemical Essays on Cognitive Science and the Philosophy of Mind (Cambridge, Mass., MIT Press, 1998).
Frankena, William K.
'Obligation and Ability,' in Max Black (ed.), *Philosophical Analysis: A Collection of Essays*, Ithaca, Cornell University Press, 1950, 157–75.
'Obligation and Motivation in Recent Moral Philosophy,' in A. I. Melden (ed.), *Essays in Moral Philosophy*, Seattle, University of Washington Press 1958; reprinted in K. Goodpaster (ed.), *Perspectives on Morality*, Notre Dame, University of Notre Dame Press, 1976, 49–73.
Frankfurt, Harry
'Identification and Externality,' reprinted in *The Importance of What We Care About*, 58–68.
The Importance of What We Care About, Cambridge, Cambridge University Press, 1988.
Volition, Necessity, and Love, Cambridge, Cambridge University Press, 1999.
Freud, Sigmund
The Psychopathology of Everyday Life, (1901) *SE* vi.
'Obsessive Actions and Religious Practices,' (1907) *SE* ix, 116–27.
'Notes upon a case of Obsessional Neurosis,' (1909) *SE* x, 155–320.
'The Unconscious,' (1915) *SE* xiv, 161–215.
Introductory Lectures on Psychoanalysis, (1916–17) *SE* xv–xvi.
'A Childhood Recollection from *Dichtung und Wahrheit*,' (1917) *SE* xvii, 146–56.
'Some Elementary Lessons in Psycho-Analysis,' (1938) *SE* xxiii, 281–6.
The Standard Edition of the Complete Psychological Works of Sigmund Freud, ed. James Strachey, et al., London, Hogarth Press, 1958.
Freidman, Michael
'Explanation and Scientific Understanding,' *Journal of Philosophy* 71 (1974) 5–19.
Gallie, W. B.
Philosophy and the Historical Understanding, New York, Schocken Books, 1968.
Gardner, Sebastian
Irrationality and the Philosophy of Psychoanalysis, Cambridge, Cambridge University Press, 1993.
Gauthier, David
'How Decisions are Caused,' *Journal of Philosophy* 64 (1967) 147–51.
'How Decisions are Caused (But Not Predicted),' *Journal of Philosophy* 65 (1968) 170–1.

'Assure and Threaten,' *Ethics* 104 (1994) 690–721.
Morals By Agreement, Oxford, Clarendon Press, 1986.
'In the Neighborhood of The Newcomb-Predictor (Reflections on Rationality),' *Proceedings of the Aristotelian Society* 89 (1988–9) 179–94.
'Reason and Maximization,' in *Moral Dealing; Contract, Ethics, and Reason*, Ithaca, Cornell University Press, 1990, 209–33.
'Rationality and the Rational Aim,' in Jonathan Dancy (ed.), *Reading Parfit*, Oxford, Blackwell, 1997, 24–41.

Gilbert, Margaret
'Walking Together; a Paradigmatic Social Phenomenon,' *Midwest Studies in Philosophy* 15 (1990) 1–14.
On Social Facts, Princeton, Princeton University Press, 1992.

Ginet, Carl
'Can the Will Be Caused?' *Philosophical Review* 61 (1962) 49–55.
On Action, Cambridge, Cambridge University Press, 1990.

Ginsborg, Hannah
'Reflective Judgment and Taste', *Noûs* 24 (1990) 63–78.
'Kant on Judgment' (MS).

Goldman, Alvin I.
A Theory of Human Action, Princeton, Princeton University Press, 1970.

Grice, Paul
'Method in Philosophical Psychology,' *Proceedings and Addresses of the APA* 48 (1975) 23–53.

Griffin, James
Well-Being: Its Meaning, Measurement, and Moral Importance, Oxford, Oxford University Press, 1986.

Griffiths, A. Phillips
'On Belief,' *Proceedings of the Aristotelian Society* 63 (1963) 167–86, reprinted in *Knowledge and Belief*, 127–43.
Knowledge and Belief, Oxford, Oxford University Press, 1967.

Hampshire, Stuart
Thought and Action, London, Chatto & Windus, 1959.
'Feeling and Expression,' in *Freedom of Mind and Other Essays*, Princeton, Princeton University Press, 1971, 143–59.
Freedom of the Individual, Princeton, Princeton University Press, 1975.

Hampshire, Stuart, and Hart, H. L. A.
'Decision, Intention and Certainty,' *Mind* 67 (1958) 1–12.

Hansson, Bengt
'Risk Aversion as a Problem of Conjoint Measurement,' in Peter Gärdenfors and Nils-Eric Sahlin (eds.), *Decision, Probability, and Utility; Selected Readings*, Cambridge, Cambridge University Press, 1988, 136–58.

Hare, R. M.
'Brandt on Fairness to Happiness,' *Social Theory and Practice* 15 (1989) 59–65.

Harman, Gilbert
'Moral Relativism Defended,' *Philosophical Review* 84 (1975) 3–22.
'Practical Reasoning,' *Review of Metaphysics* 29 (1976) 431–63.

Change in View: Principles of Reasoning, Cambridge, Mass., The MIT Press, 1986.
'Willing and Intending,' in Richard E. Grandy and Richard Warner (eds.), *Philosophical Grounds of Rationality: Intentions, Categories, Ends*, Oxford, Oxford University Press, 1986, 363–80.

Harris, P. L., E. Brown, Marriott, C., Whittall, S., and Harmer, S.
'Monsters, Ghosts and Witches: Testing the limits of the fantasy-reality distinction in young children,' *British Journal of Experimental Psychology* 9 (1991) 105–23.

Hollis, Martin
The Cunning of Reason, Cambridge, Cambridge University Press, 1987.

Hooker, Brad
'Williams' Argument against External Reasons,' *Analysis* 47 (1987) 42–4.

Howard, J. V.
'Cooperation in the Prisoner's Dilemma,' *Theory and Decision* 24 (1988) 203–13.

Humberstone, Lloyd
'Direction of Fit,' *Mind* 101 (1992) 59–83.

Hume, David
A Treatise of Human Nature, second ed. L. A. Selby-Bigge and P. H. Nidditch (eds.), Oxford, Clarendon Press, 1978.

Hursthouse, Rosalind
'Arational Actions,' *Journal of Philosophy* 88 (1991) 57–68.

James, William
'The Will to Believe,' in *Essays on Faith and Morals*, New York, New American Library, 1974, 32–62.

Joyce, James M.
'A Nonpragmatic Vindication of Probabilism,' *Philosophy of Science* 65 (1998) 573–603.

Kant, Immanuel
Groundwork of the Metaphysic of Morals, translated and analyzed by H. J. Paton, New York, Harper & Row, 1956.

Kavka, Gregory
'The Toxin Puzzle,' *Analysis* 43 (1983) 33–6.

Kneale, William
Probability and Induction, New York, Oxford University Press, 1949.

Korman, Abraham K.
'Toward an Hypothesis of Work Behavior,' *Journal of Applied Psychology* 54 (1970) 31–41.

Korsgaard, Christine
'Skepticism about Practical Reason,' *The Journal of Philosophy* 83 (1986) 5–25.
'Morality as Freedom,' in Y. Yovel (ed.), *Kant's Practical Philosophy Reconsidered*, Dordrecht, Kluwer Academic Publishers, 1989, 23–48.
'The Normativity of Instrumental Reason,' in Cullity and Gaut (eds.), *Ethics and Practical Reason*, 1997, 213–54.

Kripke, Saul A.
Wittgenstein on Rules and Private Language, Cambridge, Mass., Harvard University Press, 1982.

Lear, Jonathan
  'The Heterogeneity of the Mental,' *Mind* 104 (1995) 863–79.
  'Restlessness, Phantasy, and the Concept of Mind,' *Open Minded: Working Out the Logic of the Soul*, Cambridge, Mass., Harvard University Press, 1998.
Lecky, Prescott
  Self-Consistency: A Theory of Personality, Hamden, Conn., Shoe String Press, 1961.
Lehrer, Keith
  'The Gettier Problem and the Analysis of Knowledge,' in *Justification and Knowledge*, George S. Pappas (ed.), Dordrecht, D. Reidel, 1979, 65–78.
Leon, Mark
  'Rationalising Belief,' *Philosophical Papers* 21 (1992) 299–314.
Lewis, C. I.
  An Analysis of Knowledge and Valuation, Lasalle, Ill., Open Court Publishing Co., 1946.
Lewis, David K.
  'Counterfactual Dependence and Time's Arrow,' *Nous* 13 (1979) 455–76.
  'Desire as Belief,' *Mind* 97 (1988) 323–42.
Lillard, Angeline
  'Making Sense of Pretence,' in *Children's Early Understanding of the Mind; Origins and Development*, Charlie Lewis and Peter Mitchell (eds.), Hove, Lawrence Erlbaum, 1994, 211–34.
MacIntyre, Alasdair
  After Virtue, Notre Dame, University of Notre Dame Press, 1984.
  'The Intelligibility of Action,' in J. Margolis, M. Krausz, and R. M. Burian (eds.), *Rationality, Relativism and the Human Sciences*, Dordrecht, Martinus Nijhoff, 1986, 63–80.
MacKay, D. M.
  'On the Logical Indeterminacy of a Free Choice,' *Mind* 69 (1960) 31–40.
McCann, Hugh
  'Rationality and the Range of Intention,' *Midwest Studies in Philosophy* 10 (1986) 191–211.
McClennan, Edward F.
  Rationality and Dynamic Choice: Foundational Explorations, Cambridge, Cambridge University Press, 1990.
McDowell, John
  'Are Moral Requirements Hypothetical Imperatives?' *Proceedings of the Aristotelian Society 52, Supplementary Volume*, (1978) 13–29.
  'Might There Be External Reasons?', in J. E. J. Altham and Ross Harrison (eds.), *World, Mind, and Ethics; Essays on the Ethical Philosophy of Bernard Williams*, Cambridge, Cambridge University Press, 1995, 68–85.
McNulty, Shawn E. and Swann, William B.
  'Psychotherapy, Self-Concept Change, and Self-Verification,' in *The Relational Self; Theoretical Convergences in Psychoanalysis and Social Psychology*, Rebecca C. Curtis (ed.), New York, Guildford Press, 1991, 213–37.

Mele, Alfred
'Motivational Internalism: The Powers and Limits of Practical Reasoning,' *Philosophia* 19 (1989) 417–36.
Merton, R. K.
'The Self-fulfilling Prophecy,' *Antioch Review* 8 (1948) 193–210.
Milgram, Elijah
'Williams' Argument against External Reasons,' *Noûs* 30 (1996) 197–220.
Miller, H. B., and W. H. Williams (eds.)
The Limits of Utilitarianism, Minneapolis, University of Minnesota Press, 1982.
Millikan, Ruth
'Truth Rules, Hoverflies, and the Kripke-Wittgenstein Paradox,' in *White Queen Psychology and other Essays for Alice*, Cambridge, Mass., MIT Press, 1993, 211–39.
Mink, Louis
'On the Nature and Role of Narrative in Historiography,' *History and Theory* 10 (1971) 153–171.
'Philosophical Analysis and Historical Understanding,' in Fay, *Historical Understanding*, 1987, 118–146.
'History and Fiction as Modes of Comprehension,' in Fay, *Historical Understanding*, 1987, 42–88.
Moran, Richard
'The Expression of Feeling in Imagination,' *The Philosophical Review* 103 (1994) 75–106.
Nagel, Thomas
'Death,' in *Mortal Questions*, 1979, 1–10.
The Possibility of Altruism, Princeton, Princeton University Press, 1970.
'The Fragmentation of Value,' in *Mortal Questions*, 1979, 128–41.
Mortal Questions, Cambridge, Cambridge University Press, 1979.
The View from Nowhere, Oxford, Oxford University Press, 1986.
Nehamas, Alexander
Nietzsche: Life as Literature, Cambridge, Harvard University Press, 1985.
Neu, Jerome
'A Tear is an Intellectual Thing,' *Representations* 19 (1987) 35–61.
O'Shaughnessy, Brian
The Will: A Dual Aspect Theory, Cambridge, Cambridge University Press, 1980.
O'Connor, John
'How Decisions are Predicted,' *Journal of Philosophy* 64 (1967) 429–430.
Oldenquist, Andrew
'Causes, Predictions and Decisions,' *Analysis* 24 (1964) 55–58.
Parfit, Derek
Reasons and Persons, Oxford, Clarendon Press, 1984.
Peacocke, Christopher
'Deviant Causal Chains,' *Midwest Studies in Philosophy* 4 (1979) 123–156.
Pears, David
'Predicting and Deciding,' *Proceedings of the British Academy* 50 (1964) 193–227.
Motivated Irrationality, Oxford, Clarendon Press, 1984.

'Intention and Belief,' in Bruce Vermazen and Merrill B. Hintikka (eds.), *Essays on Davidson*, Oxford, Clarendon Press, 1985, 75–88.

Perry, David L.
'Prediction, Explanation and Freedom,' *Monist* 49 (1965) 234–247.

Perry, John
'Belief and Acceptance,' *Midwest Studies in Philosophy* 5 (1980) 533–42.

Platts, Mark
Ways of Meaning, London, Routledge & Kegan Paul, 1979.

Quine, W. V., and Ullian, J. S.
The Web of Belief, New York, Random House, 1970.

Railton, Peter
'Facts and Values,' *Philosophical Topics* 14 (1986) 5–31.
'Moral Realism,' *Philosophical Review* 95 (1986) 163–207.
'What the Noncognitivist Helps Us to See the Naturalist Must Help Us to Explain,' in John Haldane and Crispin Wright (eds.), *Reality, Representation, and Projection*, New York, Oxford University Press, 1993, 292–94.
'Truth, Reason, and the Regulation of Belief,' *Philosophical Issues* 5 (1994) 71–93.
'In Search of Nonsubjective Reason,' in J. B. Schneewind (ed.), *Reason, Ethics, and Society: Themes from Kurt Baier, with His Responses*, Chicago, Open Court, 1996, 117–43.
'On the Hypothetical and Non-Hypothetical in Reasoning about Belief and Action,' in Cullity and Gaut (eds.) *Ethics and Practical Reason*, 1997, 53–79.

Rawls, John
Political Liberalism, New York, Columbia University Press, 1993.

Rosati, Connie
"Naturalism, Normativity, and the Open Question Argument," *Noûs* 29 (1995) 46–70.
'Morality, Agency, and Regret' (MS).

Rousseau
The Social Contract, (1762) trans. Maurice Cranston, Hammondsworth, Penguin Books, 1968.

Rozin, P., and Nemeroff, C.
'The Laws of Sympathetic Magic: A psychological analysis of similarity and contagion,' in J. W. Stigler, R. A. Schweder, and G. Herdt (eds.), *Cultural psychology; Essays on comparative human development*, Cambridge, Cambridge University Press, 1990, 205–32.

Salmon, Wesley C.
'Four Decades of Scientific Explanation,' *Minnesota Studies in the Philosophy of Science* 13 (1989) 3–219.

Savage, Leonard J.
The Foundations of Statistics, New York, Dover, 1972.

Sayre-McCord, Geoffrey
'Deception and Reasons to be Moral,' in Vallentyne (ed.), *Contractarianism and Rational Choice*, 1991, 181–95.

Schick, Frederic
'Dutch Bookies and Money Pumps,' *The Journal of Philosophy* 83 (1986) 112–19.

Schueler, G. F.
  'Pro-Attitudes and Direction of Fit,' *Mind* 100 (1991) 277–81.
Searle, John
  Intentionality, Cambridge, Cambridge University Press, 1983.
  'Collective Intentions and Actions,' in Philip R. Cohen, Jerry Morgan, and Martha
    E. Pollack (eds.), *Intentions in Communication*, Cambridge, Mass., MIT Press,
    1990, 401–15.
Sen, Amartya
  'Utilitarianism and Welfarism,' *Journal of Philosophy* 76 (1970) 463–89.
  'Plural Utility,' *Proceedings of the Aristotelian Society* 81 (1981) 193–215.
  'Well-Being, Agency and Freedom: The Dewey Lectures 1984,' *Journal of Philoso-
    phy* 82 (1985) 169–203.
  'Rationality and Uncertainty,' *Theory and Decision* 18 (1985) 109–28.
Shapiro, David
  Neurotic Styles, New York, Basic Books, 1965.
Sherman, S. J.
  'On the Self-Erasing Nature of Errors of Prediction,' *Journal of Personality and
    Social Psychology* 39 (1980) 211–21.
Sidgwick, Henry
  The Methods of Ethics seventh ed., Indianapolis, Hackett Publishing Co. 1981; first
    ed. first published 1874, seventh (ed.) first published 1907.
Simon, Herbert
  'A Behavioral Model of Rational Choice,' *Quarterly Journal of Economics* 69 (1955)
    99–118.
Sinnott-Armstrong, Walter
  '"Ought" Conversationally Implies "Can,"' *Philosophical Review* 93 (1984)
    249–62.
Slote, Michael
  'Goods and Lives,' *Pacific Philosophical Quarterly* 63 (1982) 311–26.
  Goods and Virtues, Oxford, Clarendon Press, 1983.
  Beyond Optimizing: A Study of Rational Choice, Cambridge, Mass., Harvard Uni-
    versity Press, 1989.
Smith, Holly
  'Deriving Morality from Rationality,' in Vallentyne (ed.), *Contractarianism and
    Rational Choice*, 1991, 229–53.
Smith, Michael
  'The Humean Theory of Motivation,' *Mind* 96 (1987) 36–61.
  'Reason and Desire,' *Proceedings of the Aristotelian Society* 88 (1988) 243–58.
  'Valuing: Desiring or Believing?', in David Charles and Kathleen Lennon (eds.),
    Reduction, Explanation and Realism, Oxford, Oxford University Press, 1992,
    323–60.
Snyder, Mark
  'When Belief Creates Reality,' *Advances in Experimental Social Psychology* 18 (1984)
    247–305.
  'Motivational Foundations of Behavioral Confirmation,' *Advances in Experimental
    Social Psychology* 25 (1992) 67–114.

Sorensen, Roy A.
  'Uncaused Decisions and Pre-Decisional Blindspots,' *Philosophical Studies* 45 (1984)
    51–6.
Spangenberg, Eric R., and Greenwald, Anthony G.
  'Social Influence by Requesting Self-Prophecy,' *Journal of Consumer Psychology* 8
    (1999) 61–89.
Stalnaker, Robert C.
  Inquiry, Cambridge, Mass., MIT Press, 1984.
Stampe, Dennis
  'The Authority of Desire,' *Philosophical Review* 96 (1987) 335–81.
Stocker, Michael
  '"Ought" and "Can,"' *Australasian Journal of Philosophy* 49 (1971) 303–17.
  'Desiring the Bad: An Essay in Moral Psychology,' *Journal of Philosophy* 76 (1979)
    738–53.
  'Values and Purposes: the Limits of Teleology and the Ends of Friendship,' *Journal
    of Philosophy* 78 (1981) 747–65.
  Plural and Conflicting Values, Oxford, Clarendon Press, 1990.
Stone, Tony and Young, Andrew W.
  'Delusions and Brain Injury: The Philosophy and Psychology of Belief,' *Mind and
    Language* 12 (1997) 327–64.
Taylor, Charles
  Sources of the Self: The Making of the Modern Identity, Cambridge, Harvard Uni-
    versity Press, 1989.
Taylor, Richard
  'Deliberation and Foreknowledge,' *American Philosophical Quarterly* 1 (1964) 73–80.
  Action and Purpose, Englewood Cliffs, N.J., Prentice-Hall, 1966.
  Metaphysics, Englewood Cliffs, N.J., Prentice-Hall, 1983.
Thibodeau, Ruth, and Aronson, Elliot
  'Taking a Closer Look: Reasserting the Role of the Self-Concept in Dissonance
    Theory,' *Personality and Social Psychology Bulletin* 18 (1992) 591–602.
Trzebinski, Jerzy
  'Narrative Self, Understanding, and Action,' in *The Self in European and North
    American Culture: Development and Processes*, A. Oosterwegel and R. A. Wicklund
    (eds.), Dordrecht, Kluwer, 1995, 73–88.
Tuomela, Raimo, and Miller, Kaarlo
  'We-Intentions,' *Philosophical Studies* 53 (1988) 115–137.
Tuomela, Raimo
  'What are Joint Intentions?', in R. Casati and G. White (eds.), *Philosophy and
    the Cognitive Sciences*, Austrian Ludwig Wittgenstein Association, 1993, 543–
    547.
  'We Will Do It: An Analysis of Group Intentions,' *Philosophy and Phenomenological
    Research* 51 (1991) 249–277.
  'Actions by Collectives,' *Philosophical Perspectives* 3 (1989) 471–96.
Urmson, J. O.
  'Memory and Imagination,' *Mind* 76 (1967) 83–91.

Vallacher, Robin R., and Wegner, Daniel M.
  'What Do People Think They're Doing? Action Identification and Human Behavior,' *Psychological Review* 94 (1987) 3–15.
Vallentyne, Peter (ed.)
  Contractarianism and Rational Choice; Essays on David Gauthier's Morals by Agreement, New York, Cambridge University Press, 1991.
Van Fraassen, Bas C.
  The Scientific Image, Oxford, Clarendon Press, 1980.
Velleman, J. David
  'The Doxastic Theory of Intention,' in Michael P. Georgeff and Amy L. Lansky (eds.), *Reasoning About Actions and Plans*, Los Altos, Cal., Morgan Kaufmann, 1987, 361–93.
  Practical Reflection, Princeton, Princeton University Press, 1989.
  Review of Bratman, *Intention, Plans, and Practical Reason, Philosophical Review* 100 (1991) 277–84.
  'Self to Self,' *Philosophical Review* 105 (1996) 39–76.
  'Identification and Identity,' forthcoming in Sarah Buss and Lee Oveston (eds.), *Contours of Agency*, Cambridge, Mass., MIT Press.
  Review of Bratman, *Faces of Intention*, forthcoming in *The Philosophical Quarterly*.
  'From Self-Psychology to Moral Philosophy,' forthcoming in *Philosophical Perspectives* 14 (2000).
Vonnegut, Kurt
  Slaughterhouse Five, New York, Dell Publishing, 1969.
Wallace, R. Jay
  'How to Argue about Practical Reason,' *Mind* 99 (1990) 355–85.
Walton, Kendall
  Mimesis as Make-Believe; on the Foundations of the Representational Arts, Cambridge, Mass., Harvard University Press, 1990.
Watson, Gary
  'Free Agency,' *Journal of Philosophy* 72 (1975) 205–20; reprinted in *Free Will*, Oxford: Oxford University Press, 1982.
Wegner, Daniel M., Coulton, G., and Wenzlaff, R.
  'The Transparency of Denial: Briefing in the debriefing paradigm,' *Journal of Personality and Social Psychology* 32 (1985) 338–46.
Wegner, Daniel M., and Vallacher, Robin R.
  'Action Identification,' in *Handbook of Motivation and Cognition*, Richard M. Sorrentino and E. Tory Higgins (eds.), New York, Guilford Press, 1986, 550–82.
Williams, Bernard
  'Imagination and the Self,' in *Problems of the Self*, 1973, 26–45.
  'Persons, Character and Morality,' in Amélie Oksenberg Rorty (ed.), *The Identities of Person*, Berkeley, University of California Press, 1976, 197–216.
  'Deciding to Believe,' in Williams, *Problems of the Self*, 1973, 136–51.
  'The Makropulis Case: reflections on the tedium of immortality,' in *Problems of the Self*, 1973, 82–100.

Problems of the Self, Cambridge, Cambridge University Press, 1973.

'Internal and External Reasons,' in *Moral Luck*, Cambridge, Cambridge University Press, 1981, 101–13.

'Internal Reasons and the Obscurity of Blame,' in *Making Sense of Humanity and other Philosophical Papers*, Cambridge, Cambridge University Press, 1995, 35–45.

'Replies,' in J. E. J. Altham and Ross Harrison (eds.), *World, Mind, and Ethics*, Cambridge, Cambridge University Press, 1995, 185–224.

Wittgenstein, Ludwig

Philosophical Investigations, trans. by G. E. M. Anscombe, Oxford, Basil Blackwell, 1967.

Wolf, Susan

Freedom Within Reason, Oxford, Oxford University Press, 1990.

Woolley, Jacqueline D. and Wellman, Henry M.

'Origin and Truth: Young Children's Understanding of Imaginary Mental Representations,' *Child Development* 64 (1993) 1–17.

Wollheim, Richard

The Thread of Life, Cambridge, Mass., Harvard University Press, 1984.

'Wish Fulfillment,' in Ross Harrison (ed.), *Rational Action*, Cambridge, Cambridge University Press, 1979, 47–60.

INDEX